W9-AAW-343

Forbidden $\dfrac{\text{Sex}}{\text{Texts}}$

Forbidden $\dfrac{\text{Sex}}{\text{Texts}}$

new india's gay poets

Hoshang Merchant

 Routledge
Taylor & Francis Group
LONDON NEW YORK NEW DELHI

First published 2009
by Routledge
912–915 Tolstoy House, 15–17 Tolstoy Marg, New Delhi 110 001

Simultaneously published in the UK
by Routledge
2 Park Square, Milton Park, Abingdon, Oxon, OX14 4RN

Routledge is an imprint of the Taylor & Francis Group, an informa business

Transferred to Digital Printing 2009

© 2009 Hoshang Merchant

Typeset by
Star Compugraphics Private Limited
D–156, Second Floor
Sector 7, Noida 201 301

All rights reserved. No part of this book may be reproduced or utilised in any form or by any electronic, mechanical or other means, now known or hereafter invented, including photocopying and recording, or in any information storage and retrieval system without permission in writing from the publishers.

British Library Cataloguing-in-Publication Data
A catalogue record of this book is available from the British Library

ISBN 978-0-415-48451-0

for
my teacher
Virgil Lokke
and
for Whabiz,
my sister

A new truth is ridiculed at first,
it is vehemently opposed next —
only finally is it taken as a self-evident truth,
which it always was.

There can be no longer any grand narratives...
only smaller communication circuits, conducted
through private language-games.

contents

preface

In the summer of 2007, I visited America reluctantly after a gap of 13 years. My elder sister is seriously ill and we two spent the summer before her TV like two invalids tending each other. Not surprisingly, of the 64 available channels, sister's favourite is the medical channel. She told me about a program she had seen. She prefaced her narration by saying that nowadays Americans record their entire lives on video practically from the time the child is born. A certain boy of 3 refused to be called 'he'.

—'No, she!', he'd correct his mother.

He refused to go to school in boys' clothing; he insisted on a pretty dress. His mother consulted the school principal.

—'Let him come, dressed as a girl,' the principal said.

I blame mothers.

At three the brain is bombarded with estrogen, hence the gender change, explained my sister. I trotted out the familiar excuse that mothers make sons gay.

—'Stop blaming Woman!', my sister countered.

—'Do you think, then, my brain was bombarded with estrogen at 3?' I asked.

No reply. But yes, that sharp disapproving look met my look.

In the West the law, religion and psychological sciences have kept in pace with the aspirations of modern gays. In India, the law still criminalises us, religion ostracises and punishes us and the science of the mind abnormalises us. Lots of gay Indians today are poets, dramatists, film-makers, writers. They choose these professions to locate alternative worlds which they present to the world, thereby joining it and enriching it with their contributions. It is this work my book analyses and critiques and I salute these brave, gay Indians.

acknowledgements

To my editors at Routledge, Omita Goyal and Nilanjan Sarkar, for their ideas for the book and their fondness for and patience with me.

To Seth for Seth.

To my student friend Amitendu Bhattacharya for getting me library books and help with the Internet, with e-mails and for the *Chocolate*!

To my student friend Saradindu Bhattacharya for work on Mahesh Dattani's *Dance Like a Man*.

To my student S. Anand and Akshay K. Rath for parts of their thesis on Padamsee and Namjoshi respectively.

To my American student Michael Fieni for his analysis of single poems by Padamsee.

To my friend Nagarajan Ramanathan for cheerfully typing a difficult manuscript.

queering India

Identities are the names we give to the different ways we are positioned by, and position ourselves within, the narrative of the past.

~ Stuart Hall[1]

If gender transpositions aren't real entities, then laws dealing with them don't make sense.

~ James Weinrich[2]

In her introduction to *Facing the Mirror: Lesbian Writing from India*,[3] Ashwini Sukthankar mocks the 'nonexistent' status of Indian lesbian: '...we don't live outside the law, as gay men do in our country, we live between its lines. "Section 377" of the Indian Penal Code makes homosexual acts between men illegal but it does not technically have lesbianism in its purview, since the legal definition of intercourse requires penetration.'[4] The act and public/social discourses on same-sex love are still illegal; it is against the Indian 'tradition' according to people, both for the left and right; and a sense of 'history' is seriously problematic when we dig out for a past tradition of homoerotic love and desire. Neither do we find technical synonyms for terms like 'homosexual', 'homoerotic', 'queer', 'gay', 'lesbian', or 'sodomy', nor do recent constructs like *samalinga*[5] help us define the act and practice appropriately. Nor do they fulfill the gap of a vocabulary for the study of this identity construction movement. A sense of historical 'self-representation' is thus complex, and it signifies, in principle, that the movement has to offer a sense of 'existence' in historical relics and the cultural sphere.

Ruth Vanita and Saleem Kidwai, however, claim that there is a genealogy of queer tradition in India. They anthologise passages from the *Mahabharata, Panchatantra, Kamasutra, Bhagvata Purana* and other *puranas*.

India, still a land of Other Victorians, continues to hold its traditional beliefs on 'the love that dares not speak its name' even today. No love outside heterosexual mono/polygamous marriage, or no love that cannot take a spiritual form is accepted; any articulation of such love outside these two institutions sees social rejection, violence, punishment or judicial action.

Two negative forces against same-sex love, concurrently, must be addressed to understand queer studies in India. The first erratic notion is that queer sexuality is not Indian; and second, that it is against Indian tradition and culture. The first negative force, which forms the root of homophobia in India, draws critical attentions to explore the standpoints, belief systems and hypotheses of what is called 'queer discourse', the identity construction movement of the 'third sex'; it becomes a creative impulse in and after the late 1990s and strengthens its basis/arguments in relation with European queer theory. And the second one, which blindly looks at Indian tradition as a religious/spiritual articulation of love, virtue, sacrifice, devotion and friendship, would mean, in turn, a belief system that is neither questioned nor properly investigated or debated about. The second force, a maturing framework of homophobic guilt, holds the management policy against any love outside 'productive' penetration and criminalises it.

A visible gay or lesbian category in India is perceived as a threat to mainstream Indian culture; any articulation of such love would destabilise the 'dominant model of history', and hence homoerotic love is constructed as 'deviant', 'unnatural', as 'sin' and as a 'vice'. 'Unnatural though the vice is,' M. K. Gandhi, father of the modern Indian nation, nails down in an article from *Young India*, 'it has come down to us from times immemorial.' He does not deny its existence, rather confirms it from 'personal letters received from boys'. Gandhi, who took the leadership of *swaraj* that encompassed the rights of all victims — of the poor, peasants, women and 'untouchables', gave homosexuality a new phrase — the 'unnatural vice'. However, he complicates the issue, advising '...not to treat sex between men as a different category from sex between men and women' (Vanita and Kidwai 2000). Gandhi's perception is just an explanation of his own feelings and has nothing to do with a possible solution. His idea, however, becomes problematic, to a significant degree, when he refers to the gospel according to St John, where in a chapter Jesus tells the people to stone a 'bad' woman if only they are free from all evils and vices. Moreover, the whole issue indicates, in a broader sense, a culture's perception towards same-sex love or homosexuality. Its origin is unknown, but its existence, according to our culture, is a vice. Gandhi's statements clearly unwrap cultural attitudes, which make same-sex love 'deviant', a 'sin', and a 'vice' in the Indian tradition.

This constructed 'myth' is, however, further strengthened with western ideas on homosexuals and homosexuality. One of the major contributions of recent queer scholarship, thus, has been to question the misrepresentation of queer subjects/sexualities. Over the last three decades, western queer scholarship has highlighted several problems and difficulties which queer subjects face living in a homophobic and heterosexist society. Queer subjects characteristically face homophobic abuse and harassment, neglect by schools and families; and in some cases, they are subject to judicial actions (Plummer 1981). They are thought to be isolated, lonely, 'at risk' of unsafe sex, homelessness, drug and alcohol abuse, and most prominently 'at risk' of attempting suicide. Reality of gay and lesbian historiography, as we understand today is a social construct (Weeks 1977; Foucault 1979; Seidman 1996). Michel Foucault documents its construction in *The History of Sexuality*:

> As defined by the ancient civil or canonical codes, sodomy was a category of forbidden acts; their perpetrator was nothing more than the juridical subject of them. The nineteenth-century homosexual became a personage, a past, a case history, and childhood, in addition to being a type of life, a life form, and a morphology, with an indiscreet anatomy and possibly a mysterious physiology. Nothing that went into his total composition was unaffected by his sexuality. It was everywhere present in him: at the root of all his actions because it was their insidious and indefinitely active principle; written immodestly on his face and body because it was a secret that always gave itself away…
>
> (Foucault 1979: 43)

Foucault's work exclusively deals with the nineteenth century western homosexual who forms a category, possesses an ideology, categorises his/her strengths and weaknesses, codifies the act, and seeks for an identify fighting against a tradition that has subjugated his/her 'sexual preferences' throughout the ages. Critics of queer theory, especially in educational institutions and in social spheres and queer activists look back and read histories for gay role models and celebrate the canon. One could stress the beginning of this discourse in western society with Edward Carpenter's writings on Walt Whitman; as well as with further re-readings of Shakespeare, Siegfried Sassoon, even J. P. Ackerley, E. M. Forster and T. E. Lawrence. John M. Clum sums up institutionalisation of queer studies '…there was some notion of a gay literary canon, shared by an intellectual subculture, even if there was no openly gay critical writing' (1992). Clum goes on to see the beginning of western queer literary studies with Oscar Wilde's celebration of same-sex love, and the shaping of this pedagogy with the writings by Jeffrey Mayer, Jeffrey Weeks and Kenneth Plummer. He goes a step further to describe its historicity: '…our sense of homosexuality becomes historically shaped and ever changing.'

Significantly, this is not the case with the modern Indian homosexual. In India, we find a few gay/lesbian activists; institutions still oppose the idea of introducing courses on queer sexualities; and further, we have only a few historians who possess a proper understanding of the queer tradition. It is further complicated because we do not see open homosexuals in our society. In *Yaraana: Gay Writing from India* (1999) I had lamented: '...most men are bisexuals', or most men who have a homosexual relationship in their early age become complete homosexuals and marry because of social pressure.

Queer sexuality possesses a critical history in India. It is centred on law, religion, and social in/acceptance; the act is destabilised by law, thought to be 'deviant' by culture, and presented as a 'low-grade' act by ancient literatures. Construction of the homosexual as a category thus sees social un-acceptance, destabilises the code of law, participates against judicial actions, and sees violence.

On 13 November 1998, India's Censor Board of Film Certification, headed by Asha Parekh, former film star, released *Fire*, uncut, stating that it was an important movie for Indian women. Geeta Patel in her essay 'On Fire: Sexuality and Its Incitements' documented its results:

> ...Newspapers report that (on December 3, 1998) two hundred Shiv Sainiks, men and women, storm into two theaters, the New Empire and Cinemax, in Mumbai (Bombay), break the glass on the display windows, damage a ticket counter, and burn posters of *Fire*. In the photographs, women of the Mahila Agadhi, the women's wing of the far-right organization, Shiv Sena, are seen brandishing sticks in front of the theatre. *They allege that the film is against 'Indian tradition.'* A portion of the burden for defending 'Indian tradition' is given to women.
>
> ~ Vanita and Kidwai 2000

Representation of homosexuality/homoeroticism, as it is understood today, is thus a western import, and it is viewed against the 'Indian tradition'. However, it is not true. Ancient texts like the *Kamasutra* proscribe oral congress (*Auparishtaka*) and other 'non-productive' penetrations, strictly for a learned *brahmin*, 'a minister who looks after the matters of a state or by a man of good reputation' (Anand and Dane 1982: 148), and make alternative and queer sexualities a 'low-grade' act. People practicing these sexual acts would be liable to severe fine and punishment according to the *Manusmriti*. Punishments like loss of caste, heavy monetary fines and strokes of the whip for gay and lesbian behaviour are prescribed by the *Manusmriti*. Ruth Vanita and Saleem Kidwai (2000) provide instances of homoerotic articulation from the *Mahabharata, Kamasutra, Bhagavata Purana, Shiva Purana, Padma Purana* and *Krittivasa Ramayana* to argue that same-sex love is Indian; and hence, they attempt to construct a queer literary history in India. Furthermore, in my 'Introduction' to *Yaraana: Gay Writing from India,* I documented several aspects of Indian religions (which I call 'culture'), exploring religious sentiments towards homosexuality and pointed out that 'Islam's strict strictures on any sex outside heterosexual polygamous marriage and strict social segregation of the sexes has spawned both homophobic guilt plus a vast literature on homosexuality.' Although the Quran proscribes any kind of a sexual intercourse outside heterosexual polygamous marriage, at least the court during the Mughal period seems to be indifferent towards homosexuality. Surprisingly, in Muslim culture during the Mughal period, male homosexuality entered court life in India. Homoerotic articulation during this period was used as a metaphorical expression to show the spiritual relationship between God and man, and it finds it best culmination in Islamic Sufi literature and much Persian poetry.

The colonial government, however, on the other hand, marked by a deep sense of homophobia, proposed anti-sodomy laws, and enacted them in order to suppress homosexuality and masturbation, and thus a history of complete repressive sexuality begins during the colonial period. Kenneth Ballhatchet 'Memorandum' (1979: 10):

> For a young man who cannot marry and who cannot attain to the high moral stand required for the repression of physiological natural instincts, there are only two ways of satisfaction, viz., masturbation and mercenary love. The former, as is well known, leads to disorders of body and mind; the latter, to the fearful dangers of veneral disease.

The colonial government thus establishes brothels and lock hospitals, and enacts laws to suppress alternative sexualities. Ballhatchet, furthermore, adds another important aspect of memoranda and shows the British attitude towards homosexuality, which directly or indirectly leads to laws against the homosexual act. Mahesh Dattani explores the prevailing silences on the discourse of homosexuality in his article 'Last Word: Queering the Other':

> Over the decades, conservative British society has changed. Sexuality is no longer sublimated to flamboyant behaviour and witty repartee. It is so in-your-space that it raises not even an eyelash.... But closer home, the same British laws that condemned the likes of Oscar Wilde to imprisonment for

life are still a part of the Indian Penal Code and, although rarely used to arrest anyone, silence many political voices.

Owing to the nature and function of queer theory, queer writers/scholars in India attack the base or root of Indian tradition/culture, which is deeply rooted in homophobia, and re/read Indian culture(s) in the light of western queer theory. The present chapter investigates religious/cultural/historical instances of queer sexualities (same-sex love and cross-dressings are important here; hijra identity is another form) to show that same-sex love is Indian whereas 'queer identity' is a western import. Ruth Vanita and Saleem Kidwai's anthology (2000) is an important pioneering investigation into the history, and historical documents on same-sex love. Here, I investigate Indian discourses on the love 'that dares not speak its name' to propose a historical dis/continuity. I propose to read Indian myths, folk tales, religious and legal documents to propose the position of same-sex love in Indian society.

Notes

1. See Hall (1994).
2. See Weinrich (1992).
3. See *Facing the Mirror: Lesbian Writing from India*, India's first lesbian anthology, edited by Ashwini Sukthankar (1999).
4. From 'Introduction', Sukthankar (1999).
5. *Samalinga* and *Kliba* are recent terms constructed to represent same-sex love or sexuality.
6. See Vanita and Kidwai 2000.

introduction

I am supposed to be India's intellectual gay. When R. Raj Rao interviewed me for his book on India's gays and asked me about Lacan, I simply said western theory was not relevant to India. I do not theorise first and then live. I live my life as an Indian gay in India, write about it and then leave it to NRI's in the West to theorise about gay lives in India. Having said that I will, later, helpfully summarise recent critical theory on gays in the West, called 'Queer Theory', to help my readers.

This brings us to the matter of nomenclature. Naming and shaming, we once said. Then 'homosexual' became a badge of honour instead of an abuse. Still later came the kinder word 'gay', which seemed les abusive but took away all happiness from folks 'happy and gay' for ages. Now, in my 60th year I'm suddenly 'queer', which only meant 'strange' during my primary school days. Even so a 'fag' may call himself a 'fag' but to others, politically correct, he must remain forever 'queer'.

India has its own local name equivalents for 'active' and 'passive'. 'Active' in an eunuch's in-group lingo is *panti* (NOT *panthi*) meaning 'husband'; 'passive' is a Telugu word *koti* (NOT *kothi*) meaning, literally, 'monkey'. In an interesting twist, 'passive' gays or castrated men made eunuchs call their own male sexual organs *nikkam*, meaning 'useless' in Hindi. All this shows self-hatred brought about by centuries of social exclusion. These days, *kotis* bravely man AIDS awareness programmes. This does not end self-hatred. Socially elite gay men who head these NGO's still cannot bring themselves to call themselves publicly gay. They moved a petition to decriminalise Article 377 (anti-sodomy law) of the Indian Penal Code as AIDS activists wishing to identify potential gay disease carriers more easily. The Supreme Court threw out the petition saying they had no locus standi in the case because they would not identify themselves as gay. Ashok Row Kavi told me that the only way India would accept gays was via AIDS awareness. This is too little, too late. Freedom is not begged for; it is snatched.

However, self-hatred does not go away in a day thanks to the fairy wand of political correctness. We still feel guilt which makes literature possible. And some shame that Adam and Eve must have first felt in Eden which makes our very humanity possible. And, I dare add, which makes 'love' possible. 'Love is a literary genre,' says Ortega Y. Gasset (1957).

To wish it away as a bourgeois feeling or a class construct is, again, to diminish our humanity.

And yes, there is violence. We feel orgasms at being beaten not because we are Marquis de Sade but because nature made us so. Violence in love and sex cannot be wished away by the Cartesian rationality of the Enlightenment. Marquis de Sade haunts us still as he indeed did Jean-Paul Sartre, Roland Barthes, Michel Foucault, Gilles Deleuze. Violence in India's gay life consists of straights beating gays, active gay lovers beating passive lovers, lower class gays beating up upper class gays. This is not to say gays are criminal but to say that the class system based on power vitiates love and makes criminals and accomplices of us all.

There is no monolithic homosexuality; there are only homosexualities. By this I mean there are as many reasons for being gay as there are gays. It does not mean there is no reason why one is gay. It is not like being left-handed, nor a fashion, nor a preference. Some people are born gay, some have gayness thrust upon them, to paraphrase the bard. And some, like me, do indeed achieve to great gayness. 'I had no more choice in my sexuality than a Negro has in the colour of his skin,' said Jean Genet. There are as many escapes from homosexuality as there are roads leading to it. Drink is one escape route; macho-criminality and sadism another. These days neuroscience puts all social malaises down to brain chemicals. But writers cannot make stories out of chemicals as lead characters. 'Oedipus was at least good for something: He was good for telling stories' said Barthes. Poets, painters, film-makers, dancers, sociologists need stories. Even literary critics do. They are not scientists; these are humanists. And mine is not a rant but a plea for sanity.

It is also an intellectual fashion to equivocate: those who are not for us are not against us but are indeed for us in a veiled way. Really! In other words, the closet queer is not the queer's enemy but his ally, because from the closet he brings queerness into a hostile public consciousness. Tell me another! So Ugra in colonial India and Karan Johar in independent India are not closet queers but 'making space' (a favoured leftist cliché) for queers. Politics is about making alliances; art is about seeking truth even at the expense of making enemies. Wake up and smell the hooch!

Another American obsession catching on in India is wanting to be 'of the moment'. So you have instant nirvana and instant love like instant coffee. Hoshang should instantly become a twenty-first century 'queer' because 'gay' is so 1960s and passe. Queer theory takes off from Jacques Derrida.

Gay studies is nothing but a deconstruction of gender: men as women; women as men; and a third gender in-between. Gender too can be liminal, i.e., on the threshold of masculinity or femininity. I like Judith Butler best: she calls the bluff of all the bleeding heart, leftist feminists. Sympathy is not enough. Sex is performative. If you sympathise with a lesbian, do you actually sleep with her?

Liminality is a term conjured up by Homi K. Bhabha (1994). He says all postcolonial men and women are hybrids. Hybridity, culturally, means belonging to both East and West: like born in the East but thinking in western ways. All of us are hybrids. Postcolonial Queer Studies, something attempted here, focuses on gender in the postcolonial world — a queer aspect of postmodernism, indeed.

I

Book of the Self

introduction

When my editor approached me with a proposal to write a poet's account of homosexuality in India, I was a bit surprised. I'm no sociologist and his company's list only brings out heavyweight sociological tomes. But my editor, a youthful, fresh graduate from SOAS in London, convinced me that literature was also a kind of sociology.

My long life in the gay world began at 12 in India and I've seen gay life at close quarters in America, at different epochs, in my 60 years. What I have given here is a distillation of what I hope are universally valid truths, tropes and axioms about homosexuality as it is practised today around the world. Since the poet's knowledge, like the dancer's, emanates primarily from his or her own body, I have decided to name this first general section the 'Book of the Self'.

When you make the world tolerable

for yourself, you make it tolerable

for others

~ Anais Nin

There is no need for privacy where there
is love.

~ Osho

1

subterranean sex in the subcontinent: is homosexuality 'Indian'? a (personal essay)

The short answer is 'yes'. If 'violence is as American as apple pie and Mother', homosexuality is as Indian as *'amma* and *avvakai'*. I could add ' *aam-ka-achar', 'sadra* and *kusti'*, 'feni and sorpotel', *'rasgolla* and *maccherjhol'* and so on for the 14 states of desire, and the 18 erotic languages of union.

When I wrote *Yaraana* 10 years ago, it was hailed as a bestseller at number 2 for two consecutive weeks by *Outlook*, got a few tepid reviews and dropped off the radar screen. It has been selling steadily, bringing me new friends and detractors in my old age. Both are a nuisance at my stage of life.

There is a whole new generation of men — gay and straight — in both India and America, since I wrote *Yaraana*. The American gay has grown up like the rest of the 'civilised' West without god and consequently without guilt. Now, such a state of bovine bliss I cannot even imagine because to be without god is to be without guilt and to be without guilt is to be totally non-literary. Because gay guilt produces gay literature and it is literature that life imitates. No gay literature in India, no modern Indian gay.

Yaraana created a new canon of gay Indian literature to replace Nissim Ezekiel with Sultan Padamsee and Ranjit Hoskote with Dinyar Godrej. In between were a plethora of stars, Indian English and regional. But what is needed is not to replace an old hierarchy with a new one, an old hegemony (straight) with a new one (gay), but to shift the periphery towards the centre and to let ever-new voices be heard.

Now in what voice, rather what register, should (or do) these new voices speak? Surely not professorese of Oxford exotic but common demotic speech of everyday discourse which says: 'I'm Indian, I am gay. I want to articulate my pain or joy. So that I may be able to live and not commit suicide.' Surely this cry or plea or dry statement is understood as such if it is linguistically couched as such.

The time of artifice is over
The time for life has arrived.

Since *Yaraana*, I have grown in confidence as a teacher, as a writer, as a public speaker in the Deccan for a gay consciousness. I, as a passive gay, have concentrated on the question of motherhood punningly, since 'mother' in the gay subculture means both our biological mothers who make us gay (read 'neurotic') in the nursery and the 'gay mother' who is an older passive homosexual who gives a straight young man his first homosexual experience, births him into a gay, new world.

Since I am a teacher, I have expended a lot of writing on the creation of a gay discourse in a heterosexist academy. We leave our genitals at the university gate, but do we also need to leave our hearts behind?

So I can say with honesty, if not modesty, that I have been one of many new Indian writers writing the gay experience, that is to say, *creating* the modern gay experience. I would be most honest if I said that the way for my work was already paved for me by Ashok Row Kavi's homophiliac movement, Bombay Dost. I enclose, as a second part, my amateur anthropology of 'Gay-India from Mohenjo-Daro to Merchant', as I'm fond of trumpeting it. In poetic terms I call it 'The Book of the World'. Since Narcissus looks into the nursery mirror and becomes a genealogist of Boy at five, I call this personal historiography 'The Book of the Soul'. The mystics have always said that the body is in the soul (since everything is soul and not body as the heathens of the modern age believe).

Since there is no Dalit history, the new Dalit literature will primarily be autobiography. So too with women's writing and gay writing. This should not be mocked as narcissism but should be seen as a creation of a gay self by gays away from the macho fascism of heteronormality of the patriarchy (matriarchy, again!).

Is this articulation of a gay Indian identity western? Yes, it is. In the West, 'gay' is an identity. In the East it is one form in the cosmic flux, not *'the'* only form. After all, Siva is bisexual, both masculine and feminine, so is the Quranic 'god', unlike the all-male Judaeo-Christian Creator. In fact, there is no creationism in the East. God is eternal. There is no beginning, hence no end. This mindset would churn static sexuality as well into a carousel of changing colours, desires and moods. Then there can be no (moral) judgement. Only acceptance of our varied humanity.

But I am being carried away. Before we establish the Gay Millenium we face daily humiliation, rape, torture, even murder, without recourse to law. Even if I am not raped or beaten up on a daily basis, I am royally ignored in my neighbourhood decade up on decade and hooted at by young Lotharios. I know what humiliation ordinary women face in the Indian street. 'Raste ki gaali suna jo uski', so I ignore the kids. The hypocritical oldies I bait by getting younger lovers as I grow older, never keeping a boy longer than two years ('if they want a fag, give them a fag'), mourning their joys and celebrating their losses just as they do mine with Confucian detachment. This, too, is a yoga of survival. Article 377 of the IPC still reigns supreme and all the belated breast-beating of a Vikram Seth or the prestige of a Nobel laureate like Amartya Sen has not moved the honourable judges on the bench to bend an inch. Under such circumstances, gay writers still do write; gay listeners listen; and gay sex does flourish under the gaze of the nanny State just as it did under the law of our own nursery nannies. I should place here on record the fact that I once counted having 17 jobs in a 10 year period and seven homes within 11 months during my first year in Hyderabad. This shows that human sadism as well as masochism is almost limitless.

The modern electronic revolution has brought the western gay media circus into Hindu and Moslem homes. So our children have grown up with concepts like 'gay pride' and 'gay marriage' which my generation invented in the West. Is this globalisation of sexual identity? Yes, it is. But it should be noted that the identity existed before globalisation.

Do I approve of gay marriage? No, I don't. Why? Because I'm impossible to live with and do not wish to recreate the trauma of my parents' marriage. But also because no children/no marriage is my warcry. Yes, western lesbians and now homosexual men are allowed adoption. But why be gay if only to mimic straight patterns? We invented love (Plato) because we cannot have children. Why not make love, write books, make movies, paint portraits, teach other people's unloved children, rather than mimic pregnancy like the male seahorse or sit on a stone egg like the much touted gay male penguin of the Bronx zoo? Are we of the natural world alone or do we wish to create a new civilisation? To redefine 'family' as a gay unholy trinity of daddy-daddy (possibly) 'gay' baby is as pernicious as the holy trinity of father–mother–baby or God–Mary–Baby Jesus.

It's the Church creeping into the gay bedroom. Worse, it is consumerism. Thou shalt have babies who consume goods. Thou shalt allow yourself to be consumed by consumerism. Thou shalt not abandon the path of glorious capitalism. Thou shalt never be non-bourgeois. If you are a proletarian gay you deserve to perish with the straight proles: from Vancouver to Vietnam it shall be so because ABC and CNN rule the waves. Welcome to the Grave New World! Difference, then, is again ironed out by the marketplace, if not ruled out by the law.

There is more tolerance now than ever before because of more literacy. A new generation, the generation of sons rather than fathers, is willing to listen to the other.

But in a globalised world, othering takes many forms based not just on sexual preference or racial branding. The diasporic market place makes a Jew an other in Ramallah and an Arab an other in Tel-Aviv. Perversely enough, we all want to live in another person's country instead of our own, thereby 'othering' ourselves. And god help you if you are a gay foreigner. They were the first to go into Hitler's gas chambers. They were also the first to optimistically support the Bolshevik Revolution and the first to end up in Stalin's gulags. 'Go home (gay) Paki!'

Now the mainstream western media says there was not multi-culturalism in the street (only in professors' brains); the 9/11 and 7/7 bombings prove this point on both sides of the Atlantic. Conversely, our multicultural universities have produced straight young men willing to listen to gay young men and even gay old men like myself. This, as they would say in 1950s Indiana, is 'just peachy'. 'Something is better than nothing', the Parsi schoolgirls of my childhood used to say. My irate Iranian roommate, an Ayatollah's son, would thunder: 'Nothing is better than this little something.' Do I sound tired? Yes, I am tired.

All I can do here is put together my new diverse pieces which branch off from the main gay theme. I wanted to call the collection 'A New Gay Science' after Nietzsche. But in Nietzsche's day 'gay' only meant happy. For him Apollo was the gay god, for Dionysius' diathrambs only pulsated into eternal sorrow. Was Nietzsche gay? Was anyone? If they were, they did not know it. We are and we know it, and are here to say it.

As a footnote I add the gay man's friendship with straight women. Straight husbands see us as 'little bitches' and 'shameless fairies' because we share women's secrets. But translating an Urdu woman's poems is the gay mind's triumph over the transsexual/transvestite body. In the Brahminical Indian university everyone becomes a Brahmin.

Some More Esoteric Issues

Homosexuality is supposed to be the end of male chauvinism. No such hope in India. The penetrator is not even considered a homosexual; he considers himself 'male'. It is the female role in bed that is feared, fought off and ridiculed outside bed. This chauvinism allows a 'male' to 'experiment' under the dispensation: 'A man can do anything': even, sometimes, play the female in bed once at *his* will and whim. A 'male' can get away with murder. This role-playing in bed is more or less permanent. Top is top; bottom, bottom. Top can never be bottom; bottom never tops. A corollary is that 'He who is at bottom, pays.' Pays by way of sacrifices in bed and with time, effort, labour and money outside bed. The 'husband' in a gay marriage in India is 'kept' (in lolly) by his 'wife' (a wealthy *koti*: something akin to a dowry!) 'S/he pays to *get* fucked' is a term of ridicule. S/he may never fuck, only be fucked. 'A man should never be made into a *koti*; *he* is the 'only' male in the *koti's* universe, the *koti* is a *pativrata*, a chaste Hindu wife. 'She' does not demand orgasms: role-playing. In Brindaban Krishna is the only male; in sufism, Allah. All humans are female.

Hindus like to say there is no punishment for gays. But *Manusmriti* says a gay should be 'sewn up in the vagina of a cow'. Is this a fantasy punishment? I think an offender's penis would be sown into a cow's vagina and be left open to ridicule on the village commons. Cow, cow-dung, cow-urine, all are holy, of course, therefore purifying. Shame, not guilt, cures all in hypocritical India. No one is executed for a sexual offence. A holy bath restores normality. But a lesbian's two offending fingers were cut.

Macaulay's IPC gave the offender 10 years in prison. Technically lesbians were exempt, since the law dealt only with penetrators. The Empress of India had stated ex-officio, anyway, that no such creature called a 'lesbian' ever lived in her lands. In 1956, Nehru's India, under the Hindu Mahasabha moral brigade's prompting, made homosexuality punishable 'for life'. Stanley Wolpert's biography of Nehru shows the pretty Jawahar as an ephebe at Baroda's drag ball in 20s London. Why would Nehru agree to this? Probably because no judge would, nor had ever, put away a cocksucker for life! It's death in Saudi Arabia; no one's ever been killed there for the droit de seigneur of pederasty! It's only a deterrent.

In Iran, if a foreign gay and an Iranian man are seen by five (Islamic) witnesses sleeping together and if so much as their heels are touching, the foreigner is killed, the Iranian flogged 40 lashes. A second offence on the Iranian's part would entail death for him as well. In Khoemeni's Iran they booked you for being gay, sodomised you in gang rapes at the police station all night, dragged you out at dawn, shot you in the yard and sodomised the warm body one last time! Ah, justice!

The classic Freudian pattern of sexual development is auto–homo–hetero. But let me tell you the story of the red-blooded, Iranian descent, old city Hyderabad poet. He peaked in the 60s and was a natural heterosexual. At 14 he impregnated his maidservant, who delivered and was not seen again. The trusting mother soon replaced her with a 14-year-old girl, much to the delight of our budding poet. She soon enough started having morning sickness on the job and became visibly pregnant. It was then the mother realised who was the fox in the hen-pen. A 'boy's room' was given him. Across the road was a boy with a bum like a peach. Both being in the same class in high school they began 'night, combined-study', as the Indian English phrase goes. Our roaring heterosexual was made, by life's cruelty and society's prudence, into a raging homosexual. Married and divorced, he is today a compulsive womaniser at 60. His 'boy', a father of five, is a respected immigrant doctor in the US.

Another unfortunate child was brought up in a Bombay brothel by his prostitute mother. He was sexually used by the homosexual pimp during his childhood. Sent back to Hyderabad to gain respectability and an education, he had become 'an eve-teaser' (another Indianism) to prove his heterosexual credentials to himself over and over. Iqbal Mateen has such a story in *Yaraana*.

More astonishing is the story of a tea plantation boy whose parents were so busy in 'their loving marriage' that he was allowed to grow up with the young managers. The boy spoke the Chotanagpur dialect of the women tea pickers whose children he socialised with on the playground. The horny young managers used this kid as a procurer since they themselves did not speak the dialect. The kid used to hang around and watch the drunken, sexual orgies of his manager-friends. I also suspect one of the bisexual managers had made the kid gay. Soon enough, he was having sex at 14 with his landlord's 16-year-old daughter every single afternoon after school while the parents of both napped. He told me he had to stand on a stool to quickly finish the act performed standing up. After this, there was no looking back. Girls galore in college and university wooed in the manner of Dev Anand and Rajesh Khanna. There were still wildlife safaris with the tea estate managers, and some impossible crushes on male teachers. I fell a prey to him. The boy had become a destructive secret bisexual, destructive to both the men and women he seduced with practised ease. I joined hands with his then girlfriend after coming clean to her and we both booted him out to teach him a lesson. Already, he had a new girl waiting in the wings. Soon enough, she caught him red-handed with another girl in her own bed and fled back to her mother. The boy loved no one; only the mother he could not seduce. We all **had** to pay the price for this. Today he is alone. This is not only sociology **but** a morality tale. Sometimes it is the student who seduces the teacher. Political correctness does not take into account human vulnerability. How does the Indian boy turn gay?

This is Rauf's (20) story. I met him at the Yusfain Dargah at Nampally. He wet his lips when I gave him a come-hither look ('bade pyar se dekhna'). He laughed when I asked if I too should be a lipsmacker in reply. He came home:

> 'I was 14. In the ninth standard. I am from Delhi's Nizamuddin. I met my friend and went to his village, Chandni Chowk, and refused to come home. He started

selling clothes like my dad so I joined him in business. We live together, eight boys. But my friend and I share a room, the others use the other room. In sleep I put my head on his broad shoulder. We show each other, we hold each other. Sometimes we kiss — we've been together seven years. One day he said: Give it to me now. I can't hold out any more. I said: Please say again what you said. He said: I want you. I said: Sir, it's the first and last time you're demanding this of me. He said: Let's sleep. Don't be angry. I was only joking. I'll sleep with others but I need one 'pure' friendship. He's willing to sleep with anyone I bring for him — beggar or prince. But I won't sleep with him. He goes to whores. I don't. Girls die for me. But I won't marry them now. If you leave me I'll leave Hyderabad. I'll go to Lucknow. I won't go home.' Lucknow is the gay mecca.

As can be seen from this story, friendship includes everything up to but not including sex between male friends. Love is for friends and mothers; sex for whores and gays.

What about the bisexual? Is he only a homosexual masquerading as a heterosexual, as modernism thinks? Because modernism thinks either/ or; not this and that as in postmodernist thought which is complicated, poetic and kinder. There are real bisexuals, if sex is a continuum. There are very few men who are 50–50. Most are 40–60, 70–30, 20–80. I could be 95 per cent gay and 5 per cent straight. You could be 95 per cent straight and 5 per cent gay. There's no 100 per cent in anything: not in sex, not in love.

My neighbour's boy aged 18 wanted me. 'No,' I said. My friends warned that I would be driven out of the neighbourhood on a donkey. 10 years later he got engaged but broke the engagement. Then he married for real but did not wish for kids. He insists on becoming gay with me. Is he gay or straight, bisexual or bitch? One cannot legislate on or label human sexuality. I think he could be a gay who was brought up straight. Once he got a semblance of social autonomy he could dare to experiment with his true, secret nature. Perhaps his is the sexuality of the future. One day we will all be bisexual (as we once were before patriarchy; before colonialism in the East). Meanwhile, he's a bother.

This brings us to the nature/nurture debate. Are gays born or made? Some are born, some are made; most are both born and made. We all suffer due to our genes and because of our conditioning. We do not know enough about brain chemistry to understand the brain's role in human sexuality. What I have given here are case histories which you can judge for yourselves.

What about Dalit boys? The Dalit homosexual is akin to the Black Jew. So no Dalit boy, if he is straight, will experiment with his sexuality.

Being Dalit is bad enough. Dalit gay boys who have become bourgeoisified at school (under reservations) have inherited middle-class sexual neuroses. But 'the primitive' is also a myth. Village landlords humiliated peasants by forcing them into fellatio or anally raping serfs. Bourgeois communists who went into Telangana in the 1940s and 1950s to liberate peasants see the new Gay Movement as a continuation of sexual exploitation, as unemancipated sex. They are behind the times.

For city gay intellectuals, working-class men in bed are all the rage. Rural fantasies, working-class fantasies, blue-collar fantasies (firemen, policemen, railworkers, soldiers) are the stuff of gay bourgeois men's dreams. The Hyderabad autowallah is a special fetish for some. 'Rustic fantastic', it's called. Who wants an intellectual discussion in bed à la Eric Rohmer's films? Give me action any day. For that 'real men' will be very necessary; not brainy pansies.

Does my sleeping with a rickshaw-wallah bridge the class divide? Yes. But only in bed; *not* outside it (see Rao 2003). This is better than heterosexual same-class marriage and 'love-at-first-sight' between the sexes which happens only when social conditions first are met. It is better than 'feminists' who enslave maidservants; liberal professors who make wives and daughters serve them for life.

Since so many of my friends are Moslems I should discuss purdah. It is purdah that makes men homosocial in Islamic lands. These men are *not* homosexual. Since the zenana, harem (forbidden zone, i.e., women's area in the house forbidden to men between ages of 14 and 60), *gosha* or *anderooni* (in Dakhni) are forbidden to men, they socialise publicly (chai and backgammon) and go home to their wives after 10 p.m. They are straight married men who were probably gay in their youth. The young like Rauf have each other for company. Irani homes have a room on the street occupied by the young male heir of the family where he is allowed male guests (not female ones). This premium on the virgin bride allows for the homosociality of Islam. It encourages male bonding, male friendship; the flip side is the ever constant threat of homosexuality (especially fear of becoming a passive gay to a friend one idealises). A mullah in an Isfahan mosque told my sister who questioned him on the inequality of purdah for women: 'Men too have a purdah. They have to draw it over their eyes.' That is, Islam enjoins modesty for men. However, whereas a woman has to dress from head to foot, a man in public needs only a covering from waist to knee (if poor). Veils were not there in Arabia. Ayesha appeared barefaced before the Prophet's friends. 60 years after the Prophet, Moslems imitated the veil of Iranian aristocratic women they conquered. Male misogyny also crept in from Zoroastrianism, which considers a man 'cleaner' than a menstruating woman.

How I Met My Friend

This is not a universal morality tale but a story of a time and a place: pre-computer age Hyderabad, that is before Hyderabad become Cyberabad. Now a friend is a click of a mouse away but then (1990)! We oppressed gay men of India saw a light from the shores of California (Ah, Walt Whitman! This is thy hour!). It was called *Trikone*, 'a magazine for NRI Gays', as it billed itself. There, Indian gays advertised for American and NRI lovers. An ad said:

> I love to cook and garden
> in Hyderabad. Will you be my
> man?

We wrote to a box number in California. *Trikone*, under strictest confidence, sent our replies to the advertisers' box numbers in India. It took months.

I got a phone call at the office. It got cut off: 'My mother is coming.' Mother, den mother, house mother. Mother of all Mothers.

Next day: 'Meet me under Aishwarya Rai's poster at the RTC bus depot. I'll be on a Kinetic.' I turned up. No show from cook–gardener/husband–wife. The operative word in the ad was 'man'. I did not qualify!

Months later we fell in love with the same man, an Arab student. We had to. We were the same: upper-class, repressed queens. No fireworks when we met. But tons of sympathy.

It turned out Terry (for that was his name) lived on the next street from me between my house and my lover's and I passed by him several times a day without recognising my second self. Now if this isn't oppression, what is?

Inversions: At Ramadan

> Night has become day
> And day, night
> Men have become women
> And women, men
> Angels shed real tears
> Men aspire to be angels
> Do I see a hoof and a tail?

Do men still consort with devils?
Yesterday I saw a prophet in a four-wheel drive
Am I in a time-warp or has Time caught up with all prophets?
1ˢᵗ Ramadan, 1994
Sharjah

Hinduism/Buddhism has no time for this claptrap of the body. The Dalai Lama's monks told me, 'We have no answer to your sexual suffering. We do not discuss sex here.' Sexual love is an illusion. 'Love is a real illusion,' I learnt at the end of a life of love-suffering. So, in the end, everyone is had. Hence the Buddhist emphasise 'Right Thinking'; the Zoroastrians 'Right Thought, Word and Deed'. Love is maya in a life that is maya. End of desire is end of suffering. Etymologically, 'passion' means 'to suffer', as in 'Christ's passion'. Before leaping into shark infested waters the gay poet Hart Crane cried, 'I'm Rimbaud, I'm Baudelaire, I'm Christ.' Buddha tells me 'I' is an illusion.

But that does not mean that you can beat up on me with your fists. If you do, I'll scream. This book is my 50-year long scream.

Basant Panchami, 2007
Hyderabad

Some Issues

'Mother'

How did plain Hoshang become Mother Hoshang? I have lost the Oedipal battle to my father. An Urdu poet-son writes to his enormously reputed dead poet-father: I feel now that I'm dead/And you're still alive.

'Mother' in the gay world is a passive homosexual, usually older, who initiates a young boy into active homosexuality. S/he usually looks after the child for the rest of its life as a mother does. Let me tell you a real story: A Delhi boy I picked up at a dargah told me how at 15 his services were utilised by the local slum queen. He told 'her': I feel bad. 'Everyone does', she said. The boy would not eat or sleep for three days. The slum doctor immediately detected a sex episode. The boy, being cleverer and less truthful than me, heterosexualised the fictional account of his life to the doctor. He frequents prostitutes and prefers men. I look after my men.

I looked after my lover for four years in Hyderabad. He took my money and went to brothels and drug dens. He died inebriated, under the wheels of a public bus at 27. By way of expiation I gave a Hindu boy my five years' savings in five weeks so he could marry. Sacrifice turned sour.

Passive boys who go after active ('straight' acting) men initially have no one to help them. Victims of child abuse blame themselves, becoming masochistic. Boy love, in medieval Delhi and Lucknow, cannot be labelled 'pedophilia' or 'child abuse' as practised in the modern West. These terms (like the new term 'AIDS: The Gay Disease') are used to discredit homosexuals. Our *'laundé-baazi'* is more like it is in Plato's *Symposium*: ours is more philia (love) than sodomy. Poor parents are happy that a good-looking boy will be educated by a rich 'patron'. In ancient Greece, it was a chance for the 'pede' to grow up educated and become a free man from a slave childhood.

Mother-fixated boys, not daring incest or homosexuality, go to women who least resemble mother, that is, prostitutes or impossibly young women. A film star, the late Vinod Mehra, a classmate of mine, married (four times) vampish actresses. He was the quintessential *mata-bhakt*, impossibly Oedipal. He died at 40. He hated homosexuals.

I have heard that there is no sexual apartheid in the West. Gay and non-gay men mingle socially. The Delhi gay scene is dominated by Sylvie the hairdresser and Rohit Bal the dress designer (he put men in skirts: *read* sarong). Not very encouraging for young gay intellectuals to come out of the closet.

The hated father figure is replaced by friendships with older men. The young 'queen' in some Parsi households in the old days used to be sodomised by a father-in-law who was in the closet, a variation of the Parsi 'keep it within the family'. I read this between the lines in Gieve Patel's play *Mr. Behram* (XXXX), much to the author's surprise. I cultivated impossible crushes on my American professors in graduate school: never once did they abuse me and I am today what I am because of them entirely. I still look up to successful older male teachers. Male homosexuality is only *an* answer to the woman problem and a socially less acceptable way of solving an Oedipal crisis.

Men/Women from Movies

What is the fascination that the modern gay male feels for older women (mother) and the impossible-to-get woman (the film star/diva)? The two women are two faces of a coin; two sides of one ambivalence, attraction and a repulsion. Oedipus is attracted to his mother but fearing incest, he hates her. Love/Hate. The impossible-to-get woman is no threat. You can dream of her because she is at a great distance from you. She is also '...

at a great-distance' in her allure, set apart from our homely, motherly moms. The diva is a creation of the gay film director (George Cukor in 1930s Hollywood made stars out of mannish girls like Joan Crawford, Kate Hepburn, etc. These women were imitated in the 1940s Bombay, Hindi films where the horsey Nargis was dressed and filmed from below (to add height, stature) in the mode of Griffith and Cukor. I, a gay man, am much in demand as a translator of women's poetry!

Here in India, we are plugging into a globalised, US-dominated, mass culture. Fashions are made by gay dress designers. Fashions repeat every 40 years. This year the 1970s bell-bottoms have made a comeback. It reminds the gay male of mother (60) of 40 years ago when she was young and 20. The misogynistic gay, male fashion designer mercifully does not have to wear the stilettos, tight skirts, low necklines, high skirtlines he designs for women he alternately desires at a distance and hates in his heart for being so unreachable. I mention Manish Malhotra's uglification of Sushmita Sen.

In 1930s Hollywood the great male star was gay (Rudolph Valentino), the great female star a lesbian (Greta Garbo). Millions of gullible men and women patterned themselves on sexually ambivalent models. This means that movies plug into the deep ambivalences of our psyche; they feed our dreams but also soften our nightmares. In ballet we had the darlings of the gay crowds, Nijinsky and in my day, Nureyev; the female dancers all long-haul warhorses like Pavlova and Fonteyn. In current Bollywood the women are mannish (Madhuri, Kajol); the men effeminate or boyish (Shah Rukh, Aamir, Salman). Rachael Dwyer, London-based historian of Hindi film, says the boys in films are all gay. So indeed they are, if the gay grapevine is to be believed. The fans are little boys who grow muscles to be men, patterning themselves on these gym-built, testosterone powered fantasy men. They applaud their heroes, who, from being runts, went on to win the world.

Karan Johar, that abomination passing for an apostle of love and family values, merits more than a paragraph. He tried to bring homosexuality out of the closet in *Kal Ho Na Ho* (KHNH). So we have the tickle-nudge-wink nod at closet homosexuality in the scene between Shah Rukh and Saif Ali Khan in bed watched on by the homophobic housekeeper Kant*aben*. And who's rolling in the aisles? The audience, of course. Slap-tickle-wink! Johar epitomises the worst in Hindu heartland kitsch. He has done the gay community a disservice by further lowering the tone of the discussion of a serious subject to the level of farce. More charitably, a woman critic states that Johar is commendable: he brings a hidden subject into public thinking, although disapprovingly.

Latent/Blatant:
The Classic Gay Pattern of Two Men Sharing a 'Woman'

The pattern was set in modern literature by D. H. Lawrence sharing his wife with his best friend, G. Middleton Murray. This was fictionalised as the Birkin (Lawrence)–Gudrun–Gerald romance in *Women in Love* (1920). The critic wrote: 'Birkin is not interested in Gudrun but in Gerald!' There were howls of protest.

This is a commonplace of Indian cinema now. In Mehboob's *Andaaz* (1949), Raj and Dilip love each other but both also love Nargis. Alternately, the men threaten suicide to solve the triangle but it is the 'liberated' woman Nargis who shoots one of the men and goes to jail. She is adequately punished for being a 'modern' woman and at the end, the surviving male marries her when she has served her sentence.

In Raj Kapoor's *Sangam* (1964), Vyjayantimala battles for (and almost succeeds in getting) audience sympathy. She is the bone of contention between Raj and Rajendra Kumar. Of course, the latter shoots himself at the end but throughout the film the two are 'romancing' each other, 'dost dost na rahaa', etc.

My friend Terry sleeps with two brothers who won't sleep with each other (behind their backs). Or better, s/he sleeps with two friends simultaneously, both of whom will have sex with 'her' but won't as much as touch each other. Seeing (and comparing), however, is allowed so that homosexuality between the two 'brothers' ends over the exhausted (if not, dead) body of the gay.

Gay Icons and Their Makers

Who are the gay icons of contemporary India? From the cricket team it is Zaheer Khan (my personal favourite is Irfan Pathan, until he talks, that is). From the movie business it is Shah Rukh Khan, the King, the *Badshah*.

Who made Shah Rukh Khan? The Delhi theatre director Barry John (he declined to write for *Yaraana*). From his stable have come some remarkable actors who ultimately went into films: Manoj Bajpai, Rajpal Yadav. Manoj Bajpai confessed his debt to Barry John on television: 'For five years I lived night and day with Barry Sir!'

Among the women Micki Contractor, make-up man (sorry, 'stylist'!) and matinee heart-throb Madhuri (the *'dhak-dhak'* girl) tie-up' is famed. My Parsi hairdresser in Bombay told me how Micki 'put together Madhuri every evening from head to toe': hair extension, hair highlights, facials, facial highlights, false eyelashes, lip gloss, teeth polisher, falsies and padding to indent the waistline, false nails for hands and feet. A product called 'Mads' was assembled. Then, being all dressed up and with nowhere to go, Micki took ('invited') Madhuri out to dinner every single night to assuage her week-long loneliness. That put Micki out of pocket to the tune of Rs. 4,000 nightly. Yes, she did book him exclusively for about a lakh monthly (we're thinking the 1990's).

(Who put together the bicepital Roshan? The bisexual Khan, in his personal gym, if the gossip-vine is to be believed.)

Liz Taylor is famously believed to have said of Marilyn: 'Get that dyke out of my sight.' Sharmila sent the junior artist Madhuri back to the greenroom to fix her chipped nail polish.

Do I sound like Shobha De of *Savvy* Hinglish fame? Who put together Shobha? I knew her in college. Kitsch is always our contemporary.

'Fag Hags' and Gays

'Fag hag' is a gay endearment for straight women who love us. This is how we repay our women loyalists — with tongue-in-cheek linguistic misogyny. To give the scientific name 'fruit-fly, in Latin *drossophila melagaster*, in plain English, 'dirt lover and shit eater'....

The literary prototype, of course, is Gudrun's love of Loerke, whom Gerald really detests, in *Women in Love* (1920) (Mrs D. H. Lawrence famously picked up fags).

In recent Indian fiction we have Paro of *Dreams of Passion* (1999), who rejecting men and having 'liberated' herself, finds she is fit company only for a gay. I mean, where do you go after screaming, 'Fuck me, fuck me because I'm a five-star whore' in a hotel lobby. Here, I am merely quoting Paro's creator, Namita Gokhale, who is quoting D. H. Lawrence to the effect that if women get so liberated no man can stand them, except gays in non-sexual friendships.

In R. Raj Rao's novel *The Boyfriend* (2003), all boyfriends leave at the novel's end. The protagonist is left with a pushy, loudmouthed fag hag. She is nevertheless, dripping with kindness for the hero (read: 'Raj'). Raj told me he modelled this womanly kindness on his own mother, a great support for him.

Father

What about fathers? Why does the patriarchy repress the male homosexual as severely as it does heterosexual women and lesbians? Because the sons stole power from the matriarchy and they do not wish to lose this power again. Why was my father, a Parsi man of the early twentieth century, so repressive? I understood him from Ashis Nandy's *The Intimate Enemy: Loss and Recovery of Self Under Colonialism* (1989). My father was a colonised subject; colonised by the British, that is. He did not want his wealthy widowed mother or an older active, homosexual man to colonise him further. He colonised women, children, gays. He became a mimic man, a mimic brown-skinned English man in the Fort area of Bombay. He kowtowed to the British and Anglicised Indian males because that is who held the power then. It is not a matter of political collaboration; it is a matter of sheer personal survival of a besieged manhood.

How did my father show his hatred towards a gay son? At five, when I had resolved my Oedipal conflict by succumbing to the mother image, he sent me off to boarding school without warning. When I would not play cricket he would bowl straight at my shins. When I stood between my quarrelling parents he aimed straight at my genitals at 16, to tell me what he could do to my incipient maleness. I bore testimony against him duing my mother's divorce trial where he had hired paid witnesses, 22 of them, against poor Mother. No one dared to stand against my wealthy father. I did at 19. Later I felt compassion for him in spite of his increasing senility but a father rebuffs overtures of friendship from an estranged gay son as he, the father, fears arousing the homosexual in himself that he thought he had successfully slain in his own adolescence. I now believe my father — a neurotic, violent misogynist and control freak — was not the dominant heterosexual patriarch he pretended to be, but a destructive heterosexual hiding his basic homosexual bent. 'If you can't love, at least forget', E. M. Forster said. This essay is a step towards a long forgetting.

Johan August Strindberg, in his *The Father* (1907), discovered the truth of men and women in 'straight' marriages. He says that it is weak husbands who make for strong wives and mothers who then breed weak (read 'gay') sons.

In my love manner with men I imitate my shrewish mother; and with women I imitate the misogynistic behaviour of my father. Doubly doomed. It takes a Mahatma Gandhi to practice celibacy. So far now we have to settle for neurotic, even if aware, relationships.

The fact is, we cannot talk of a thing without talking of its opposite. We cannot talk of straight women and men without talking of gay men and women. After all, in Bismarck's Germany, Kurt-Benny invented the term 'homo (gk) sexual (Lat)' to denote the kind of man redundant in the dream of a new industrial–military set-up in resurgent Germany of the late nineteenth century. Its opposite term, 'hetero-sexual', was only dreamt up a full 10 years later.

These are the *douleurs* of the patriarchy. Around the Mediterranean basin were the settled, agrarian, civilised matriarchies (see the many-breasted Diana of Ephesus, modern Turkey). The barbarians swooped down upon the surplus civilisation from the north and east and imposed their father gods, beginning the reign of sons over the usurped Mother. Thus began male chauvinism, a chauvinism that even gay males practise to this day.

There is no proof of the matriarchy either in Europe or Asia. We have Sappho's account of lesbianism, Homer's of homosexuality (Achilles–Patroclus). The Judaeo-Christian god put paid to all that. In India we have the matrilineal Nairs of Malabar: the home, *tharavad*, goes from mother to daughter, with the maternal uncle administering the estate. In the north-east too, we have matrilineal clans: the Meitis, for example. Of course, in neighbouring Burma it is women who buy and sell in the bazaar commerce to this day, as in Mexico, though both societies are patriarchal. The eastern bisexual male (Arab/Persian/Indian), inspite of his homosexuality, does not give up the eastern potentate's right over his female harem. So homosexuality in the East in no way guarantees an end to male chauvinism.

Father Complex

Queens suffer from a father complex. They want to become their own mothers who have won for themselves husbands (our own fathers). So we snatch somebody else's husband or father. In other words, queens want a straight man to sleep with. We don't want another queer like ourselves to sleep with. This certainly shows self-hatred on the part of the gay. In swinging London and New York this is called 'The Queer Eye for the Straight Guy'. If the guy is so straight then what's he doing obligingly becoming eye-candy for the guys?!

Anyway, as Edmund White put it in *A Boy's Own Story* (1982): 'I wanted to sleep with a straight guy. But I knew, the moment he slept with me he would no longer be straight. I could never be happy.' The neurotic had painted himself into a box of insoluble, ever-constant neurosis.

The obverse of father is 'baby'. Young straight fathers (in their 30s) used to be my fetish at 20. I was looking 'to conquer' my father in bed, conversely to lose to the father in bed as I had to him in life. The need to be fucked, to be humiliated by an older man. Conversely, also the need to be solaced through sex.

Allen Ginsberg, in his *Indian Journals* (1996), tells of a dream of the famous Khajuraho sculpture of a mother holding her baby in her arms. In the dream Ginsberg is the mother; the baby, his younger lover Peter Orlovsky. In the dream, as in life, Ginsberg, the mother, fellates her baby. In childhood I fellated older men (father); now (as mother), I fellate younger men (son). This is not so far-fetched when we learn that some women have orgasms while breast-feeding infant sons, sexual feeling then being transmitted through touch to the male baby who becomes Oedipal: The beginning of life-long mental (latent) homosexuality. Most Indian men are latent homosexuals.

Ifti Nasim, in a bad later American English (non-grammatical) poem, talks of non-Moslem queens sucking dry Moslem youth and killing future Moslem babies (finishing the *quom*). Really!

When finally our lovers deign, condescend, decide to reciprocate out of generosity (or simply to end their sexual blackmail), we queens feel we have indeed become mothers suckling our infants. (This is not so perverse when we think some husbands drink up their wives' milk meant for the infant son.) I have always maintained that sex is a metaphor. Metaphor is a fulfillment of fantasy, a restoration of sanity and an end to neuroses as in dream. What you do or don't do in bed tells you what you are outside bed.

Some Erotic Exotics

The Gay Institution of the 'Sugar Daddy'

A gay 'kept' boy is not a prostitute. A 'Sugar Daddy' is not a customer. Daddy is father and boy is son. 'You do not have sex with your children' is a law that does not apply here, because the whole institution is a clever, age-old (as old as the Greeks and the Arab Caliphate) device to circumvent the sex taboo between father and son. The boy is nurtured. His (usually) poor family is looked after, but not upon demand. There is no obligation, only voluntary sacrifice. Call it 'love', if you will. The old man is 'daddy' and his boy is 'sugar'. This misunderstanding of the sugar trade as prostitution is akin to the West's misunderstanding of Japan's geishas as sex workers. It is a trade only in the sense of a voluntary exchange. There is no bargaining allowed here. 'No bargains in friendship' is a favourite slogan of the Persian and Hyderabadi boys. At worst, you can call it a sexual barter (Shakespeare's 'what is mine is thine and what is thine is mine'). The painted boy who sits in the Kuwaiti 'souk' to sell 'pots' or 'meat' (read 'ass' and 'penis') is also *jaāyez* (Islamically 'legal') if the boy and client enter into a *sigeh* (contract marriage) lasting from anything between three hours to three months (but it won't last up to 3 years — that is an American 'gay relationship'!)

The Transvestite

They are called hijras (eunuchs) in India and *khosri* in Pakistan. There are the street hijras and the *kotha* hijras. The latter are wealthy singers and dancers with powerful patrons like the sons of the last Nizam of Hyderabad. They kept a lamp burning at dusk in the street-level door to their rooms to indicate they were ready for business. If the lamp was out, it meant they were otherwise engaged. They were prized for their sexual stamina and muscular buttocks which could 'milk the penis'. Some amassed great wealth and had their own *addas* or *kothis* of ill-fame. Some earned repute for their art. Under the guise of art prostitution flourished, as in Hyderabad's Mehboob-ki-Mehndi and Lahore's Hira Mandi.

During the Afghan War, the boys of Peshawar went to the border to sell 'meat'; they were called 'gosh-fouroush' (meat-sellers). Their innocent mothers and sisters in usually fatherless houses took their boys literally at their word.

The *khosri* of Karachi sleeps with politicians (some said Zardari) and imitates Rekha. Field Marshal Ayub Khan, who famously 'kept' Noor Jehan, also was fond of keeping *khosris*. These transvestites become politically powerful; very few of them, though, among thousands.

Ifti Nasim, Pakistan's first gay poet in Urdu, worked as a boy prostitute in Faislabad (Abbotabad) to feed his sisters when abandoned by the father. Later, he was a used car salesman in Chicago, wearing lipstick to work. He picked up American business efficiency as a Detroit student earning pin money. He had a Body Menu — Fellatio: $15; Ass: $25; Full Night: $50, etc. To work the streets in the night and write poetry by day is also heroism.

The Transsexual

'A man trapped in a woman's body'. The only one of my acquaintance is Farrokh Rustom, classical pianist, now Farah Rustom (aka Mrs Beal of Colorado). She made it to the covers of gossip magazines and Mithun Chakraborty told her, 'For a week you were more famous than me.' We are in contact on e-mail. She told me she had 'a mother from hell'. Her abiding passion is to equal and outrun the mother in social respectability. She is very emphatic that she is not a homosexual. She considers that her plastic surgeon merely gave her her true nature by correcting God's little mistake. She took offence at my statement in the autobiography: 'A phoney way of making phoney men and women as a cure for a disease that does not exist.' She's over 60 and hopes to adopt a child, but 'he will never know my deep, dark secret'. At last report, she was left for dead by sissy-beaters in Hamburg. But true to her style, she resurfaced on e-mail to say that the report of her death was highly exaggerated. She should know as she is no stranger to that figure of speech.

Gay Murders

The most sensational gay murder was of a high-end Vasant Vihar, Delhi gay who was murdered by his two servants just after he returned from a diplomatic party. No convictions yet but an obnoxious anti-gay opinion page article was published in *The Indian Express* by a *bhadralok* critic. In Hyderabad, two gay murderers sodomised six boys and killed them with stones after first drugging them. This is what repression does in our society. More sensational was the murder of a gay man by his 'squeeze' (both NRIs) who said the lover was blackmailing him and pressing him for money.

In *Yaraana*, I have written about a one-year jail sentence for a Christian teacher who murdered a gay student for refusing his advances. The trial of gays by a jury reminds me of Pasolini's murder trial where his murderers, viz. members of the Communist Party/Catholic Church tried and acquitted their own accomplice to the crime.

The Police

R. Raj Rao will tell this story in his new book of gay interviews. I have read the manuscript and this story is haunting and illuminating. A semi-literate Pune teenager, son of a constable (Dawood was one), failed as a male prostitute to find a sugar daddy. He ambushed a high society girl into a gang rape by his gang of boys (the girl committed suicide) and went in for three years. He served two years of the sentence, during which he found a cute, fair boy as his fag in the jail and sodomised him daily under the guards' eyes: 'We are their blue-film,' he says. Out now due to 'influence', he has joined Dawood's gang in Bombay: his dream come true. This is the nightmare India lives because of its refusal to come to terms with homosexuality.

Riposte to Sunday Indian Express *anti-gay-opinion-piece (after Vasant Vihar Gay Murder, 2006)*

Homosexuals are murdered with impunity in India because there is no recourse to law. Article 377 of the IPC make sodomy illegal and a punishable offence. I met the then Solicitor General Soli Sorabjee at Bellagio and he told me he had advised the Government of India to decriminalise homosexuality (the gay NGOs from Bombay and Delhi had petitioned for such a move). Atal Behari Vajpayee, then India's Prime Minister, a bachelor himself, had then said that the time is not ripe for such a move and 'the majority will not accept it'. He should know that in India this law was introduced by the British along with English education in 1859. Since 1963, UK's sodomy laws have been repealed. It is 40 years now that this move is due in India. If private sexual activity were not criminal, gay men would not have to cruise in public, putting themselves at the mercy of blackmailers, torturers and murderers.

The Curse of the Eunuch

There is a widespread belief in India that if you do not pay a fee to the hijras who dance and sing at the birth of your child, your child could even die of a curse. Recently a Bombay eunuch drowned a child in the family's own water storage cistern, feeling offended. Every man who does not use his sexual organ (Sanskrit *kliba*) for whatever reason is called *napunsak* (non-male), hijra (eunuch) or *chakka* ('sixer': a pejorative for gays since eunuchs beg on the sixth day of the week, which is associated with Venus).

Another theory doing the rounds on TV is about '*manglik*' women. They have Mars (*Mangal*) badly placed in their horoscope (fourth house of family life). They kill their husbands. They are called *narbhakshu* (man-eaters) or *vishkanya* (snake women). I have had three lovers, all now dead. AT 16, I had a crush on a classmate from a wealthy family. I dreamt of running away with him. When that did not happen, I tried suicide at 16 (I was a drama queen but my dramas were real, then). He died at 36 from stomach cancer, probably from drink. (Alcholism is veiled homosexuality.)

My lover in Iran went to Khomeini's war against Iraq and was never heard of again. A statistic now: 'one of 2 lakh Iranian men dead on the front in a 10 year war.'

My Hyderabad lover died under the wheels of a bus. Moslems donate money to the mosque to expiate a guilt. I did too.

If my curses come true (Hindus call me *Durvasa*) will my blessings, too? I still haven't learnt to bless.

Negotiating Modernity

The Indian filters modernity through traditional values (see Pandey 2005). This allows for continuity as well as cultural schizophrenia. The Islamic world exemplifies it as religious paranoia. Saddam exemplified it as a return to the Arab chivalric past. In gay Hyderabad, it means a gay nawab taking his male lovers home to satisfy his wife since he cannot. It means a Parsi aristocrat, always nameless but enormously promiscuous, kicking his gigolo's backside after drawing immense pleasure from it. This restores the lost traditional value of masculinity. It means the new generation of gays in the same family dying of AIDS in USA and Europe leaving their mothers to prepare face-saving exercises. Social hyprocrisy comes from the need to pursue outdated values in a chaotic world.

Decolonising the Self

W. B. Yeats was the first decoloniser in poetry, followed by Tagore. I am in their tradition. My speaking Urdu to my lovers is actually denying the English; Macaulay, the same who introduced English education as well criminalised homosexuality in the IPC he drafted. Gay love was not a crime, the English made it so. (Conversely it gave us terms for that love and bisexuals had to love one sex or another permanently!) So my simple act of convenience becomes an act of rebellion against deep-seated neuroses brought on by colonisation.

Nomenclature

This bring us to nomenclature: English and Hindi, viz. gay/straight, active/passive, top/bottom, *panti/koti* (i.e., husband/wife). As you can see, gays have unthinkingly adopted the straight paradigm of penetrator/penetrated possible between one negative and one positive pole (female/male), but not applicable where there are two males in a relationship.

Koti (Telugu for 'monkey') is the Bombay–Hyderabad term for passive gay, queen — an outré, campy creature. It is a creation of homophobia in society and gay self-hatred. *Panti* is the slang for husband. The 'male' gays refer to us queeny gay men as 'she'. It has nothing to do with my misogyny which is actually a projection of the male mind. Passive gays derive a lot of support from female friends and are less misogynistic than males who sexually depend on females, something a female can take pleasure in denying them. Sex discussions go on between gay men and their female friends unabashedly because, as Gilles Deleuze and Félix Guattari remind us in *Anti-Oedipus* (1983) gay men can spare their blushes in such a situation (so can the women) as the two parties in the conversation are not sexually interested in each other. Straight men do not understand this and call us queens 'bitches', 'sluts', etc. Lorca, the straight-acting gay man, the poet, descended to calling queens names in his *Poet in New York* (1998), in which old world meets new world and the old crumbles.

The Western Agenda

This book comes out of a western agenda (Routledge, London). What is the agenda? Is it still a civilising mission of the West for the East? 'Elite' gays like myself lead a vanguard to win 'freedoms' for their less bold, hence less articulate, fellow sufferers. I am actually 'orthodox' and 'conservative' (Parsi traits) though I'm gay. I never push the envelope too far, though I hope I've pushed it far enough here. Does the West like to congratulate itself? Is the West doing on a moral scale to India's gays what Europe and America's 'shock and awe' troops did in Iraq in politics? I never badmouth India in literary conferences (with 'Marxist' agendas) in the West. One does *not* bad-mouth one's 'parents' (though I do here since I must). When asked how gays are treated in India, I say, 'We too have (Clinton's) 'Don't ask/Don't tell' policy; we're at least as civilised as the West.' My Dalit colleague fits nicely into the western agenda by playing 'the put-upon Third World Woman', something the West likes to hear in order to congratulate itself.

In my defence I should say that in 1975, when I was 'radicalised' at Purdue, I did not know what forms our gay revolution would take in the twenty-first century. The West (with its economic and ecological *douleurs*) has become 'conservative' since then. Consequnetly, the gays have become more radicalised. Every 'Revolution eats its own children'. Once I was the beaten child, now I'm the eaten grandfather!

'Gay Marriage'

Gays re-enact the neuroticism of their straight parents' marriages in their own marriages. After all, gays are born into straight households, not gay ones. Gays are a living reminder to everyone of the inadequacies of straight marriages. Hence they are hated. Liv Ullman, star of Ingmar Bergman's *Scenes from a Marriage* (1973), says in her autobiography that after this film's release, gays used to come up to her in the streets of Stockholm (early 1970s) and tell her : 'This is *our* marriage you've portrayed.'

I used to wonder as a child why my mother, an educated woman in a second marriage (in the 1940s), took a lifetime's beatings from my father. The answer, of course, is that my mother had become 'masochistic'. She had internalised society's diktat that any woman who fulfills her (sexual) needs is a 'fallen' woman. My father, for his part, specialised in 'rescuing fallen women' (a typically Victorian hypocrisy learnt by Parsis). I say this because he did the same thing in *his* second marriage: bullied an illiterate girl he 'rescued' (never mind that he had first taken advantage of her impecunious circumstances).

The Sissy-beater

The fagbasher comes in many forms. He came to me at 21 in the form of an ex-Purdue footballer with a crushed knee and an aborted football career who had gone into making 'souped-up' cars (converted into more powerful cars, that is) for Derby racing — not quite Indianapolis 500. He weighed 200 lbs. He wanted to be fucked. I was 21 and weighed 51 kg. at that time. I was bashed up and left for dead (see *Autobiography*).

The more interesting thing was what came later. The campus police probably knew him (he was a serial offender) but they booked me, 'a foreign fairy'. I was the colonised subject in bed, the police station and then the psychiatric clinic. The offender didn't need psychiatry, the victim did. I knew where power lay, then. 'Why did *he* do it?' I kept asking. Of course, I was too good a masochist back then to ask 'Why me?' Complicity!

Later, when my Iranian boy-lover used to slap me after asking to be fucked in bed I realised that 'masculinity', a false notion of it, was being restored. For me, then, it was the end of the world, or at least of my love for my lover, but for the sissy-beater, the person who stole his masculinity in his own bed does not even have a right to exist.

Gay Spaces

Christopher Benninger, Pune's gay architect (who designed Mahindra College, Pune; now buildings in Bhutan) says gated communities are an end to cruising; to gay street-life. The Indian leftists say the malls are designed to separate Bharat from India; the have-nots from the haves. There are two peoples now: the poor and the rich, in the same city, with demarcated borders. Floodlit parks that charge fees are designed to keep out poor, cruising gays. Public toilets with guards are meant to discourage the use of public spaces as gay sex havens. But gay subversion finds a way out. The Bombay Churchgate midnight local had become a moving orgy room for gays, specially the freight car. Washroom attendants in Hyderabad cinemas could be gay, kept there by a gay manager to service the gay clientele after show time. Anyway, the San Francisco gay ghetto — 'dogs on top of fags on top of dogs' — never fascinated me. I'd rather have the whole world as my oyster. But again, I'm dreaming. The world is changing; cities too change. The *paan*-bidi shopkeepers that Bhupen Khakhar cruised in Khetwadi and Baroda exist no more. So gays and straights won't mix; the rich and poor don't mix; and men and women never mixed socially in India anyway. So why have lesbian fantasies (sorry, Sohini Ghosh) of gay Indian women cruising one another at Kolkata cinema-houses? Gays live on in nostalgia of their boyhood cities, be it Bombay or Barcelona.

Is 'Gay Identity' an Answer to Identity Crisis?

I will give here two literary examples — one historical, Sultan Padamsee's and the second contemporary, Shani Mootoo's.

Padamsee, a Bohra brought up as a Christian, an Indian mimic man masquerading as a Brit, a speaker of Gujarati writing in English, a gay living socially as a straight and a gay writing as a straight finally at 24, committed suicide from the strain. Which came first: the social crisis or the sexual one?

Shani Mootoo, born in Ireland of a South Indian Brahmin sugarcane plantation family in Trinidad and currently in Canada says, as a lesbian writer, ' by writing she *creates* a memory'. Very moving. It allows her not to go mad, not become a cripple, not commit suicide. Which came first: the social crisis or the sexual one?

Both R. Raj Rao and Mootoo think sex came first.

I posit that a gay child, male or female, is very aware of its 'separateness'. If it is a poet, it goes into fantasy missions of making the world safe for gays later on in life. The sex urge does go under at five. From five to 15, the child takes stock of the world in its sexual quiescence. That is, it takes stock of the social crisis. Then, the recurring sexual crises of teenage alert the child that the social malaise fits neatly in with the sexual malaise. If the child is a fantasist she becomes a brilliant writer, a Shani Mootoo, a female Rimbaud. If he is a realist he becomes Padamsee and commits suicide. If he goes mad he becomes Hoshang, just in order to be able to live on.

A Note on Genre

Gender is genre. The third gender will produce a third (new) genre: not prose, not poetry; not fiction, not fact; not discourse, not effusion; but a mixture of all these.

If you bend gender, you can bend genre. Gays are gender-benders and genre benders.

It was said of Leonardo da Vinci that he left everything, including the Mona Lisa, incomplete because he was a gay genius. His genius and his gayness always led to boredom. He was always being called elsewhere.

Picasso left his harlequins incomplete because in Spain, they believe the harlequin represents the Devil. He might come alive if finished in paint.

Gays are both harlequins and devils. Out of compassion, then, should we gays leave rough cuts instead of finished artifacts behind us for newer generations to contemplate and finish?

Feminists complain they write with one hand while stirring the home fires with the other hand with a baby on the hip. Has anyone thought of a gay's time devoted to his profession, home making, and husband hunting (every single night for a new one)? I am not making excuses but stating facts.

Former professor Meenakshi Mukherjee's complaint is that I write as I talk, i.e., not academically. Jargon is an epidemic of academia. I'm not writing for former professors like her but for thousands of homosexuals dying of shame and guilt in the gullies of Hyderabad, Nizamuddin and Lucknow. I should also mention Bangalore, Calcutta and Bombay, three cities I know. Also Hebbagodi (outside Hubli) where Ganesh, a young gay who barely speaks English but can read simple English, decided not to end his life at 20 after reading *Yaraana*. I know this because he wishes me on the phone every year on my birthday. To connect with these men I speak Hindi, not English, leave aside Derrida and Foucault's language. I speak Urdu to my lovers — intimacy does not develop in foreignness.

The likes of Mukherjee will say, 'How many Indians read English?' I did not take on to save the world like Christ. Yes, I have taken it upon myself to give a modicum of self-respect to India's English-speaking gays because I was given none when I was growing up in India 40 years ago. And I still have to fight to be respected by the *aam-janta*.

Notes on Deleuze's 'Minor Literature'

1. *All* literature is minor literature as it belongs to a group. For example, there is no one unified, major Shakespeare. But there are many Shakespeares, e.g., of the academics, of the tourist industry, etc.

2. Art does not re-present reality but creates realities (in the plural), i.e., there is no world present which art then represents but that art creates the new worlds of gays, women, blacks, Dalits, i.e., a creation, rather than an expression, of identity.
   N.B. We put these four 'minor' groups together because oppression is oppression, though modes and characteristics of the oppression differ, e.g., though none can change their birth, Dalit and black men look down on gay men and gays look down on women.

3. Each group had an allegiance to a totem sign: Brahmin's thread, she-wolf of Rome, phallus for gays.

4. Language becomes a sound, a stutter: *not* communication or representation but sound as an incantation, a chant (e.g., Gaddar's ballads, American Indian chants.) The staccato effects of my writings, unable to say but saying it nevertheless.

5. It disrupts and dislocates tradition: e.g., Aga Shahid Ali's 'Americanised' 'gay' ghazals.

6. The power of eternal return of Art :

   (a) Each generation uses traditions of art differently, e.g. Andy Warhol's Marilyn of the 1960s different from the Hollywood Star of the 1950s.

   (b) Each generation re-reads the work of art by its own light: we *are* 400 years 'older' than Shakespeare!

Literatures

On Love

Love is a literary genre

~ Ortega Y Gasset (1957)

The first book on love in the western World is *Ta Erotika* (*On Love*) by Plato. He is teaching love to the ephebe he is enlightening sexually and socially. Love is an activity to build young minds and hearts (just as the gymnasium at the baths built bodies), which then built society. It was an activity between men: older men with younger men, teacher with pupil.

There is no text comparable in India. The *Kamasutra* is a sex manual of prostitutes. Hindu wives could not read, and Hindu husbands were loath to coax wives when prostitutes were freely available in Gupta India. Love does not occur in marriage; only outside it, with prostitutes. Marriage is a social contract and love has nothing to do with it.

This homosexual convention of love invented in pagan Europe was Christianised by the early Church fathers who banned prostitution and brought Love into the marital home. It has led to the American anomaly today of 'the sexy mom of 2 kids!'

In literature, gay men wrote as if they were straight. Arnaut Daniel, the troubadour in Provence at Eleanor of Aquitaine's court, was gay. They invented 'heterosexual love' (influenced by Sufis of Andalusia). The question of these young gay men physically loving their queen did not arise as she was an old, lonely, grass widow (with her gay husband Richard off on a Crusade), who ostensibly would give her chastity (note: not virginity) as a prize to the best poet. No one won because the queen was ever-chaste and the poets were gay or uninterested in anything but poetry. So literature was invented in name of love, and courtly love began to be imitated from books into life. (Note that Dante's twelfth century lovers go to Hell for reading a book on love which physically inflamed them to sin.)

In nineteenth century Victorian England, Mathew Arnold, Alfred Lord Tennyson, Walter Pater, all homosexuals, wrote as if they were heterosexuals. No one except Oscar Wilde was bold enough to declare gay love. He got jailed and the prostitutes danced in the streets: 'Let them do what they want, but let them not frighten the horses!' Alfred Edward Housman, a closet queer, was happy Wilde 'got his come-uppance', as indeed Wilde was blowing Housman's 'cover' (the very homoerotic *Shrophsire Lad* notwithstanding).

In India, our parents of the nineteenth and we of the twentieth centuries were fed this bilge of 'great Victorian poetry' (read 'heterosexual) by probably gay colonial schoolmasters. (Fagging and ragging were gay rituals of British public schools still going on until recently in anglicised, upper class India.)

It was left to the gay, Gallic Rimbaud to cry, 'Love has to be reinvented,' before committing literary suicide at 19! American Puritanism and political correctness has put paid to Platonic love in the academy. America, however, did learn 'living-in' and 'the bath culture' from the gays before AIDS shut down America's bath houses.

My diaries are an attempt to re-invent gay love in the modern world of Mafia-run gay brothels which had transformed Platonism into a kind of Whoredom.

Western Theory in the Gay Indian Bedroom?

Queer is a continuing moment, movement, motive-recurrent, eddying, troublant. The word 'queer' itself means across-it comes from the Indo-European root twerkw, which is German quer (transverse), Lat. Torquere (to twist), English athwart….queer is multiply transitive. The immemorial current that queer represents is antiseparatist as it is antiassimilationist. Keenly, it is relational and strange.
~ Eve Kosofsky Sedgwick, *Tendencies* (1993)

Totally useless; abandon it, immediately! Queer theory is no good in India: no Indian gay wants to be a queer unless he's a queen or a hijra and has to be happy being just that.

I did, however, find the following western theorists profoundly liberating:

(a) **Michel Foucault**: In his *History of Sexuality, Volume I* (1979), has a profoundly liberating passage on bourgeois repression in nineteenth century Europe. He says that industrialisation enjoined sexual repression, which led to the effeminisation of sons (me) and hysterisation of women (my mother). This key unlocked the secrets to my family's attic. Ashis Nandy (1989) builds on Foucault's research with respect to colonised subjects in India (which I have referred to while dealing with fathers of Indian gays).

(b) **Jean Genet**: I have read everything ever written by Genet: prose, poetry, fiction, polemic, film. I have also read everything written on Genet by way of biography and criticism. The most affecting book was Edmund White's magisterial biography (1993) which provided an insight into the mechanisms of making western colonialists. The first 'colony' was a penal (pun!) colony where 'juvenile delinquents' (seven-year-old boys who stole a single pencil at school, as in Genet's case) were sentenced. Once they came out they became 'repeat offenders'. Three times and you're out' or rather you're 'in' (for life). The panopticon was created, where the jailer sat like an all-seeing God at the centre of a circular jail where the corridors were the wheel spokes, at the end of which was a solitary-confinement cell under 24-hour surveillance. The inmate had to sleep, eat, defecate and masturbate under 'God's' watchful eye. He could become gay, being sodomised (brutally) year after year, until he became an adult when the sentence was commuted. Boys stripped of all childhood, of all social links opted to join the army, the French Foreign Legion. They were fed, educated and could travel to Algeria and Tunisia where they brutalised the colonised Berbers or Arabs as colonialists. Having known only brutality, they became brutal men. (The connection to our Indian family is not hard to make here.) But Genet was gay and he fell in love with the Arab whom he allowed to sodomise him! You can see here that the gay literally and figuratively 'fucks up the system', i.e. *humanises* it by sexualising it. We postcolonials have a lesson to learn here. Enough said.

(c) **Pier Paolo Pasolini**: is the greatest gay artist of the twentieth century, after Genet. He died young (was murdered) and he had two enemies instead of Genet's one, viz. not only the Church but also the Communist Party. What I like more than his hatred of the Church (sorry Roman Catholics!) is his love for the proletarian youth. His *Roman Poems* (2001) allowed me to understand my fascination for urban slum kids: the autowallah, the welder, the store-keeper (Bhupen Khakhar painted the petty tradesmen he cruised on lazy Baroda afternoons). To go over to the class enemy is to vanquish class pride. I can only quote a poem; I've done this, been there, similarly, in a different but similar place (Philadelphia Roman Amphitheatre Ruins, downtown Amman, Jordan) at a different time (my 1970s to Pasolini's 1950s).

I was walking near the hotel in the evening
when four or five boys appeared
on the field's tiger fur,
with no cliff, ditch, vegetation
to take cover from possible bullets — for
Israel was there, on the same tiger fur
specked with cement-block houses, useless
walls, like all slums.
I happened on them at that absurd point
far from street, hotel,
border. It was one of countless such
friendships, which last an evening
then torture the rest of your life. They,
the disinherited and, what's more, sons
(possessing the knowledge the disinherited
have of evil — burglary, robbery, lying —
and the naïve ideal sons have
of feeling consecrated to the world),
deep in their eyes, right off, was the old
light of love, almost gratitude.
And talking, talking till
night came (already one was embracing me,
loved me) they told me everything about themselves,
every simple thing. These were gods
or sons of gods, mysteriously shooting because
of a hate that would push them down from
the clay hills like bloodthirsty bridegrooms upon
the invading kibbutzim on the other side of Jerusalem…
These ragged urchins, who sleep in open air now
at the edge of a slum field —
with elder brothers, soldiers armed with
old rifles, mustached like those
destined to die the ancient deaths of mercenaries —
these are the Jordanians, terror of Israel,

weeping before my eyes
the ancient grief of refugees. One of them,
sworn to a hate that's already almost bourgeois (to blackmailing
moralism, to nationalism that has paled with neurotic
fury), sings to me the old refrain
learned from his radio, from his kings —
another, in his rags, listens, agreeing,
while puppylike he presses close to me,
not showing, in a slum field
of the Jordan's desert, in the world,
anything but love's poor simple feeling.
(1963)

This is a Christian (*nazaari*; 'Nazarane' in Arabic) and foreign (*ajnabi*) view of the Palestinian refugee camp fedayee (freedom fighter) in Israel (a revolt south of Italy in West Asia, hence 'Southern Dawn').

I have an even more chilling story from Israel about Arab fedayee told by an upper crust Israeli queen (even Jewish gays have to fight for Israel). On the Lebanese border, the fedayeen would belly crawl the no-man's land to be fellated by Israel's queens at night, who in the morning would target them dead anonymously, from their America-supplied tanks.

(d) **Gilles Deleuze:** Foucault called him his heir; another gay man, dead of AIDS like his mentor. In his 'What is a Minority Literature?' Deleuze has pointers for gay literature, western and Indian. He says that all great literature is minoritarian in the modern and pre-modern ages. The modern example is Kafka: an Austrian Jew writing in German rather than his native Yiddish. Shockingly, we learn from Deleuze that Shakespeare was minoritarian: he was not of the aristocracy, not patronised by the King (though he performed at Court), not a university wit, but he got his material from folklore, old tales, old historical chronicles, in short, the sixteenth century equivalent of our pulp fiction. His strengths were the groundlings: he thrived on their humour, and they thrived on his plays. What's more, he was the first postcolonial writer digesting the implications of the Bermuda Voyage (his Milanese sailors flounder at Gibraltar). It is plain to see how Deleuze opens literary respectability to someone like me.

(e) **Sigmund Freud and Frantz Fanon:** are respectively the grandfather and father of the afore-mentioned writers. Freud, in his 'Civilisation and Its Discontents' (1929), writes the seminal essay for our times. As a Viennese Jew of the late nineteenth century, he longed for the un-neurotic life of the uncultured savage. But the price of civilisation is neuroticism. 'Gay', then, is nature and marital bourgeois discontent culture (hence un-nature breeds neuroticism), the polymorphous perverse being straitjacketed into monogamy.

Fanon, in his *Wretched of the Earth* (1961), talks as a western-educated, brown-skinned man who practised psychiatry in colonised Algeria and saw the horrors perpetrated by that colonisation not only on the colonised but more so on the coloniser. In a statement that sums up Fanon, we can say: 'the hand that holds the whip is as brutalised as the back it brutalises.' He says with Shantideva, Tibet's first medieval Buddhist psychologist, that no one can victimise anyone unless the victim first makes himself available. Of course, the ravages of colonialism were well-planned with the victim's mind first being seduced (read: colonial education) and then the body follows (read: the Oriental land and riches). So the way out is to re-educate the coloniser and the colonised. Now that we have kicked the coloniser out of our lands, when will we kick out the coloniser from our beds? 'I am a colony,' says an Indian English poet (Sudeep Sen). But we are all colonisers in our homes and in our beds. We need a pedagogy of the oppressed. And now I'm not talking of pimp, prostitute and gigolo but men and women in heterosexual marriage. The implications of the other impinge upon the self: in fact, it is only in light of 'others' that 'we' are defined, whoever we may be.

The Strange Case of Lacan

Jacques Lacan found male homosexuals strange (his French Roman Catholicism wouldn't let him accept them). Lacan's critics and friends found this blind spot in Lacan's thinking somewhat strange. So, soon enough, he came out in full praise of lesbians. According to him, man is sexually an incomplete creature. The complete sexual being is a woman who has a clitoris (vestigal penis) that fully functions to an orgasm and ovaries to reproduce (men have orgasms but can't birth). So lesbianism is understandable and to be encouraged (by extension). Male homosexuality still remains a puzzle for Lacan as Lacan remains a puzzle for us. This, of course, would spill into linguistic implications: the male bias of all languages would have to go. (Hoshang makes *everyone* into a 'she' except God and his lover. When Hoshang is the Lover, like Krishna in Brindaban (read: 'bed') then Hoshang is a 'he'. However, Hoshang/Krishna is usually in 'Radha-bhava' wearing a saree!)

Anais Nin calls lesbianism 'making love like fish without sexual organs'. She is referring to cunnilingus and mutual masturbation. Fellatio is the preferred method between fag hags and their fags who the women with their 'golden-pussy-syndrome' ('once you fall into it/you'll never fall out') think have gone 'straight'.

Recently, an American girlfriend of mine confessed her taste for old, impotent Italian men who sodomised her with dildos. They gifted her electronic sex toys for masturbation. She went by a boy's name. This Jewish New Yorker had got around her lesbianism with older, latent gay men. The mind conjures new forms to circumvent society.

Modern Indian Psychology

In a book on India's Freudian psychologists, *Vishnu on Freud's Desk: A Reader in Psychoanalysis and Hinduism* (1999), a tribute is paid to the 1930s psychiatrist Dr Bose who spoke on the Indian Oedipus succeeding in 'castrating' the father. In Hinduism, after *grihastha* ashram (50), men are enjoined to give up, go to the woods, meditate, attain *moksha*. The son is, at 30, 'freed' automatically of his father. Therefore in youth Indian men are homosexual; after the father 'retires' (to the forest or from his offices), the son can be a husband and father in his turn between the ages of 25 to 50. In the West and in (superficially) 'westernised' Indian homes, the father never gives up and the son turns gay. Hence, the incidence of homosexuality is higher in the West than at home.

(Recently the BJP's Hindutva brigade sent 10 boys to my class. 'We must not say anything against Dr Merchant but we do not agree with his ideas.' Was it a case of the fear of being found out?)

It can be argued that India's western-educated elite (Jawaharlal Nehru) conducted an Oedipal rebellion against the father (British in India) by achieving India's independence. If Nehru was first Mountbatten's lover and then Edwina's, it can be said that he first succumbed to his ideological father and then castrated him by marrying the mother (Lady Mountbatten).

His daughter Indira understood her own symbolic value as 'India's Mother' and rode a tiger, Durga-like, during the Emergency (M. F. Hussain painted her as such). A 'son' (her bodyguard) assassinated her.

Appendices
(a) The Homosexual/Dalit Interface
(This is a personal essay on one man's sexuality)

Marxist intellectuals amid us believe that there is no connection between bourgeois homosexuals and Dalits. They even refuse to admit that homosexuals are treated today as badly as Dalits, or worse.

A Reddy friend told me that homosexuality, as it existed in Telangana up to the 1970s, usually took the form of a Reddy or Brahmin landlord askng a Dalit farmboy to fellate him. This was pleasure for the landlord and humiliation, rather than pleasure, for the Dalit at the landlord's hands. This class, caste and social position were re-established once the act of pleasure for both or either party to the sexual transaction was over.

The Marxists, who went out from the cities of the then Nizam's domains into the countryside to liberate the toiling farm labour, took the master–servant sexual bond as a harking back to feudal lord/fief–serf relationships. This was true in the 1940s during the Independence struggle and the 1950s during the Telangana Movement. But to stick to this idea from a bourgeois–Brahmin viewpoint is an anachronism.

The fact today is that through extreme social struggles and education (thanks to reservations), some rural Dalits have escaped humiliation and joined the ranks of the city bourgeois. A gay Dalit boy could certainly not be expected to give up bourgeois social respectability gained through at least two generations of struggle merely in the name of gay liberation. I find this true in my classes at University of Hyderabad where, as a gay teacher, I find Dalit boys dying for bourgeois respectability even refusing to give me a hearing (in my instance it was perhaps an unofficial fiat from the student wings of the BJP and the RSS where all-male militant social groupings flourish). So, in the name of right-wing political activism, a chance for personal liberation for Dalit gays or bisexuals is lost.

An explanation: in *The Indians* (2007) Sudhir Kakar explains two kinds of homosexuals in India, both married to women. The first type, the anal type, explains (rather fantastically) that he collects male semen all day in his anus to transfer it to his wife from his penis at night. The second type, the oral type, mostly includes the great gurus like the teachers of physical education in *akhadas* and *vyayamshalas*. They fellate their young charges to attain eternal youth and are seen as males, not passive gays.

In south India, the passive gay is called *koti* (Telugu for 'monkey') and the active is called *panti* ('husband' in *chakka* language). 'Active/passive' are ultimately mere heterosexual categories. As the poet Muriel Rukeyser says:

'In Love do not ask who gave, who received
only, who most enjoyed!'

The other interface is the bourgeois passive gay/Dalit (untouchable) interface. To make such a grouping of passive men with women reflects the false tendency to force straight paradigms (active/passive) on gay culture. However, like the untouchable Dalit prostitute a bourgeois, largely passive gay like myself, becomes eminently touchable in the act of sex. As soon as the sex act is over, a religious ritual or quasi-ritual bath in hygiene's name redresses the balance and puts back the clock by making us untouchables touchable again.

Arudra, poet Sri Sri's nephew, shared with me once his personal intuitions about the birth of the devdasi dancers in Dravidian Hindu India. The land was owned by the kings (Rajus/Kshatriyas) and the temple (Brahmins), plus the citizenry (Vaishyas) wanted their share. To ensure equitable distribution, a Shudra woman was used to throw the dice. She took steps east–west–north–south in the four directions and parcelled out the land. The steps evolved into the intricate footwork of Sadr (later Brahminised as Bharatnatyam by Rukmini Devi) and the hand gestures at dice-throwing became the hand gestures or *mudras*. The woman was for public use. She was a public woman, a prostitute. Because Mother Earth was parcelled out among sons, her body was offered to whoever paid for it and she bore sons for men of all castes (the daughters become the future *devadasis*, i.e. dancers and temple prostitutes). This was ritualised by a bath and puja to the Siva-linga (phallic father-god authority) before and after the sexual congress. She could not refuse anyone as she had to establish social and sexual democracy between brothers and society at large at the expense of, and literally over, her own body.

Prostitution historically played a role in keeping the middle-class family together by allowing husbands to stray and then return to their wives. Frederick Engles, Marx's friend and patron, said as much. He was following Dostoevsky's notion: 'Prostitutes allow our mothers and sisters to remain our mothers and sisters.' Prostitutes are trade. Elite Dalits are game. He has taken over the function of sacred sex from women. Sex is a way to sainthood. It is self-defeating but also sacrificial.

Today a gay friend of mine, another passive homosexual whom I call 'sister', shares his/her body with three brothers, two blood brothers and one paternal cousin. 'You can be shared between us brothers but do not go to anyone else', is their understanding. Thus, competition and sibling rivalry is sexually resolved by sharing a gay's body without explicitly stating so.

I cruised the Hyderabad Public Gardens for years. A Dalit boy who was part of the 'trade' working the park told me, 'You can go elsewhere. You're doing this for fun. I do this for a square meal in order to survive.' It was then I stopped cruising the Public Gardens.

My personal experience is that as a passive gay I am 'used' sexually, but my users (friends, neighbours, students) refuse to recognise me socially. They would lose caste (I never had one to begin with) in their own eyes. (A gay son in a high-born family soon loses all his position — and possessions — even in his own bourgeois family.) Property is linked with progeny in the urban middle class just as the *devadasi's* body was linked to the land in the king/temple struggle in

Indian history. I go back now to the bourgeois survival strategy of what Ralph Ellison had called 'invisibility' in the Negro context (he used the word 'Negro' in late 1950s, and early 1960s America) and what I call here the 'untouchability' of the passive gay. (Active gays are excluded from the social humiliation because they can 'pass' for 'straights', as some mulattos once passed for whites in the context of colour.) I am socially boycotted. This is an extreme form of social and spiritual violence, if not physical violence. Not to talk to a neighbour or a colleague for 15–20 years because he is gay is violence of the highest order. (I don't even want to talk of 'sissy-beating' and 'fag-ragging' which has been well-documented at least in the West, if not in India.)

I do admit that my suffering as an upper-class urban gay pales before the suffering of a village Dalit woman. She was not allowed to eat well, bathe and wear clean clothes even if she could afford it, my Dalit woman student Swathi Margaret tells me. I should add that violence against me in my own family and during my student days in the American mid-West radicalised me as nothing else could or would. (I lived in the closet. The stakes of my elite family 'losing face' socially were too high.) I could come out only after my father's death. So paternalism is ingrained into the minds of even those like me who rebel against and give up the father role.

I have to address here the issue of class. I will sleep with a Dalit boy (waiter/autowallah) but will not socialise with him publicly. Nor will he due to his internalising false notions of respectability. Here, class wins over caste in the cities. I hold myself as guilty of violating that Dailt boy's social dignity as my neighbours who, by boycotting me, violate my dignity and self-respect. Gays congratulate themselves on obliterating caste and class in bed and some feminists congratulate gays on this. (Of course the Marxists cry foul; they see bourgeois men taking rural Dalit boys, called 'rustic fantastics', to bed as nothing but social and sexual exploitation by higher castes and classes of lower ones.) I submit that caste in the city is flexible but class is not. Intellectual men cannot even lust well! 'Only the brute can fornicate lustily' (Baudelaire 1897). I will lose 'social class' if I go out with my low-class bedmates, just as my bourgeois neighbours will lose theirs in 'straight' society if they are seen hobnobbing with an openly gay person like myself. R. Raj Rao (2003) delineates both the pathos and the comedy of his association with Dalit men in gay love (Raj himself is by birth half Yadav, a Shudra fishermen's caste from coastal Andhra, though socially he belongs to the highest echelons of Bombay society. He insists on using the old name rather than 'Mumbai' for all that 'Bombay' implies for modernity).

To conclude: I have ruffled a few feathers by writing this. I have put my own body on the firing line again. But if it makes my Marxist male colleagues and Dalit male students sit up and think on this issue, this effort would have been worthwhile.

To live my life from 1973 to 2007 as openly gay has taken great courage on my part in inviting difficulties and surmounting greater existing ones. To divide minorities and prevent them from coming together on a common platform is just another male heterosexist ploy to preserve their power. Just as bourgeois feminists were mocked initially for taking up the Dalit cause (e.g. by asking 'Can the Dalit Speak?' The answer is 'No'), now elite gays are similarly mocked. My struggle is unimportant unless it also opens up a possibility for generalised liberation and living.

A Personal Note on R. Raj Rao's *The Boyfriend's* Dalit Hero

Yudi, who belongs to the upper class, loves the lower-class Milind (I almost wrote 'lover class'!). The critics go crazy applauding the inter-class gay marriage. Could I call it a class struggle? Milind is trying to rise in life. Bourgeoisification. There's no blame in that. But why doesn't Yudi/Raj go over and start living in the slum? Isn't 'love' going over to your lover's life? Why is it that the slum takes over the high-rise? Or better still, why is it that the city high-rise always annexes the slum? Is there not a Dalit culture, a Dalit way of living and loving? Why should the Dalit leave all those riches and go over to the middle class? Cannot a third way of life be found from a mixture of two potent groups in a gay 'marriage'? Why is it that the bourgeois vices become intensified, leading to 'scenes' in a 'marriage' (with apologies to Ingmar Bergman here).

In real life, Raj adopts his peon-lover's child. There is a constant tug-of-war between the child's biological mother and Raj. She accuses Raj of trying 'to steal' her child by offering 'bribes'. Why does all this never find its way into the novel? Why is the new gay novel lily-livered like the bourgeois novel? Titillation without insight! Why are the women stereotypes? 'Mother' is also a woman. She does not have to be a wife only in a novel. Jean Genet creates a great heroine out of his lover Hamza's mother. She becomes Umm-Falastin, Mother Palestine. Raj first gives us a large woman, a caricature fag-hag; she's repulsive. He tells me she is the one who takes care of Yudi. I suppose he has fused the black and the white Marys together.

This interracial marriage (the rich and the poor being two separate races) does allow comedy. So Milind imitates Yudi's talk, mimes his fairy gestures, dishes his lifestyle. Yudi puts up with it laughingly initially, then gets angry. The Palestinian boys imitate Genet's limp and squint when they suspect he dares aspire to sleeping with them, the future heroes of Palestine (Genet (1986).

(b) Transforming Pedagogies
My Gay Indian Literature Course at Hyderabad Central University (HCU)

Do pedagogies transform us or do we have to transform pedagogies before they transform us? It is a truism that our current Humanities syllabus consists of Brahmanical assumptions with Macaulay's nineteenth century Victorianism imposed on it. Brahminism is thousands of years old, Victoria would be 200, at least, were she alive today. I have news for you. She is alive in our English syllabus.

It is the genius of the Indian mind to absorb and transform whatever touches it. Hence, we have the syncretic Mughal–Rajput culture of north India in the sixteenth and seventeenth centuries which has left us some magnificent buildings and the philosophy of Dara Shikoh (it was his Persian translation of the Upanishads that the German translators picked up to start European Orientalism). The land of Khajuraho and Konark, with all the wisdom of the body displayed at those two holy places, adopted the crabby philosophy of a middle-aged Victorian gentleman as its educational policy. Why? Because there is a whole strain of Puritanism in Brahminism which found affinity with Macaulay, in the name of modernising India. 'We will take your bombs but we do not want your nude beaches', is the argument. What is more dangerous — a bomb or a sex bomb? How dangerous is a sex obsessed person to society? The answers to these questions are at once self-evident but beyond the scope of my small inquiry.

Suffice it to say that I introduced gay literature to India because I am a gay teacher and there was no place for my likes in the Indian academy; because there are gay students, men and women, studying literatures in English in India who feel unenlightened about their human and socio-sexual condition at the end of two boring years of MA classes; and most importantly, because there are a host of Indian writers writing the gay experience in the cities and small towns of India in both English and the Indian languages since 1940.

Kunika Batra, an MA student at the University of Delhi, helped start the gay literature classes there under the title 'Literature of Sexual Dissidence'. The assumption is that a university is a place to diffuse social tension by giving a place to socially unaccepted practices before they blow up society. That is, another social bomb to diffuse before it goes off. Batra, however, simply states in a published article that she felt left out personally in her English classes as nothing in them spoke to her intimate, personal knowledge from her own lesbian experience (she now lives in the West).

Taking a cue from her, I started my first gay literature class in south India at Hyderabad Central University, first stealing her title and then simply calling it 'Gay Indian Literature'. (to call it Indian Gay Literature would be to give primacy to Indian rather than gay. I'm conscious of being gay first and Indian later). As you can see, we are stuck again with the chicken-and-egg situation of which came first. To put it simply: do I make a poem or does the poem make me? At the simple level it is I who makes the poem; at the profoundest levels of human psychological transformation it is the poem who made me. My teacher Anaïs Nin always said 'Begin with yourself' — and society will follow.

I do not wish to waste time on the profound shock the stupid people in our midst would have received due to my innocent academic messianism. The University of Pune has an active gay discussion group cutting across disciplines but Gay Literature was not an official, recognised MA course until last year. It has now been grouped under Minority Literature — II, Minority Literature — I being Dalit Literature, for the purposes of the Academic Council of that University. As recently as last year, the uncle of a Tripura student of mine, commenting on my course, said: 'So is this what English Literature has degenerated to in India?'

Mark the words — 'English' and 'degenerated'. The implication is 'English' was pristine and we local monkeys somehow made it degenerate. So the great-grandsons of Victoria ride on and on in independent India. Or the implication is that English education was to save us from our native degeneracy and now, having become free, we have chosen to become degenerate again.

Thank God he did not say what Ahmednejad, Iran's President, recently did at Columbia University, that homosexuality is a western degeneracy and that there are no homosexuals in Iran, not one. It is like *The Hyderabad Times* recently writing: 'Hoshang Merchant is the only gay in Hyderabad.' God save us from that rag because I can't! So this is the RSS take on Indian homosexuality — That it is a western import. It is not. It is as indigenous as *amma, rasam* and *avvakai*! It is this nineteenth century prudery and horror at sexuality which has been imported into India with Macaulay's syllabus. For an extended discussion of this read my *Yaraana: Gay Stories from India* (1999), and for a most extended version read Ruth Vanita and Saleem Kidwai's *Same Sex Love in India* which followed my book.

Now why is that Hyderabad allowed gay literature before Pune, though it can be argued that Poona is a more liberal city than any southern one? The simple answer is that Hyderabad is a central university (hence the 'c' in HCU) and is allowed to experiment by the centre, while state universities like Poona are bound by local considerations. In favour of Brahminism let it be said that my Brahmin boss, Professor (now Emeritus) S. Viswanathan, supported me throughout as did then professor and now Dean Mohan Ramanan. Then came the examination question paper: 'Discuss Suniti Namjoshi as a lesbian poet.' Professor Makarand Paranjape, then a young hothead, roundly stated that my paper would be tabled in Parliament and could not contain the 'l' word as it would 'shock Parliamentarians'. Now I ask you: does a Hindi-speaking Bihari Parliamentarian really bother about my sisterhood (adoptive) with sister Suniti? (Let it be said in Makarand's defence that he has mellowed now.)

This brings us to the larger question of: 'Who is really transformed by my transforming pedagogy?' Certainly not the Bihari bumpkin, in or out of Parliament. 'Art is local' is what Maurice de Vlaminck, the Surrealist painter, taught us. I am a local lad. I write of local things. Local people read me, damn me or praise me. True, I went to school at Purdue and came back with a few airs (which my strict Parsi father soon beat out of me, not to speak of India's heat, cholera and crowds). So I have gone global to turn local again. (I also know where my bread is buttered.) I am sorry to use that horrible neologism, but we have all gone 'glocal', i.e. global and local at once.

Talking of local globality or global locality brings me to my third point: our home-grown Indian gay poets in English. These men are mostly from cities, English-educated, belonging to minority groups — Parsi, Christian, Bohra Moslem. (Ah! They're not Hindu. They're not Brahmin! Pity one Hindu Oriya gay man dared a gay novel *Root and Flower* and the local goons pulled him and his book out root and flower!) They've been writing since the 1940s in Bombay (Sultan Padamsee) till today in India and the West (Firdaus Kanga, Adil Jussawalla,

Dinyar Godrej, myself — what's with these Parsis?!) The problem is the solution; minoritarianism is its own reward. We can articulate our angst as a gay from a social minority, i.e. as twice-marginalised beings, because a third pariah status 'gay writer' won't matter. Indeed, it is a badge of honour for us vanguardists of the currently ongoing sexual revolution in India.

This brings me to our last point: in literature, what is in the centre and what on the periphery or the margins? Lionel Trilling reminds us, in a now famous essay, that *Moby Dick* by the gay Herman Melville or Nathaniel Hawthorne's *The Scarlet Letter* about on unwed mother are tales of marginalised characters written as warnings to nineteenth century America going full speed toward Mamon. But today they are the pillars of American literature. So too with our Indian poets — Sultan Padamsee, Adil Jussawalla, Suniti Namjoshi, Ali are our most important post-independence poets in English. And they happen to be gay (not to talk about a plethora of lesser lights like R. Raj Rao, Dinyar Godrej and myself). So is gay literature on the margins or has it, due to its avant-gardism and relevance, become the centre? I suggest this is the literary equivalent of the political problem of the provinces' relation to the federal centre. Should we allow Brahminism to proclaim its President's rule on all the states of literatures in the Union, in their various states of excitement?

(c) Gays with Critical Disability

In every population, 2-5 per cent people will be gay. This includes the high-born (such as Brahmins and Parsis), the Dalits of north and south India as well as the tribals of the south-west and north-east (I merely mention here the large groups that populate my university in order to show that no group is exempt from the rule of having a representative gay population). Critical Disability Studies is a discipline just starting out in India.

I was recently presented with Kenny Fries' *The History of My Shoes and the Evolution of Darwin's Theory* (2007). I base my inquiry on this book. Fries writes:

Before I was ten years old, five reconstructive surgeries were performed by Dr. Joseph Milgram, the head of orthopedic surgery at the Hospital for Joint Diseases, then located in Manhattan at 125th Street and Madison Avenue. Dr. Milgram was the first doctor who did not recommend amputation of both my legs. This bespectacled doctor's doctor, by force of his gruff yet endearing personality, convinced my parents to let him begin the course of surgery that would enable their son not only to walk but to live, according to Dr. Milgram, 'a normal life.' (ibid.: 15)

Then he tells us the story of Charles Darwin because do-gooding is termed 'Social Darwinism', that is, the strong taking care of the weak.

Since his return from the *Beagle* voyage, he had been vexed by questions about the distribution of species: Why are animals on islands so different from those on the nearest mainland? Why were the fossils he found in Patagonia so similar to what currently lived in Patagonia? Why does each island of an archipelago have its own endemic species that are more similar to each other than to related species farther away? What is the origin of species?

By October 1838, he had consolidated his theory, using what he had learned about geology. This theory of "gradualism" made colleagues, such as the *Beagle*'s Captain FitzRoy, realise Darwin was in the process of transforming the earth's history into an entirely secular story. (Fries 2007: 27)

Then he tells a story parallel to Darwin's, that of Alfred Russel Wallace.

'If we look at a globe or a map of the Eastern hemisphere', wrote Alfred Russel Wallace, 'we shall perceive between Asia and Australia a number of large and small islands, forming a connected group distinct from those of great masses of land, and having little connexion with either of them.' The spice islands, now largely known as Indonesia, are situated on the equator, surrounded by the warm tropical oceans. Wallace considered the region more hot and moist than any other part of the globe, teeming with collectible plants and animals that were elsewhere unknown.

Arriving in April 1854, Wallace used Singapore as a base, learning about his new environment and collecting beetles and butterflies. (Fries 2007: 41)

Then Fries very cleverly goes on to show us how the current teleology or rather theology of disability developed:

Disability studies theorist Lennard J. Davis echoes Bagemihl, showing how, when we speak of disability, we associate with a story, place it in a narrative. A person *became* deaf *became* blind, *was born* blind, *became* quadriplegic. The impairment becomes part of a sequential narrative.

By doing this we think of disability as linked to individualism and the individual story. What is actually a physical fact becomes a story with a hero or a victim. Disability becomes divorced from the cultural context, and becomes the problem of the individual, not a category defined by the society. The dialectic of normalcy — for someone to be normal, someone has to be not normal — is kept intact. (ibid.)

This misquotation of Darwin's 'Survival of the Fittest' theory allows some powerful individuals (doctors, lawyers, parents) to throw some less endowed beings (children, the physically challenged, gays) on to the scrap heap.

But Darwin also talked of 'adaptability'. Fries gives us the example of those afflicted by cerebral palsy. They flail their hands and legs as they move or walk because of lack of motor coordination. But then, everyone gets backaches. Man walked upright, unlike animals, to carry food and babies that gave us backaches, which occur simply because we are human. 'Every re-adaptation is a process of make-do and mend.'

Those who adopt survive. This includes the so-called normal and the so-called abnormal. Those who don't, in both categories, die. 'Dead as a dodo', we say. The dodo did not adapt. It could not fly away from club-wielding seafarers who clubbed it into extinction for fun. So those who use Darwin against the gay handicapped should remember Darwin on adaptability.

Then Fries tells what to most Indians will be a shocking story (who knows, with globalisation such delectations might reach our shores too). I quote the short story in its entirety:

Disability Made Me Do It

In 1991, I am living in Provincetown when I get a call from Tom, a local artist. Tom has been hired to do the drawings for an updated version of a well-known guide to gay sex. "I want to make sure different types of men are represented in the drawings", he begins. "I wanted to talk to you about how to best portray a disabled man having sex."

"Don't use a wheelchair to signify the man is disabled", I tell him.

"Where can I find a disabled guy to model for me?" he asks.

"Beats me", I say.

"Would you do it?" There is a pause. "I'll take photos of you having sex and use them as the source for what I'll draw", he explains.

"Sex with whom?" I ask.

"That's easy", Tom assures me.

Why did I so easily agree to model for the cause?

In 1988, I was working for a San Francisco theater services organization when I was asked out to lunch by a man interested in getting to know his way around the theater community. "I was an understudy in *A Chorus Line*", the man tells me as we sit down for what I expect to be a business lunch. "What can you tell me about directing a play in San Francisco?"

Over salad I tell him what I know about getting a start: classes, the theaters, some people I suggest he call.

After the waiter removes the plates from the table, my lunch-mate looks across the table at me and asks, matter-of-factly: "Do you like to be humiliated?"

I know right away what he is talking about, where this conversation is leading, even though no one has ever asked me that question before. "Why do you ask?"

"Because I know this one guy in Los Angeles who told me that's the only way he can enjoy sex. Pain and humiliation bring up all the times he got attention when he was a kid, so he gets off on it."

For me the operative words are *this one guy in Los Angeles*. I could answer him by pointing out how many nondisabled men, gay or otherwise, enjoy experiencing sex that way, or offer him other enlightened responses, but at this moment all I can muster in reply is, "Really?"

In 1990, a nondisabled gay male editor who is interested in my work takes me out to lunch at a ritzy New York restaurant.

"I was very interested in the sex in your book", the editor tells me.

"Oh?" I say. As I eat I keep nodding encouragement for him to continue.

"I have a cousin who is disabled. We spent a lot of time together growing up in Texas", he says. My family wasn't very happy about how swishy I was. We lived in oil country and I guess I didn't live up to, well, what they expected a boy to be. My cousin was my only friend. People are very interested in how disabled people have sex, aren't they?

Puzzled, my first thought is that not many people would be interested in the way I have sex, being that my sexual practices are probably similar to the experiences of most gay men. My unspoken response is: No, most people aren't interested but you obviously are.

Taking into consideration that I might have to work with this well-intentional man sitting across from me, and that he is paying for this rather expensive lunch, I simply correct his assumption. "Actually, most people do not think of those of us who live with disabilities as being sexual at all."

What happened to Russel? Darwin gets all the prizes, Russel got none. Late in life when he was offered an honour, he declined it. Could a future psycho-biographer tease out a story of sibling rivalry in science and of suppressed homoeroticism between brother-scientists in the largely untold story between Darwin and Russel?

II

Book of the World

introduction

This book is called Book of the World because it deals with history. The politics of yesterdays is today our history. This book deals not with kings and queens but ordinary men and women like us who battled the world's prejudices in their day with their writers' pen. I include here not only the pioneer writers Firaq, Ismat Chugtai and Ugra but also the current writer of the theatre, Mahesh Dattani, whose concerns are worldly. My quarrel with him is that he is no poet of the theatre like his mentor Chekhov. Otherwise I'd have gladly placed him in the next book, viz. the Book of the Soul.

This section also briefly touches upon the entertainment medium of our modern-day world, namely cinema and TV. I deal here with the image of the eunuch in some Hindi films and television.

2
Indian narrativity: fiction, film, theatre

Narration in Indian epics is cyclic: stories within stories; stories turning in upon themselves; stories throwing out new offshoots like Deleuze's rhizome or the many-spired (banyan tree-like) cathedral at Milan; stories which are the obverse or reverse of each other; stories which are repetitions or mirror-images. This can also be seen in the Persian *Thousand and One Nights* which obviously bear an Indian influence.

Ramayana (Rama's story) and the *Mahabharata* (the Great Indian Epic) tell the stories of the gods and have provided heroes and villains to every film and every Indian story down to the present day. Even R. Raj Rao's eponymous *The Boyfriend* is called Yudi, short for Yudhishthira, the truth teller, the eldest of the five Pandavas in the *Mahabharata*. But to go down the line finding analogies in every character and incident in Rao's book with that of the epic, as a Canadian professor and fan of his has done, is a bit far-fetched. Rao is certainly not writing an allegory akin to Edmund Spenser's *The Faerie Queene* (1596)!

But in *One Day I Locked My Flat in Soul City* (2000), Rao has 'Indian' stories. This is the liminality and hybridity of all postmodern/postcolonial fiction. So Rao's English language homes, Indian experiences like the high-born gay hero being thrown out of a Dalit village where he had gone searching a lover. At the same time, you might say it is an inverted search-for-the-father of a Stephen Dedalus where the 'father' for searches for a 'son'; or a sugar daddy, a young lover. Hence, liminality; hybridity. The unending search is its cyclicity. Old mistakes with new lovers; each time you board a train, be sure your devils are on it, too (Freud and Lawrence on Freud). But the search also could be the Sudama–Krishna story in a gay reversal where Sudama rejects Krishna unlike in the *Puranas*, where the happy god clasps his lowest friends to his breast. There are a multitude of such unconscious epic motifs running through Indian writing in English which, by its appearance, seems superficially affiliated to the West.

Conversely Urdu writing, which prides itself of being the vox populi of the Indian masses, actually has literary luminaries schooled in English literature. Sa'adat Hasan Manto read Emile Zola and the Naturalists. You can smell them in his prose. Ismat Chughtai read English Literature at

Lucknow's Isabel Thoburn College for Women. It was an eye-opener for her because all she read till then were vapid women's romances written by (gay?) men under the names of their own sisters! She was ready to become Urdu's Collette or George Sand. Of course, her mega hit movie script, *Aurat*, of the 1940s, is a straight rip-off from Emily Brontë's *Wuthering Heights* (1847), with Dilip Kumar as Heathcliff and Kamini as the great heroine.

The great western hero of the Progressive Movement in literature is Louis Aragon, the staunch French Communist poet who supported Stalin. He confused Utopia with Stalin. In Hyderabad, Raj Bahadur Gour, 90, still eulogies Aragon (and by extension, shamefully enough, Stalin). Of course, they have all read Marx (sure enough, many more have not but call themselves Marxists). They also excommunicated Manto and Ismat Chughtai for 'obscenity' (i.e., bourgeois decadence), innocently failing to see that their horror of obscenity, too, was very bourgeois. Ah, Trotsky, Gramsc!.

In Hindi, Kamleshwar, a modernist but a postcolonialist, uses humble characters, low language, descriptions of low life as in a socialist novel from Russia, say Mikhail Sholokhov's *And Quiet Flows The Don* (1934). But he also uses the native forms of the Nautanki and the Burra Kathas; one lewd, the other sacred. Hybridity again. Master Premchand invented a new spoken Hindi for the new age.

For modern Indian theatre we have to look at three antecedents, viz. epic Sanskrit theatre, the dance dramas and Parsi theatre. Modern Indian theatre partakes of all three.

Famously, Sanskrit theatre has no tragedy. Since all action has a re-action (karma) there can be no tragic hero. Also sensitively and sensibly enough as in Shakespeare or more aptly, Aeschylus there are linguistic registers. The learned men speak Sanskrit; untaught women and rustics speak Prakrit. I understand the Greek Chorus, mostly men dressed as women, spoke rustic dialects rather than standard Greek. The ancient curses were uttered in ancient Greek; but the curses of the high-born Medea (played by Aeschylus himself in women's weeds, mask and wooden platform heels) are in exceptionally beautiful high Greek. But Gieve Patel's Parsi men, women and children all speak standard Bombay convent English even in rural Gujarat of the 1890s! The curses of the proto-Dravidian, cross-dressing Theyyam oracle of Kerala could be reminiscent of the Greek chorus in a bizarre way. In Sanskrit drama time itself is spatialised.

The other dance dramas are the Rasleela played all over India (Assam's is given here) and the much misunderstood Meiti, all male, Sumangali

Theatre of Manipur. They are invited to perform at Avignon and the gay Parisians think it to be gay theatre. Wrong! Just as the priest at the Akhilendeshwar Temple in Thanjavur cross-dresses for rituals, just as the male Theyyam oracle wears breastplates, so too did the Manipur priests cross-dress at the ancient Lai-Haroba New Year festivities.

Now, Mahesh Dattani's *Dance Like A Man*'s male dancer, who wants to perform the female dance form Bharatnatyam is labelled queer. Until Vyjayanthimala taught the dance to the Parsi male dancer Rohinton Cama, no man had dared to perform women's dances on stage. Now Cama is out of circulation, but he has spawned a host of less meritorious imitators throughout India.

Dattani himself is a product of Anglo-Indian schools. His drawing-room farces recall W. S. Pinero, Terence Rattigan, Oscar Wilde *et al*. His homosexual melodrama, of course, is the High Modernism and Southern Gothic of Tennessee Williams. The postmodernist gay alienation is Edward Albee's. But he does remember going to the Gujarati theatre brought by itinerant Bombay troupes to his childhood Bangalore.

Bombay's Gujarati theatre of my childhood was centred in Kalbadevi. (Haribhai Jhaveri, a Gujarati stage-actor, became the Hindi 1970s film star Sanjeev Kumar; Sachin, then child actor, was rumored to be his pede.) I remember titles like *Zehr to Peedhan Jani-Jani* (Knowingly We Drank Poison) and *Preet, Piyu ane Panetar* (Love, Lovers and Sacrifices) running a whole year in Sunday matinees. Social melodramas, again. It is Dattani's staple too.

But the greatest modern theatrical influence in India was Parsi theatre. It involved grand settings, rant and bombast for dialogues; noble, historical characters (Sohrab Modi as Sikander, i.e. Alexander), cross-dressing males for comedy, lots of songs, lots of pageantry and spectacle to drown out inanities. Shakespeare's *Hamlet* in Gujarati had the Parsi ghost famously complain of death-by-vinegar ('He poured vinegar into my ears' came out in literal Gujarati as 'Mara kaan maan sarko nakhyo', blissfully unaware that by 'vinegar' Shakespeare meant 'rumour'). But Marathi theatre was influenced by it. Bal Gandharva as well as *Begum Barve* owe a debt to Parsi theatre. A word must be said about female leads in Parsi theatre — they were always played by women. The cross-dresser Sundari was a notable exception. Since the actress' profession was looked down upon Parsi upper-class women did not join the stage. Girls from Moslem courtesan families did join, as the courtesan culture had fallen into disuse after 1857. Lucknow courtesans came to Hyderabad.

Mushtari Bai Begum was patronised by Mehboob Ali Pasha, the Nizam. She wrote:

> What a pass these times have brought me to:
> My pulse beats and my wrist hurts

The actress Nargis was the courtesan-singer Jaddanbai's daughter. Nadira's (the 1940s film heroine) parents acted in a Parsi troupe at Alexandra Theatre, Grant Road, now Bombay's red light area. Parsi women's fashions of the 1920s, 1930s and 1940s were imitated all over north India. The Hindi film of Bombay gets its song sequence narration from Parsi theatre (which, of course, goes all the way back to Sanskrit drama).

So, no modern Indian art is wholly indigenous or wholly western.

Chughtai's Story

When Ismat Chughtai started writing, no respectable, educated Moslem woman in Uttar Pradesh wrote. But there was a great hunger for devouring stories during the lazy afternoon hours in these same ladies. Moslem men wrote stories of moral turpitude that begets a befitting Islamic justice at end. So the ladies could mentally indulge in immorality and morality while simultaneously spending their long summers and winters reading. Male fiction writers asked their sisters for the life stories of their girlfriends (*saheli*, also a code-word for 'lesbian') and then cheekily also assumed these poor girls' names as feminine pseudonyms. A vast literature was thus churned out. (Source: Saleem Kidwai's unpublished paper presented at the Gay Film Seminar, University of Pune, March 2007)

Chughtai really thought she could do better. And she did. She took the Victorian female writers she read at college as models. But she, as a woman, spoke to the maid (*khadima*), to the washerwoman (*dhoban*) and got not only gossip on neighbours from them but she also recognised their *boli* (colloquial talk) which she put into the mouths of her appropriate characters (e.g. the woman servant in 'Lihaaf', translated as 'The Quilt').

She certainly could be funny. 'There is nothing so consistently funny as us human beings in the act of sex' (Barth 1957). The whole lesbian sex scene under the quilt is described through a child's eyes. What the child imagines she sees could surely be funny to an all-knowing adult reader.

She has been adopted by the new lesbian feminists of India. Was Ismat a feminist? (All the women called her 'Ismat Apa', i.e. elder sister). She negotiated her terrain between marriage and a career in 1940s India. But she called her marriage 'a friendship'; there was not much lust there.

Her husband, Shahid Latif, who directed her scripts for films, almost threatened divorce during the 'Lihaaf' obscenity trial in the Lahore High Court. Unlike Nora in *A Doll's House* (Ibsen 1879), Ismat did not walk out on her marriage. I think, like Elizabeth Bishop who refused to be in gay anthologies, Ismat would also say, 'Literature comes first, ideology later.' Is that an evasion? Perhaps.

Was she a lesbian? She always looked mannish in photographs (after all, she had Chughtai blood). Her husband looked, as his name suggested, 'Latif' ('delicate'). When she was thrown out of the Progressive Movement she did not care (she was never really a part of it). She had her own way of dealing with men and women. She was my mother's hostel mate at the University Women's Settlement, Bellasis Road, Bombay in the 1940s. All the girls were 'modern': they had premarital love affairs with men they later married, my mother included.

Films can be a cruel world for single young girls hoping for stardom in Bombay after coming out of Punjab villages. Chughtai threw these girls into her husband's lap. That way he left her alone and she had time to write. This could be read as repressed lesbianism. Chand Usmani, 1950s side heroine, ran a halfway house for runaway girls in Bombay films at her Mahim residence.

I heard Ismat say on Doordarshan Television that her contribution to Urdu is the freshness of local women's dialect she brought into fiction for the first time. A dishonoured life found honour at last.

The Story: *Lihaaf*

At the end of her life, Ismat Chughtai told the story of meeting a begum from her remote past who fell weeping into her arms. The recognition, in spite of time's passage, did not surprise Ismat as much as the fact that the begum had a beautiful son, because as far as Ismat knew the nawab was probably gay and so was probably the begum. Ismat had written a story about her, 'Lihaaf', which was so scandalous for the times that she had to face not only her husband's wrath but also the Crown Court's in Lahore. She was tried for obscenity.

Brought up a tomboy among many brothers, she was sent to a girls' school and trained as a teacher. Her first story was written under her brother's name as good ladies did not tell bawdy tales. Of course, the true identity of the writer was soon apparent to the cognoscenti.

As a girl, she listened to the tale of a fat begum who spent her time under a quilt being 'massaged' by a little servant girl. This is what she knew and this is what she told in the story. She probably did not know much herself then. She never uses the word 'lesbian'. Anais Nin would say, 'Never use the word 'homosexual' or 'schizophrenic'. She would find poetic reasons for the off-centric behaviour which she, a trained psychoanalyst, was hard put to poeticise in her prose as a pioneering feminist writer.

Here is an excerpt from 'Lihaaf' — 'She was guiding my hand wherever she felt the itch. With my mind on the *babua*, I was scratching mechanically, unthinkingly. She continued talking. "Listen, you don't have enough clothes. Tomorrow I will ask the tailor to make you a new frock. Your mother has left some material with me. "Silly girl, don't you see where you're scratching? You have dislocated my ribs." Begum Jan was smiling mischievously. I was red with embarrassment. "Come, lie down with me." She laid me at her side with my head on her arm. "How thin you are…and, let's see, your ribs," she started counting. "No," I protested weakly. 'I won't eat you up! What a tight sweater," she said. I wanted to run away from her, but she held me closer. I struggled to get away. Begum Jan started laughing.'

Ismat's own marriage was more a friendship. Shahid Latif was considered 'disreputable' because he was a Bombay film director. But 'Lihaaf' strained their marriage. Her name was in every Urdu paper. She was feeding the baby when the summons came and she couldn't help laughing. The Court clerk soon brought her to her senses.

In Lahore Manto accompanied her, eating mangoes in Anarkali Bazaar, as he too was similarly charged for writing 'Thanda Gosht', a short story. (His 'Bheegi Dopahar' is another Urdu lesbian story from the 1930s). In Court, the Judge accused him of comparing a young girl's breast to luscious tomatoes. 'Would you rather I called it "lentils"?' he countered, to general mirth. The court was brought to order and cases against both writers were dismissed.

But the stigma remained. Manto had to go to Pakistan, where he died penniless and mad. Ismat became known by a single story. Her works were always inclusive of the servant classes (sweeper women, housemaids, washerwomen, masseuses) that frequented a *khata-peeta* ('well-off') family of feudal Lucknow. She wasn't taken seriously initially because she was a woman though she had been to Isabelle Thoburn College and even heard some professors lecture in men's colleges from behind a curtain. She was no card-carrying socialist, and did not care when she was thrown out of the Progressive Poets' Movement.

Her characters do not speak high Urdu but the local dialects women use in Lucknow. She thus made the unknown face of the unseen woman labourer known to the elite. Herself from the elite, she used her art for social inclusiveness. She was recognised as a pioneer stylist in Urdu just prior to her death.

Being a poet at heart, she said she felt that she had a part in making that 'flower-like child' of the Begum by 'watering' the soil of the Urdu short story with her own 'heart's-blood'.

3
Urdu gay literature: Poetry

Urdu is generally believed to mean 'camp' in Turkish and the language of Delhi soldiers. New research says it began in Gujarat, went to the Deccan and came to Delhi. Its first poet is Amir Khusro, a Sufi. The Sufis used oral transmission of knowledge between master and pupil. Hence intimacy grew between the two men. In fact, so close was Khusro to his master Nizamuddin, that he died a mere year after his master's death. Another Urdu poet, Mir Taki Mir, wrote poems to a fairy (male) from the moon! Firaq is in this old romantic tradition. Following him were the Deccan poets Shaaz Tamkanait and Suleiman Arib, who wrote the occasional gay lyric.

Urdu

Gay readers would like to know that Urdu's first poet (twelfth century Delhi), Amir Khusro, was a gay man. He was Turkish ('Urdu' means 'camp' in Turkish) but his mother was Indian ('Hindi'). He called Urdu, his mother tongue, Hindawi. He invented the Urdu *ghazal*, wrote tens of thousands of them and was called Tut-e-Hindi, the Songbird of India. He also invented the *qawwali* form, still performed in *dargahs*. He invented the sitar. Most importantly he was Nizammuddin Aulia's student and lover and died a mere year after his master's death. Khusro was married to a woman hand-picked by his master but spent most of his life singing and meditating with his master, like Rumi and Shams-i-Tabriz. They were politically powerful Sufis.

'Firaq', India's 'closet' gay poet, is in this tradition. I put 'closet' in inverted commas because though he never said so, everyone knew him to be gay. The 'secret', if any, was the name of the Beloved. It was the Lover who wrote *ghazals*, never mind that the lover could be an adult catamite in bed. 'Firaq' taught the English Romantics at Allahabad University and his literary mode is post-Romantic rather than Modern. Towards the end, he did turn to political themes. The nation is the Beloved and Love is the only patriotism, as in Faiz. The Progressives were modernists of the 1940s (modernism came late to Urdu with N. M. Rashed's poetry). They had a

Marxist credo: No Art for Art's sake but Art for Society's sake. They were the dispossessed north Indian Moslem feudals who embraced education and communism rather than the Congress Party later became hard liners. Sardar Jafri is their best poet, along with Kaifi Azmi.

Poetry: Firaq's Trope of Substitution

It is well-known that Firaq did not need the help of alcohol to attract boys and young men to him. A recent Doordarshan TV serial on Urdu poets showed as much. What is important in Firaq's case is that like Stefan George in Switzerland, a gay fascist poet, Firaq attracted young men to the leftist cause. As a moderate he was Nehru's friend (and the Allahabad connection helped) and Nehru enlisted Firaq and his homoerotic circle in the task of nation building.

The poet, however, remains anonymous. Once Firaq fell down on a road in Allahabad. No one recognised him until one of the cognoscenti did. It reminds us of Edgar Allen Poe's death in a public square in Baltimore. 'This wall paper has killed me,' said Oscar Wilde in his hired Paris digs. Who killed Firaq? The rumour-mongering bourgeois forgot his poetry and perpetrated the rumour. Here is a poem, a 'gay' one, by Firaq. It is the soul of indirection. Or, say, 'substitution'. Born a Hindu, he took a Moslem name. An Urdu poet, he became an English teacher. A closet gay, he passed for a straight. On his wedding day, another woman was substituted for the girl of his choice on the marriage *pandal*. A gay man, he wrote *one* gay poem. I give it here.

Public Meeting and Parting As Private Acts

Look at your face in the mirror, friend
After our reunion it shines twice as bright

I am besotted with the scent of his words
His each word brings the scent of his lips

This isn't a public meeting since
My eyes are raised only to you

Loving grudgingly is no love, friend
Go! Now you have no sorrow from me

Nevertheless my life is spent
Either remembering or forgetting you

Your tearful shadow is the sorrow of the age
Before my sight plays this shadow eternally.

The poem's crucial line is the lightning playing like a snake under the green of the grass (of the male beloved's green *kurta*). This is a high state of excitement (youthful rebellion) but it must be covert, for the authority (parent/British) will know. This sorrow of secret love for boy-lover, mother/ motherland becomes 'the sorrow of the age'. Gay love is turned into nationalism.

'Witness the mystical devotional obsession of our literature, its furtive and sentimental attitude towards sex, its emotional exhibitionism and its almost total lack of rationality. Such literature was produced particularly during the past two centuries, one of the most unfortunate periods of our history, a period of disintegrating feudalism and of acute misery and degradation for the Indian people as whole.' This is part of the Progressive Writers' Movement manifesto. It was against this background that Firaq and Chughtai wrote. When the party line hardened all writers writing openly on sex including Manto, N. M. Rashid, Miraji along with Chughtai were thrown out of the Party in 1948. Chughtai did not toe the party line. She knew her novel transformed readers better than any pamphlet.

Manto

Manto, like all writers, was a lover of the physical body. Too much sex leads to a sense of perdition of the flesh. His description of the body is always as if it is a hunk of meat in a butcher's shop. This he learnt from Zola and the European Naturalists. He never drew back from realistic descriptions. He called breasts 'breasts'. When taken to court for obscenity he asked the Judge, 'Would you call them lentils?' Case dismissed. Excommunicated from the Progressive Movement. Not that he cared. He made money in Bombay films. He went to Pakistan. There he saw the Partition's carnage and necrophilia. The great stories came then.

'Wet Afternoon' (1930s)

Sa'adat Hasan Manto is known for his controversial stories. 'Toba Tek Singh', set in a Punjab madhouse, satirises the Partition as madness. In the babble of the mad, all life is reduced to gibberish. In 'Khol Do', a woman raped during the Partition opens her pyjamas, drawstrings when she hears the hospital doctor tell his attendant 'Khol do', meaning 'open the window'. She has become a mechanical victim in the violence perpetrated upon her. 'Thanda Ghost' is what we call a corpse, 'dead-meat', which is the fate of all human flesh.

'Wet Afternoon' is about a cold north Indian winter during adolescence. A boy goes home from school on a day a worker at his school dies and a holiday is declared. Other children are at school so he tarries at the butcher shop to touch quivering meat hung on hooks. At home, his equally adolescent sister asks for a back rub. (Father is having his temples rubbed by mother.) In the Indian family, there is an incest taboo. So 'massage' is a legitimised touch. Under his feet, the boy finds that his sister's buttocks quiver like the freshly cut meat at the butcher shop. This is a favourite Manto metaphor. Dead or alive human bodies are just meat.

But what allure do young bodies hold for minds not yet fully developed which is the comedy of all flesh? Soon the boy goes to his lonely game of cricket, creating a racket with his ball. He strays into a room where he spies his sister staring at a girlfriend's naked breasts.

So we have scopophilia (looking), we have incestuous touch and we have incipient lesbianism. All ingredients of an 'obscene' Manto story. To write so boldly in the 1940s in India was really brave.

The story takes us through the Freudian auto–homo–hetero triad of sexual development. The quivering flesh under the boy's hand, a private pleasure he stole in public, is akin to masturbation. The sister's voyeurism with her girlfriend is specifically homosexual, lesbian. Manto reminds us these are grown or growing children. Heterosexuality is outside the story's frame. As in a poem, it is highlighted by its absence. What is *not* spoken is as important as what is told, if not more. Like a good poem, this story too teaches us how to read. But gay sex is immature.

Of course, the law givers of colonial India did not know how to read human sexuality nor a story about it. They were busy imposing punitive, man-made measures on a man, a poet who was trying to understand the human psychology of sex.

The undercurrent, philosophic, is that if even live human flesh is akin to freshly cut, dead meat, hot and quivering, then we are all practicing necrophilia upon each other in our various states of desire.

4

hindi gay literature

Ugra's *Chocolate* (1927)

Pandey Bechan Sharma's (hereafter Ugra) short story entitled 'Chocolate' is considered to be the first written on the subject of homosexuality. The story begins with the protagonist Babu Dinkar reciting verses of love in Urdu. His selection of Urdu as the language to express his love for a boy is interesting, for although he is a Hindu, he has chosen to express himself in a language mainly associated with and spoken by the Moslems of India. Urdu is a rich language containing both subtlety and playful and ambiguous expressions that suggests more than what can be read on the surface. Urdu poets recorded homosexual love in their poetry much before it was actually done in other Indian languages. Mir Taqi Mir, the greatest of all Urdu poets, surely dabbled on the subject of homosexuality. He records the love of at least 20 male lovers of his in his verses and, at times, his language is vulgar and bawdy in these poems. No sophisticated interpretation can cover up the presence of homosexual themes in some Urdu poems.

Dinkar's verse recitation evokes a feeling of incomprehension in the minds of his listeners. The narrator believes that Dinkar is keeping secrets from them, whereas Manohar Chandra is disgusted by his riddles. The author makes the reader safely assume in the beginning that the verses speak of Dinkar's heterosexual love. But in the second part of the story, this carefully crafted illusion is broken as it becomes apparent that Dinkar Babu is enamoured by 'a beautiful lad of thirteen or fourteen'. Manohar informs the narrator that the lad is Dinkar's 'chocolate' and 'pocketbook'. These terms are evasive in this context. Nevertheless, an argument could be made in order to maintain/establish a relationship between homosexuality and the words 'chocolate' and 'pocketbook'. The universal popularity of chocolates could be read in the present context as homosexuality being rampant in human societies and the concept of the pocketbook makes us aware that homosexuality is essential but it is always kept under wraps—just the way one stuffs a small notebook in the pocket, away from public gaze. Manohar condemns homosexuality in unequivocal terms and calls it a disease more deadly than plague or cholera and also compares it to prostitution. He says:

> … This chocolate disease is spreading in our country faster than plague or cholera. Society sees it all but pretends to be blind. People oppose prostitution, and are angered by widow remarriage, but will not even mention this. Why? Because people feel ashamed. The house is on fire but these *gentlemen* are too ashamed to put it out!…
>
> 'Chocolate' is a name for those innocent, tender and beautiful boys of our country, whom society's demons push into the mouth of destruction to quench their own desires. Highly respectable people in our society destroy these boys and make them bad-charactered. There are many different names for them in different regions. In our United Provinces, people call them 'chocolate' and 'pocketbook'. There are also many names for them which cannot be written in civilised language.

Undoubtedly, Manohar is a homophobic intellectual who is dismissive of Dinkar when he sifts through historical details to defend his homosexuality and prove that his behaviour is not unnatural. He says:

> …He (Dinkar Babu) will sift through history, finish off the Puranas, and prove to you that love of boys is not unnatural but natural. When I talked to him about it, he told me, on the basis of an English book, that even Socrates was guilty of this offence. He said that Shakespeare too was a slave of some beautiful friend of his. He spoke of Mr. Oscar Wilde as well. If you don't believe me talk to him yourself and see if I am right.

Manohar obviously believes that homosexuality is alien to India and is an imported vice since Dinkar's defence of it is based on ideas drawn from 'an English book'. In a letter to the narrator, Manohar mentions to what extent boys would go to make themselves handsome for the purpose and also enlists the name of 'all kinds of places in this country where boys can get ruined'. He writes in the letter:

> …Most of the efforts to mislead boys occur at *boarding* schools, Brahmacharya Ashrams, Company Gardens, fairs and festivals. One often hears of teachers being responsible for boys' ruin. There are few schools where five to ten such cases do not come before the headmaster each year. Despite this, people do not think of reform.

Evidently, Manohar's hostility towards homosexuality colours the opinion of the narrator, who also begins to consider it as an ailment afflicting 'enslaved India'. The narrator pities Ramesh, the teenage beloved of Dinkar, as 'a beautiful flower' thrown into the furnace. But the narrator does not reserve any such sentiments for Dinkar and does not even think of considering his situation sympathetically. Dinkar Babu simply disgusts him.

We can identify the narrator with a large segment of our population which does not mind peeping into other people's private business and slinging mud at their characters. His attitude seems to be quite biased in the end where he takes Ramesh away to his father after 'rescuing' him from Dinkar Babu and wishing for his protection. Strangely enough, he does not care to wish for that protection on his friend, who disappeared abruptly after the fiasco at the residence of the narrator. Dinkar Babu's escape/self-imposed exile is an indicator of what fate awaits an Indian homosexual if he unfortunately gets caught or exposed. It is a life of humiliation and obscurity.

The *hungama* that ensued on the publication of this story nearly eight decades ago is still heard whenever such incidents are reported both in life and in literature. It is sure that despite globalisation and a constant emphasis on the several forms of human rights, we have not been able to clean the grease of Victorian Puritanism from our society even today.

Was Ugra a Closet Queer?

Ruth Vanita and Saleem Kidwai's book (2000) is exhaustive. But they deal in contexts, not in texts. I shall go over the contexts here and then use the texts in support of my hypothesis that Ugra was actually homophobic, possibly a closet queer. (By definition, 'hypotheses' don't need proofs; and intuition is 99 points in literature.)

The context, then, first. In the first three decades of the twentieth century, India under the British was in political turmoil. The late nineteenth century reform movements were bearing fruit. Some were homoerotic (see Kirpal 1995, on Ramakrishna's sex life and his attraction to Vivekananda). The Maharaja of Seraikela, a homosexual, founded the Gotipua School of Odissi boy dancers whom he sodomised. But he kept the art alive. The king as queen. Another ruler, Dewas Sr patronised E. M. Forster. Dewas Sr was a guilt-ridden homosexual who fasted and prayed to wash away his sins. Forster fell in love with a sweeper boy of the lowest 'Mehtar' (sweeper) caste and wrote him a love-poem as a short story called *Kania*, after his name, which was published in the *Illustrated Weekly* in the

1970s. 'Kania' could also mean in slang 'blind in one eye' or 'jug-eared' (from *kaan* = ear), i.e., a bit queer or strange. Of course, nothing happens. Forster was a frightened virgin who lost his virginity at the ripe age of 42 to a Moslem train conductor in Alexandria. The boy, Jiddu Krishnamurty's mentor A. C. Leadbeater, was taken to court on the charge of sodomising boys. The court papers, which Mary Lutyens helpfully re-publishes (1973) mentions the old Englishman's penchant for lathering the boys between their legs at bath. Another Englishman, C. F. Andrews, was 'sublimating' his homosexuality into *seva* at M. K. Gandhi's Wardha ashram on Gandhi's orders (see the Gandhi Correspondence published by the Sevagram Trust). How come after all the *seva* Gandhi could not suppress his libido and had to sleep naked between two nubile virgins in a moment of devastating self-doubt (devastating to the virgins, that is)? But then Gandhi was 'Mahatma' and father of many sons (one of whom turned both Moslem and alcoholic in an abusive moment, abusive to the Father of the Nation, that is). Rabindranath Tagore was not impressed with a freedom without discipline or international culture. But then he was already 80 and passé. (Tagore himself at 14 had to be taken to the Himalayas to visit the *kali bhaktas*, viz. naked sadhus in order to cure him of his 'possession' by the Great Mother, read, his 'incipient homosexuality'.) This was told to me by Professor Probal Dasgupta. So India was forever finding Indian cures to a 'western' malaise. Jawaharlal Nehru was soon to sleep with both the Earl and his wife, Edwina Mountbatten. He was introduced to these delights in 1920s Soho (see Wolpert 1996). Christopher Isherwood was boy obsessed and god obsessed simultaneously in 1950s Westwood, Los Angeles. Prabhuvananda told him to look at his boy, Don Bachardy, as 'Krishna' (see Isherwood 1976). This is the advice Ugra gives posthumously to Oscar Wilde!

There was much opposition to Ugra in the press (see Vanita and Kidwai 2000) because in India, anything sexual has to be immediately spiritualised. So Draupadi's audacious polyandry in the *Mahabharata* is aetherialised as the female human soul wedded to the five earthly brothers, the five very sensual senses. Also, pederasts can become lovers of the child-god, the blue-hued Krishna, just as easily.

The fact of the matter is the Indian soul had been christianised by the Brahmo Samaj (not least in Bengal). The British introduced Indian Penal Code's (IPC) 'sodomy law', viz. Article 377, in the wake of the Oscar Wilde trials in London. India's white rulers could not be seen as patsies and pansies by its colonial populace. But the actual fact of the matter is that it was the coming of the 'memsahibs' out East in 1857 that caused the army mutiny when the bond between master and manservant (homo-erotic if not downright homosexual) broke down in the wake of feminine intrusion. This is a documented historical fact and one of the causes of the Mutiny. (See Allan on the Raj.)

Ugra became a transvestite child actor to escape Brahmin childhood poverty in the United Provinces. He played Sita. Villagers touched his feet. Troupe managers sodomised the boys. Ugra says he escaped. He perfumed his hair like prostitutes. He frequented them, some say. He never married, 'a wife to gods' in his childhood (Vanita 2006: 21–22).

Now, you can see from Ugra's posthumous advice to Oscar Wilde that he, Ugra, was talking from both sides of his mouth and took his pleasure, probably, from both sides of his anatomy. The biography talks of his peregrinations in British India as a 'journalist' and a 'freedom fighter'. A freedom fighter, in our eyes, can do no wrong. He was probably a closet queer. His writing (badly written and badly translated) gives him away. To paraphrase Dr Graham's advice to his dancing daughter Martha, 'writing never lies'. The author's unconscious is naked on the page for all to see only if they have eyes in their hearts, i.e., intuition.

In Ugra's day, gay boys were called 'Chocolate'. Their youthful sod-omisers, of course, loved them. The 'moralists' (read other 'closet queers) used to see to it that these boys' faces were blackened (*kali potna*) and then they were soundly thrashed and driven away. You'd bother to do that only if there was a little queer in you which bothered you. Otherwise why take the trouble?! So Ugra's boys are alternately loved and thrashed: loved when Ugra feels love and thrashed when Ugra is beset by homosexual paranoia.

This is much like Mozart's opera *Don Giovanni*, where the Don loves women much to rakish Vienna's rapture and approval and is then killed by the father Commandant and dispatched to Hell. This way, both the bohemians and the bourgeoisie are pleased. And the boy Mozart can go his merry genius way. But Ugra is no genius. He is a closet queer who is also, more unforgivably, a bad writer. Specious leftist reasoning among India's gays has made them take him to their hearts. Like Queen Victoria, I am not amused.

Another unforgivable sin of Ruth Vanita's edition of Ugra's 'Chocolate' is the pilfering of a Bhupen Khakhar painting as cover art without any citation. Gays are still exploiting gays, even dead ones.

A Street With 57 Lanes (1957)

Kamleshwar's *A Street With 57 Lanes* is a symbolic depiction of low-life in India's heartland of Uttar Pradesh. His protagonist is a bisexual truck driver who loves both his truck cleaner and a *nautanki* dancer (the stuff of Bollywood dreams). These are not freaks but ordinary Indians. The eponymous streets are the winding lanes of a red-light district but they are also the lanes of the hero's heart, vast as the Indo-Gangetic plains and convoluted as a seashell. The lanes around a street also conjure up an animal's backbone with ribs from which the meat is successively stripped away, as in a butcher's shop, to show the elemental man within. For man is his body moving in a vast space as in a Russian novel, a Soviet era film or as in our own Mehboob Khan's *Mother India* (1957), which is of the same vintage as our novel. (Mystics, both eastern and western, have taught us that the body is in the soul.) The soul may be of primary and ultimate value but what we have here are three bodies stripped down to their basic urges for food, sex and social survival driven to their doom by machinations of social forces they do not fully understand, viz. British law courts and transport conglomerates. Men are vermin crawling under the sky's inverted bowl. The innocence of the Raj Kapoor starrer *Teesri Kasam* (1966) is missing here. What we have instead is an altogether more stark and sinister human drama which is the stuff of everyday life in India's badlands. That Kamleshwar chose a prostitute, a homosexual and Gainda, a poet as organs for his voice way back in 1957 is altogether to his credit. The poet is Gramsci's proletarian intellectual! He is against 'suttee' (widow-burning)!

Naquib Mahfouz considered the novel to be the art form of the industrial age. Its facts appeal to our need for science and its romantic plots appeal to our imaginations. Charles Baudelaire said 'Sex is the poor man's romance.' And sex we have in plenty in this novel with a bisexual for a hero.

Here are some excerpts in the manner of a film trailer. In a translation the earthy Bhojpuri of Premchand's vintage, of course, is missing.

When Shivraj woke up in the morning, he found Sarnam lying with him in his cot. His hand was resting on Shivraj's chest. It was nothing new for Sarnam and Shivraj should have got accustomed to it by now. In the beginning, when Shivraj protested, Sarnam said, "You remind me of my own youth. Sixteen years ago, I was very much like you — smart, agile and simple." He sighed. "Alas, those days will never return.' He held Shivraj's hand in his own, looked wistfully at his finger-nails, pressed his knuckles, and moved his hand over his soft downy arm. Then, as if the spell had broken, he said, "Run away!"

Once Sarnam clutched Shivraj in his arms and digging his face into his hair, sighed deeply. "Shivraj, look at me," he said lifting his chin. Shivraj, fluttering to disengage himself from his clasp, stared at him like a helpless bird. Relaxing his grip, Sarnam said, "Shiva, I'm sure you were related to me in your previous birth. No? Once I caught mother like this. She slapped me in the face and then overwhelmed with maternal affection, started crying." Shivraj's heart which was filled with revulsion suddenly melted. Sarnam did everything to please Shivraj and bought him the nicest things currently in vogue.

What kind of love was it? Shivraj wondered. But why did it stink? Where did it begin and where did it end? Shouldn't he draw a line somewhere and keep him from overstepping it so that their love was saved from festering.

Pushing away Sarnam's hand, he got up and went into the inner room. It was still dark.

His meeting with Bansari seemed to have cast a spell on him.

But that was two years ago and her face had got obliterated from his mind. He was going round a country fair. Fortifying himself with a shot of toddy, he entered a tent to witness a *nautanki* show. He got a jolt as he looked at the stage. Wasn't it Bansari, standing among the companions of Laila? Once a simple, country girl, she had now learnt to be coquettish. She gave a provocative jerk to her shoulders, uttered '*hai daiya*', with a copy lisp, and winked at the audience. Sarnam threw a coin on the stage but its jingle was lost in the loud bearing of the drum. He was not sure. Perhaps, she was not Bansari. While speaking her lines, she bandied words with the audience and even mouthed profanities. Her eyes roved over Sarnam.

Sarnam returned to his place and spent the remaining part of the night in great agitation. The next evening, before the start of the show, he happened to run into Bansari.

"Out on a prowl?" she asked.

'I've kept the thing safe for you. Are you game?' Then she started laughing. What a brazen girl! Sarnam looked fascinated at her *pan*-stained lips.

Her love drew Shivraj like a magnet.

Bansari was pleased at Shivraj's decision. For one thing he would be released from Sarnam's stranglehold. For another, Sarnam's loneliness would ultimately drive him into her lap. He would feel repentant and she would gleefully watch the lion at bay. If woman is helpless, man too has his moments of defeat. "Go away somewhere Kamala," she told Shivraj. "And give a damn to what the world says."

Sarnam was busy consulting lawyers about his case. But he was equally worried about Shivraj. A wall seemed to have risen between them because of Kamala. "A girl who lives openly with the music master can have no scruples," he told Shivraj. "If it is a girl you want, I can arrange another girl for you."

He took him to the red light district to give him a glimpse of the world of sin. "See them for what they are," he told Shivraj. "The one you want to fall for is only a gilded butterfly. When you see her under her skin, the fire will go out of your heart."

The dacoity case came up for hearing before the court and Sarnam Singh surrendered himself before the magistrate. He found Rangeelay, his friend from childhood days, standing before him as an approver. He knew that he was only a pawn on the chessboard and its manipulator, a hennaed-hand wearing bangles — the same band which one night at the country fair had caressed his hair. "What a broad forehead you have!" The words now reeked with vengeance; he was still in love with them. If these hands had lifted in protection, he would have gladly submitted to them. But they held out a challenge instead, and he was not the one to recoil.

"Yes, Maharaj," a bystander said. "These days even friends have turned into foes."

Could anyone believe that Rangeelay would turn against Sarnam Singh? The river had started flowing upstream. Now it was Sarnam Singh's turn. He would surely wreak his vengeance on Rangeelay's family.

They saw two shadowy figures emerging on the road, one walking behind the other. As they came nearer, Gainda poet's eyes bulged with surprise. "Is it you Sarnam Singh?" he asked.

Sarnam Singh stopped in his tracks. "Yes, Maharaj, it's me."

"Who's she? A relative?"

"It's Bansari, Gainda Maharaj. I've brought her from the hospital. That's no place for her."

Sarnam Singh resumed his walk. Bansari, as she followed him, looked at his stone-like rugged, broad back. Crossing the road, Sarnam Singh handed the child he was carrying back to Bansari and unlocked the door of Rangeelay's house. "Go in and light the lamp," he said. "I'll go now. Send me word if you need anything. Now that Rangeelay is gone, don't think that there's no one left to look after you. Go in."

He turned away. As he reached the end of the lane, he heard the sound of sobbing. He wondered why Bansari had started crying.

With bowed head, he walked away towards his empty house.

Kamaleshwar's hero is high-born but he falls from grace because of his unintelligent behaviour. The new caste code says: 'You're a Brahmin not only because you're born one but also by your behaviour.' Yet, you lose caste the same old ways by associating with the impure, namely, homosexuals and prostitutes. To construct a mystique of purity, a notion of impurity was first created. So Kamleswar's novel, on inspection, does not turn out to be as radical as it seems at first glance. He was of the New Story Movement (Nayi Kahani Andolan). His criticism of the Nehruvian dream is mild because he, like the leftist Urdu Progressives, took patronage from the same state they wished to criticise.

The novel has a base in 1930s Hindi film and Bhojpuri folk music. It reminds me of B. R. Chopra's *Naya Daur* (1957) where machinery is seen as villainous, a regressive message if ever there was one.

The New Story Movement (in Hindi) is at least as old as Premchand. Kamleshwar is its post-independence exponent. He is a socialist and a liberal. That means that his characters are humble, his story realistic, his genres native. So we have a truck driver, a lover (the lorry cleaner) and a woman (a golden-hearted prostitute). Social registers blur in love. The lorry cleaner can boss the driver in bed. The lowly prostitute is the queen of the trucker hero's heart. But the main story is of social change. New syndicates put the truck out of business. These are little people caught by big forces and helpless to resist. The love triangle remains unresolved. Who has time for love if they cannot eat?

The genre is native (*nautanki*) but it is mixed with the storytelling of the European novel from Dostoyevsky to Sholokhov. It is wrong, of course, to say that the modern novel in India of Tagore, say, comes from the *burra katha* (legends of gods' boon or 'burra'). Jane Austen, Sir Walter Scott and George Eliot are the nursery of the Indian novel. Aurobindo Ghosh's brother Manmohan, the poet, did not rub shoulders with Oscar Wilde in London for nothing!

Gay Prose in Indian English

R. Raj Rao's Short Stories

One Day I Locked My Flat in Soul City (Rao 2000) went through two editions: an ini-tial one and a slightly expanded one post-1993. The first story, chronologically the earliest, deals with his love for a Dalit (Mahar) student in Pune; the middle story in the collection, 'Tandoori Nights', deals with his love for a Moslem boy in Leeds (where Rao was a graduate student and British Council scholar in Postcolonial Literature at the University), and the last story, 'Landiya ko Maar', is set during the Bombay riots (of 1993).

The first story, 'Confessions of a Boy Lover', is the most spiritual; the last, the most political one in this collection. Raj falls in love with a Dalit boy at the University (Pune). But the boy takes fright and runs off to his village. The boy is shielded by his Dalit villager relatives and refuses to come out of his house when Raj follows him to the village. Raj is beaten, thrown out of the village and has to nurse a bruised body and ego all night at the railway station because the last train has left. After cruising Bombay V. T., Raj finds a spiritual love. The boy used to place his feet on Raj's heart in love play just as a devotee places his heart between the guru's feet. The boy too has spiritual stirrings but cannot detect spirit in the body. He joins a monastery; Raj becomes a Sai Baba *bhakta*. But he keeps his spirituality out of his work though he privately says all his work is a gift of Sai Baba's.

'Tandoori Nights' is a tortuously told tale of a cat-and-mouse love game between an Indian graduate student in England (read: Raj) and a Pakistani Moslem Tandoori cook, a delicious 20-year-old. But the Moslem culture has homophobia, homosexual paranoia and gay guilt. On the day Raj finally leaves for India and is taking his last crap with the toilet door open, the Moslem boy comes in and allows Raj to fellate him. Spirit has fled out the loo door and Raj is back in the loo where middle-class guilt thinks gay love belongs.

The tenant has to go through the restaurant kitchen where his lover works to his upstairs rental. Love and food are insistently mixed as one appetite. The last oral love act takes place in the latrine. The homosexual conflates the digestive and reproductive tracts so that oral sex replaces the penile sex of heterosexuals.

Redemption will come through politics. 'Landiya ko Maar' is a pun meaning sexual anal rape as well as beating up the political opponent (of the Hindu Shiv Sainik), namely, the *landiya*, a Bombay slang for 'Muslim'. A newly married couple living in a slum with the groom's mother is confronted by a Hindu mob. The groom is hidden in a box beneath the bed and the women face up to the mob, which leaves. But not before the Hindu leader notices lustfully the groom in the wedding photo. He returns to the house to make love to the groom in the kitchen while the women cower outside. He leaves, giving dire threats for 'next time'. This is Rao's most mature story. He frames it as a traveller's tale: one told by a (gay) journalist (read: Raj) to a probably gay army officer on a night train in order to seduce him. But the reader gets disappointed as the officer gets off at the next station. Onir (of *My Brother Nikhil* 2005 fame) wants to film it. But Onir is unintelligent and Raj deserves better.

The anarchic Shiv Sainik returning to the Moslem household to have gay sex (sodomy) with the householder is a metaphor for the attraction of opposites. I go one step further and say 'Opposites are One'. William Blake says as much in his 'Proverbs of Hell' in *The Marriage of Heaven and Hell* (1790–93).

R. Raj Rao believes that the great age of literature is over and we live in lesser times. By writing in a colloquial style, he is challenging the received notions of high literature. So style points to content here, low style for a literature about low-life.

gay theatre

Mahesh Dattani: *Dance Like a Man*

Dance Like a Man is a dramatic exploration of the performative nature of gender in a patriarchal system. The title of the play itself clearly indicates that dance as 'art' is not a neutral domain where one may be able to break free of the constraints society constructs and imposes on the biological entities 'man' and 'woman'; rather, dance encodes and is itself implicated in the division and reinforcement of gender roles as 'masculine' and 'feminine' that is the foundation of patriarchy. Thus, the ironic reference to a manly/masculine way of dancing in the title is really a probing into the power structures that render the relationship between 'dance' and 'man' seemingly contradictory. The protagonists, Jairaj and Ratna, are torn between their passion for their art and the need to sustain their personal relationship within the structure of a (compulsory heterosexual) family.

The patriarchal economy does not recognise dance as a vocation suitable for a man, or for that matter, as a legitimate vocation at all. Dance is seen either as a means by which supposedly immoral women like Chinni Amma gratify male sexual desire, or, conversely, as an 'evil' that self-appointed reformers like Amritlal take up to justify and perpetuate their agenda of 'social reconstruction'. In neither case is dance perceived as an art form that could possibly, if ideally, exist independently of these mainstream discourses of patriarchal power; rather, it is perceived as belonging to the 'feminine' domain that always needs condemnation or rescuing by the 'man'. Patriarchy allows the 'man' only to appropriate dance for his own sake, not to participate in it himself as a learner. The conflicting views on the nature of dance as art vis-a-vis its morality within a patriarchal structure come to the fore in the debate Amritlal and Jairaj have about the cult of the *devadasi*s:

> Amritlal: We are building ashrams for these unfortunate women! Educating them, reforming them…

Jairaj: Reform! Don't talk about reform. If you really wanted any kind of reform in our society, you would let them practise their art.
Amritlal: Encourage open prostitution?
Jairaj: Send them back to their temples. Give them awards for preserving their art.

In deciding to take up dance both as passion and profession, Jairaj transgresses the artificial boundaries that set apart the personal and the public, the artistic and the economic, the feminine and the masculine — distinctions on which patriarchy itself is premised. Jairaj's choice of dance as his vocation thus offers a challenge to patriarchy: the choice automatically also poses a threat to the gender distinctions that dictate a strict division of roles between men and women. As Jairaj points out:

The craft of a prostitute to show off her wares — what business did a man have learning such a craft? Of what use could it be to him? No use. So no man would want to learn such a craft. Hence anyone who learnt such a craft could not be a man. How could I argue against such logic?

Evidently, Jairaj is aware of the self-justifying nature of such logic, but this awareness alone does not enable him to break free of the restrictions that patriarchy imposes on the sexes. Dance does allow Jairaj to swap gender roles and perform as a woman, an experience he seems to relish, especially in the instance in which he recounts performing an erotic number in drag to a delighted audience of army men. Jairaj is clearly aware of the homoerotic implications of such an 'act' and the challenge it offers to patriarchy. But his transgression is not a simple act of liberation from the pressures of binary gender division; rather, it is a source of anxiety not only for Amritlal but also for Ratna and even himself. Not least of the reasons behind this is the strict law of inheritance which is the chief means of transference of patriarchal power from one generation to the next. Amritlal's reluctance to let Jairaj continue with his 'obsession' with dance is indeed a refusal to let economic currency flow into a channel that has traditionally been considered 'unproductive' and has therefore been kept outside the realm of mainstream economic activity. In a desperate bid to 'make a man' out of his son, Amritlal not only concedes to let his daughter-in-law to continue with her career as a dancer, but even conspires with her to sabotage Jairaj's career:

Amritlal: A woman in a man's world may be considered as being progressive. But a man in a woman's world is pathetic.

Ratna: Maybe we aren't 'progressive' enough.
Amritlal: That isn't being progressive, that is … sick.
Ratna: Then why did you tell him just now that he could dance?
Amritlal: Tell me. How good is he as a dancer?
Ratna: He's good.
Amritlal: Good? Not brilliant? And you?
Ratna: Well, if I practise hard then …
Amritlal: Then you might become famous?
Ratna: I might.
Amritlal: Just as I thought. He is wasting his time. Poor boy.
Ratna: He isn't …
Amritlal: It's up to you now.
Ratna: What?
Amritlal: Help me make him an adult. Help me to help him grow up.

Thus, in a paradoxical act, Amritlal, the symbol of patriarchal authority, tries to bring his son 'back to the fold' through a sort of transference of power from his son to his daughter-in-law, thereby assisting to legitimise dance as a respectable vocation in spite of his obvious dislike for it. A greater paradox is that this act ultimately backfires to render Ratna 'masculinised' and Jairaj 'feminised' in terms of the active/passive roles that patriarchy lays down for 'man' and 'woman'. The gender roles are reversed insofar as Ratna takes charge of her own career and of Lata as well while Jairaj is reduced to drink and cynicism, but the power equation between the two continues to remain unequal. Consequently, this kind of role reversal comes with its own share of guilt and sense of loss on both sides. Even in their chosen field of dance, the same principle of fierce, destructive competition, manipulation and dominance that underlies traditional patriarchal economy is reduplicated, with the result that 'success' and 'failure' remain the binaries that work by means of unequal distribution of power. Dance thus becomes only a part of a larger exploitative system that traps Jairaj and Ratna in a self-destructive game of role-playing.

The situation is further complicated by the interplay of familial duties and expectations with the already strained professional relationship between the two. Even forgiveness becomes a performance that both must indulge in to survive their sense of guilt — Jairaj's guilt for not being 'man' enough to live on his own independently of his father, Ratna's guilt for not being 'motherly' enough to save her infant son's life. Each must forgive the other, or at least pretend to do so, in order that they are able to live up to the choices that they have made. Lata becomes the living, dancing embodiment of these choices: Jairaj's indifferent approval of Viswas as her prospective husband and Ratna's frantic efforts to establish her as a promising dancer are fittingly ironic tributes to the uneasy positions they have created for themselves within the patriarchal economy. The fact that the actors are made to exchange roles — Jairaj becomes Amritlal, Viswas becomes Jairaj, Lata becomes Ratna — draws our attention to the insidiousness of patriarchy, to the resilience of a power structure that must involve performance, whether of dance or gender.

The final harmony of the perfect dance is achieved only through death — an expression of regret at being 'only human', at lacking 'the magic to dance like God'. And that is the final point: the players are never 'only human'; they are 'man' or 'woman', trapped in predetermined roles that patriarchal society choreographs for its members. The 'magic', therefore, is shown to lie beyond the confines of the house Jairaj and Ratna have lived in, in a transcendent domain where their voices and movements become indistinguishable from one another and they declare:

> We dance perfectly. In unison. Not missing a step or a beat. We talk and laugh at all the mistakes we made in our previous dances.

A Personal Note on Mahesh Dattani's Plays

Mahesh Dattani has found full length critical treatment in *Mahesh Dattani Contemporary Indian Writers in English* (Chaudhuri 2005). Every single interview Mahesh has ever given is listed, plus Derrida, for good measure, in her bibliography (she could have expended her attention and affections on Edward Said and Homi Bhabha, in Dattani's postcolonial context more profitably). One thing that Dattani isn't is an egghead. And he's sly in his wit. Someone asks him:

> Why don't you write in your mother-tongue?
> He: (in a high-pitched voice) But I do!

This is Dattani. It is a well-rehearsed and well-timed line and it always, always brings the house down. So all the drama the shy Dattani can't play out in his life he puts on-stage. I visited his Bangalore pad: an amphitheatre with Warli paintings on the walls in the yard. And you ascend to a stage setting living room with bare white walls and two staircases leading off left and right to two bedroom doors at middle level (the level where Prospero usually appears in Shakespeare, as also the queeny Richard II just before death: 'And down, down I come like glistening Phaeton', etc) He knows how to use space on a set. Dattani read literature at school and claims his teachers did not know Whitman and Shakespeare were gay. (No, Dattani, they just did not tell you!)

More importantly he saw the 1960s Taylor-Burton film version of Edward Albee's *Who's Afraid of Virginia Woolf?* (1962) (The same Albee who shocked us in *The Zoo Story* [1958] by spelling it out: 'I am a H-O-M-O-S-E-X-U-A-L!')

Perhaps Dattani did not know then that *Who's Afraid of Virginia Woolf?* with its two bickering, heterosexual couples was originally written by Albee for two gay couples (the 'hysterical' pregnancy in the play than makes perfect sense). It would be too hot for 1960s Broadway and for Albee's genteel, Westchester country adoptive mother, whom he would only posthumously forgive in *Three Tall Ladies* (1994). So Albee 'heterosexualised' *Who's Afraid of Virginia Woolf?* All little Dattani then knew was he wanted to write plays like that.

He did in *On A Muggy Night in Mumbai* (1998) which begins with two men kissing in bed in a Marine Drive penthouse. Then the bitchiness between men and women begins. Someone asks:

Why don't gays get married?
...They do! To the same sex!

Two male lovers find that the sister of one wants to marry the other gay's ex-boyfriend. Mercifully, she discovers a photo of the two men in bed and saves herself the meows. Gays in India are trapped in families. Even in the gay world the sensible sex is the woman. This is Dattani's straight take on the gay world. Gays are completely normal except for a kink in the head or in the bed: the '80s American take on gays. No wonder Dattani and I part company. 'If I were a woman I'd be Madhubala', is a Dattani quip.

Mango is the Indian apple. In *Mango Soufflé* (Dattani 2002, queer cinema), the film version of *On a Muggy Night in Mumbai*, the movie camera is free to roam the swimming pool and the mango orchard of a suburban farmhouse. Dattani is credited with coining the term 'metrosexual'. Men frolic in swimming pools with men but all the action is 'above the belt'. Neither he nor any of his characters ever spell out the term 'homosexual'. The bisexuals in the audience and the Indian Film Censor Board are pleased.

Mango Soufflé won awards abroad. This is the West's patronage of India's gays. In Copenhagen, 50 years of gay freedom have still not rid the Danish gay of his macho swagger nor kept the gay nightlife out of the clutches of an American style mafia that trades on gay bodies and gay souls in baths, saunas, clubs and dance halls. In India, we are at least as progressive as Clinton's America with its 'Don't Ask/Don't Tell' policy. Indians look the other way. No coming-out-queens here. Anyway, Dattani is praised for showing normal gay lives in an India which criminalises homosexuals and sees them as 'mad' or 'abnormal.'

Dattani himself could get the Sahitya Akademi's award only if he did not come out as a gay in interviews. This was when Sonia and Rajiv Gandhi had invited for the first time gay fashion and design icons to the Presidential Palace to felicitate their work on the Festivals of India abroad. So it is a game of hide-and-seek in life as in art.

Dattani's wit is devastating on stage and in person. He says he learnt Anton Chekhov's wit. But where is the poetry? He says the poetry is what transpires between audience and actors on stage in the magic of the theatre. But this is too easy. India's haute bourgeoisie need a swan song as Chekhov's Russia got one in his plays (and I don't mean Gurcharan Das's *9 Jakhoo Hill* [1962] which is a straight Chekhov rip-off). Dattani says he is influenced by Henrik Ibsen and Tennessee Williams. His plays are 'well-made plays'. His farce is Georges Feydeau's; his gay fun and games, very serious.

Dattani could say that poetry is lacking in India's urban lives so why force it on-stage? I hate cross-over movies, i.e., Indian actors mouthing inane English dialogues ('If you were a straight, we'd be married. Eeeks!') in Oxbridge accents. But that is where the nation is heading: towards one protracted night at the call centre, as Chetan Bhagat's novel (2005) has it. Dev Benegal wanted to film this in *English, August* (1994). He called 'Pack up' after one day's shoot. He couldn't handle the accents! Dattani sees this as a matter of cultural assimilation. He says India survived because it assimilated the cultural influence of its invaders; the American Indians could not and hence have died.

Dattani's lasting insight could be 'phobo-genesis' (Fanon (1952), where he explores how the mechanisms of 'othering' influence the self. The homophobe who tries to 'expose' the homosexual on-stage is himself revealed to be a closet queer. Thus, homophobia is explained. It was such a story Dattani sent me, entitled 'The Night-Queen' ('Raat-ki-Rani' in Hindi, meaning the night-flowering jasmine) for *Yaraana*, and we became friends for life.

Gieve Patel: Parsi Play with a Gay Surprise

This four-act play is a poem to the powers of the Earth Mother, i.e., to the earth's reconciliatory powers and a description of the males, both primitive and socialised, who live in an all male society devoid of woman and who ultimately fail, the balance between the male–female polarity restored at the end.

One has to understand that Gieve Patel is a poet and poetry transcends politics. He is a Parsi doctor with a rural practice who lives in Bombay. The play is set at the turn of the nineteenth century, the heyday of the Parsis and of the British Empire. It is roughly set in the period between the 1857 Mutiny and Jalianwallah Bagh (1919). The story is that a Parsi lawyer in rural Gujarat adopts a tribal Warli boy, makes him into a lawyer with his wife's help and marries him to his daughter. In nineteenth century India, there was not much of a class divide between master and servant of the same caste. It was a matter of reward for hard work for a servant to be socially accepted as a master. The play, however, gives us an 'enlightened' Parsi who adopts a wild child whose wildness he romanticises. The child, called Nahnu ('Little One'), later Naval ('Newborn'), hero-worships Behram. The question the play posits is: Can we worship anything other than the Earth and Sky? Is man worshipping man of any use?

The play mentions *Pericles* (Marina, the daughter, lost and found after 20 years), but the obvious Shakespearean echo here is that of Caliban being 'civilised' by Prospero. Prospero, at the end, breaks his pen; Mr Behram goes mad. The play begins and ends with two birth scenes.

Naval, a lawyer, comes flushed with his first victory from court. He sees a goat birthing and has an epileptic fit. He confuses goat and woman, he tells his wife Dolly. Mr Behram cannot brook the young couple's independence at the play's end, suffers a paralytic stroke and becomes as helpless as a baby. A wife with whom he has long ceased having sexual relations can now communicate with him in silence for the rest of his life.

There had been tension between husband and wife over Naval. 'Set him free', the wife would plead. 'Call him back', the husband would bellow. There had been tension between father and daughter over Naval as well. Finally, the pregnant daughter confronts the father at the play's end and asks him if he did not make her marry Naval only in order to keep him (Naval) for himself. Now, this is a classic Parsi solution to a homoerotic conflict. The entire play is a mystic communion between Naval and Mr Behram. For want of a better word, we would have to call this communion 'love'. To characterise it as a homoerotic mania on Mr Behram's part would be reductive. But he abuses his wife over the boy going so far as to bang her head on a table when she wants to return the boy back to nature. Politics is negated by love, love by madness.

But the boy grows into a man. He consorts with rival lawyers Bharucha and Hegde, one a Parsi, the other a Maharashtrian, over a case involving the town's common grazing lands on which the British District Collector wants to build a cantonment. Behram loses the case and he alone gets blamed for it. People would talk about Naval and Behram but Naval is not implicated in this failure. He can now practice alone as a new ('naval') lawyer.

Behram feels unloved. He'd rather love his shoe, he says in his Lear-like final madness. He bangs his own head retributively on the same table on which he had banged his wife Rati's head. The shoe is the same shoe Naval had kissed and fawned upon towards the end of Act III.

So the play is choreographed as a series of rises and falls. We see bodies physically kneeling and rising on stage. The body is important to the play. Gieve Patel, a physician, himself ill in childhood, is no stranger to the body. His last book of poems is entitled *How Do You Withstand, Body* (1976). The body moves physically in space. The body is also imaged (in the mind) before we can love it. This imaging (romanticising) has political implications. The earth's body is ploughed. We are all earth's children, especially so the tribal who lives off the earth's produce. We Parsis are interlopers in Gujarat. First we collude with the local Rana, then we collude with the British. In a way Mr Behram, paralysed at the end, gets his just dessert. But the trope of paralysis is poetic: whenever he moved he caused disaster, now stilled, he can nurse his insight; that is, if you love a thing you let it grow, go.

In the first act Naval is made to literally regress to childhood, being forced by Behram to wear his childhood loincloth and vest. He is a young earth god, a Dionysius. Naval feels humiliated. Their love is such silent contemplation of each other that Behram knows each eyelash of Naval's intimately. At the play's end, Behram breaks down and is willing to enter Naval's bowels, feel his faeces and drown in his body fluids. All Naval knows is that he was considered short, thin and dark when in England. And that he'll never know English Literature like Mr Behram, who knows it better than the British District Collector, himself a poet and soon to become a village tyrant.

So there is the body politic and the sensate body. Triumph in the body politic, as a self-ruled, influential lawyer means nothing to Behram as he has failed to reconcile his sensate body to the body politic. Behram, at the end, quotes Sophocles who, in his ageing years, said of his vital drives and desires: 'Most gladly have I escaped the thing of which you speak; I feel as if I had escaped from the hands of a mad and furious master.'

Who is the mad and furious master here? Is it the body? Is it the British? Is it the Parsi over the Gujarat tribal? Behram over Naval? Or is it, indeed, the tyrant dark lover Naval over poor Mr Behram who disintegrates?

Naval feels that his marriage is sacrificed to Behram. When he asserts his independence, his daughter is saved from immolating her marriage for her father. 'I feel like I have been saved from Sati,' Dolly tells Naval. The District Collector saves Indian women from 'suttee'. Naval saves his wife from becoming a living sati. I submit that Naval, the mystical 'bride' of Behram, has to commit sati before he can be saved from Behram. The Parsi male as Sita! Men become women become men.

Meenakshi Mukherjee, in her unpublished paper 'Gender and Nation' (delivered at the University of Hyderabad), states:

> Women as loyal wives upholding traditional values and women as veeranganas — empowered creatures who can make things happen — are two opposed symbols in the narration of the nation in the colonial period. But there is yet a third paradigm. In the nationalist agenda, the figure of woman that had emotional potency was that of mother. This resonant image brought together three different discourses — the discourse of the family (biological mother), discourse of religion (devi or goddess) and the discourse of nation (the motherland).

And again,

> Worshipping the nation as mother and essentialising women as the source of spiritual power are parallel processes — one perpetuates the bondage of women, the other exalts the abstract notion of the country over the people who constitute it.

Rati can do no wrong. She is mother. She carries even a jug with great beauty. Parsi women had personhood before other Indian women. They had limited education under male patronage, like Rati does. But Rati's salvation first and last is through her husband. Dolly, Rati's daughter and younger avatar, has made, shall we say anachronistically, a pan-Indian marriage and goes off with her newly and truly liberated husband at the play's end. Naval, then, has a new personhood from his mixed Parsi–tribal heritage. Dolly too had been only partially educated since Behram wished to educate his adoptive son Naval fully. But Portia-like Dolly had donned lawyer's robes and gone off to court. And people mocked one more innovation of the imaginative Behram.

But imagination has its limits. The life of Marquis de Sade showed the Enlightenment that the mind cannot go where the body wishes to go. So too with Behram. Poetry becomes pornography in the male mind devoid of women's personhood. It is only the body of the women, the Earth Mother, that finally reconcile Naval and Behram, if not to each other then at least to their own, individual fates.

Gieve Patel gives here a Parsi trope of coping with homosexuality, the Parsi way, (like marriage between first cousins to keep the money within the family). Nineteenth and twentieth century Parsi homosexuals used to have gay pairings of sons-in-law with fathers-in-law, made convenient by three generations living under one roof in joint families. Incest is also a way to secrecy. It is a kind of 'homotopia' that the two generations of men made by keeping their secret from their womenfolk. Homotopia means the topography of a place inhabited by a homogenous sex group, e.g., women's brothels or men's gyms. It is a kind of in-joke that should never have got out!

As noted before, the dialogue in one register for man–woman–child mars this otherwise perfectly chiselled, gem-like cameo of Parsi society in the early years of the last century.

The Transvestite Rasleela of Assam

400 years ago, Shanti deva established monasteries on the banks of the Brahmaputra river. These monasteries are repositories of great art and culture, viz. religion, music and dance. The monks are celibate and children as young as five are brought in to be dancers in the Rasleela of Krishna and the milkmaids (*gopis*). The temple is dedicated to Vishnu whose incarnation Krishna is. The monks are celibate and if they wish to marry they have to leave the monastery. The dance of Krishna's dalliance (*leela*) is danced to the accompaniment of a drum (*dhol*), slung on the neck and played with both hands, and cymbals. The old monks are the dance teachers and musicians. There can be only one Krishna but many *gopis*, each one longing for him. This is clearly an allegory of the human soul's longing for the divine. The adolescent boys do not feel sexual loneliness as they find 'love' and 'kisses' from other boys; strictly no sex is allowed. These men are lifelong celibates. The performance is preceded by elaborate make-up sessions. Blue powder for Krishna, white rice paste for the *gopis*. All eyes are kohl-ed. The young boys playing the *gopis* are clearly not professional transvestites. They transform their male physiques into females with cotton balls stuffed into bras for female breasts. No one cuts his hair in

monkhood, so all the dancers have a lush head of hair. They live with cows for milk and with stray dogs for pets. Life is resolutely pre-industrial. The drums announce the beginning of the Rasleela in the dance hall painted blue in memory of the dark-hued (blue god) Krishna. He dances at the centre and the *gopis* are entranced. The demon, all black and old and fat, remains outside the charmed circle. The dance goes on in circles. The dogs go on with their doggy lives. The earth moves around the sun in circles just as the 'female' dancers move all day around the male principle at the circle's centre, each human 'female' soul thinking that the Lord dances with him/her alone. But in reality Krishna only dances with Radha, a married woman, symbolic of the soul wedded to this world. It has to wed God. The day ends. The dance ends. River geese from the Brahmaputra find a night's rest on a tree-perch. Boys go to their beds after ritual ablutions to guard against impurity. If anything or anyone is touched the boys have to bathe again. Floors are smeared with cow dung, a pesticide and a cleansing agent. The boys are content with their loving lives with other boys. Embraces are allowed. Tomorrow will be another day. But nothing will change. Just as we are curious about them, they are curious about us. Nothing has changed in the monastery on the banks of the Brahmaputra for 400 years. Each day men will become women again, pining for their male god, Krishna.

Sumang Lila and Modern Theatre

Theatre in Manipur, as in many parts of the world, has a social commitment. Manipuris, in fact, are a cultural people. The cultural spirit has never been allowed to be blown out despite its geographical aloofness from the outside world. This is the main reason why theatre is thriving valiantly in Manipur. Theatre culture, per se, has travelled a long journey with meandering courses. It has always been part of the Lai Haraoba festival since time immemorial. But what we call theatre in contemporary usage is a later acquisition of this culture.

Theatre in Manipur today can be broadly divided, based on texts, into religious and secular. The former is the adaptation of religious epics or some episode from them, they are performed mainly in the sacred sphere such as temples. Within this we may incorporate Gouralila (stories of the childhood days of Gourana Mahaprabhu) and Udukhol (episodes of Krishna childhood days).

They are seasonal performances commanding spiritual devotion among the audience. On the other hand, secular theatre is mostly confined in themes, which are not religious and performed in the secular or profane sphere. Within this, we may include Sumang Lila and Phampak Lila (stage drama). Though the religious genre is loved profoundly by the audience, the torch of theatre is being held a lot more by the secular one.

Among the latter, Sumang Lila commands a very large rustic popularity among the audience though the stage drama still does not lack its serene and dignified position. This is because of its community-based themes and styles.

History and Development of Manipuri Theatre

Etymologically, Sumang lila is the combination of Sumang (courtward) and Lila (play or performance). It is also known as Jatra or Jatrawali, which is imported from Assam and Bengal as a result of their historical contacts. It is performed in an area of 13 × 13 feet in the centre of an open courtyard or playground or *mandap* (pavilion). It is performed in a very simple style without any raised stage or any set design or heavy props such as curtain, background scenery, visual effects, etc. The only things used are two chairs and one table kept on one side of the performance space. Its claim of being the theatre of the masses can be exemplified by the way it is performed in the middle of an audience which surrounds it from all sides, leaving only one passage that serves as both entrance and exit, connecting the space with the green room.

Sumang lila is performed by a touring band of 12–13 professional artists on invitation. These troupes may be exclusively female or exclusively male. In the case of Nupa Sumang Lila, the male characters are enacted by female artists, but what is the most intriguing is the enactment of the female roles by male artists or *nupishabi* (read male actress) in the case of the latter. These male actresses are profusely popular and are the main attraction of any Sumang lila.

Historically, the actual seed of Sumang lila was sown in *phage lila* (farce), performed during the reign of Maharaj Chandrakirti (1850–86), though traces of it were already present in episodes of Tangkhul Nurabi Loutanba of the Lai Haraoba festival. Then it was succeeded by such plays as Ramlila, Sabha Parba, Kabul lila, etc. But the real Sumang lila with various *rasas* (sentiments) was ushered in with the epic play *Harichandra* (1918). Others, such as Sabitri Satyavan, Meiraba Charan and Thok lila, then followed it. One of most successful play of this era was *Moirang Prabha* (an epic play based on the legendary lovers Khamba and Thoibi of Moirang).

Manipur has been a storehouse of rich culture, art and theatre. While the modern stage theatre is performed for a selected audience, the community-based theme and style of Sumang lila makes it widely popular.

6

gay films

Eunuchs in Hindi Films

Hijras are phenotypic men who wear female clothing and, ideally, renounce sexual desire and practice by undergoing a sacrificial emasculation — i.e. an excision of the penis and testicles — dedicated to the goddess Bhedraj Mata. Subsequently they are... endowed with the power to confer fertility...This [is] their 'traditional' role though currently half of the hijra(s) engage in prostitution, which seniors disparage. They (figure) in the narrative linking of India with sexual difference. As the 'third sex' of India they have captured the Western imagination as an ideal case in the transnational system of 'alternative' gender. The hijra (Thai 'kathoey', Omani 'xanith') Rosalind Morris notes, becomes 'an interstitial gender occupying the liminal space between male and female', or 'a drag queen who is a hero(ine) in a global sexual resistance' (1994, 16).

~ Reddy 2005

There are many kinds of eunuchs. Most are castrated at a Gujarat temple of goddess aka Bahuchare Mata. Some in Maharashtra and Karnataka are male *devadasas* (called *jogtin* also). They grow dreadlocks, *devadasi* style or in the style of *sadhus* (mendicants) who have renounced the world. In Maharashtra at Khandoba's temple (see Kolatkar 1976) they are called *vyaghyas* and dedicated to the temple. These hermaphrodites, if they happen to be the only child of wealthy parents, are given away in childhood itself along with their property, so that the property is in safe hands after the parents' deaths. Usually illiterate rural folk follow this practice. In Tamil Nadu, a yearly festival is arranged in the name of the god Aaravaan (Arjuna). The cross-dressed men (not necessarily hermaphrodites; some are householders dressed up for a day in their wives' sarees) become the god's brides for a day and at the day's end, when the god dies, they become his widows and become men again (see Appendix). Hijras are mimic women. Their mannerisms slutty, some adopt babies to mimic motherhood. They are associated with, conversely, fertility, Venus and Friday, the sixth day of the week when they go begging, dancing and clapping in the streets. Hence they are called 'sixers' or '*chakkas*'.

They feature in the comic gags of Hindi films. But these days they negotiate the liminal space between genders in both popular and serious cinema. *Sadak* (1991) is a potboiler from the Mahesh Bhatt camp. It shows a typical *chakka* brothel-keeper, 'Maharani', who is villainy personified. The hero (Sanjay Dutt) loses his girlfriend (Pooja Bhatt), only to find her in Maharani's brothel. Maharani plays all kinds of tricks on the poor boy and girl before s/he admits defeat and the couple is reunited, Bollywood style, at the film's end. Maharani is a cross-dressing, campy, foul-mouthed villain; a caricature eunuch.

But in Mani Ratnam's *Bombay* (1995), the twin boys of mixed Hindi–Moslem parentage lost in the city during communal riots are rescued by a eunuch who is neither man nor woman, neither Hindu nor Moslem, since he is abused by both communities, in a city polarised by religion. This breaks the stereotype of hijras as baby stealers and baby murderers. Hindus do allow eunuchs to bless their weddings and subsequent births in the family while eunuchs are rejected by the Moslems even at Hajj. Till recently eunuchs couldn't hold passports, bank documents or even railway travel passes.

In another movie from the Mahesh Bhatt camp, *Tamanna* ('desire', 1997) a eunuch is shown as a myriad-shaded, living human being. The 'desire'of the title is a desire to love, to nurture and to grow. The eunuch in *Tamanna* feels all these feelings. And 'her' dream is answered when s/he finds a foundling. S/he names the girl 'Tamanna', meaning desire fulfilled. (Pooja Bhatt plays the role and has said she knew such a kindly 'uncle' in her childhood without realising then 'his' sexual identity, so dignified was this person.) In the film, too, the girl grows up not knowing that her nurturer is not a true man nor her true parent. But when she learns this she accepts him because he has fulfilled an orphan's desire for a normal girlhood. 'Abnormal' people can give normal people love. Love has no gender or it is myriad-sexed.

While *Sadak* gives us a stereotypical '*chakka*', *Tammana*'s eunuch breaks the stereotype by not cross-dressing but wearing a manly *lungi* (sarong). He lives with a brother rather than with a 'husband' (*panti*). The eunuch (Arif Zakaria) in Kalpana Lajmi's *Darmiyaan* ('In Between', 1997) is humanised before our eyes by suffering from his 1940s film star mother's (Kiron Kher's) social rejection due to the stigma of her having birthed him, a eunuch; by his being raped mutely by the mother's film producer (a factual detail from real life in the film; in fact, the same producer's Juhu bungalow is used in the film as a setting for the rape); and by his finally giving up a boy-foundling he rescues from certain castration at the hands of hijras to his mother's moviedom rival Chitra (Tabu) and her boyfriend (Shahbaz Khan) to be reared in relatively 'normal' circumstances. Hence all the characters, normal and abnormal, friendly or feuding, accepting or rejecting, are finally reconciled at the film's end in great magnanimity as in a Shakespeare comedy.

Cross-dressing in Indian Films

Cross-dressing in Indian films (from Bombay) constitutes both men dressing as women and women dressing as men. The ultimate 'manly' woman was Nadia, the Hunter Queen ('hunter' being a local name for a whip). I will limit myself to Amitabh Bachchan dressing as a woman to sing 'Mere angane mein' as an example of cross-dressed film stars.

I personally feel the need for men to dress as women goes back to the anxiety of maleness, to the time the sons snatched the power from the mothers' matriarchy to establish a patriarchy. It is son bowing to Mother (the goddess as well as the biological mother). In the West its first manifestation is Euripides, *Bacchae* (Dodds 1977), the gay dramatist's last, unperformed play. Bacchus the god comes down to earth and sows confusion; Penthius the king cross-dresses as a woman in one moving scene to woo his lady love away from Dionysus who is torn to pieces by the frenzy-driven female mobs of Bacchus the God. The lesson, of course, is to the patriarchy: Bow to the woman within; you do not do so at your own peril.

Shakespeare's men who become women — who become men and women who become men — who become women not only point to the above cosmic and philosophic truth on gender but also play with the convention of the Elizabethan boy actor. Women were not allowed on-stage for moral reasons and boys were used instead of actresses. Hindi film directors of the 1950s and 1960s all read Shakespeare in colonial India's schools. But in Indian theatre too is a deeper tradition of men dressed as women on stage. The great Marathi female impersonator Bal Gandharva is a case in point. Jatra village theatre too had female impersonators.

Shakespeare also uses the stage convention of cross-dressing to image concretely on-stage philosophic love dimensions in his comedies. In *As You Like It* (XXXX) Rosalind cross-dresses to embody on-stage the gender confusion of the hero, Orlando. In *Twelfth Night* (XXXX) the twin brother–sister couples are separated and the girl dresses as a boy for safety. Here, the incestuous love motif is represented by the fact that brother and sister have not only exchanged bodies but Viola and Sebastian have also exchanged souls.

There is no Shakespearean echo in the Hindi film plugged to the lowest common denominator in the audience. Nadia's is an interesting case. She was an Australian Jew who became Indian on marrying the Parsi Wadia of Wadia Movietone who cast her as a woman playing a man in a hundred films. (She lived and worked till a ripe old age and was no stripling when she entered films.) Considering that she was a heart-throb of boys in colonial India, something political was coded into the message beamed at a colonised male audience by a 'foreign lady' dressed as a man performing incredible derring-do. The message cut both ways: 'You men are less than women' and/or 'if a woman can do it on-screen', so can you lesser men rouse yourself to do it in real life, the 'it' here being the overthrow of the British in India. Towards the end of her life Nadia (not quite white; she was a Jew) was whitewashed by postcolonial film critics (some of them members of her husband's family like the great-nephew Riyad Vinci Wadia) as a harbinger of freedom.

Amitabh Bachchan was indeed preceded in the cross-dressing routine by I. S. Johar. Khushwant Singh tells us in his gossipy memoir on film stars of the 1950s that Johar was gay. God forbid if such aspersions are cast on Bachchan. He is more male than male; the 1970s macho man. He is cast opposite Rekha, more female than female; the impossibly feminine (read coquettish) woman of the 1970s Hindi film. Male and female are constructions in, for and by the movies. So let's relax the pressure a little on all those street thug clones of Bachchan and all those Gujarati housewives wanting to be Rekha. Let Bachchan be a woman; then the street urchins can be as girlish as they want, the housewives as virago-ish as they wish. It is the topsy-turvydom of comedy. But cross-dressed Bachchan sings a peculiarly misogynistic song in *Laawaris* (Mehra 1981) with refrains like 'Jiski bibi moti' (he who has a fat wife) or 'Jiski bibi kali' (he who has a black wife), etc. All the men with black, fat wives can relax and laugh because Bachchan himself has now become their wife before their very eyes.

'Fire': Next Time

There are two 'Fires': Deepa Mehta's film and the reception it got in Hindu India. This is the burden of Ratna Kapur's argument in her essay 'Too Hot to Handle: The Cultural Politics of *Fire*' (2003). Hence also the title to my essay here.

Deepa Mehta is a second generation Canadian Indian of Punjabi descent who looks at the Indian family 'as she remembers it' across time and space of generations that went over the 'Kala Pani'. She says it is not a lesbian film; it is about the hypocrisy of the joint Hindu family.

But two sisters-in-law, Radha and Sita, do turn lesbian in the film because their husbands neglect them. One husband is dedicated to business, the other to spirit. Our souls like the divine Radha's are indeed wedded to God (Krishna and Rama, here) but also to this world. Hence Radha, wedded to another man, who loves Krishna in the myth, is actually an adultress and Sita, who remained 'chaste' (lesbian sisters-in-law do 'it' 'within-the-family' and do not cross the 'Lakshman-rekha' of the threshold of the wedded home.) There is Beeji, the invalid grandma and a man-servant who only watches T V and masturbates. 'Love', then, is the ray of hope in a devastated landscape. The family goes on a picnic to Lodhi Gardens and there one sister-in-law begins to massage the other's feet. 'Massage' is a code word for 'sex' even in modern India as it indeed is in the *Kama Sutra*.

The film I saw was dark and grainy. It was a film made with a hand-held camera in 16 mm. and then blown up to 35 mm. for the theatres. There were lots of scenes between the two women, played by Shabana Azmi and Nandita Das, in a bed under a mosquito net. Now, adolescent incest indeed does occur during the afternoon siesta under the *macchardani*, the gauzy veil of the mosquito net which can be easily lowered to hide all intimacy. Intimacy is the only crime in a devastated landscape because it is devastation that has to triumph, what the bourgeois call 'keeping up appearances'.

So in the dark atmosphere the only light is of the fire that is lit to test Sita's chastity via a fire test, The so-called *agni-pariksha*, the test of all tests. Sita, of course, comes out unscathed from the fire because for a sister to love a sister is no crime. 'Love thy family' but also 'Do not commit incest'. This is the double bind that children try to overcome as adults by the queer twists and turns of their fates and sex-lives.

Now, do people turn gay because their heterosexual spouses ignore them? No. Homosexuality is an innate condition. In her essay, 'Same Sex Love in India', Ruth Vanita does talk of 'opportunity', 'proximity', etc. leading to same-sex love episodes. But this then is 'situational' or 'occasional' homosexuality in, say, boarding schools for girls, aboard ship or man-of-war for sailors. It is not a lifelong condition. Lacan, who rejected male homosexuality, accepted lesbianism as the double sexual function of the female sexual organs: Male-like orgasms from the penis-like clitoris and vaginal orgasms from the contracting vaginal walls. Indeed, female clitoral orgasms are infinite when compared to the once-in-three-hours male orgasm. Hence females are superior. Hence all this male brouhaha (see Bowie 1991).

Juliet Mitchell (1974) explains that the female child breastfed by a female mother has to shift its love object from the mother's breast to the father's penis. Failure to do so results in lesbianism. Hélène Cixous says, like the American feminists, that 'every woman of woman-born is a born lesbian' (1975).

The poet-feminist Adrienne Rich explains that little girls are given no option but to grow up, get married and become mothers. Could they not be given the option that they could alternately lose themselves to other women? She gives examples from literature, most notably Emily Dickinson, who loved her sister-in-law Susan. The only time Susan ever touched Emily's body was when she bathed her and prepared Emily's body for her funeral. Devastating!

As in America, so in Canada. Canada is no stranger to queer cinema. You can say Canada invented the genre. Norman McLaren, the grand-daddy of them all, was acknowledged as the 'Queen of Canada' shortly before his death. All his life, he made animated films on homosexual turning to homophobia in a homophobic society. (He also famously invented animation and sold it to Disney Studios in 1952 for $50,000!) The National Film Board subsidised films to build a national film culture. The film world, being what it is, had gay people hiding gay themes in their films and their own gay identities for years in order to make what we call today 'queer cinema'. Deepa Mehta is merely the last of a long line. As in India today, so too once in Canada there was repression of gay films.

Now what is the deeper implication of the cultural fire around *Fire*? Men sent out their wives, sisters, mothers, daughters to set fire to Indian theatres showing *Fire*. In other words, men used women as agents of their own (sexual) repression, i.e., if we take homosexuality to be sexual freedom. Those householders in the *grihasth* ashram wanted their families to remain stable. But 'stable' surely does not mean 'static'. It is a static view of Hindu society which says that every Indian wife is Sita, every man Rama. That there were no Greek, Moslem or British invasions of our country means our society is culturally 'pure' and polluting 'foreign' influences have to be rooted out. To see pollution as 'foreign' is to deny that every woman could harbour libidinal desires for both sexes.

The sexual logic of *Fire* was flowed. The technique of the film was flawed. But the *Hindutva* brigade lent the movie credence beyond all its powers. *Earth* (Mehta 1998) was a surer attempt. About the disaster of *Water* (Mehta 2005) we shall not speak.

Ruth Vanita also says that because of its moorings in the Indian freedom struggle, the Indian press is sympathetic to alternate movements like the gay and lesbian movement currently sprouting up all over India. Sangama, a lesbian support group, has chapters in the smallest of out-of-the-way towns in India. The press surely also fed this *Fire*!

Gay Documentary Films

Two Gay Films-

Bath and *The Dance of the Night Fairies*

One lesbian, another gay. Shohini Ghosh's good film, *The Dance of the Night Fairies* ([2008] about prostitutes) and *Bath*, a bad (male) gay film. *Bath* indulges in guilt: bourgeois guilt at homosexuality and in paying the 'straight' gigolo to perform gay acts for a fee. But the film-maker says: I'm a prostitute. I've sold my mind. (This is outside the film). She could never prostitute herself. She, like Meenakshi, is a Bhadralok leftist. She says 'My sister has all the markers of a prostitute: lipstick etc.' 'When I was mak-ing the film every woman appeared to me to be a prostitute', etc. She, by contrast, of course played gallant street cricket with the boys. This is intellectual dishonesty; le trahison des clercs (Sartre).

Shani Mootoo, also a film-maker, laughs today that she wanted to be a wooer of women in her adolescence in imitation of Rishi Kapoor's films. Mercifully, she has moved on. When will our leftist feminist women critics, gay and straight, drop their hypocrisy and get a life?

Or does the Indian lesbian think it's alright to laugh at sissy men because they go down the sexual pecking order while cricket-loving lesbians like themselves are admirable in imitating a higher being called the Bhadralok Kolkatta male leftist (pseudo) intellectual?

The Dance of the Night Fairies is about Sonagachi's prostitutes as seen by the lens of the Calcuttan lesbian film-maker Shohini Ghosh who familiarises us with the terrain, thereby breaking down gender stereotypes. She shows us the streets where she played cricket with the boys as a girl. She also shows us the cinema hall with posters of male matinee idols she imitated as a gay girl growing up in Calcutta.

Genteel poverty is replaced by the slum where prostitution festers in crumbling Calcutta. Some girls themselves are from poor Brahmin homes, one abandoned by a husband who did not feed her, only to be confronted by a schoolteacher father who weeps helplessly. This is the eye of the 'liberated' lesbians looking at the literally caged woman.

But all is not lost. Revolution in Calcutta will come even to the brothels. A hefty madam will come to the rescue of helpless girls whose clients refuse to use condoms. She can get physical in all senses of the term. Her son will go to college. There is hope.

Homosexuals go round the *basti* playing 'The Dance of the Night Fairies'. They distribute condoms. The republic will be saved from the 'gay plague'.

Shohini Ghosh, at a film seminar at the University of Pune, said, 'My sister wore lipstick. I always associated lipstick with prostitutes.' This casual remark meant to liberate women from the false standards of beauty imposed by the cosmetics industry was also meant to strike at gender stereotypes. Prostitution of women by men is a gender stereotyping of women's sexuality by men. The gay way, Shohini Ghosh probably meant to say, was a third way out of the two extremes of hypermasculinity and hyperfemininity.

The film is about legalising female prostitution and does not really qualify as gay cinema. But we are interested in it as its director is an outspoken, up-front lesbian.

Moreover, she uses an anti-AIDS campaign as grist for her film, showing gays and eunuchs being used to spread the message in the film. Hilariously, air-filled condoms also double as festive balloons.

It is to be noted that gays and eunuchs do this for a living. There is no other living for them to be earned. To say that such social use eradicates two millennia of shame and humiliation is just a way of salvaging our bourgeois, guilty consciences.

Manjuben Truck Driver (2002)

The Parsi woman film director Sherna Dastur follows Manjuben on a trucking expedition from Gujarat to Delhi. Manju wears a loose shirt, 'Moslem' black-strapped, shiny leather, slightly heeled *chappals*. In the first scenes she worships Ardhanarishwar ('Aprajeva' — 'he's like us', she says) and in the film is on backslapping terms with the men. She rakes in the 'moolah' ('I once had 8 trucks: if I'd kept them all I'd have gone bald from worry by now,' she says). Her aim in life is 'to make money and to travel' but at the end she says: 'No one can tell me anything'. Freedom, in a word. In the hour-long documentary's middle section, we are shown children of the wayside eatery calling her 'big daddy'; she's kind to the kids' mother. More importantly, she has a married woman of her own age who is her girlfriend. The camera focuses on the hands of the two women as they talk sitting on a bed. The truck driver wears a thick Sikh gold bracelet (*kada*); the married lady her traditional gold bangles. So the dress codes herald different 'identities' taken on by the two women socially. But they are not what they seem: Manju is a lesbian dying for love, not a tough lady-driver (she has to sandwich her trysts between business commitments) and the married girlfriend is a closet lesbian hiding behind her married woman's *pallu*. We learn at the end that Manju was married (to our horror) at an innocent 16 years of age and she had the good sense to ask for a divorce. It is the film's penultimate scene: there is a voice-over and the protagonist has flies bothering her during sleep on a charpoy at a way side pit-stop. It was all a bad dream. And it has passed. Our '*behns*' today are pilots, '*bade bade*' doctors and engineers; 'who am I?' Manju modestly asks.

Manju goes to a barber and has a 'full shave' like any man. The barber laughingly obliges her and pockets the tip. All this on camera. Identity as role-playing. Quiet poignance. Vulnerability masquerading as toughness. An embattled identity finding a way out. Quite moving.

In-between are scenes of the male lorry drivers and their cleaners (read 'fags') at the rest stops, bathing in public and making pre-dawn chapatis like any real life Hindu housewife. Role reversal. The zoom lens catches them slinking out of their underwear from behind teeth-held towels and the horror in their eyes when they realise the voyeur is a Parsi lady! Role reversal again.

Is sexuality only role-playing? And what about politics? Manju thinks it chic to wear a Taliban suit and dance the Gujarati Garba at Navratri with the men. Does she realise the Taliban would make mincemeat out of her? Or is it her way out of the Gujarati 'Grihani' trap by donning the face of her enemy? 'Enemy, my enemy I call you friend'. I become you. (Woman becomes man.) I am you. I am your other face. To go through the mirror and to come out on its other side. This is frightening to some. To the little Alices and Alexes in Wonderland it's pure fun. Leela. Pure play.

It is obvious that gays who are pioneers in India lack role models. Manjuben loves and worships 'our Shiva'; his role as Ardhanarishwar tickles her. She gets a man's haircut at a men's haircutting saloon and gets the superflous hair on her face shaved with great glee. The young boy-barbers are tickled, too. On the job, men do her bidding. She cannot repair her truck but she knows what goes into it and the repairmen cannot fool her though they laugh at her. Most importantly, her girlfriend is a middle class married woman like Radha. So like Krishna's, Manjuben's love too is not *sva-kaya* but *par-kaya* and hence all the more poignant. The woman she loves is somebody else's *maal* (stuff). This also shows a gay's aspiration to be accepted. Even Lord Krishna's Radha was married to another man. Manjuben is only following a very ancient example.

From *Mother India* (1957) to *Mother Hoshang* (2007)

Mother India (1957) is Mehboob Khan and Nargis's most famous film. It represents India of the 1950s worldwide (from Egypt to Russia, from France to China, with Greece and Turkey thrown in). It is about our Indian obsession with motherhood. It not only means 'nation' but also pure, asexual passion. It is the love of mother for son.

Geja Poeto: Mother Hoshang (2005), is Kathy Maloney's 26 minute epic with me. A gay Indian poet serving as her muse, turns Nargis's *Mother India* on its head. Here son becomes mother to love other sons without lust. Ezra Pound writes about 'Men wanting to do good/Doing evil.' But at least we did not fail due to lack of ambition.

The *foisson* of India. The Indo-Gangetic plain. The billion strong population. The Birju's as heroes. The Black son and the White. Fertility versus sterility. Birju as a sex icon. Birju, mother-fixated and gay? Nargis complained about Sunil Dutt's 'parasites', that they became Amitabh Bachchan, Manoj Kumar, Vinod Khanna. Mother Hoshang lusts after all of Mother India's sons, black and white.

Usury. The *bania*'s usury. The percentage of interest rising with a Churchillian grandeur', to quote Pound's *Cantos* (Byron 2007) again. Sterility. 'If we don't buy their cotton/We don't have to buy their guns' — Pound quotes M. K. Gandhi. Does this sound like a critique of globalisation?

What can we place against usury? Pound sees usury as buggery, sterility. But when the buggers in the banks are all out to make us beggars, what can a single gay poet do? (Pound finally appreciated Pier Paolo Pasolini.) S/he comes out of big city Bombay, from a narrow Parsi household. Escapes to the big, bad world. America, here I come! S/he is Elpenor, 'a man of no fortune/with a great name to come' in *The Odyssey* (Homer XXXX). S/he has seen Circe, been Circe. S/he has tried and abandoned the Circe role. Pure mother, Nargis, the Lady in White. Men have become *lotophagi*, their heads between their legs. How again to walk upright?

To escape Mother, become the mother! Escape sterility. In Greece they catcalled after me 'Nargis!' (1976). The fertility of the cultural world is celluloid, paper, ink, paint, terracotta. These fragments we have shored against the ruins'. Epics these days are 26 minute long. The world lit by lightning.

The camera follows one gay man for one day: *The Inferno* (Alighieri n. d.) of lust, the purgatorio of the social life (classroom/gay bar), the paradiso of the pure poem. Kathy often forgets her audio equipment at home as she follows Hoshang throughout the day. Words are not necessary in Hell. Hell has its own images, with their own justification. The autowallah (this is Hyderabad — city of minars and seminars), the paanwallah, the doodhwallah, the paperwallah, the shop clerk, or storewallah are all fair game (You can add your own items to this fantasy fair : How about rastawallah, the unsuspecting, gullible passer-by?…)

Why this is Hell
Nor are you out of it

Blind imitation of the West. The flailing of arms and legs of possessed men, dancing. More images from purgatory. The south Indian teacher-*amma* trying to make sense of a Parsi queen: He too is my son! Mother wins *this* time! Boys in the classroom, boys in the Band. Plato as Father and Mother, standing patriarchy on its head. The teacher as the taught. 'Learn us, teacher…learn us,' the Palestinian boys would implore their English teachers in unself-conscious English. Ascent/Descent: the rickety elevator to the top floor of the first high-rise in Andhra Pradesh. The purgatory of gossiping neighbours, all 300 of them, 100 to a building in three blocks. A, B and C. The scandal of university boys jeering beneath my balcony.' And I am quoting Pasolini from 1960s Rome. Do I see a new archetype there? Washing dirty linen too can be a purgation.

Sar pe lal topi Russi
Phir bhi dil hai Hindustani

'Jiya bekaraar hai' from the 1950s Raj–Nargis film in 1990s gay bar in India. Finally arrived 50 years too late. Why blame Hoshang for being a 1950s queen? At least there is some tinsel there; beneath is the grime. Cacophony. Flagellations. The night is lit by strobe lighting and the masochists' lust for defeat. Let this be my physick. Physician cure thyself!

I'm here. It is now.
This is India. Not Rome
or Greece, nor yet N. Y.
It is not globalisation.
This is all pure homespun.
Local boys. ('All art is local' — Vlaminck)
Accept. Accept…

Once I borrowed from the banks at 22 per cent interest to feed a rat. Once a cruel queen sat on Delhi's throne. Then a lame *randwa*. (Nehru made homosexuality punishable from 10 years to life in 1953). Why then blame the *chakka*? These are labels. These are names. These are terms, hardly of endearment. Terms of being, alright.

I write this in Italy. I'm chasing the forméd trace of Pound and Pasolini. Shobha De, eat your heart out! It is the night before the dawning of my 60th birthday. I'm fat, old, bearded and 60. No mustachioed Mona Lisa. No one screams 'Nargis'! after me any longer. What a relief! They call me poet. And a good day to you too, Papa Whitman and Auntie Raj (Kapoor, that is). 'Camp' is a way of being in the world. Can we be sure the manly Nargis wasn't really only a man playing a woman?!

Gay boys now come to study with me from America. They too want to be gay poets. They're tired of the bar scene, the bath scene, of AIDS, safe sex, no-sex celibacy, condoms, dildoes, S&M…you name it! Open the window and let the warm Love in! wrote poor Keats ridden with tuberculosis in Rome. Garden Towers, my address, is sought out not only by gigolos and blackmailers, but also by poets and would-be poets. You can be a poet of biryani-making, of tall tale-telling, blaspheming or plain gossping. You could be male, female or in-between. Young, old or in-between. But for a single moment do hold your breath! Kathy has forgotten the sound equipment again. Her muse has fallen silent. What a relief…

Can't ride a train
Won't write a paper
What can you do?

This is R. Raj Rao's e-mail diatribe sent my way.

I CAN WRITE A POEM.

The poem is my life. This is not narcissism. It is survival. It is 1947. The country is divided into India and Pakistan. This wound will never heal. This is brother against brother. What is better — to make love or to make war? This is Father against Mother. Father Time and Mother Earth. And the newborn son, the newborn nation torn between them.

I slowly read a poem on the bleeding province of Sind. It could be Palestine, Kurdistan, the Basque country, Occitania, Corsica. Take your pick. Each homeless nationality is me. The unhoused homosexual. Un-accommodated man. I'm not talking nostalgia, nor romance, nor elegies.

I'm talking politics. A politics of survival. My book *Yaraana: Gay Stories from India* (1999) saved one gay life. That is, one life other than my own. What have you saved? Memories of old loves? Yesterday's books? A few *paise* in a bank? This is not subjectivism. The poet's 'I' touches others' I. On this page and in the film, the poet is naked as the day he was born. All art being local.

Author. Authority.

Nothing is easy. Mother India kills her son. This son, standing before you, in order to survive becomes Mother India. Two-and-a-half cheers for all the Mother Hoshangs of the present and future.

In *Mother Hoshang*, as in *Mother India*, national tragedy is bisected by personal tragedy. Mother India suffers physical hunger. Mother Hoshang's is a spiritual hunger for love. Out of your sorrows you make your song. Nargis became the tragedy queen of India. Mourning becomes Hoshang. Finally, the Sufi transcends gender.

Love. Love is outside the tribe. Pride, jealousy, possessiveness are the three attributes of Hell.

Kuanon, your fingers are silk and water (Byron 2007). Love, poetry, life flow. Let it go…

Appendices

(a) The Eunuch Festival of Aaravan

Recently, I returned from Koovakam, a village 30 km. from Villipuram, which plays host to the largest annual gather of hijras in India. I spent a night on the roof of the Koothandavar temple and watched as an otherwise dormant village transformed itself in a brilliant display of colour, vitality and spirit. Koovakam has come to mean many things to many people. For hijras, it is the most important event of the calendar year, a time when they are reunited with friends, a place where they are a given a platform from which they can be seen, heard and applauded, where they get to embody all the things they want to be: woman, bride, goddess. In Villipuram, which is where they stay during the five-day lead up to the actual festival, they overtake the town, strolling up and down the main streets in bright clothes, with flowers in their hair and bangles on their wrists, frequenting the various roadside restaurants and bars; confusing, teasing, beguiling onlookers about what is true and what is false, what is man, what is woman, and what is the place in between that defies definition. It is precisely their sexual and gender ambiguity, their ability to move within an apparently boundary-less world, that has made them a fascinating community for me to study, and the reason for accompanying a group of them from their home in Perungalathur with a friend and cameraman to document their journey to Koovakam.

But four days in Villipuram are enough to realise that Koovakam isn't merely about hijras, although they are the star attraction — how can they not be? Koovakam is about the basic right to express oneself — a startling revelation that has developed from a culture struggling with issues of identity and repression. The trend of moving towards an increasingly dichotomous way of viewing the world, of classifying, pigeonholing, pinning down all manner of things, be it problem, opinion or concern, in a bipolar fashion, has created a stultifying atmosphere which gets to be aired out only once in a long while in places like Koovakam. The result is a strange display of exhilarating liberation paired with unsettling sordidness.

What is most visible is the intensity of physical experience against the backdrop of spirituality with the ever-present ghost of sexuality hovering about. People come to Koovakam without any apology. They come because it is a time for them to be what they want to be. This includes not only hijras but a vast array of men — homosexual, bisexual, straight, cross-dressers, married, single, divorced, college boy, autowallah, tea shop owner, businessman — walking up and down the streets along with the hijras, mingling and intermingling in various combinations of the aforementioned — physical, spiritual and sexual. For people not taking part in these interactions, the spectacle forces contemplation.

What is obvious is that there is a need to address issues of sexuality and gender conflict within the framework of our society, especially with the growing menace of AIDS crashing through the horizon. Koovakam is a microcosm of a country caught in contradiction because it shows simultaneously what is right and wrong about our society. The fact that hijras are not only treated with respect, but welcomed by the ordinary townspeople and village folk during their short stay here every year is heartening proof of how the basic Indian philosophy that envisions a universe boundlessly various, including all possibilities of being, proscribing the notion of plurality of selves and allowing opposites to confront each other without resolution, is still alive and kicking. By the same token, hijras as a community are still struggling to regain their place in the world, denied the most basic rights — the right to own a passport, ration card, property, equal opportunities in the areas of education and employment, simply because they to be categorised as either male or female and wish to claim a third gender for themselves. Hijras have always occupied the fringe of the Indian subconscious; they are accepted without question, even if it is with a mixture of fear, ridicule and contempt, because of their inherited centuries of old court history combined with the eternal wellspring of mythology, which constantly affirms and validates their existence. This is quite unlike their western counterpart, the transsexual, who must resolve sexual anomalies one way or the other without the luxury of floating in man–woman limbo. But acceptance does not mean openness; it could simply mean that you don't care one way or the other because a thing has no bearing on your life. It is the same veil through which we view the problems of poverty, war and disease. Unless problems come steamrolling into our own immediate lives, we don't feel the need to address them.

So what does it say about the young, homosexual men who come to Koovakam every year to dress in women's clothes, their parents unaware of their son's double life, plotting weddings with girls who are equally uninformed? What does it say about the hundreds of straight young men who flock to Villipuram because sex is cheap and easily available? This is not an attack on men, but rather an attack on the ruthless nature of sexuality in our society.

It is dangerous thing when sexuality is linked with confusion and dishonesty. The dilemma is not so much what one says to these young men who are questing — whether for their identity, their sexuality, the ambivalent feelings of their gender — but what does one do about the existence of repression in a society which perpetuates a rigid demeanour of prudery, while kicking all disparity and deviation under the rug, refusing to accept it as a part of our existence? Koovakam should be seen for what it is: a possibility in transformation and liberation, of crossing over boundaries and erasing lines. The festival at Koovakam celebrates the life of Aravan, who in the Mahabharata must be sacrificed for the Pandavas to emerge victorious. Aravan is willing, but wants to be married before he is to die. No woman will come forward to marry him because she knows that what lies waiting for her is the doom of widowhood. So Lord Krishna, taking the form of a beautiful woman, comes down to satisfy the desire of coital bliss. For the thousands of hijras who throng Koovakam dressed as brides for Aravan, theirs is a martyr's role; they experience these important stages of womanhood symbolically and sometimes physically. They are brides, wives and widows in a span of two days, and for many of them, this annual pilgrimage to Koovakam is their way of asserting themselves.

The life of the hijra is a dubious chimera of sexual ambiguity, but it is also a life that has embraced this ambiguity and called a spade of spade, so to speak. Hijras should be saluted for taking this stand, for disallowing for pretence, for wearing their hearts on their sleeves and parading around the streets with them. They stand in stark contrast to the unhealthy display of magnified need expressed by the other actors of Koovakam, who have also left their normal lives for a few days, but have come draped in veils and other secret layers in which to get lost. It is to them that Koovakam must teach its transformational lessons to, and to society, which is continually turning its face at the slightest rustle of confrontation.

(b) Transsexual Hosts on TV Talkshows

A transsexual calling herself 'Shobha' is to host a daily question–answer hour on a local Tamil TV channel in Chennai. Her motto is 'Here am I! — So, I have to think!' She is India's answer to the saree-clad 'Begum Nawazish', TV talkshow host in Pakistan who is actually a boy called Ali. Shobha will answer questions usually on sexuality from mostly rural viewers. There is a great dearth of information on sexuality in villages and both homosexuals and transgendered people live very lonely lives there. Shobha hopes to be able to afford a sex reassignment surgery soon. S/he is not the only one of her kind. Shohini Ghosh, film-maker, recently made a film on Laxmi, a transgendered person whom she calls 'the most beautiful woman in India'. S/he says, 'you insult me when you call me a man. I am less than a man and more than a woman.' Witticisms aside, these people are active in India's AIDS eradication programmes among the hijra community. Another such Mumbai personality, calling herself 'Muskan', is similarly occupied. As can be seen, all of them are educated in English-medium schools and come from middle-class homes.

Hypocrisy, however, is still rampant. A TV poll showed 100 per cent of the viewers disapproved of homosexuality in Hyderabad, a city teeming with same-sex lovers. The poll showed 89 per cent disapproval in hi tech Bangalore where actually sexual mores are changing fast. Chandigarh showed a 79 per cent disapproval rate. No Indian will publicly support homosexuality whatever be his private belief.

Rose, a 27-year-old transsexual, says that the talkshow concept is hers. Though trained as a bioengineer in Louisiana, s/he says s/he returned to India to 'change the system.' Transgendered sexual identity does not conform itself to male or female genders but combines both or moves between the two to form a third sex. This is not understood in the media, where transgendered people are butts of cheap jokes. Rose wishes to open a forum to discuss homosexuality and relational issues. Her models are American: TV soap star Rose O'Donnell and

Ellen Degeneres who proclaim their sexualities openly and are opinion makers. Her talkshow is eagerly anticipated. No one knows if it will garner brickbats or bouquets in conservative Chennai. Maybe Rose is banking, like many others, on Brahmin tolerance. But other stars haven't been lucky with their radical pronouncements on the Indian cult of virginity ('If virginity concerns women, let the women decide'). Begum Nawazish of Pakistan shares these views. Though the Begum believes in Allah she says she makes his creations, the men, very happy!

Begum Nawazish Ali

Ali Saleem, aka Begum, has crossed borders, namely gender borders and the one dividing the subcontinent. The Geo TV star will be on Aaj Tak channels' 9x. Eldest of an army colonel's three sons, he loved cross-dressing as a child in his mother's boudoir. He is six feet tall in three inch heels and is campy. Examples: 'What border are you talking about? Saree borders'? (Women imitate his fashions.)

He is in the tradition of the Japanese Noh play's 'Onnagata' (cross-dressed female leads) and of the Kuchipudi dance gurus of Andhra Pradesh who taught high-born girls both dance and deportment. What this shows clearly is that gender is a performance, an act.

Nawazish Ali is a name borrowed from a neighbour, another colonel's wife. He says, 'Ali Saleem was a coffin within which the Begum was buried. When she was born Ali was liberated.' His parents sent him to a psychiatrist at 14 but now they are proud of his success.

What does this success mean? It means that there is a woman in every man and this peepshow keeps the TV ratings going. Since Nawazish interviews Pakistan politicians and figures from society, 'her' own topsy-turvydom might be a comment on the confused state of Pakistan today. She is an 'abnormal' lens focused on so-called 'normal' society which then questions the very notion of 'normality' itself.

It is certainly not her wit that keeps 'her' going. Her camp is old hat. Examples: 'I like being manhandled'; 'I'm not a bisexual, I'm a trysexual; I'll try anything since the age of 13.' She told the Railway Minister on her show, 'I'll like to do a special number in your minister bogey.' He stormed off the show. 'She' helpfully tells us that the minister is unmarried and there are all sorts of rumours about it.

This says something deeper about the moral corruption in Pakistan in particular and in so-called 'Islamic' societies in general. During the Zia regime, a *khosri* calling 'herself' Rekha, after the Bollywood star, used to service a high-end clientele. Boys from lower middle-class homes from Lahore and Karachi used to pose as 'meat-sellers' and prostitute themselves to the Taliban on the Afghan border. 'Purity' is another name for sexual repression which manifests itself in covert homosexuality.

Of course 'Nawazish' santises this sleaze. She imitates the 1960s star Mumtaz. 'She' brings sex kitsch into our living-rooms. 'She' lets closet transvestites breath easy'; 'she' is an inspiration to all the drag queens out there. (Sometimes we wondered if all the fag-hags like Liz Taylor and Liza Minelli are not also an inspiration for drag-queens.) On the subcontinent the tradition goes back at least to the cross-dressing hijra or *chakka*. (If he does not cross-dress he is a *gandu*. So there is a choice!)

What Nawazish does is provoke, protest and promote. Her guest-list is always an incendiary mix: a female model with a mullah. The model is skimpily dressed on the show and the mullah is protesting about women in advertisements. She has also had brave women like Mukhtar Mai, the outspoken rape victim, on her show to shame macho men and honour their victims. She was banned when she allowed the suspended Pakistan Chief Justice's lawyer to speak on her show.

The battle lines are drawn. If you are for her you are democratic, standing for free speech and Mrs Bhutto's party (she does wicked Benazir imitations). If not, then you're pro-dictatorship and possibly, horror of horrors, an 'Islamist'. All this is on the Internet too. She likes Bollywood 'gay icons' like John Abraham too. When young, her heroine was Empress Noor Jehan. Now she is seriously thinking of dating a girl in Goa for Christmas. The dude is no more a lady! Normality catches up with best of us.

Both 'Shobha' and Begum Nawazish are cross-dressing men. They are basically homosexual men wishing they were born women. Nawazish, a bisexual, had an absentee father and was brought up by a single mother and her girlfriend. What do homosexuals want? They want nothing less than an end to patriarchy. They want the father dead. They wish that the father should never return. Here is the reasoned voice of the Marxist Herbert Marcuse (1955):

> Sexual perversions express rebellion against the subjugation of sexuality under the order of procreation, and against the institutions which guarantee this order. Psychoanalysis sees in 'perversion' an opposition to continuing the chain of reproduction and thereby of paternal domination — an attempt to prevent 'the reappearance of the father'. Perversions reject the enslavement of the pleasure principle by the reality principle. Claiming sexual freedom is a world of repression they reject the guilt accompanying sexual repression.… Against a society employing sexuality as a means for a useful end, perversions uphold sexuality as an end in itself. They are a symbol of the destructive identity between freedom and happiness.

What these drag queens want is the removal of unjust patriarchal laws. If Nepal can do it, why can't India?

(c) The Pakistan Poet as Eunuch: Ifti Nasim

A militaristic society punishes the sensitive. Conversely 'Begum Nawazish', gay TV host, gets police patronage, in all senses. Ifti Nasim's essay 'Why am I not like my father?' ('Main mere baap ke jaisa kyun nahin hoon?') explains, via an evidently concocted mythology, that he was a Hindu child lost at the border in Pakistan during the Partition and picked up by a Moslem woman who reared him as a Moslem son. Whatever the 'truth' of the matter it works superbly as myth because it twice alienates Ifti, first as a gay in heterosexist Pakistan and second as a Hindu in a Moslem nation. (Nasim's father in Abbottabad made his money as a popular journalist writing anti-India diatribes, but Ifti was poor because exiled by a stepmother.)

This is not to say that Islam's gays do not live at peace with their own consciences. Saudi Arabia has the death penalty for gays but no gays are routinely hanged. A new American documentary, *Jihad*, uses the word in its meaning as 'a struggle with one's own conscience'. It focuses on Moslem gays in the New World and the old Islamic World. Not every Moslem gay commits suicide any longer. Ifti's life and work are a case in point.

In India, the homophobic Urdu literary establishment defames him as a saree-clad gay. Nasim wore men's street clothes to work with a camp dash of lipstick. I let his work speak for him by giving here his poems.

Her/Man

I am a two-in-one
I use back and front
I change sides
I do not hide
An in and out
Or up and down
Above/below: all reversible for me

Only a man can complete a man
Only a woman can complete a woman
I am Man/Woman
I am complete within myself
O divided ones
Do not try to tear me apart

Heal thyself!

~ Translated from the Urdu by Hoshang Merchant

An Answer to the Female Liberationists

Where were you?
— You who screamed for women's rights
Why were you silent
when I washed dishes :
the eunuch going house to house?
You should have understood
Why did you not speak?

I kept travelling
city to city/alley to alley
dancing and singing:
amusement of the crowds
a man in a saree ...
Where were you?
Why were you silent?
You should have understood
Why did you not speak?

And the man who tormented you
was the man who tormented me
I took on your disguises
Your ruses and your vices
You should have understood
But you kept silent

I kept washing dishes house to house.

(for Kishwar Nahid)

- Translated from the Urdu by Hoshang Merchant

'Nath' of the Gay Prophet

I will press your legs
tired after hunting the beloved
I will kiss your feet
even when you reject my kind of love
I shall wash them with my tears
a male Magdalene
And I shall follow your flag
Even if you deny me
When wounded in battle
I shall enter your tent
and kiss every wound
and body's every pore
and orifices wounding which themselves
are wound-like
And from dung I shall sprout roses
When all have gone home
after golden oratory
I shall stay the winter
burning pages of the *Koran,* if need be
to keep you warm
And since no boys, nor birds

fall out of the sky these days
I shall forage for physical bread
for the physical body
And when it's found
lay it at your feet as trophy
When you've done with the repast
I shall wash your dishes
so that, just so that, you shall say:
This man has done for me more
than any woman, my own mother
included.

(after Ifti Nasim)

~ Translated from the Urdu by Hoshang Merchant

The first poem depicts the male/female syzygy in the gay body and soul. The second poem is a slap on the face of the feminist Kishwar Nahid (a good poet herself) and the last is an impassioned plea to homoeroticise the faith for gay believers. This poem remains unpublished. Pakistan could erupt in flames. All Ifti is doing here is making a boyfriend into a god, and making God into a friend: very Sufistic. It is not blasphemy. At worst, it is merely sentimental; at best it is highly Platonic.

In America Ifti had a hard life as a male prostitute, a go-go dancer (patronised by a Cuban Mafioso) and a Chicago used car salesman. He has abandoned the Urdu ghazal, a nod to the beauty of the Lucknow *tawaifs* kept alive by gay poets, and chosen to write in Black slang. The once beautiful poet stands twice castrated: once wrenched from his masculinity, now severed from his lovely mother tongue because bereft of his beloved motherland. What Ifti was doing in his ghazals was difficult and important; difficult because you can't flog a dead form and important because he homosexualised the heterosexual Urdu ghazal form.

(d) Gender-fuck in Namdeo Dhasal's 'Gandu Bagicha'

'Gandu Bagicha' created a stir when Namdeo Dhasal first recited it in the 1980s at a Bharat Bhavan (Bhopal) Poets' Meet. He was up to something. But what exactly? Dhasal, reared in Golpitha (aka as 'Pila Haus' after the English 'Playhouse'), Mumbai's red-light district, uses the diction of his birthplace and views Indian Society from the bottom-up (so to speak) instead of from the top-down, which is what most middle-class poets do.

Gandu in working class Marathi literally means a catamite. In *chakka* language it means a *koti* or a eunuch (castrato) who does not cross-dress. 'Gandu Baghicha' could mean a park or playground where gays gather. In ordinary parlance, anything substandard is called *gandu* as in 'the municipal school system in Mumbai is totally gandu'. 'All balls', as the Indian schoolboys of my generation would say. To translate it as 'gay' is to narrow its connotation.

Dhasal, who is a product of this 'inferior' schooling (as opposed to private English education, called 'convent' in Indian English), bursts upon the Marathi world with this poem. The Brahmin critics do not know what to do with him. So they appropriate him by making the right noises and giving him a few awards. He goes to the extent of calling the Indian nation *gandu*. His politics drive him to join the Dalit Panthers, and now the Congress. It is a political suicide of sorts. Anyway, he is dying of Amitabh Bachchan's disease, Myasthenia Gravis. He is 70 years old and does not have Bachchan's money for a cure. He has just been celebrated with a deluxe edition from Navayana Press, a minorities' press. He's done his work. And a castrated nation has paid him homage, just as he probably expected.

These are literalisations of metaphors: A wimp is called a eunuch, a *chakka*. Congress Party members who could not right the nation for 60 years are called *chakka*s. All politicians who hold office for personal profit instead of social service are called *chakka*s. So, hermaphrodites are fielded as candidates and they win elections with the help of local goons, probably their once or future paramours. Shabnam Mousi of Bhopal is an example of a eunuch councilor; he is a metaphor literalised!

This is not to diminish Dhasal's work. He got the tenor of a nation, well ahead of others, in the 1980s itself. The lame get shoes in his free India; Henrik Ibsen's 'Doll' becomes Sita in free India, the prostitute's saree is a rag stretched against the sky, the *gandu*s fuck each other to the strains of the national anthem 'Jana gana mana...'. Who is exempt from being screwed? The metaphor for exploitation is expressly sexual for this Dalit boy from Golpitha.

The recurring refrain is 'Fry my heart on onions!' The poet as martyr. The inspiration is probably Marcel Carne's *Les Eenfants du Paradis* (1945), and its parody, Guru Dutt's *Pyasaa* (1957) for the motif of the poet as martyr, specifically, the poet of the sewers and the whorehouse, that is.

But all is not bleak. The bird of paradise spreads its wings in this public, gay garden. Is it a peacock, India's national emblem? Is it a Hawaiian flycatcher, the white bird with a crest high in the air and its plumes hanging down to earth, an ornithological metaphor for a rainbow joining heaven and earth, aspiration and reality, and in the Lawrentian sense man and woman, because a eunuch is literally both the sexes fused into one? Most purely it is the bird of poetry that presides over the disillusion and illusions of the poet in this microcosmic public garden which is also his private Hell.

Knowledge in a Dhasal poem is always hard-won. The men in the whorehouses lose their 'Galileo's pendulums' and go home castrated from a place where they had come to test their manhood on mere downtrodden women, 'the cheapest women in the world', at one dollar a throw. Everyone gets to go 'home' except the poet. Home is a name for a compromise. The poet is one who never compromises. Hence a poet is always a child, always alone, always able to exult in all kinds of language games.

Dilip Chitre's Translation of 'Gandu Bagicha'

Dilip Chitre, a noted bilingual Pune poet in both English and Marathi, has done commendable service in bringing out the English translations of Namdeo Dhasal's Dalit Marathi poems (2007).

Having said this, the translation of the poem 'Gandu Bagicha' leaves much to be desired. For starters, Chitre begins translating the poem from the middle, not from its beginning. Why? My guess is because the first part deals with homosexuals, a breed Chitre, a married heterosexual father of one son, cannot stomach. It is not then an exaggeration to say that gays should translate gays and not straights; Dalits should translate Dalits and not the bourgeois. The Brahmins co-opted Dhasal when they could do nothing else. This is an old Brahmin trick: not to lose out on any new trend, even trends which portray them as villains. Can the Dalit speak?

The title 'Gandu Baghicha' could also be translated as 'Hermaphrodite Garden'. Now we know from high school botany that trees and flowers can be hermaphroditic but I'm sure we are not referring to flora in this title. Chitre flinches from using the world 'homosexual'. It would not serve to say we do not know English, because he also writes in that language. Chitre uses 'Arsafuckers' Park'. I have never heard gay gardens referred to so archly, ever.

At the poem's end there are unflattering references from a Dalit's viewpoint about the Indian nation and the Congress Party (then, as now, in power). All this is left untranslated. Should timid translators take on the task of bringing bold, radical new poets before the public?

Four letter words (including the 'F' word) end the poem. The reference is to homosexuals fucking each other to the tune of the national anthem 'Jana gana mana...'. Perhaps Chitre blushed to translate these too. 'Eunuch' is another English word the translator dislikes. How to translate a poem about them?

Chitre's translation of Marathi Bhakti poet Tukaram is legendary. I cut my poetic teeth on them as did a host of other young poets. Why then this let down of gays? Bourgeois propriety? Personal prejudice, perhaps.

I have met Chitre and he treats us younger poets with the avuncular concern befitting an elder poet like himself. But he slips now and then. Surely it is not 'I am a sore *in* the private part of language' but *'on* the private part'. The larger debate is: Should Indian poems translated into English read like Indian poems or English poems?

(e) Jameela Nishat: Muse as Poet

The state of close embrace is a symbol of Moksha, final release or reunion of the two Principles, the Essence (Purusha) and Nature (Prakriti)... (and the) symbol of Purusha and Prakriti as Moksha is Mithuna, 'the state of being a couple.' Mithuna, as symbol of Moksha, ultimate release, means a union like that of the Fire and and its burning power which is inseparable from the beginning.'

— Kramrisch 2002

Woman comes to us in symbolist poetry as sea, cloud, fog or water. Jameela Nishat's poetry is full of such dream images. Jameela, the person, comes to me as food, home, conversation, poetry, sisterly concern, laughter, the imagination. Hence, I call her my sister-spirit and my twin-in-writing.

Hélène Cixous, the French feminist critic, says women writers write not out of phallic compulsions but out of a sense of lack. So do homosexuals. She lists Collette, Marguerite Duras and the gay writer Jean Genet as the only three feminine voices in France. All the other women write as men. Among India's feminine writers I would list Kamala Das, Nabaneeta Dev Sen, Amrita Pritam, Jameela Nishat and myself. All the others, irrespective of their gender or lack of it, write as men.

Cixous also says that all women of woman-born are necessarily lesbian. Jameela threw off patriarchy and her father's name, that of the painter Saeed Bin Mohammed, and took on the name of her first love, Nishat, a motherly shape I met later in her life.

Jameela, a teacher, is woman-centred, concerned with children. She talks of listening to Maqdoom, M. F. Husain, Alam Khundmeiri, Shaaz Tamkanait, Mughni Tabassum, Suleiman Arib (a veritable Hyderabad who's who) from behind a curtained zenana door, talking to her celebrity father. She can identify loneliness in others immediately. She can also identify with the incestuous current running through the lives of other artist-daughters of artist-fathers, such as Anais Nin, whom I introduced to Jameela.

Main kabr mein kood padi.
Mere ungliyon mein /khoon ka rang ghulne laga.
(I leap int your grave
There my finger mix your blood as paint)

This is my translation of Jameela's celebration in death of her love for her father. She still dreams of him, of his paintings, now priceless, which she has kept before the public eye not only out of daughterly piety but out of a sense of herself as an artist that springs from the image and imagery of the artist-father.

Jameela is a Piscean, so is Nin, as is the ascendant in my astrological chart. Pisces is the sign of the poet, of the poet's late arrival also of imprisonment, infamy. Christ was a Piscean (and not Capricorn, as forcibly made to be by a Pope Gregory to make Christmas in his calendar coincide with the pagan December Saturnalia). What does that mean for poetry? It means the two fish swimming up and down, eternally together and eternaly opposed. Jameela, the free soul, descends from her mother's side from a mullah of the Deoband seminary. Her moon is in Scorpio (my sun sign). Scorpio, the ninth house, is the house of sex, death and regeneration.

When Genet goes to retrace the footsteps of his Palestinian lover, 14 years after the fact of love in his swan song, *Prisoner of Love* (1986), he does not say, on seeing locations of past love, 'I think or 'I see'; he says, 'I feel'. Jameela's locations of love come to us as feeling made flesh, made poem. It is the musical phrase (say Bismillah Khan's *shehnai*) that evokes an entire night of love in a strange location, say, a night terrace or a room in a boarding house.

The daylight, if not the police, breaks in and Jameela bursts into a poem like lesser mortals burst into a sweat from the pores of their skin, or, say, as Ramakrishna burst into (menstrual) blood cycles bodily during the miracle of his *Radhabhava*.

Lest you dread to meet this metaphysical monster, Muse-as-poet, let me assure you. I met her walking down a street with a young son (also a Scorpion) and she instantly recognised me as a twin and her little boy, justifiedly, took an instant dislike to me. What I mean to say is that interestingly, unlike myself, Jameela has also the tact, finesse and diplomacy to balance a domestic life with her public life as a poet.

Her husband, a communist and an apostate Moslem, whose name Jameela has abjured like her own father's name, is in the slightly ridiculous position of abnegating himself in order to encourage her poetry. If she should go to a sooth-sayer, the first thing the Teresian clairvoyant says is: '*Aap ke miyan bahut acche hain*' (You have a good man for a husband). He is known to have encouraged a rural boy into theatre because he wanted to see the birth of the proletarian artist (of his Marxist textbooks). Jameela's politics is her art; Jameela's religion is her art; Jameela's true society is provided by her art — 'the soul selects its own society,' as Emily Dickinson well knew.

I write of the struggle of the woman as artist and the artist as woman while detailing the symbiosis between Jameela's poem and my own. For nothing is born comfortably full-blown like Minerva out of Zeus' brow. Each day is wrested from the dark as that now much ridiculed Victorian of our childhood, Alfred Lord Tennyson, taught us. It is not for nothing that Jameela translates my English poems into Urdu and that I translate her Urdu poems into English.

And no, she does not write in Dakhni as a recent anthology of women's writing erroneously states. She writes as she speaks, she writes as she feels, she writes as she dreams. Her vocabulary is the vocabulary of the household, of the Indian woman, whether Moslem or Hindu, her imagery is that of blood, birth, broken pitcher, desert, caravan, a search for water, a movement away from sterile poetry into the dirt and detritus of our shattered lives, broken loves and unfinished dreams. Her Eden is the paradise of first utterance, of languages, of saying as a woman — 'I am'. She births her poems out of semen and blood, as ordinary women birth children. And she does not write out of a make-believe womb as I do. She's for real.

No wonder she scares a few people. But her Scorpion-like diplomacy sees her safely through life. I cannot quarrel with Jameela. She will 'not' quarrel with me;

she will only love me as a sister and a younger poet. Popular talk has us making babies in bed. The fact is we have entered each others poems we babble each other's sentences, we have submerged ourselves in each others' dreams.

My nature is wealth
Man, reason, deeds,
Oath of salvation
Hope for being 'narman'
The lava in my veins
The flesh around my bones
Politics in my hand
The strength in my being
Relationship swings in a balance
A chemistry is in my breath.
The sun drinks darkness
I sometimes become homosexual
You who are Hindus and Muslims
Sikhs and Christians
You put masks on your faces
I drown in a sea of faces
Existence, meditation.

– Translated from the Urdu by Hoshang Merchant

Beyond the Female Eunuch:
Three Urdu Lesbian Lyrics by Jameela Nishat

Jameela Nishat is by now a famous Urdu feminist poet of the Deccan. She is not a lesbian. She has, however, written three lyrics to women (and has probably had as many love experiences with women). She is a daughter of the well-known Deccan modern painter Saeed bin Mohammed, whom Nehru persuaded to stay on in India after Partition and whom he appointed as the first principal of the Fine Arts College of Hyderabad. Since childhood, Jameela does not use her patronymic nor did she take on her husband's name as her last name. Instead she took her first girlfriend's name as her pen name (*takhallus* in Urdu).

On being introduced to the first unexpurgated Henry and June: From "A Journal of Love": the Diary of Anais Nin (1931–32) Jameela was inspired by the June Miller/Anais Nin love affair and wrote her poem 'Henry and June'. She is dancing within Nin's *Diary* when the poem opens. Then she becomes June: 'June ki choot par ubharti huyi mardangi'. ('A maleness grows on June's cunt). This taboo word is used for the first time by a Urdu woman poet in Jameela's poem. In the third and final stanza of the poem the Jameela persona has become Anais: 'Henry ki safedi bait-ul-khala mein ghoul gayi' ('Henry's sperm was lost in the toilet'). A woman treads the tightrope of bisexuality in India, trying to find her essential freedom.

Anais Nin's *Henry and June*

Henry's white blood
slipped Anais' diary-pages
and dripped into my eyes

June's cunt
with its little penis
opened the doors of the mind
to reveal a perfect androgyne

Henry and June
dancing
leaves of the *Diary*

I drink leaves
and words turn music
in the bloodstream

My womb hurts
In the toilet drips
The pure blood of words

The whiteness of words
becoming loss
in the dark drains…

~ Translated from the Urdu by Hoshang Merchant

The second gay poem is addressed to an otherwise engaged lesbian. Jameela does not give titles to her poems; she finds them constricting. This poem is included in Jameela's bilingual book *Lava*: 'tere kamre ki khidki mein kal raat ko ulloo jo aaya tha/shayad who meri rooh ka halka sa saaya tha' ('The owl last-night in your window-tree/was perhaps the nightshade of the soul of me'). It is difficult for a married woman to commit herself to a committed lesbian. But God sees all, knows all ('Mere Allah ne bhi sar ko pallu mein dhak liya hai' that is, God Himself is shy and averts His eyes like an Indian woman covering the head with her saree-end'). To break hearts is easy/To join hearts hard.' So the ominous owl remains as an ending refrain in the lover's tree and our lady poet goes home to her husband and sons.

Meri sanson se lab-a-lab tha samaad ka tere pyala
Magar wo lolki khulna lagi thi mere honthon mein

This third poem is a couplet recently written to a girl pupil, Asma. The two line poem describes a woman trying to undo the earring clasp of a young girl with her lips. The reference to cunnilingus is unmistakable in the clever pun on 'lips'. The cup of the lover and beloved overflows at the effort.

Jameela has gained notoriety with her poem named 'Burkha'. Girls in burkas (veils) were not allowed to go to the cinema by the moral police. 'Hey girl! Burkha not allowed', a girl in a veil was greeted by the squad 'wagging their rods' (as an unchaste translation has it; there are chaste translations too). But the girl throws off the veiled oppression for she 'completed degree', 'and also (done) computers.! This is a far cry from Ismat Chughtai's coyness.

For Jameela, to live is to love. She deals with bride burning cases in the old city of Hyderabad. She writes about it too and is admonished by the mullahs for it. It seems, to hate is very easy; to love, difficult. As St Theresa once wrote, 'Love is difficult and hard; like Hell.'

Juliet Mitchell (1974) explained that the young girl is fixated upon the father's phallus. But to avoid incest she shifts her focus to the mother's breasts and turns lesbian. Jameela is obsessed with her dead father. In one poem she enters his grave and begins to paint with her fingers with mud and blood as he did with paints on his canvas. 'Meri ungliyon mein/teri haddiyon ka ras nayi zindagi gholne laga' that is, 'I got new life from his fingers' is the poem's last line.

Gemaine Greer called the woman obeying male stereotypes of femininity *The Female Eunuch* 1970. This Urdu woman poet has broken stereotypes. I end with a musical poem by Jameela, translated by me:

The red of my palms
Wasn't henna but blood
One cry from my heart
Burnt this earth to cinders
You smouldered/I turned air
And flowed away your way
What did I know which way
The dew on my grass
Shone by your Sight
Becoming a rainbow by light
Becoming honey at night
Was it a dream behind my eyes
Or a mirage made of your sighs
All I did was ponder this
I went nowhere
Neither here nor there
The one my sight searches
What do I know where she is
Come let us break all riddles
Come let us make a new world
And search out new roads
New dreams New loves
New feelings New music
All of us queens and fairies
All stories, love-stories.

(f) Rukmini Bhaya Nair's 'Hermaphrodite'
Sappho: Contexting Rukmini Bhaya Nair's Poem

Some say there's nothing more beautiful
than ships at sea
Some say horse's hooves
Some, men's marching feet
But — I say what I love most
Is most beautiful to me.

~ Sappho of Lesbos

How does Sappho negotiate lesbianism in ancient Greece?

Plato in Book III of The Republic' speaks through Socrates to voice his opinions on how the guardians of his republic should comport themselves. As regards relationships he says:

> Apparently then, in the state we are organising, you will legislate to this effect, that though a lover may be attached to a favourite, and frequent his society, and embrace him as a son, for his beauty's sake, if he can gain his consent; yet in other matters he shall regulate his intercourse with the person he affects, as that he shall never be suspected of extending his familiarity beyond this, on pain of being censured for vulgarity and want of taste, if he acts otherwise.

It is evident from this dialogue that same-sex love did exist in Greece and was perhaps considered superior to a heterosexual relationship. There was pleasure, but pleasure within limits.

In an epigram ascribed to Plato in the 'Anthologia Palatina', he calls Sappho from Lesbos the 10th Muse; he was therefore aware of her and considered her writing worthy of being called a 'Muse'. The third century Philosopher Maximus of Tyre on Socrates and Sappho:

> What else was the core of the Lesbian woman except Socrates' art of love? For they seem to me to have practiced love with each other in their own way, she that of women, he that of men. For they say that both loved many and were captivated by all things beautiful. What Alcibiades and Charmides and Phaedems to him, Gyrinna and Atthis and Anactoria were to the Lesbian.

Sappho has also strong ties with her homeland and is referred to as the 'Lesbian'. History suggests that she was exiled from Lesbos sometime between 604 and 594 BC for political activities. Apart from being the original lesbian, she could have been the first 'witch' of sorts too, for a 'witch hunt' by definition is 'a search for and persecution of political dissidents on the pretext of public good.' Were the witches hunted down also because they loved women?

In the given poem, the three things mentioned as beautiful are ships at sea, horses, hooves and men's marching feet. The first half of the poem seems to be about war, for the ships, horses and men marching signify battle. All of them are moving usually under orders — the ship its helmsman, the horse its rider and the men their captain. Sappho uses the word 'some' repeatedly in the first three lines, that is to say that different people love different aspects of men on the move. And yet ships at an estuary, men standing about randomly, horses sniffing at grass or a battle ravaged ship, ragged filthy men and miserable worn out horses have nothing to recommend them. Perhaps the poet is hinting at the fact that people find beauty in them only in sending them away to disfigurement, grossness and death. The poet does not use the word 'love' in their descriptions of what is beautiful, these are things that cannot be loved, for their beauty lies only in their going for war.

Sappho believes in the triad of truth, beauty and goodness which in Plato's words (*The Republic*) are truth, harmony and proportion. However, Plato seems to glorify poetry that whips up a patriotic fervour during times of war; he is not averse to it. Sappho's triad is one of peace. One may also presume that Socrates (not as Plato's mouthpiece) was for peace, for how can one send what one loves to death?

The classics, while belonging to the Greeks, have been adopted by the English as their literary ancestors and the English would like to believe that their literary and cultural traditions have been influenced to a large extent by the ancients. Brian Doyle (1989) refers to what constituted the national spirit of colonial England as portrayed in the Newbolt Report (1921):

> Although commercial enterprise may have a legitimate and desirable object…that object cannot claim any satisfaction of any of the three great national affections — the love of truth, the love of beauty and the love of righteousness.

The statement is important, for the commercial enterprise led to the slave trade and wars to conquer other nations through the centuries. In sending their own men to death, by plundering and destroying other nations, one wonders as to how the 'national affections' of 'truth', 'beauty' and 'righteousness' were maintained. These national affections seemingly adopted from the Greeks have been fostered onto the Christian religion. And just as in the case of Judaism and Zorastrianism, Christianity too encourages a culture of shame and regards same-sex love. The word 'same' is defined as 'identical, agreeing in kind, degree or amount'. And since war is about unequal relationships, same-sex love is to be feared. Berth Brant puts this rather succinctly (1994) when she says that 'Homophobia is the eldest son of racism', and colonialism is another face of racism.

For Sappho, an object, a person, is not beautiful in itself, but rather becomes beautiful because she loves it. This beauty is permanent in the eyes of the beholder because it is love that makes it so. It is constant in a sense, unlike the love of men for men going to war. These men do not love men, but only transient notions of glory, power, honour, etc. associated with war. War which arises from a desire to subjugate, to establish a superior–inferior relationship, is built on heterosexual parameters, where one is always on top and another below. Audre Lorde, black lesbian feminist, talks of this relationship in *A Burst of Light* (1988), where she says:

The linkage of passion to dominance/subordination is the prototype of the heterosexual image of male–female relationships, one which justifies pornography. Women are supposed to love being brutalised. This is also the prototypical justification of all relationships of oppression — that the subordinate one who is 'different' enjoys the inferior position.

In not believing in this sado-masochistic concept, Sappho, as other gays and lesbians is a lover of peace, and hence perhaps her exile.

The Poem

Rukmini Bhaya Nair steps into the world of androgyny with her poem 'Hermaphrodite'. The action of the poem is straightforward, it could happen to anyone on an Indian city street: Rukmini gets her purse stolen by a eunuch who jeers at her.

But the incident provides the poet with an opportunity to meditate on the polyvalent sexualities a human being is capable of. She has always maintained, as a professional linguist, that language is gendered and the mind which produces language is not male or female but male, female and hermaphroditic, all at once. So, Rukmini mentally accepts homosexuality, by extension, in her own self.

This calm, academic knowledge of the poet is brutally tested in reality as she alights from a Delhi city bus, a harassed teacher, housewife and mother of two when a purse snatcher, who also happens to be androgynous, rudely tests her cosy notions of human autonomy and a 'liberated' woman's self-sufficiency.

The shock is multiplied by the 'jeering'. How male is male? How female is female? Is she herself not Germaine Greer's 'female eunuch'? Who is she then to be of the upper class that sneers at or jeers at or fears hijras? The shoe is on the other foot (or her purse tucked away in the wrong bodice) as the hijra makes off with 'his' loot.

What is being looted here? Who is disabused of what notion? With the poet's purse being relieved, we are relieved of our received notions of sexuality. There is an empathy between the stealer and the stolen from, not only in the sense that the victim is always her aggressor's accomplice, but in the profound sense that a mechanical, female, doll-like, university educated, Indian woman is not so different from a castrato!

Bhaya Nair does not mince words. There is nothing delicate about her diction. She always tells me I don't push the linguistic envelope far enough in my gay poems. She sent me this poem of hers to teach me what a 'gay' poem is or should be. A gay poem challenges gender — biological and mental.

Bhaya Nair is our sister. She has always shown empathy with us gay male poets, R. Raj Rao and myself. She invited me to teach gay poetry to her 40-strong IIT class of highly intelligent and irreverent undergraduates, and kept their wisecracks in check as I sought intellectual chinks in their adolescent male armours. Rao once explained to her that we gays have to go out seeking a new bedmate every single night because gay marriages are not allowed in India. This was something even the brilliant Bhaya Nair hadn't sorted out for herself in her own head. She became Rao's friend for life.

'Hermaphrodite Longings'

In her latest *The Ayodhya Cantos* (1999) Rukmini Bhaya Nair takes her old 'Hermaphrodite' poem and reworks it, throwing in Sappho's two lyrics and references to Megasthenes' *Indica* and to Siva as Ardhanarishwar ('half woman god', as she translates it).

Even in Hades I am with you
Andromeda…Gongyla…My desire feeds
On your beauty, Gonglya. Each time I see your gown
I am made weak and happy…You of all women whom
I most desire, come to me again…

The first Sappho poem addresses Andromeda which is also a galaxy's name and so universalises the poem. The reference to India specifically as 'Indica' puts the poem in a postcolonial context, Megasthenes being Alexander's Greek satrap, Seleukos Nikator's ambassador to the Maurya court. So women's writing, gay writing and Dalit writing, all of which 'Hermaphrodite longings' is, does not remain marginalised anymore but becomes universalised as a specimen of a universal, postcolonial literature.

Then listen, Sappho, to this…

A man snatched at me this afternoon
He was a woman, his eyes rimmed with
Kohl, the veins red with memory. I could not
Look at him. My eyes fell…
Because it was your face
It was your face I saw
In the mutilated body, in the coarse
Horsewhip tactics of that hijra, scintillating with oils
Jasmine, the blouse a gaudy trap, her hand
Across me, a sinewy band of teak…I could not
Pass…I had to face

Your terrible longing, Sappho.

The second Sappho poem addresses Death which Nair 'Indianises' as a crossing of a 'lotus'-filled River Styx in Hades. Death is also our Sappho's very sensuous last 'petite morte' in her bedroom. Sappho and the street eunuch ('knuckle and satin') become Ardhanarishwar. Sappho becomes a god. The sordid is beautified.

Sappho, this was the catastrophe you feared

Hermes came to me in a dream. I said
My master, I am altogether lost…

And my many riches do not console me
I care only…to die…and to watch the dewy lotus
Along the banks of Acheron, river of hell…

If a eunuch is capable of preying on (thus being complicit with or identifying with) the female poet persona then the 'Hermaphrodite longing' is the female poet's. The woman poet bravely implicates herself in the high rituals of lesbianism which occur to her from a brush with contemporary low-life in an Indian city. By extension, every housewife could be a lesbian, only if she accedes to the lesbian in herself because René Descartes' disciple Francois de la Barre has already told us that the mind has no sex. But our professor poet pushes her research further to say that the mind has several sexes, viz. male, female and androgynous. This poem is in praise of her own androgyny and by extension, everyone else's. The poem ends thus:

Sappho, history comes winding back
Persistent as a woman…

How you shocked me, Sappho!
But I see now why you wore
The face of a eunuch this afternoon, held me
Captive with your street smart tongue, straining
Under a shameless lift of skirts, that sequined
Body to reveal your damaged sex…

You crossed black Acheron, Sappho, to rob me of my vanity

Kleis in Indica, distracted by bright ribbons
Sappho does not spare her daughters wherever they are…
In Indica, in Hades

Sappho, *Ardhanarishwara*
Sings to her vulnerable daughters
In the perfect, androgynous voice of God…

Only Sappho shows

The true hermaphrodite face of love
Under the still moon, the harsh
Bullying stars…

(g) Satish Alekar's *Begum Barve* (Marathi, 1993)

The eponymous Begum Barve contains within 'herself' two strands of Maharashtrian culture, the earlier Chitpavan (Konkan) Brahmin culture and the later Moslem culture. S/he is born a Poona Brahmin male but fantasises him/herself a female. S/he is a female impersonator: men fall in love with her, especially the theatre owner who contracted her professionally; the females in the audience copy her style; the males in the audience fall in love with her in their onanistic fantasies. This is 1930s Poona. Today they love Kareena, Madonna. Divine!

'Fantasy' is a keyword here. Everyone dreams of money, sex, love, fame. The 'Begum' fantasies herself a female because not being able to find a woman s/he *becomes* a woman. Shyamrao, the theatre owner, falls in love with 'her' because he too can't find a woman. The Begum's fantasies are full-blown. S/he thinks she's pregnant and goes through the seventh month rituals. This is when Shyamrao thinks enough is enough. For every illusion there is its opposite: disillusion. Shyamrao proceeds to strip Barve of her finery until s/he is left bare on-stage in her dirty male underwear. The lady is a man! See Edward Albee's *Who's Afraid of Virginia Woolf?* (1958) for a similar 'hysterical' pregnancy and abortion.

They sing 1930s drama songs on stage ironically. There is a lot of cross-referentiality: Raja Ravi Varma's idealised Indian woman of his paintings, the female impersonator Bal Gandharva who is referred to again and again. Only Dalit women acted on-stage. They would 'pollute' ritually an all-male homosocial Brahmin drama troupe. Hence female impersonation on the Marathi stage. Lata Mangeshkar's father, a singer, sang the boy/girl roles on stage.

When Hirabai Barodekar finally entered the stage she was compared to female impersonators and found wanting. A man acting a woman is more real than a real woman. Illusion!

Begum Barve brings us into the contemporary world with the figures of two clerks: Bawdekar and Javdekar. They want 'a government job', they 'postpone marriage', their repression finds vent in nocturnal bedtime talk. They wear 1960s street clothes. 'All men's lives peter out in incomprehensible frustration,' Sadegh Hedayat writes in *The Blind Owl* (1937). They live in an illusionless world. Alekar saw two homeless men staying under a staircase — one was once a female impersonator, the other was in love with him. The play was born.

So what are we left with at the play's end? Barve is not a homosexual, not a transsexual, not transvestite. S/he feeds her master's gay fantasies, s/he is physically a male (not a eunuch) and s/he cross-dresses to earn a living, not for mere fun. What then is s/he? S/he is a fantasy feeding other man's romantic fantasies. So life and love are illusions. Romantic love is an illusion within an illusion we call 'reality'. As Novalis says, 'When we dream that we are dreaming, we are about to wake up.'

III

Book of the Soul

introduction

I call this book the Book of the Soul because it is about Art, viz. poetry and painting, art being the best emanation of our souls. The book includes the pioneer gay poet of Bombay Sultan Padamsee and his friend the poet film-maker Jehangir Bhownagary, both now deceased. The next two chapters deal with the greatest, in my opinion, male and female poets of my generation, viz. Agha Shahid Ali and Suniti Namjoshi, both avowedly gay — the first recently dead, leaving us a rich legacy and the second, the youngest poet in this constellation, still battling cant in England, Canada, Australia and India (places where she publishes). She shares with me my mentor, Ezra Pound, who though himself not gay, has inspired poetry with a social conscience from poets as disparate as Pier Paolo Pasolini Robert Duncan, Namjoshi and myself.

If Freud and Wilhelm Reich are to be believed, the phenomenon of a male leader leading male followers is homoerotic attraction between a charismatic leader and his followers. Similarly one enslaved people (Kashmiris) empathising with another proto-typical lot of sufferers (Palestinians) is a brotherly bonding both incestuous and homoerotic at its root. Shahid Ali's translation of Darwish is hence archetypal, having to explain the gay male archtypes of our literature, viz. a hero and his men. Ali is among our epoch's most important gay Indian poets besides Sultan Padamsee and Namjoshi. It is true Padamsee died young but he starts our history. Adil Jussawalla lost two decades to alocoholism but is writing well again for future historians. What we have from him already is important.

My work and R. Raj Rao's has archival value. But our various readerships have trouble with our varied styles. My style is too high ('Orphic') and his, too low, called 'scatological' or 'Ginsberg-like.' The Appendix is on the painter Bhupen Khakhar, also recently dead, who is not only India's first gay painter but is now compared to both Pieter Breughel and Andy Warhol.

A nation's history will be written not by its
politicians but by
its poets.

The Schemata of Book Three

The glue holding these chapters on gay poets together is their diction's progress from inhibition and imitation to freedom of ideas and language.

Every new literature defining a new 'nation' begins in imitation. America imitated Britain, Blacks imitated Whites, women imitated men, gays imitated straights in their writing. The next generation breathed free. Pioneer Sultan Padamsee imitated T. S. Eliot. Adil Jussawalla still imitates Eliot but also goes to Frantz Fanon for inspiration. R. Raj Rao, the Bombay lad, breaks free of all inhibition in language. (Anais Nin and I wrote as if we were virgins.) Shahid Ali goes to America and 'Americanises' the ghazal, he said; what he meant is he introduced the ghazal to mainstream western poetry. (At the Ghalib centenarary in 1964, five prominent poets 'Americanised' the ghazal first, in their 'trans-creations'.) Suniti Namjoshi breaks new ground as a third world feminist residing in Devon and publishing in Canada and Australia. Dinyar Godrej and Ian Iqbal Rashid go 'abroad'. Godrej, a Bombay Parsi, lives in London; Rashid, a Tanzanian of Indian descent writes of the 1940s film *Elephant Boy* directed by Sabu Dastagir in Canada. Old cultures mix with new ones, gay people write a new history for themselves in a new literature. At a moment in every nation's history a new consciousness bursts onto the world stage. Given globalisation's interest in sexual minorities, the literary moment for India's gay writers is now.

7

sultan padamsee: a pioneer gay poet?

Buddhadev Bose wrote, much to the anger of practitioners of English poetry in India, that such poetry

> …was an outcome of the anglomania which seized some upper class Indians in the early years of British rule. Sons (and sometimes daughters) were sent to England even before they had reached teenage, and there they spent all their formative years. Thus it was that English became the poetic vehicle of a number of gifted Indians. (Lal 1969: 3)

Sultan 'Bobby' Padamsee was one of those 'sons' sent to England when he was in his early teens. Even while he was in India, in Bombay — then backwater London — his mother saw to it that he was not so much as exposed to Indian languages and cultures. He was dashed off to a private school in Bombay at the age of five to board and study with two Irish ladies who 'gave him his idealistic turn of mind and an early love for dramatics' (Padamsee 1975: 7). At 12 he was transferred to a Jesuit School in the Kumaon hills. Here began his poetry along with the acquisition of Latin and later the study of Greek language, thought and philosophy. In 1936, when he was all of 14, it was time to try his luck in England. And in spite of being accepted by Christ Church College, Oxford, Padamsee was forced to return to Bombay in 1938 because of the War.

Padamsee's sister Roshen Alkazi recalls how they were kept away even from their mother tongue, Gujarati (personal interview, 1996). The emphasis was on a thoroughly westernised upbringing, where any 'Indian' influence was considered undesirable. So strong was this belief that the Padamsee children were not subject to any religion except the one they were exposed to, incidentally, due to their acquisition of western literary and cultural traditions, viz. Roman Catholicism.

That India's wealthy middle class was keen on westernising in order to integrate with the 'enlightened' colonial elite would be Probal Dasgupta's way of looking at it (1993). One may term it anglomania, if one were the other Bengali — Buddhadev Bose.

Left to their businessman father, that generation of this Khoja family would have simply had to deal with the making and selling of glass.

Thanks to the 'foresight' of the 'shrewd mother', the adult Padamsees of post-Independence India found themselves launched into modern careers in art and culture. Akbar — the painter of renown; Roshen — costume designer, dance, critic, patron of art; Alyque — theatre and media personality; and the eldest, Sultan — poet, painter, theatre man. Had he not taken his own life at 23 he would have been, we are told, the greatest of them all. (What is not difficult to surmise is that, but for the economic base provided by the glass merchant father, the mother could not have envisioned a 'different kind of future' for the children.)

So, the loss of mother tongue was something which only higher middle class or upper class Indians could, literally, afford. Padamsee's use of English, coming as it does along with a closure of access to anything tangibly 'Indian', has to be placed in such a paradigm. The result: an Indian too westernised even to be apologetic about it in his writings. (In other words, it would be pointless to enquire as to why Sultan Padamsee did not have existential problems using English.)

Sultan Padamsee (1922–45) did not publish his work in his lifetime. But he did participate actively in theatre and painting. And the staging of Shakespeare and Wilde for an elite Bombay audience in a manner that anticipated Orson Welles is no less a public declaration of one's alliance with a minority westernised community than the fact of Sultan Padamsee not publishing his poetry in his own lifetime. It may be safely said that irrespective of whether Padamsee wrote poetry in English, the position he occupied owing to his westernisation stands.

Padamsee's *Poems* published in 1975, 30 years after his death, would not have meant much to even the increasingly self-aware tribe of Indian poets in English being churned out then by P. Lal's Writers Workshop. One should remember that in the 1970s poetry written in English by Indians achieved a status of sorts. What with, on the one hand, well-placed academicians and scholars like C. D. Narasimhaiah, K. R. Srinivasa Iyengar, V. K. Gokak and others making a strong claim for the study of Indian Writing in English (IWE) as an alternative to 'English' literature, new anthologies being compiled, and people like Lal leading the other side — of writers — with unprecedented self-assurance, it was boom time for all those who could arrange finance to publish their 'poetry' with the Workshop, where Lal welcomed writers with the zeal of a missionary.

Around this time, Roshen Alkazi had herself published her verse with Lal and it was quite natural that her brother's work also saw the light of day, during what was turning out to be a 'momentous' decade for Indian Poetry in English (IPE). But the fact remains that Padamsee's work has gone unnoticed. So much so, that today, even unabashed promoters of IPE would ask 'Sultan Padamsee who?'

What are the 'differences' in Padamsee's poetry that render him irreconcilable to a rubric, IPE, which today claims quite an undeserving following. Is it his exclusive westernisation alone that sets him apart to the extent that he is not self-conscious about being — for all purposes — an Indian who fits neither in the Anglo-American tradition nor in the non-native English literary tradition.

To begin with, it needs to be argued that Padamsee is not an 'Indian Poet in English', especially when such a label necessitates his being viewed as a part of a tradition which has been variously addressed as Indo-Anglian to simply Indian Poetry in English. In 'placing' Padamsee, we are then faced with the question of assigning an identity to him: Padamsee the artist, Padamsee, whose artistic leanings were basically informed by the westernisation he was subjected to; Padamsee the artist as homosexual who killed himself in a grand manner; the connections between Padamsee's westernisation and his art, his homosexuality and death.

At one level, claiming exceptionality for Padamsee would perforce mean that we claim also an autonomous space for him. But is he that important? Should we at all toil about finding him a 'place', something which he perhaps very intentionally denied himself, by choosing death. What promise does Sultan Padamsee's veiled exploration of homosexuality hold for contemporary society, literature and culture? In answering such questions as these we might only end up confronting more questions, as one shall see.

Padamsee was born in 1922, which for the critic Harry Levin was the modernist year with its miraculous yield of James Joyce's *Ulysses* (1922), I. S. Eliot's 'The Wasteland (1922), Rainer Maria Rilke's *Duino's Elegies* (1939) and *Sonnets to Orpheus* (1936), Bertolt Brecht's first play, Virginia Woolf's *Jacob's Room*, Marcel Proust's *Sodom and Gomorrah* (1922) and Eugene O'Neill's *Anna Christie* (1922). And if we are to accept the oft made claim that 'modernism', in short, is synonymous with internationalism and that our poet belongs to that 'moment', it does not sound all that convincing in spite of Padamsee's extensive westernisation. Modernism's 'internationalism' cannot be extended to the non-European parts of the world. Paris, Vienna, Berlin, London and New York, says Raymond Williams, 'took on a new silhouette as the eponymous City of Strangers — the most apt locale made by the restlessly mobile émigré or exile, the internationally anti-bourgeois artist'. Just as much as Bombay might at best be the backwaters in London (and later Bobby was in war-torn London), so also in Bobby's poetry we see not just an imitative modernism but also perhaps an imagined one, i.e., one constructed by the mind. A modernism born out of a read cultural experience rather than a lived societal experience.

Colonialism, especially after the introduction of English education, brought with it, to an extent, to British India, cultural values that would have been current at that point in England. But there is also this famous question of Nehru's (addressed by Dasgupta 1993): 'Which England came to India? The savage one or the liberal democratic one…;' that has to be answered. Life in London in 1940 could not have been the same as that in British Bombay at that time. A rejection of simultaneity of modernism has to be thus understood.

Hence comes the need to go to London for the artist who wants to take modernism head-on. The real thing. Padamsee did go. And so did Nissim Ezekiel, Dom Moraes, Adil Jussawalla. As did Nehru, Gandhi and a host of nationalist leaders, including right-wingers like M. S. Golwalkar and Dalits like B. R. Ambedkar.

According to Makarand Paranjape, a contemporary anthologist in IPE, 'a ready-made aesthetic was available to the new [I-E] poets — the modernism of Eliot and Pound, or Richards and Leavis, and of Picasso and jazz music'. For Paranjape, the 'sources' of modernism are 'literary rather than political or social; moreover they are imported and extraneous, rather than indigenous and locally engendered. Also these influences become dominant only after 1947, during the early fifties and sixties.' The literary 'source' is not political and social and the problem, if any, of writing in English is 'the tension between English medium and the Indian experience' (Paranjape 1993: 15). English, here, is seen as no more than a linguistic fact.

Let us juxtapose such a sentiment with that of Ashis Nandy's who argues for non-modern India's ethnic universalism that takes into account the colonial experience including the immense suffering colonialism brought, and building out of it a maturer, more contemporary, more self-critical version of Indian traditions.

> It is a universalism which sees the Westernised India…as a 'digested form of another civilisation that had once gate-crashed into India. India has tried to capture the differential of the West within its own cultural domain, not merely on the basis of a view of the West as politically intrusive or as culturally inferior, but as a subculture meaningful in itself and important, though not all-important in the Indian context. (Nandy 1989: 32)

For Nandy, even 'the exposed sections of Indian society' (i.e., exposed to western onslaught) 'have not been fully deprived of their self-confidence vis-à-vis the West.' Nandy, in fact, talks of how the 'Indian had his [*sic*] own theory of the West and used the occident for his [*sic*] own purposes' (ibid.: 3). But somehow, if IPE were to be treated as a category (of representation) through which the West has been theorised by the Indian bourgeois order (in the manner in which Nandy sees it), then, disappointingly, there is a lot that is lacking. That body of writing produced in English by Indians as 'poetry' has in fact made no contribution thus far in enlightening us about the East–West encounter and our colonial or postcolonial realities. It has been the onus of the discursive English of Nehru, Gandhi, Ambedkar and the like which has substantially theorised upon such political and cultural complexities. And it is in this tradition that Ashis Nandy on the one hand and the Kancha Ilaiah (1996) on the other operate today. This tradition of Indian Writing in English has substantially responded to the intellectual challenges that colonialism/English/West/modernity has thrown up, unlike the highly impoverished genre of IPE, as defined for the purposes of anthologies and Eng-lit courses in our universities.

Therefore, we achieve nothing really in trying to find for Padamsee a place in this artificially hoisted, elitist (and for Hindu writers) upper caste tradition of Indian poetry in English. We had better look elsewhere since neither IPE in its presently defined form can accommodate the demands Padamsee would make, nor can Padamsee's work be comfortably explained in an exclusive heterosexual setting which in all aspects makes for not very stimulating reading.

Writing about 'a new discovery', namely, Shahid Suhrawardy, Paranjape introduces us to him quite dramatically:

Suhrawardy's recovery...is nothing short of a major find in the historiography [sic] of Indian poetry in English; it tantamounts to the discovery of the 'missing link' between the contemporary poets [the modernists — Ezekiel onwards] and their predecessors [the romantics — Naidu, Tagore etc]. (Paranjape 1993: 235)

We lay claim to no such discovery of a 'missing link'. A 'missing link' with which the petty politics of anthologies/anthologists (exclusion versus inclusion) need be concerned. More than a 'forgotten modernist poet' like Shahid Suhrawardy, Padamsee may at best be regarded as a 'lost' poet who interests less because of his affinity to (literary) modernism and more because of his explicit treatment of same-sex passion.

And the reasons for uncovering him (rather than discovering) are not as simplistic as filling the gap between the 'nationalist–idealist–romantic' school and the 'disillusioned modernists' of the 1950s. Nor is the intention to hoist up a poet only to point out that Nissim Ezekiel was not the first modernist Indian poet in English, but some other fellow was.

Neither Suhrawady and Ezekiel nor the Indian English Romantics offer us much of a challenge as far as categorising and placing them are concerned. But not Padamsee who writes about a (male) lover thus:

He smiles and you can see his tongue
Within his widened mouth,
The expert practitioner of perverted love
His tongue is smoothened
With the sauce of years.

Fed on a cultural diet that ranged from Greek literature to Shakespeare to Oscar Wilde, Padamsee would have acquired enough acquaintance with the homosexual (sub)culture to understand the place assigned to it in the literary and cultural history of the West. He would have probably realised that his passion was something which one learned to talk about by simply practicing discretion, a discretion which W. H. Auden espoused. As Alan Sinfield suggests (1992), 'Auden founded a theory of poetry on the indirection he felt was required of homosexual men.'

Padamsee's poetry was one art that he did not publicise unlike his theatre and painting for which he was better known in his own lifetime. His sister, Roshen, does inform us that he did once give a public reading of the dramatic verse of 'Golgotha' (a section in his *Poems* published in 1975) and this upset a couple of Catholic priests whom Padamsee had cheekily invited over for the occasion.

Padamsee, we must remember, committed suicide at the early age of 23, when his peers and friends were in awe of his brilliance. His sister, Roshen, recalls how he was really hard-pressed for intellectually challenging company. There were, reportedly, not many persons who could stand up to Padamsee and make him feel that he was not all that hot. He was head, shoulders and a cock above the rest, and this is how his (now) old sister remembers it. But why did he decide that he had had enough of life when everyone around him thought that he had a great future ahead of him as an artist? 'Somehow he started feeling that he had already started repeating himself. He harboured this feeling that he had started becoming repetitive and that there was no point in continuing to live on to just see what would happen next' (personal interview,

January 1996). He is supposed to have said something to this effect even in his suicide note, according to Roshen.

However, on carefully reading his poems, one cannot but make a connection between Padamsee's homosexuality and his 'pact with death'. He took his own life, but how! That night he dressed himself up in royal fashion — in dramatic death robes, a pendant with a precious stone dangling from his neck. As he consumed sleeping pills, the gramophone was playing Chopin's 'Funeral March'. This suicide, as described by Padamsee's sister, has every element of a 'performance' in it. It is as if he took to death with the kind of pleasure he took in living. The artist as homosexual seeking death in his own hands. Yukio Mishima's hara-kiri — a loud public performance. Padamsee's meditative, music induced sleep — private, personal, yet celebratory.

Let's see how in the 1980s Michel Foucault meditates on the theme of suicide, and the right to commit suicide, in a gay magazine *Gai Pied*, according to one of his biographers David Macey:

> Taking his cue from an observation culled from a treatise on psychiatry, that 'homosexuals often commit suicide', he (Foucault) muses about 'slender boys with pale cheeks' who, being 'incapable of crossing the threshold of the other sex', spend their lives entering the antechamber of death and then leave it, slamming the door on their way out. He argues for the right to commit suicide, the proviso being that it should be a right to die in dignity and comfort, without the horrors (duly catalogued) that often accompany suicide bids... he suggests that potential suicides should enjoy the benefits of institutions modeled on Japan's 'love hotels' (which he saw in 1978), with 'weird decors... in which you could seek out with nameless partners a chance to die without any identity'. To die in that manner would be 'such a simple pleasure'.

And now AIDS has taken care of this (!) though it is hardly dignified or comfortable.

A consideration of the lives of Thomas Chatterton (1752–70) and Richard Savage (1697–1743), two 'unsuccessful' eighteenth century poets, helps us speculate on the problematic nature in which an aspiring artist seeks to project his identity. For that matter, the identity of any artist (or public figure) becomes contestable in terms of 'projected' and 'real' versions. For instance, the discovery of William Wordsworth's relationship to Annette Vallone as late as the 1920s (thanks to literary sleuthism) resulted in feminists and deconstructionists urging readers to (re-)evaluate Wordsworth's politics and understand his poetry in this new light.

However, even today 'introductions' to this celebrated Romantic poet in English literature courses do not account for this suppressed incident and its significance as regards Wordsworth's changing reactions to the French revolution and his political position in general (see Spivak 1987).

In most cases that we learn about, the artist and others around him (followers, admirers, friends and literary critics) project one version of identity as the real one. When the artist in question is a 'strong' poet like Milton or Wordsworth — someone who has produced a considerable body of work and has managed to project himself as an important voice by aligning himself with the state (through a laureateship or at a secretaryship to the king) — then the chances of the artist's own efforts at presenting to the world his identity being undermined by counter-claims become weaker. It is for this reason that Richard Savage's claim to be the son of Earl Rivers is considered (by literary historians today) as inauthentic despite the fact that this poet had the support of one of the most authoritative figures of his time — Samuel Johnson. (Though it needs to be mentioned that when he wrote the *Life of Savage* [1744] Johnson himself was a hack in Grub Street. Today, ironically, Johnson's biography of Savage has come to be more regarded by the English studies establishment than the work(s) of Savage as such.)

Toni O'Shaughnessy, taking into consideration David Hume's conception of personal identity as nothing but a bundle or collection of different perceptions, writes that, 'if identity is nothing in itself but consists only in imaginative connections drawn between perceptions, then not only is identity itself a fiction, but the identity of any person has the potential to become a multiplicity of conflicting fictions, as various as its interpreters' (1990: 489). However appealing such a philosophical position may sound, we must recognise that within the 'multiplicity of conflicting fictions' certain interpretations override others, and the dominant version gets presented as the 'true' identity.

O'Shaughnessy questions the justification we give ourselves for the 'comforting narratives of self-coherence whether fictional or not'. And she writes this in the context of examining Samuel Johnson's *Life of Savage*. But we should realise that the 'comforting narratives of self-coherence' is something that holds together only perhaps in the case of strong/great poets like John Milton, Edmund Spenser or Eliot. Lawrence Lipking, a significant voice when it comes to the dominant understanding of the life of a poet in English literature, notes in that 'great poets forge their own identities. They invent an image…and project themselves into it' (1981), and cites Milton on himself. Further, Lipking lays down that 'what he does and what he is, is less important than what he may become. The future will forget all facts except those the poet has put to use'.

The future did indeed forget Wordsworth's Annette Vallone but refused to accept the 'facts' that a poet like Chatterton put to use. From Thomas Walpole to Thomas Warton to Donald Taylor (the modern authority on Chatterton), each one is unanimous in his suspicion of Chatterton's disclaimer.

Chatterton was claiming that he was not the poet he was accused of actually being. Whereas Lipking's 'young poets' (Keats or Milton) as a norm make well-planned claims about their identity as poets:

> Keats, ability to grow, like Milton's depends on a vision of his future: his range of possibilities, his moment in English poetry, the latent principles of his development, the ideal work he hopes to accomplish, the legacy he hopes to leave.

None of these 'norms' are comparible with Chatterton's life and/or work. If anything, he seems obsessed with a vision into the past and this resulted in the 'pseudo-antique' Rowley poems.

It is interesting to note the kind of 'moment' in English poetry Chatterton chose to place himself in. Thomas Warton, the early nineteenth century historian of English poetry, examines the poetic claim of authors during the reign of King Edward IV. One John Herding is dismissed as 'the most important of our medical historians' (1824: 328). Warton does not spare John Kay, who was poet laureate to Edward IV, and another John Scogan, the King's 'joculator'. Also belonging to this uneventful period are two didactic poets on chemistry, John Norton and George Pipley, 'whose pieces have no merit other than serving to develop the history of chemistry in England. They certainly contributed nothing to the state of our poetry.' And finally, Warton writes with some relief:

> ...but a want of genius will be no longer imparted to this period of our poetical history, if the poems lately discovered at Bristol, and said to have been written by Thomas Rowley, a secular priest of that place, about the year 1470, are genuine.

Thus we see Chatterton displacing himself onto a time when good poets are not easy to come by. Usually we see a genius being described as one ahead of his time. But our genius chose to look backwards. Hence the question — Why did he do it? — is asked more earnestly and with greater curiosity in this case. Warton answers, 'From lucrative views, or perhaps from the pleasure of deceiving the world.' He further speculates that Chatterton 'probably promised himself greater emoluments from this indirect mode of exercising his abilities.'

The act of operating in an indirect mode, an oblique fashion, rattles the faculties of scholar-critics who are used to the normative 'great/good' work that looks 'ahead' of its time, or at least represents its own time in such a fashion that it becomes 'a key to our understanding of the temperament of that age' (Tennyson's 'In Memoriam' or Eliot's 'The Wasteland' come to one's mind). Thomas Hammond Chatterton's 'Rowley Poems' can perhaps not stand the 'test of time' because they radically question this very conception of time in two obvious ways. First, by their (pseudo) antiqueness, and second by the fact that a 'boy' could go thus far in deceiving the world. Chatterton's career, if there was one at all, is not marked by the 'planning' which goes into the making of a Milton's poetic career, or Alexander Pope's.

In the case of successful (great) poets, the 'greatness' of their work keeps us engaged and in the process our interest in their lives is limited, limited in the sense that we approach their life through their work. In the case of a Chatterton or Savage things start working quite the other way round. Their life seems to hold critics' interest rather than their work. For instance, one could, on keenly searching, find critical pieces here and there on Johnson's *Life of Savage*, but nothing as such on Savage's work treated on its own terms, like we do if the poems are by a 'successful' poet (for instance, on Keats' odes or Pope's *Rape of the Lock* [1714]).

Such questions are likely to be answered by pointing out to us obvious facts: Savage or Chatterton are not important poets, as much it would be said that Padamsee, too, is not. We are also told that the psychological, aesthetico-cultural and quasi-Orphic factors in the shaping of poets' lives lie in danger in ideological approaches that view the self-fashioning of the poet as a social formation.

To begin with Chatterton, Thomas Lovell Beddoes, Thompson, Savage and Padamsee are not poets in the same sense in which we are given to understand Spenser, Milton, Wordsworth, Keats and Eliot as poets. In case we are to view both these sets of poets with the same conception or understanding of what constitutes the psychological, aesthetico-cultural and quasi-Orphic factors, then, we yet again run the risk of only emphasising the already constructed differences — simply put, of good/strong/great/successful versus bad/weak/minor/failed poets. That is, there is a dominant understanding of what these factors are as seen in the Spenser-to-Eliot poets. And when those poets — who 'failed' for the very reason that they did not live up to the standards set by the dominant aesthetic — are again studied on these very terms, the exercise (of studying their lives/work) remains unjustified. (What we argue here also applies to poems whose reception we view as representative of how supposedly 'technically incorrect' Indian English poems are dismissed as bad poetry instead of being understood on their own terms, as products of a certain sociological and cultural critique.)

It may be more fruitful to view factors like the psychological, aesthetico-cultural and quasi-Orphic as themselves a social formation. It is only because these factors are socially/culturally constructed that the self-fashioning of a poet also becomes a social formation.

The present exercise of studying Padamsee (and because of him others like Chatterton, Savage, etc.) will be rendered a redundant indulgence unless one effects a change in the optic with which one reads poets and their lives. To put it crudely, there is no point in studying a subaltern group using those very techniques of the mainstream which resulted in their becoming the subaltern. The poetic philosophy which believes in the (unquestionable) supremacy of poets like Milton and Spenser over Chatterton and Savage has to be given up. It must be realised that the lives/work of subaltern poets like Chatterton, Beddoes, Thompson, Savage and Padamsee are in danger when viewed through a dominant notion of psychological and aesthetic factors that have informed the self-fashioning of poets like Spenser or Milton.

Some facts: Spenser was almost ready to do anything to win the Queen's favour (including being sodomised because the king then — James I — was a queen!). At the most he managed to get himself posted as the Governor of Ireland (where he slaughtered 70,000 Catholics). Milton, the most self-prepared, self-conscious poet, opposed the king but served Cromwell. During a change of regime, he had to go into hiding and surface later. Wordsworth, who abandoned the pregnant Annette Vallone, became poet laureate, as did Tennyson. Charles Baudelaire (1930) writes, 'to consent to being decorated is to recognise that the state or prince has the right to judge your merits, to dignify you, etc.'

The politics behind Wordsworth's 'pleasure of deceiving the world' (Warton's words with reference to Chatterton) as regards his French lover and suppressed paternity being relegated to the realm of the invisible, while at the same time the politics of considering Chatterton's 'deception' as central to our understanding of his work, I think have now become clear. One poet disavows, the other embraces and claims — an identity. Wordsworth maintained silence on Vallone and the child.

Chatterton passionately told the world that he discovered the Rowley poems, only to find himself discovered. Savage was denied the pleasure of being addressed as the son of Earl Rivers.

In David Hume's words, it becomes a question of drawing connections between different perceptions. Savage's claim to be the son or heir of Earl Rivers was to several contemporaries 'at least somewhat a doubtful story', though 'there was considerable sympathy for Savage'. Even in Johnson's account, we must remember that Savage's experience with patrons becomes an alternating case of assignment of identity (as Steele's son Tycronnel's 'equal') and its subsequent withdrawal. In my opinion, why a Chatterton refused to write 'normally', i.e., as himself, and why a Savage felt so driven to prove his identity (other than claiming to be somebody's son, his voluntary laureateship, his homelessness, his being a 'pardoned murderer', etc.), are questions we might not be able to answer definitely. But these 'whys' are as important as other such questions that are brushed aside. Why did Wordsworth not tell us about Annette Vallone, how Milton managed to remain close to the blueprint he devised for his career in spite of several handicaps, etc.

Some reflections on the question of the (author-itative) author would not be out of place here. Chatterton is essentially an absent presence in the Rowley poems. He simply withdraws from the work, dissociates himself from it. What the gay French philosopher Michel Foucault has to say in this context finds a startling echo in Chatterton's work. Elaborating on the connection (in western literature) between author, his work and death, Foucault observes that the writing subject

> using all the contrivances… sets up between himself and what he writes, cancels out all the signs of his particular individuality. As a result the mark of the writer is reduced to nothing more than the singularity of his absence; he must assume the role of a dead man in the game of writing.

Chatterton very much assumes the role of a dead man — Rowley's; and he was perhaps so disillusioned when he could not pass of his contrivances successfully that he 'cancelled' himself out by committing suicide.

The author's name, according to Foucault, assumes a classificatory function. Such a name permits one to group together a certain number of texts, define them, differentiate them from and contrast them to others. In addition, it establishes 'a relationship among the texts'. It is for this very reason that the author's name assumes such importance in the work of Donald S. Taylor, the authority on Chatterton. Taylor's thesis has it that 'less than a year was devoted to Rowley [i.e., to the Rowley Poems] out of a life of nearly 18 years, and out of a creative span of seven years'. The classificatory function of the author's name — accuracy — in this aspect is crucial for Taylor's scholarship. Foucault also points out that there was a time when the texts that we today call 'literary' were accepted without any question about the identity of their author. Their anonymity caused no difficulties since their ancientness, their status'. However, with a 'reversal' in the seventeenth or eighteenth century — Chatterton belongs here, 'literary discourses came to be accepted only when endowed with the author-function'. The importance or status of a work depends on how well questions like where the work comes from, who wrote it, when, under what circumstances, or beginning with what design are answered satisfactorily. Literary anonymity, in this scheme of things, cannot be tolerated because it hinders the answering of each of these questions as best illustrated in the case of Chatterton. A Milton, Eliot, Wordsworth, etc., are grist to the mill of the modern criticism industry. The poets in question — Chatterton, Savage or Padamsee — cannot be constructed as 'rational beings' in such a kind of discourse, and hence pose problems which are not easily resolvable within the existing frameworks of modern literary criticism.

Foucault's constructionist claims, however, pose some crucial problems when women, Dalits, lesbians, homosexuals and other subaltern categories try to trace/create a 'tradition' of their own. What Foucault says is that in the manner in which modern period literary discourses came to be accepted only when endowed with the author function, does not apply so easily to women, lesbians, Dalits or homosexuals. In such cases there is rather a tendency to suppress such identities than create 'scholarship' around the subject. The fact that 'successful' women authors had to assume male names and perhaps even learn to write like their male contemporaries (as proven in the western literary tradition) exposes the patriarchal bias in Foucault's theorising of the place of the author. And that men and women, who today are identified and claimed as lesbian/gay, had to learn to write indirectly, discreetly and obliquely about their same-sex passions; and how such writings have been healthily incorporated into the standard, universalist, humanist project of 'Literature' by suppressing/silencing their difference(s), also exposes the heterosexist bias of such a scholarship industry, nuances to which Foucault is surprisingly and ironically not alive.

The author function, according to Foucault entails that 'the author is also the principle of a certain unity of writing — all differences, having to be resolved, at least in part, by the principles of evolution, maturation or influence. There must be…a point where contradictions [in a series of texts] are resolved.' The underlying principles are forcefully rejected by Chatterton and it is almost impossible to find a point in his Rowley poems where contradictions may sought to be resolved. To use Toni O'Shaughnessy's phrase (quoted earlier), Savage and Chatterton offer us no 'comforting narratives of self-coherence'. However, I would, unlike her, refuse to generalise this as applicable to the identity of any person. Authors/artists, because of the elevated positions they occupy in our (westernised (?)) culture, are expected to at least project/show self-coherence (see, for instance, how Vinay Dharwadker 'performs' his Introduction to A. K. Ramanujam's *Collected Poems*, 1996). The 'great' poets stand great precisely because they have responded efficiently to the demands of this scientised mechanism.

Of the poets whose lives I pursued — Chatterton, Savage, Beddoes and Thompson — not without difficulty, in the libraries of Hyderabad, whatever was available on Chatterton proved the most interesting as far as such a search enlightening my project on Padamsee is concerned. It helped, since I was myself trying to know about a poet who had defied the existing norms about how a poet should prepare and fashion himself (not publishing and committing suicide certainly not being deemed as ideal ways of launching oneself). The eighteenth century Chatterton who committed suicide when he could not pass himself off as Thomas Rowley might not have exactly been a role model for Padamsee in mid-twentieth century Bombay. But there are a few things we may learn from Chatterton's case that will prevent us from undermining the importance of the 'absence' of Padamsee (except for a memorial trophy for drama instituted in his name in Bombay) from the contemporary socio-cultural scenario.

It could be that Padamsee preferred a grand death (in his prime when his friends like Jehangir Bhownagary and Adi Marzban, Ebrahim Alkazi and followers were overawed by him) to living in hiding. Hiding his sexuality, his love for men, and perhaps, therefore, his poems too. In the 1940s we had one man, strongly believing that the nation's political destiny was connected to his ability to control his heterosexual libido. An old man who felt that he would have somewhere committed a 'mistake' when lying between young women whose temptation he practiced to resist. And when the partition took place and there was so much blood and gore, this 'father' of the nation wept within himself. On the other hand, there was this virtually obscure artist who decided to take his own life owing (perhaps) to his inability to openly exercise his right to sleep with the men/boys he wanted to.

Both men made trips to England. Gandhi talked about Swarajya, Ramrajya and several things, that apparently concerned 'Hindu' (in Ashis Nandy's sense) India. The nation decided, even here, to selectively listen to this old man, and preferred to maintain an eerie silence on his experiments with sexuality truthfully accounted for. Padamsee was fed, and fed himself, on a western cultural diet; his short stay in England further strengthened such a foundation. His art and his life do not so easily relate to modern (postcolonial) Bharat. And why would a gay man in his youth, unlike an oversexed Gandhi, think of controlling his libido when he might have hardly got to release it (without feeling ashamed about it?), a person who would have learnt enough from the Oscar Wilde trials not to try anything too wild.

It may be argued that Gandhi's experiments with sexuality (among other things) are worth attending upon, unlike a Padamsee's. For Gandhi was someone who identified himself with mainstream Indian identity as a Hindu upper caste male (who had acquired enough knowledge of the West to try to look beyond it). Whereas Padamsee comes across as an unplaceable figure as far as the question of fixing his identity is concerned. A Khoja (followers of Aga Khan) upper class male whose upbringing did not involve ritualistic participation in any religion and whose know-ledge of Christianity and affinity to Catholicism was more a result of his westernised education. Here, the option of questioning the West (literally, culturally, socially) within himself does not so easily arise, thus resulting in his greater alienation from mainstream Indian identity.

The poems (published in 1975) hardly seem to address an Indian reader, of whatever training and background. They appear to be the product of an extensive reading of Euro-American literature and cul-ture. In Padamsee's poetry, other than the obvious immediate influence of Eliot in some stylised poems, what is most interesting is the creative appropriation of the poetic mode of Epithalamium/Prothalamium — a poetic form that was in wide currency in the Elizabethan period — whose famous practitioners included Spenser and Donne. Epithalamium is a marriage song meant to celebrate the consummation of heterosexual love through marriage (after a long courtship where the poet pens sonnets to woo his beloved). This song in its original form (as in Spenser, Donne, etc.) celebrates fertility, regeneration and reproductive love.

However, in his 'Epithalamium' and 'Prothalamium', Padamsee achieves a masterly subversion of the Spenserian model. In Padamsee's tongue-in-cheek (or should we say cock-in-cheek) presentation of the 'marriage' song, far from a celebration of heterosexual love we have Lenia, 'the harlot of high places' trying very hard to seduce Marius, a Roman soldier, in a verse dialogue that brings to fore the predicament of Marius in choosing between productive love (the compulsory heterosexuality Lenia demands of him) and unproductive love (his physical attraction to the suffering body of Christ) which he cannot easily 'rationalise'. From the beginning of their strangely constructed 'Epithalamium', we see Lenia demanding an explanation from Marius for not evincing any interest in her. Lenia fields question after question, wondering at her own capacity to make men go crazy.

> Could I not have had lovers,
> Waiting for you?
> Am I not a woman? And before you
> Many have told me, men from Araby
> And others, that the two scars on my thigh
> Kindle them to a further desire,
> So that they cannot resist my breasts
> And must couple with me many times
> Till they lie exhausted with the loss
> Of their fluid; only I waited
> With my wants not disposed of

and will not simply rest till Marius comes up with a credible explanation for his apparent 'sterility'. His responses, initially, do not satisfy Lenia:

> All this I know Lenia and I am weary? —
> Can you not understand that a man
> Sometimes desires and sometimes not?

and enraged, she accuses Marius of being untrue:

> as untrue as your love —
> Does it not even sateen your organ
> To know that you alone in a single
> Embrace completely involve me?

And this finally goads our Marius to 'explain' and he sets off in a moment of deep self-reflection where his '…thoughts/take fire and as in verse/the lines turn forth', and addresses Lenia in words simmering with anger and laced with cunning sarcasm (a tone which may be attributed to Padamsee's 'Epithalamium' as such):

> Listen then, Lenia,
> My beloved of the moment, and
> Take you fingers away from my pouch,
> For in the moment of relief I feel cool,
> And you had is irritating,
> Not enkindling, and listen —

Note that Marius curtly addresses Lenia as 'My beloved of the moment'. And in spite of such anger and resolve, Marius cannot directly, immediately tell the truth of his position. He cannot but inordinately postpone a revelation about his homosexual guilt. His attraction towards the body of Christ with the cross is something he cannot express without, perhaps, feigning ignorance, dislike, distaste and guilt. We sight the figure of Christ as Marius persistently and cautiously describes him first:

> Below the cross was a man of thirty,
> A wasted face of much beauty,
> He was made indifferently well —
> But nothing to me,
> A lover of women.

The self-instruction that he is 'a lover of women' coming five times in Marius' narrative as it does, loses more and more credibility every time he utters it since it becomes increasingly obvious that he is in fact just the opposite. After Christ is nailed on the cross, Marius tell us

> They had taken away his garments
> He was made indifferently well —
> Yet nothing to me
> But an object of pity,
> And strangely, a little love —
> But nothing to me,
> For I, Lenia, am a lover of women.

And as Christ, thus put to pain, cries out thrice, Marius concedes that 'into my belly came/ The gear of desire'. As sadism mingles with masochism,

Marius develops an erotic love of pain as embodied in the crucified Christ. Marius, describing himself 'a god, cruel and loving', pities 'the man' crying in thirst and 'wines a sponge' to quench his thirst, only to realise that the man on the cross is 'not thirsty enough'. Marius, rejected, grows angered:

> and my love
> And his pain and the dark sky
> Grew together, and I knew
> I must enter this man
> In sensuous pain.

Marius does enter him, his desire for the dying Christ shared by women in the vales waiting and watching him, and enters him as a crucifier, i.e., pierces a spear into him. This Roman also gambles with other soldiers and wins the dead Christ's garments: 'Behind a rock I buried my face/In the lice-ridden cloth.'

At this moment of truth Marius does not bother to answer Lenia's persistent query: 'Did you not think of me?' but recalls how he remembered

> The beauty of women, their thighs
> And waists and their hair,
> Their breasts…

and declares that

> They were as nothing as the
> Dust, and I was no longer
> A lover of women.
> I went from that place
> To the Jew whom we Romans call John,
> And desired him and I have
> Come here defiled.
> For the body of John stroked my body
> And the full lips of John
> Stroked my body —
> I am weary of delight.

Lenia has to make a strong heterosexist intervention when Marius is lost describing his experience (of the moment of truth) with John:

And the red nails of John
Did vile things and made
My body soft.
Lenia: Listen Marius, you are no poet

With this there is strong (self-) denial of both Padamsee's artistic
and sexual selves. He is 'no poet' nor a 'homosexual'. He has to reject the
momentariness of such realities (though it is Lenia who is earlier referred to as a 'beloved of the moment'). Lenia's words to Marius/Padamsee
here — 'you are no poet' — assume extraordinary significance, for at one
stroke Marius' experiences are all rejected as being the result of a flight
of fancy. (Roland Barthes says that only the intellectual uses irony on
his art and sex.)

Marius is told, in other words, that he is being imaginative and perhaps
that it is the prerogative of only poets to speak thus of their own sex, and
thus of their art. And, ironically, Padamsee is at once commenting on his
art and sex. He is no poet, nor homosexual. The so-called 'Epithalamium'
comes to a close with a new voice from behind (neither Marius' nor
Lenia's) declaring that

Marius slept again
In the arms of a woman.

Marius is forced to reconcile himself to the hegemonic compulsions of
heterosexuality. And thus incidentally, and again, ironically, the chief
purpose of an 'Epithalamium' (as marriage song) is sought to be achieved
with an obvious artificiality. While in several ways making the traditional
Epithalamium stand on its head, Padamsee makes sure that heterosexual love is granted a Pyrrhic victory, say, as in marriage to death prior
to any forced (heterosexual) marriage. (Jalaluddin Rumi's phrase 'the
bridegroom of death' comes to one's mind.)

Such a grand, elaborate, programmatic subversion of the original
Spenserian model of a marriage song would necessarily have to be
understood within the tradition of British poetry. To understand
Padamsee (at his best and most fascinating moments), then, would
necessitate that the reader be a person who has more than a casual
understanding/knowledge of the English poetic tradition. To be more
specific, the reader must perforce have been a keen student of English
literature (and therefore the Bible, Christianity, etc.), well exposed to
the intricate details that matter. Which is to say, keeping in mind the

1990s Indian reader, that s/he must have done a 'good' MA in English literature where a 'competent' professor should have handled Spenser and Donne's marriage songs, which again would mean a sound knowledge of not just neo-platonism, but the sixteenth century Christian (Protestant) appropriation of Platonism. For Padamsee's homosexual subversion of the heterosexuality that animates sixteenth century epithalamiums would not register on a reader who is 'unaware', a reader who has had no reason to oblige an awareness of certain nuances of Elizabethan poetry.

Accessorising Women in Padamsee and Prufrock

'The best accessory a man can have is a beautiful woman,' Joan Rivers said while hosting a red carpet fashion show. She could have been sitting down with Sultan Padamsee and instructing him on how to perform life. For his poems 'O Pomponia Mine!' and 'To a Lady' echo the underpinnings of her statement: beautiful women are accessories, that they are necessary, like neckties, to complete an image. Both poems stress the performance aspect of living, of not just mimicking the mainstream but surpassing it — performing life as it can only be lived in the movies or in Shakespeare's tragedies.

Both poems are written as monologues between the male poet and a woman, much in the fashion of T. S. Eliot's 'The Love Song of J. Alfred Prufrock', which itself is a monologue between Prufrock and a woman of less than good repute. The attitude towards living is similar in all three poems: Eliot also stresses the performance of life ('there will be time/to prepare a face to meet the faces that you meet;/There will be time to murder and create' an identity). There is a tragic overtone to all three poems as well; living as a performance cannot be maintained, something must be lost along the way.

'Gay sex, all sex roles, all genders are a performance,' I have stated in my Introduction to *Yarana*. 'O Pomponia Mine!' stresses this performance aspect right from the title. Pomponia perhaps is a reference to Pomponia Graecia, the grand roman matron who, fitting with the etymology of her name (pomp: solemn parade, with the connotation of magnificent), had coins printed with her beautiful image and a husband who had conquered the British Isles. Livy says that she was accused of subverting the state, Catholic historians claim her as an early Christian martyr. She had to hide parts of her identity and perform a life that wasn't hers.

The voice behind 'O Pomponia Mine!' is that of a gay man talking to a girlfriend (his fag hag: 'you are not my mistress nor my wife') about how they shall act, how they will perform their lives. They will go to expensive restaurants, they will live beyond their means, they will appear to be a Romeo and Juliet, and the world will never know that they are constructed images, never know that they are not Marilyn Monroe and Fred Astaire but only Normal Jean and Fredric Austerlitz.

And it will kill them, for these actions are 'the toxin that adds flavour to our lives'. In the end the toxin kills; Sultan Padamsee committed suicide at the age of 23. The conflict is that of performance verse reality:

> We shall play it bravely; only,
> Pomponia, alone.
> We shall never groan
> Even if the rolls are hard,
> And the prices on the card
> Make us feel a little lonely.

They are together, but each is alone. They are living like Madame Bovary: she too felt lonely at the prices but that did not stop her from purchasing. She bought into a material ideology, where only the best was good enough (like the Astoria). Once she was realised by the community for what she was, there was no other alternative but death.

This conflict of being figured out is present in all three poems, this conflict of being realised as 'attendant lords' and not as Hamlet himself. In Prufrock's love song, the couple 'drowns' as they face the reality of human voices. Prufrock fears being pinned to the wall for what he is, like a butterfly behind glass: 'formulated, sprawling on a pin/When I am pinned and wriggling on the wall'. This image of pins and pinning appears a couple stanzas up in the love song with reference to a tie. 'O Pomponia Mine!' opens with reference to a tie; 'To a Lady' mentions pins as well. The tie and pins evoke strangling, a caged existence. The voice of 'O Pomponia Mine!' is placing himself in the position to be strangled, he continues to knot his ties superbly, continues to go on at the Astoria, continues to try to do what Madame Bovary could not successfully do.

In 'O Pomponia Mine!', the game the couple plays is known to both of them, and so Pomponia is an accessory but also an accomplice. In 'To a Lady', the performance is strictly heard from the male voice. The narrator discusses how he loves this woman 'always while your thighs are slim'. It is conditional, and she will not stay slim and young forever. It is understood that she is just a temporary accessory.

Though temporary, she is necessary. The poet needs 'soft hands' to 'cling to the back of my sleeve to dinner' and 'lips a man takes with his wine'. He needs a lady, not just any woman, but a lady. The poem ends with 'You are not the last/Even thought I shall love you forever.' There is affection between the addresser and addressee of this poem; it is, however, a condescending one. He makes it clear to his lady that she is just an accessory to pass the time, but he loves her for that, loves her for the services she provides, for the look she completes, not for her. The first, second, third and fifth stanzas focus on physical aspects of her: 'thighs', 'cool lips', 'lips' and 'lashes', and 'auburn hair.' The fourth and sixth focus on props and scenes: 'perfume to dim the lights' and 'coffee served with cognac'. There is no mention of her as a person with emotions or thoughts, just as an accessory.

The treatment of women is similar in Prufrock's love song. He treats them as an accessory not only necessary to complete the perfect scenes (with 'skirts that trail along the floor' and 'Arms that lie along a table, or wrap about a shawl') but also for pleasure (sexually: 'restless nights in one-night cheap hotels'). He commands his woman not to ask 'What is it?' but allows himself to wonder for her if it will have been worth it — worth living this way, worth not being understood. Despite his doubts, he does not cease the performance ('I shall wear white flannel trousers' — I shall keep up even as I grow old).

The performance is inescapable — just as it was for Madame Bovary, just as it was for Padamsee. It doesn't matter that Prufrock was a seeker of prostitutes and Padamsee gay — the outcome is similar. Stigmatised and illegal actions flock together: In Mumbai's club Voodoo, on gay nights both straight prostitutes and gay men arrive. Drugs are sold out front. All these 'immoral' actions receive similar scorn from the 'they'. In 'O Pomponia Mine!', it is the 'they' in 'they shall never know'. For Prufrock, it is everything outside the 'you and I'. It is this 'they' that preach morality, they that define love, they that can pin the couples down, drown them, strangle them with their reality.

These three poems are against this 'they.' Padamsee's two poems stress beauty and youth, fantasy and performance. Eliot's Prufrock stresses beauty and youth as well as their decay of it. As I have said, again in the Introduction to *Yarana* (1999), 'it is nothing but arrogance in this world to say there is only one god or to say there is one sexual play'. Padamsee and Eliot have constructed poems that go against the arrogant, poems that define love and life on their own terms and do not seek to look for the 'they' as to what is acceptable.

In this scenario, it must also be remembered that the Indian student of English literature invariably subverts the authority of the hegemonic text in the course (be it a play/novel/poem) by almost always seeking the help of a *kunji.* (see Loomba 1992). Probal Dasgupta's argument that 'India has traditionally been an area of resistance to hegemonies — an area that handles all conquering cultural forces (such as, today, English or the 'rational and efficient' systems of the market economy) by appearing to surrender to the storm, accepting it as H [H is Dasgupta's shorthand for high culture], and then developing L-based antibodies' (Dasgupta 1993: 144), rings a bell here. The belief that Shakespeare, Milton, etc. represent the apogee of English culture and this still being reverentially studied by Indians as 'H' is undermined by the 'L-based antibodies', the *kunjis*, whose centrality in an English literature student's life Ania Loomba exposes brilliantly.

To the Indian reader who does not burden herself with a nuanced understanding of Spenser's 'Epithalamium', Sultan Padamsee would be logically more inconsequential than Spenser himself. Then, why and how should Sultan Padamsee matter in a context where Spenser himself is effectively subverted? If Padamsee's subversion of Spenser is sophisticated and literary and the average Indian student's (subversion) a more obviously political refusal to comply, is there ground for solidarity between these two seemingly polarised acts? Can we be equally appreciative of and sympathetic to both kinds of subversive gestures without risking contradiction?

It has been the attempt here to traverse both these subversive trajectories — the purpose of studying a 1940s, possibly homosexual Indian poet's use of 'English' ('not simply language, but the locus of a set of values loosely termed 'Westernisation', (Sunder Rajan 1992: 14)), and placing this in the larger context of resistance to the ideologising force of English in India and subsequently also of Indian poetry in English. The fact that we are implicitly trying to develop common ground between diverse subordinated groups may — for now — even invite ridicule, but it is a challenge this work takes up.

First, it has to be stated that the purpose of this work on and around Padamsee is certainly not to ensure a place for him at any level in the syllabi of university Englit courses. If such a thing is desirable at all, then Padamsee's place in such a framework can be negotiated, unfortunately though, only within the existing outline of what gets taught as Indian poetry in English. This, given the premises of this argument, would be simply unacceptable.

Therefore the possibility of Padamsee being read, if any such possibility genuinely exists in the contemporary scenario, has to be explored outside the purview of what a university decides is constitutive of literature. Alternately, if at all, a place for Padamsee has to be negotiated within the existing academic scheme of things, then we have to first strengthen the call for radically changing the agendas of English departments in India.

To an intelligent person, it should by now be clear that the figure of Padamsee itself could be seen as being incidental to this project at a certain level, a level from which we argue against the 'unproblematic retention and continuance [of Englit] in the post-Independence education syllabus in India' (Sunder Rajan 1992: 12).

In doing all this, and yet stressing — by the way — the indebtedness of Padamsee to westernisation, which perhaps has helped him articulate a homosexual sensibility, we throw open the possibility of a(n) (predictable) accusation which would go: 'Homosexuality is western and its manifestation in an Indian exposes his unbridled westernisation' (quite similar to the premise that feminism is western, and in Indian women a result of westernisation).

This, we simply answer — for the present — by invoking the work done by Foucault. That westernisation be seen as a prerequisite for an articulation of homosexual sensibility is a deduction that can be easily invalidated through one's reading of Foucault's work on sexuality (and power). Foucault's argument is that since the eighteenth century western man has been drawn to the task of telling everything concerning his sex (ibid.: 23). He illustrates how towards the beginning of eighteenth century (coinciding with the development of capitalism and thus modernity) there emerged

> a political, economic and technical incitement to talk about sex. And not so much in the form of a general theory of sexuality as in the form of analysis, stock taking, classification, and specification, of quantitative or casual studies. (ibid.: 23–24).

Foucault elaborates how this proliferation of discourses on sex was crucially connected to state power (it became essential for the state to know what was happening to its citizen's sex) and the discourse of modernity (modernity, whose project included a study of population as an economic and political problem, the medicalisation of sexuality, developments in architecture — be they schools, hospitals, prisons or bourgeois 'homes', psychiatry, etc). What we learn is that in the Christian

West homosexuality was not an accepted and encouraged thing, but was rather harshly treated. Along with the centrifugal movement with respect to heterosexual monogamy, Foucault argues that in eighteenth and nineteenth century West, 'what came under scrutiny was the sexuality of children, men and women, and criminals; the sensuality of those who did not like the opposite sex; reveries, obsessions, petty manias, or great transports of rage' (ibid.: 38). Though all these figures were eventually condemned, they were forced to speak and were listened to only to reinforce the claims of 'regular sexuality'. And most importantly, 'The transformation of sex into discourse was governed by the endeavour to expel from reality the forms of sexuality that were not amenable to the strict economy of reproduction: to say no to unproductive activities, to banish all casual pleasures, to reduce and exclude practices whose object was not procreation' (ibid.: 36).

If such was modern, Christian, capitalist West, the West that treated Oscar Wilde so shabbily, then how do we equate westernisation (among Indians) as a crucial input that helps one articulate one's affinity to an alternative sexuality? And for all this, Padamsee turns out to be quite explicit in his explorations of the homosexual theme, though he conducts these explorations in an impersonal, distanced form, poetic discourse itself being a veiled, covert and oblique mode of expression. Not even W. H. Auden, Padamsee's British contemporary, had practiced such a bold outlook when addressing same-sex passion. Alan Sinfield's suggestions on reading Auden's poem 'The Truest Poetry is the Most Feigning' provide us a useful reference point.

> There are similarities between 'The Truest Poetry' and Auden's essay on Cavafy (1961), in which Auden praises Cavafy's boldness on the subject of homosexuality but then defends discretion (such as he himself practiced). I suggest that Auden founded a theory of poetry on the indirection he felt was required of homosexual men, and that 'The Truest Poetry' alludes to this indirectly, of course. (Sinfield 1993: 32)

Sinfield's project also offers us an opportunity for a happy alliance when he says 'I do not want the gay reading incorporated into the standard project of Englit,' in the same essay. If Padamsee is found practicing any such discretion and indirection, it is only in the incidental non-personalising of homoeroticism in the two major pieces in his slim published work.

We should also account for the differences in the perception of homosexuality in Wilde's England, and Auden's post-Kinsey period and moreover for the perception one has thanks to post-Stonewall developments in the US (which have had an effect in the UK too). And if we today hear someone casually saying that 'homosexuality is western', then one should hope that it is the contemporary American West (where Clinton would address the problem of gay activists and would be taken on by Urvashi Vaid on primetime TV) and not the eighteenth and nineteenth century early capitalist, Christian, modern West where there was a political, economic and technical incitement to talk about sex and also a demand to hide the thing spoken about (see Clinton's 'Don't ask/Don't tell' for military recruitment of gays). Not just this, we must also be patient enough to acknowledge that

> '[H]omosexuality has not always been organized as a separate 'people'. The evidence from non-Western cultures shows clearly that relationships we call 'homosexuality' were organised in quite different ways, making the development of group identity and movement highly unlikely'. (Adam 1987: 1)

Crudely put, if one is hoping to address the 'gay and lesbian scene in India' — even if there exists none in the sense in which it perforce has to exist in the US, there are people out here busily creating one such similar scene — in this work, rather than simply shutting one's mouth after examining Padamsee's contribution 'purely' to literature (as defined in traditional Englit courses), then our hands are more than full.

8

the strange case of Jehangir Bhownagary (1921–2004)

Jehangir (Jean) Bhownagary, friend of Sultan Padamsee, wrote poems since he was 20 (1940s) but did not publish till 1997 when he was nearing the end of his life. Born in Bombay to a Parsi father and a French mother (my paternal grandfather assisted Dr Porter of Cumballa Hill Clinic at his birth), Jean considered Padamsee ('Bobby' to him) the seminal influence of his life.

Padamsee could paint, write poetry, act in theatre, don costume, do magic tricks. But he chose to die at 23. His grieving family and friends continue his work. Akbar Padamsee turned to be a great painter, not to mention *all* the painters of the Bombay Progressive Group (M. F. Hussain included). Theatre was covered by his younger brother Alyque Padamsee and his family (his wives). His sister Roshen, who published Sultan in 1975, married Ebrahim Alkazi who headed the Indian National Theatre in Delhi for decades (now the mantle has fallen to daughter Amal Allana). Roshen herself was the wardrobe mistress there and has produced a magnificent book on costumes (Alkazi 2003). The poetry fell to Nissim Ezekiel's lot whom the family sent to England and who advised Roshen on the Sultan volume; and the magic tricks fell to Jean who held the degree of Master Magician and National Councillor to the Association Francaise des Artistes Prestidigitateurs, Order of Merlin in the International Brotherhood of Magicians and Life Member of the Inner Magic Circle (London) with Gold Star. His childhood passion for conjuring consumed him till the end. And as I said before, he was a closet poet.

In the summer of 1995, over 20 years after first having met him in Paris (when he told me Sultan Padamsee was gay), he entrusted me with a bunch of poems he had written throughout his life (about 40 of them.) On his wife Freny's insistence, the early poems were taken back from my scrutiny because they 'did not want people in Bombay to know'. I was entrusted with his then current diary which had a few new poems with the instruction not to read the diary. Two years later, the poems appeared from Writers Workshop with 12 poems from the 1940s which had been unseen by me.

In the 1940s, Bhownagary was seeing Padamsee in Bombay and dating Freny Nicholson of Poona who was writing a thesis in French on Bergson which she abandoned for family-making. Bhownagary told me, while narrating Padamsee's death to me in 1975 in Paris, that the two as boys were inseparable. Bhownagary would talk with Padamsee late into the night, go home to sleep, and be at Padamsee's doorstep first thing in the morning to carry on the conversation from where it was left off the night before. Let us call this *yaraana* (my term for 'a deep male friendship up to but not including physical intimacy'). It is a mental love; the physical love went to Freny, whom Bhownagary married. On the day of his death Padamsee consumed drugs, a secret habit his friend knew about though his family didn't. He died around 3 a.m., was found by Bhownagary at 7 a.m. but by that time the poison (perhaps an accidental overdose) had spread throughout the body. Bhownagary thinks it a suicide because it was staged: costumes, candle, Marche Funébre on the phonograph. Jean told me he wept inconsolably. But everything he did later in life — making films, acting with Adi Marzban (another youthful gang member) in Parsi Gujarati plays, magic tricks, painting (the Zoroastrian Three Magis were a recurrent motif), poetry — he did with Padamsee's love and Freny's loving support. Genius is both born and made. I like to think genius is a little gay!

Seed

In the sorrow
Of twisting willow songs
My heart allow
That the stream should flow.

Our tender arms
Must take the final truth
And our seed
In the sun of our living
Will make the final truth.

Bombay 1944

Whose seed? Planted where? And for whom and what? The date shows it to be contemporaneous with both Bobby and Freny. The youth wills his love 'to flow' to both men and women. There are two stanzas in the poem: it is about twoness fused into one poem in the final extra line (a fifth line) to 'make the final truth'.

The second stanza has two parts, a couplet and a tercet: its lines 1 and 2 is the couplet; 3, 4, 5 make a tercet. The couplet has tender arms 'taking'; in the tercet the sun (read also 'son') is 'making'. 'Taking' in a youthful friendship, 'making' in a youthful marriage. Sons need both the love of men and women, of each other and of the women they marry in order to continue living. Padamsee didn't marry and died. (Remember, this is 1940s Bombay: The cosmopolitan young can experiment with lifestyles but only just so far.)

The second 1940s poem in the collection, 'Cardinal Roses', is, as Bhownagary explains in a footnote, from Bombay 1944 and he calls it 'automatic writing' and 'music'. So much the better. It is then, the young poet's 'unconscious' talking. 'Cardinal' is 'cardinal sin', 'Cardinal' is a red bird; the Bishops in the College of Cardinals wear red; 'cardinal' numbers. We are talking of primary (red) passions here. 'Fire by fight', 'ashened skein (skin?) of remorse' (at what? — 'forbidden' love?). Song, however, conquers the (physical) pain of the 'diamond scar' (anal rape?)

'The tendrils' (pubic hair), 'black hill of my birth' (the poet and his father's lingas: boys inherit their phallic proportions from their fathers), 'the night's *disgrace*', '*twisted* fist', 'forgotten *strangeness*' (emphasis mine) bespeak shame at a homosexual experience (forced: 'twisted fist' or otherwise). But the 'scar' is 'diamond' —brilliant, precious — which

> shall tell the forgotten strangeness
> of the moment in my mask of bone.

Strangeness — of the estranging adolescent sexual experience. 'Masks' like Padamsee's again! But here, the face itself is a 'mask of bone'. Appearance versus reality. What you see is what you don't get. In his introduction to Padamsee's *Poems*, Bhownagary writes about the adolescent homosexual experience:

> It would be a mistake to dismiss the conflict as adolescent. It is basic to the human condition. Only in Padamsee it is pushed to the limits, it flowers like some strange, beautiful but poisonous growth and ends only in his death at the age of 23.

Bhownagary apparently saved himself from the poison ('gift' in German) of homosexuality. 'In the Stillness' reads:

> In the stillness
> I looked into the tiger's eyes

And the tiger gave
Me the flecking of his body
Saying
These you had given me
In a forgotten time.

Please note that 'the tiger' is explicitly masculine: a male lover from boy-hood, 'a forgotten time'.

The memories must stay
Without jealousies —
I am talking of your
Memories my darling
For mine have been
A life of the wind
And a fragrance —

The future wife must not be jealous. (Bhownagary told me he did not follow the Parisian fashion of adultery because his wife took the proscription out of it by not being jealous.) 'My darling' is an address to a wife. 'Fragrance' is also hers.

The third, synthesising, final passage between the thesis (male) and anti-thesis (female) is Nature.

Between the flow of the river
And its bed
Rests the knowledge
That ours is the sea
And this sky of stars.

I submit the bed is the nuptial bed and the river is the river of blood (or semen) that flows equally from us to either a man or a woman. From it we get 'knowledge', universal cosmic knowledge of stars, sky and sea.

The sun quick' echoes the son/sun pun again. Written in Pune (then Poona) in 1944, it is probably written to Freny, whose hometown was Poona. Freny was the daughter of an alchemist and the alchemy of gold gilds the whole poem. The bisexual movement poet, Thom Gunn, talks of adolescent (gay) loves:

A first love that is wrong
Is only a place-making for the great love
to come.

First (gay) love is the alchemist's laboratory which turns base metal (gay first love) into gold. But our first gay lover (our seducer, our molester) is also our teacher. The sun quick upon the meadow (read 'son') /the planter with a song and a seed/The rich earth feeding/The roots of the song/And the tree is old/The song thrives…in tender sapling.' Father Sky and Mother Earth coupled to birth the Sun (Son) of Creation. The wisdom of the first gay lover and the wife (Mother Earth) husband the son into maturity. In gay slang, the first passive older lover is called a gay boy's 'mother' (meaning sexual initiator).

'The savages of my city', I submit, is a masturbatory revelry of an onanist who is also gay. The young James' Joyce's first book was a book of adolescent poems punningly called *Chamber Music* (1907), 'chamber' bring the Victorian solecism for a loo where the onanist could play. The book of poems gave no indication of the Joyce to come, though having all the Joycean themes in kernel. The same could be said of Bhownagary's poems. The *Poems* show us in retrospect what Bhownagary brilliantly did in film, pottery, painting. The savages are the commercial herds who mock love and the moneylenders who can't read poetry. 'Forgotten fluting', till the 'fluting bruised', is definitely onanistic and by extension loney and narcissistic. Stars are 'barren', night has 'failed'.

Is the miracle then softest
That has caught my soul
Again
In all the silverness
Of the most tensile of strings?

Bombay, 1945

The word 'tensile' is used for steel but also for a spider's thread which is a hundred times more durable than steel. Silver spider-like thread is what the onanist produces out of his own body, something that withstands like steel the mockery of the entire city. Violin strings (cat gut) are tensile and produce (chamber) music.

Those who are mocked will learn to mock. Rather, Bhownagary has the jejune young men's aristocratic disdain for what passes for 'modern art' in a colonial, cultural backwater called Bombay in the 1940s. They were going to make the modern Indian cultural scene through the Theatre Group and the Progressive Movement (of painting). He mocks the hermeticism of Eliot-like poetry. Love may be onanism but art is communication. 'May I mock' mocks our modern poets. Again, we get the onanistic and furtive, homosexual cruising in 'puzzling spirals' and 'lost breeze' to which modern poems are compared. 'Babylon' indeed: this 'tortuous wondering' (wanderings?) and 'meagre dust' (of homosexual love; the gay lover was after all his artistic mentor, too) opens out into 'poetry's endlessness', echoing 'emotion'. Prose becomes poetry, sex becomes love, life becomes pure art.

The élan vital is a Bergsonian idea. It is the flow of ideas from age to age. It is a twentieth century philosophy based on eighteenth century ideas of progress and nineteenth century Darwinism and Lamarakism brought to play upon the spiritual world from the world of biology. The 'flow' Bhownagary talks about then, is the élan vital (besides love, blood, semen, the flow of generations through birthing and dying) which unites all things through all ages and pushes it, pushes it ever so slowly towards perfection. Thirteenth century Iranian mystic Rumi writes:

> I was stone
> And I longed to be mineral
> I was mineral and I longed to be vegetable
> I became a tree and I wanted to be animal
> I was animal and I wished to be Man.

You can see the flow of longing through a spiritual progression in these lines. Jean sees such progression in music. As a potter, he believed the clay had forms longing to be set free, that the clay and the hand that molds clay were both essentially clay, essentially one.

César Franck was the avant-garde musician of choice for the cosmopolitan elite. Anais Nin alludes to his work in her 1940s novel of adolescent love, *Children of the Albatross* (1947), which has Bhownagary's theme of homosexual children turning heterosexual adults (in Nin's lucky case, with Nin herself!). In Franck's music, Nin writes, 'the staircase of fever was climbed but abandoned again and again'. Nin has learnt from Freud that love is a progression from autoeroticism to homoeroticism to heteroeroticism.

Bhownagary merely posits homosexuality and heterosexuality as two possible eroticisms among many. Poet Rukmini Bhaya Nair, in her role as Professor of Psycholinguistics, has researched the (female) brain and how it affects speech. She writes that the brain is not unisexual but multi-sexual. All kinds of polymorphous activities are thought up by the brain and put into words and action. 'Homage to the Makers of Music' has three poems: 'Cadenza' (1945), 'Toccata' (1941), Cesar Franck (1941).

'Cadenza', the latest of the three, posits the 'straight oak to dark cypress' (Bhownagary and Padamsee — 'White' boy and 'Black' boy?) 'like lovers' together 'in all the shaded perversions' (Jean's words). Jean calls it 'The tragedy, the comedy of man'. There is nothing so consistently funny as us human beings in the act of sex' (Barth 1968). 'Love is all you know of Heaven; and parting, all you need to know of Hell' (Emily Dickinson). The tragedy/comedy of love.

If the tall, straight trees were phallic, woman is the 'crystal bowl' of 'wildly fondling light'. (The tropic sun must have lit the Bohemian cut glass vases of Versova in Jean's father's home as it did in my mother's seaside home at Bombay's Pali Hill.)

Body versus soul, the surviving love, Bhownagary, remembers — The flash of minds/the sensing of a soul' (the oboe in orchestral terms) versus 'muscles rippling smooth on each other/the stroking brush/and with genius its demand fulfilled (the viol 'free' in a Brahms concerto). This conflict is genius' work, a 'saving tragedy'. Genius is defined by F. Scott Fitzgerald as the capacity of retaining two contrary ideas in one's mind at the same time and yet not losing one's capacity to function. By 1945, Padamsee is dead but not forgotten. A lover who dies young never ages in the memory of the beloved he leaves behind. 'Is this the saving tragedy'?

César Franck's music is called 'the wandering music of man's soul'. (III. Cesar Franck). 'Toccata', the second of the three musical poems, utters a Padamsee-ish death wish. Tiring of his 'own grand puny living' he desires

> With all my self to blaze my flight
> Complete to blaze and sudden die
> And thus to lose my soul
> in ashened fire floating to the sea

A young gay poet's death wish? A 1941 premonition of the 1945 suicide (Padamsee's) to come? A friend predicting a friend's death? A major poet (Padamsee) infecting a minor genius (Bhownagary's) with his own drift from Eros towards Thanatos?

But Bhownagary, as ever (like me, with basic common sense, so characteristic of Parsi practicality), pulls himself away from the precipice unlike poor Padamsee, the true poet, the truly lost soul.

> But slow the sun does rise
> Has burned my desire white
> Hiding, I climb into the rays.

So how does he live on? By submitting to 'the languor of the ages', he tells us in his next poem 'I who have felt...'. The potter's wheel to come late into Bhownagary's life debuts here as 'the wheeling wheel, of the universe itself'. 'Conched within a shell.../all the splendid swirl of sea and storm'. It is the ascendancy of the élan vital again; it is clay becoming man but 'in a moment' (emphasis mine). Does music make angels out of beasts? The nineteenth century faith in human culture to humanise human beasts. Didn't the Gestapo play Wagner as they gassed Jews at Buchenwald? Didn't Adorno say that after Auschwitz there can be no literature? To be fair to Bhownagary, he wrote in 1941, in pre-war Bombay before the Nazi terrors burst upon the world's consciousness at Nuremberg. Padamsee and Bhownagary are two precocious boys in a backwater, dreaming and making world culture. Of course, it was all unself-consciously done in English in the context of European culture that would energise the age-old roots of Indian civilisation. Westernised as they both were, Padamsee and Bhownagary wished a new, free India vitalised by a contemporary arts scene. Indeed, Bhownagary contributed to this image of India as Indira Gandhi's secretary (he was an IAS officer) when she was Minister of Information in Shastri's post-Nehru cabinet. Later, Bhownagary served at UNESCO's film division in Paris for 40 years with distinction, always showcasing eastern culture, be it with his prizewinning documentaries 'Loves of Krishna' and 'Akbar' (made for the Films Division under V. Shantaram) or his later films on Cambodia's Angkor Wat and Japanese ceramics with Freny suggesting camera angles.

The romantics want to catch ('cage') the aesthetic moment of humanising soul transformation in art and then 'free' them 'for others'. That's what poetry, painting, music, even a beautifully made ceramic pot are made for.

'I will be free' — the last but one of the 1940s poems of Jean sends him as a Magian astrologer again, or a latter-day dissenting fourth Magi (to quote Michel Tournier) into outer space, following stars yet 'unborn', if you please. I mean, if the annunciation is of Christ's birth, in its kernel lies the crucifixion too. Birth is meaningless without death. And the 'unborn' state is, after all, death's own kingdom too. Post-war, the Japanese philosopher Nishida writes:

We came from Nothing and go to Nothing
And we pass through life's Nothingness
which is everything. But we are not born
with nothing: we are born with a body.

Eyes to see, head to think, heart to feel,
hands to hold, lull and free…

Bhownagary is in his 20s. He is Hamlet. Or, he is Horatio to Padamsee's
Hamlet. Conundrums tempt him. Hamlet is subsumed, Horatio is left to
say, 'Goodnight, sweet prince'.

A voice like a bell
tolling death and birth

calls unto him but he fears to look back

For to look back is to fear
And to fear is to fall.

The Orpheus myth. Orpheus went to Hell for Eurydice but he looked
back and lost her forever. Bhownagary goes to Hell and comes back to
tell what he has seen — Padamsee's brilliant life and death and his own
youth in light of a brilliant star!
The last poem is sad:

Desert

In the desert
Among the potential pines
I stayed my hand
Although the water's gush remained
Unknown for many years.

Like some 'circumstantial navigator',
Perhaps I read the sands too long.

Bombay, 1944.

Perhaps Padamsee is dead by now. Bhownagary has renounced
poetry for 'art administration' (a vocation he single-handedly invented
for India along with Homi Bhabha, whose work is continued by brother
Jamshed). Hamlet has become Magellan. He circumnavigated the globe.
Bhownagary is ironically and parodically a 'circumstantial' navigator.
Circumstances (his mixed parentage, among others) took him around
the globe. Like a ship captain in his cabin turning over the sands of
the hour glass, hour upon hour 'he read the sands too long'. Magellan died
in the Philippines. Bhownagary was to die abroad in France. Each had

a rough 'middle passage' slavery to a workaday world. Each was guided by a 'star' (world conquest/Padamsee's love). Bhownagary lost Padamsee. In 1944 he could only read the sands, alone.

Postscript

Bhownagary took his secret to his grave. Was he Padamsee's lover? Freny is not telling because I'm not asking. The uptight Padamsee family won't tell, though Ebrahim Alkazi recently spoke of Sultan Padamsee in a recent *Outlook* article as he was not only Padamsee's brother-in-law but 'we were all in love with him'. Alkazi married Roshen, Padamsee's sister, as a classic way out of a conundrum of passionate boyhood affections (in the plural, for both sexes).

Freny is my friend (my *Juvenilia* [2006] is dedicated to her). But she is also Bhownagary's widow. I hope this gay mis/reading of Bhownagary's poems does not grieve her. I have taken her permission before printing this. Freny, like the creator and nurturer of artists that she is (not to mention 'muse' to Bhownagary, Raza and Jehangir Sabavala) will believe that art is more important than its creator because it is an expression of the Bergsonian élan vital she studied in girlhood and that art belongs to no individual but to the world.

9

Adil Jussawalla and R. Raj Rao: politics of the avant garde

Adil Jussawalla started writing in the 1960s. He was influenced by T. S. Eliot and Nissim Ezekiel in diction. While abroad, he thought deeply about his condition as a once colonial subject who also happened to be homosexual. Frantz Fanon came in handy here. I give here three poems on gay bashing by Jussawalla, R. Raj Rao and myself.

Fanon's discourse in *The Wretched of the Earth* (1961), according to an introduction by Sartre, deals with the aftermath of colonial oppression and the relationships that arise between the historically oppressed and their oppressors in a postcolonial world. Fanon preaches violent revolution as the correct and indeed natural course of action for the formerly colonised to pursue in order to raise their status from the likes of beasts of burden to men. 'There is one duty to be done, and one end to achieve: to thrust out colonialism by every means in their power,' he says, and indeed 'their mad impulse to murder [their former masters] is only the expression of the natives' collective unconscious'. Fanon explains that the violence borne out of the condition of being oppressed is only a reflection of the oppressor's violence and this 'counter-violence can heal the wounds it inflicted' because it is the process of man re-creating himself. 'When his rage boils over, he rediscovers his lost innocence and comes to know himself in that he himself creates his self' — for the first time, through violence, the person who is revolting has agency and thus is able to control his own destiny.

Adil Jussawalla's poem 'Karate' is essentially a narrative of how Fanon's theory plays itself out on individual lives; however, it goes beyond the realm of colonialism into the sexual world as well. Jussawalla describes a kind of reverse sexual colonialism, by which a gay Indian man pursues a gay White man and kills him during sexual climax. Jussawalla makes no distinction between this particular White man and all White men — 'He is the same,' — an object upon which to act out revenge. 'I pad down the streets to find my enemy,' he says, portraying more than just cruising for a lay. It is as if he is a beast stalking its prey; the prey, however, is much bigger than his predator. He is both 'my big-time twin' and a 'giant.' The narrator acknowledges his 'pigmy' status and, in accordance with Fanon's dialogue, he kills precisely because of this inferior status and to reverse it. The final stanza, 'His head will flop/My hands will chop, then fold' depicts both orgasm and murder, love and violence, two different forms of fulfilment and release, both of which put the reins of control in the hands of the narrator.

The relationship in this poem is more complicated than the typical master–slave paradigm because the two characters share a common minority as well — their homosexuality. Because of this common identity there is a kind of brotherhood between them; indeed, Jussawalla even calls his enemy a 'fratricidal fox,' though the narrator is the real murderer. Fanon says, 'In order to fight against us [Europeans] the former colony must fight against itself: or, rather, the two struggles form part of a whole. In the heat of the battle, all external barriers break down…'. Indeed, in 'Karate', the narrator is not only fighting against the enemy but against himself and his sexuality. Coupled during sex, these two men are whole; the external barriers of social stratification have broken down in the heat of sex. 'The man who raises his knife against this brother thinks that he has destroyed once and for all the detested image of their degradation,' says Fanon, and indeed there is shame in their secret homosexuality, the one thing that could bring them together. 'Symbiosis of loving that must kill,' muses the narrator, invoking the strange paradox of his relationship to his enemy, his brother, his lover. Sex can be both loving and violent, which makes it the perfect weapon — it brings about a certain vulnerability that can be easily exploited. Sex is, for the narrator, about power and domination; through sex, he is able to make a slave of his enemy. Role reversal is more acceptable during sex, than in public life and through sex, the narrator is able to recreate himself on top; by killing while he is on top he guarantees that position forever.

Not only is the climactic murder in 'Karate' a form of revolt and recreation, the poetic form is as well. Fanon speaks about how after being forced to acquire the language of the colonisers, the colonised were left in a contradictory world where they were unable to completely disassociate from their oppressors because there was no other voice for them to speak through. Eventually, however, they were able to 'bend the language to new requirements… In short, the Third World finds itself and speaks to itself through his [European] voice.' Language becomes a weapon when it no longer merely echoes but is used in the creation of new ideas. Just as the oppressor's violence can turn against him, so too can his language. Thus, by creating poetry, Jussawalla not only narrates but also demonstrates a revolt against previous colonial authority and its remaining manifestations of racism.

R. Raj Rao strictly belongs to the second generation of poets. His mentor too was Ezekiel but he calls Jonathan Swift his literary ancestor. I feel it is Walt Whitman subliminally, and Allen Ginsberg more overtly. The politics seems to be shaped by Marxism made humane by Hindu traditions of *caritas* and humanistic inclusion. In the gay world, it means having a proletarian love if you are a bourgeois gay poet.

Even the elite gay is an oppressed creature. He is exploited by straight men and women and the passive gay is oppressed by active homosexual men. I have to note here also the social hatred and physical violence between elite and Dalit gays sharing the same cruising places, generally public toilets. Both Rao and I have poems about it. His is called 'Underground'.

> You stand in your stall
> and look over the wall.
> One comes up,
> seizes you by the shirt,
> demands money and bottles of beer
> for friends outside.
> As the saying goes,
> in the company of friends
> death is a nuptial feast.
>
> You want to throw loo goo on his face.
> But you give in meekly,
> handing over cash and valuables.
>
> The meek shan't inherit.
>
> You stand bereft,
> the city your headload.

The city is Bombay, the underground toilet for public cruising is at Victoria Terminus. I have a poem 'I am Tammuz', at power failure in the gay johns of Hyderabad's Public Gardens. I set the scene: 'Water flowed at toilet…' then suddenly, lights off! The heaven of lovers and pickpockets! Romance never deserts my poet persona, even in danger.

> Fly me to the moon
> To Uranus
> Anywhere but this earth
>
> Life is elsewhere!'

Your anus, indeed! Life is love for the elite, and food bought from theft for the Dalit lover of the moment. But I gloss over the class divide, which can never be breached, by the poetry of forgiveness and self-forgiveness:

> Everybody wants to eat my body
> Everybody wants to drink my soul
> Everyone is hungry for a body
> Everyone is thirsty for a soul.

The poem is by 'Adonis,' the Arabic poet from Lebanon quoted as a coda by me for my poem. The wanderers have come home as Orpheuses in a Bombay underworld for gay poets and their predators. Poetry is only another name for the politics of nay-saying to the world of the fathers.

There are two ways of getting to the gut meaning of a gay poem. Either you get into the poetic sewer and get yourself dirtied like the physical body of the Dalit sewer cleaner. Or, you stand aloof and write a gutter inspector's report. We have had too many gutter inspections passing for criticism already. I have considered three avant garde poets of 30 years ago. In another 30 years' time they would become respectable.

Bomgay (2006)

R. Raj Rao's *Bomgay* contains 20 short poems about Bombay gay life. It is organised on the Nissim Ezekiel principle of creative writing: talk about a bourgeois experience of yours and then include your friends, lovers, family, servants, etc. The organising principle of these poems is wit primarily based on linguistic puns. The language is explosive, shocking. The original reader reaction is that of revulsion (*bibhatsa* in the Sanskrit rasa theory) or at best derision or mockery. The motive is to evoke a reaction to homosexuality from the complacent bourgeois. The gay child's habit of provoking the mother. The underlying serious intent is to shake bourgeois gentility itself. Bourgeois gentility is based on genteel language. This genteel language cloaks a lot of violence with family, within social structures. By attacking this language of hypocrisy he attacks hypocrisy itself. First appearing frivolous he turns deadly serious, making us first uncomfortable and then marvel at his linguistic jétés! Genet does this; Ginsberg does this. This is not to say that Rao is Genet and Ginsberg rolled into one. But he is the only one of his kind urban gay Indian litterateurs have and to that extent he deserves notice.

Naturally, delicacy suffers, the exquisite delicacy of saying it simply and saying it straight that I prize so highly in my own poems and which the Brahmins' tolerance can encompass and digest. But then I'm accused of being too chi-chi. I make up for it by being outrageous in life (Mother Hoshang/The Fairy Queen). Result — critical neglect. Rao presents a calculated, studied sobriety. Result — he gets his way and critical acclaim One is honest in his work, dishonest in life; the other, dishonest in his work, but honest to the core in life. What do you want — literature or love? You can't have both.

Let's take a short and relatively inoffensive poem (though it left the RSS fuming):

Five Pandava bums
Screwing seven days a week
Five Pandava bums.

Now every Indian schoolboy knows that the five Pandava brothers in the epic had one wife (because their mother told them to do so). At college we learn it is called polyandry, something Moslem India mocks just as Hindu India mocks the misunderstood Moslem marriage institution of polygamy. Now if they screw seven days a week and there are five only, what happens on the other two days? That's Rao's naughty teaser. It is sophomoric humour, but deadly serious and unsettling if you are a Hindu swearing on the epics. It is these baiters of homosexuals that Rao here baits. 'Bum' is American for the English 'buttock', 'arse'. 'Bum' is 'vagabond' in English, 'loafer' in Indian English. Five loafers practicing sodomy on each other is what the Hindu heroes are, the *panch* Pandavas upholding Hindu dharma. Allied Publishers wouldn't publish him, saying, 'You write vulgarity.' Another example:

Men, sneeze like a man
He says. Sneezes are earthquakes
that bring the house down.

Is the Raj persona here Gulliver in the Lilliput of his favourite Swift. It appears to be so. But wait, it's all about a fairy sneeze. A fairy may not even sneeze fairily. Because he will 'bring the house down', meaning both cause utter hilarity but all catastrophe on the family, who will know that their son, brother, husband, uncle is a fag! He is, of course, mocking stereotypes of manhood here. Raj can be sly. And evoke a guffaw in the bargain.

The puns multiply. Our laughter becomes rictus.

Date

Meat is what you decide to do at Gaylord's
but he chickens out…
…………………………
You are left to fish
egg him on to… a meal
…………………………
Being is becoming
…………………………..
…………………………..
Your being is a threat to society
and now you must aim at becoming
a thread.

Meat, chicken, fish. Decidedly 'non-vegetarian', as they say in Tinglish (Telugu English). The puns need no explaining. It is also precisely located — at Gaylord's, the restaurant at the Ritz, Churchgate, opposite the Churchgate station loo, the venue of pick-ups. Once Pier Agnelli, the 1950s star, dined there. So did Raj Kapoor. Now it's a bit sleazy with the other R. Raj (Rao) and his ditching dates. 'Threat' becomes a 'thread'. Rao teases us with his brain teasers. What is thread? Continual becoming unspooling like a thread? The spider's thread of pre-semen at excitement that never turns into its full orgasmic end as the gay lover here was ditched at a date.

Rao knows his gay Bombay of the nostalgic 1960s. Here it is Gaylord's. The Irani hotels (chai shops), Kyani's and Bastani's, occur elsewhere. They are along the Western Railway suburban line whose latrines are gay pick-up joints. ('anal fault lines' Rao calls them in 'Underground'). A White gay loving dark meat on an Indian holiday could use Rao's work on Bombay as a gay guide to Bombay. I am told some literary gays from Britain and Canada already do. This locale is better suited to the novel where it is more fully realised as the KitKat and Mogambo bars around Rao's childhood home at Dhobi Tolao, Bombay in his *The Boyfriend* (2003).

Nissim Ezekiel went into raptures over Rao's image of 'mirrors for walls' at 'Kyani's or Bastani's/where you have fried eggs with your lover.' He liked the realised detail in a poem from real life. He could never understand my escaping into the stratosphere in every poem at the least opportunity. This fleshed out reality in a poem is the Bombay School of Indian Poetry spawned by Ezekiel with heirs as disparate as D'Souza, Shivdasani, the late Santan Rodrigues Peeradina *et al*. With the second generation is Dinyar

Godrej with whom, thank God, I can breathe in some romance! Anyway, Rao is the quintessential gay poet of gay Bombay as, say, Jussawalla could never hope to be with his intellection. Rao's poems share their spirit with the *Kala Ghoda Poems* (Kolatkar 2005).

The late Riyad Vinci Wadia filmed *Bomgay*'s six poems — 'Underground', 'Opinions', 'Lefty', 'Eneme', 'Bom Gay' and 'Friends' (1996). This is Rao's Bombay visualised by another artist from Bombay on film. In memory, 'Lefty', 'Underground' and 'Eneme' stand out because of their respective locales, viz. the Bombay University's Library at Fort in a Victorian building (on which Manisha Koirala danced also in *1942:A Love Story* [Chopra 1993]); the V. T. underground public urinal where gays cruise; and the upperclass queen's glitzy toilet where 'she' dumps the consequences of 'her' (sexual) 'Enema'. If film is a visual medium then Wadia's visuals stand out in our memory. A (young) Rahul Bose ('I'm *not* gay') fantasises being fucked on the library tables by a queeny stud, the one from 'Enema' who now gives a longed for 'enema' to Bose. We see Bose's black bum (he displays it in every film of his from Bollywood now) and the queen's white bum advancing upon it. Bose simulates that winced pain at entry which is a staple of gay pornography. Deed done, Bose turns turtle. The fantasy continues. We see two fried eggs where Bose's dark nipples should be. Food and sex linked in fantasy; the digestive tract where the sexual should be.

'Writing gets you nowhere near the nipples.' A young girl's nipples are 'fried eggs' in Bombay schoolboy slang. Enter the librarian (the venerable late Parsi J. N. Marshall). End of fun and games. It really happened during the midnight filming. A scurrying for underwear, trousers, shorts, shoes. The tell-tale eggs plopped sadly on the floor. What fun! Fatherhood — the end of sons' childhood sex fantasies.

The daylight setting is a Bombay chawl of mill-workers. R. Raj Rao playing himself in a torn *baniyan* fantasies the neighbour, the tomato seller; all Dalits like his real-life lovers. The female domestic servant fantasies him. 'Ganga', for that is her generic name, in a Bombay household wonders who will cremate Rao, who will perform *sraddha* (*pitri* bhakti) for the gay? Here is the quintessential Hindu objection to gays. They don't have sons. They can't enter Heaven after death. Son, *putra*, literally means 'one who leads (father) out of Hell' by doing ritual *pujas* for the father's soul's benefit. The Rao persona's female domestic wonders if the Bombay Municipality will cremate him. Lightly does Rao articulate the deathly fears of India's gays.

Family members from abroad in a gay household become 'sex-tourists', the gay their 'postcolonial pimp'. He takes his gay cousins (it runs in the family) on a sex tour, the gay loos (Dadar), the gay bars (Gokul, Voodoo), the phallic symbols (not the university clock tower but the club steeple at the now defunct Apsara theatre at Grant Road).

Neighbours ask you, if you're gay, to secrete their 1970 copies of *Debonair*. Really! And then you have to secrete *their* sex fantasies about unreal erections with unreal neighbourhood woman (not their wives)!

Having done so much damage already, Rao gets bolder in the, 'Temple'. Here, in a *darshan* queue ('separate for men and women'), Rao runs into gays who paw him with 10 arms like Durga herself (it *is* a Bengali temple!). May the gods forgive him. But the gay gods are mightily pleased as they are invoked in the house of Brahma, Shiva, Vishnu. So from pornography our gay poet ventures into blasphemy. Let's see how much I can bait the bourgeoisie, how much I can get away with!

The last poem is 'Smegma'. It is no after-dinner conversation piece. Rao plays with deadly puns again. If 'Smegma' is popularly known as 'head-cheese' then it should be spread on a toast and eaten at breakfast, at least in gay linguistic fantasy. It is the most repulsive of poems but Raj is at his old trick of tearing the veils of linguistic gentility and we have to applaud him for it.

What stays with you is the menace of violence: elite gays being beaten up by Dalit male prostitutes for a watch in the gay johns in the Wadia filming of the images in 'Underground', the linguistic violence of 'Smegma'. The smell sticks in your nostrils.

10
Agha Shahid Ali's gay nation

Agha Shahid Ali is the most gifted poet of his generation, gay or straight. It is noteworthy that his was the only name mentioned among poets by Salman Rushdie in the *New Yorker* article on post-independence writing. Since Ali is an intensely private person (he has rebuffed several attempts at friendship on my part), I will concentrate on an analysis of the gay subtext in his *Poetry Review*, vol. 83 (1), Spring 1993 poem on Kashmir titled 'The Country Without a Post Office' dedicated to the gay American poet James Merrill which begins with a Hopkins epigraph:

> ...letters sent
> To dearest him that lives alas! away.

I would pick the points and put the exclamation mark before 'alas' after 'lives' to make the line read:

> ...letters sent
> To dearest him that lives! Alas away.

For the burden of the poem is a love letter to a Kashmiri lover who might be dead in the insurrection whom the poet hopes against hope is alive.

Kashmir is the background of so many of our dreams and nightmares. The 1960s Eastman colour Hindi film was shot in Kashmir. (With the civil war on in Kashmir, the film locales have moved to Switzerland.) Kashmir is now a nightmare landscape:

> And today a 14 year old boy
> was killed in Kashmir for nothing

I wrote in 1989. It is 2008 today.

Kashmir is the land where the 'Shahed' (the witness) was born. He bears testimony to his heritage, his birthright, his nation. Living as he does in the USA, he returns each summer to Kashmir like his poem's protagonist, there to find charred ruins of a lost home, a lost childhood, a lost nation and to resurrect them in memory and words. His poem on his Kashmiri grandmother pulling poems out of the air ('Dacca Gauzes') is well known. (Ali grew up knowing Begum Akhtar and Faiz; his grandmother quoted Hafez, Ghalib and Milton with equal fluency.) So this, again, is the gay poet's apprenticeship in the harem or the zenana, the veiled life, the veiled utterance being then or later no stronger to him.

Ali's passion is the passion of a Majnun, a lover of the Urdu love lyric. He blends this passion with the dispassionate eye of an Emily Dickinson. (He now lives in Amherst and is writing a cycle of poems in the style of Dickinson, his heroine.) 'Tell it but tell it at a slant.'

The poem's objective correlative (Ali wrote a doctoral thesis on Eliot's criticism) is the Kashmir paisley, an almond which then becomes the enslaved country's new currency, a stamp of its freedom from oppressors, political and of the spirit. Because war is a prohibition on love. Death is the end of all relationships. Or is it?

'When the meuzzin died, the city was robbed of every call.' Call: calling, love call, the call to prayer, the call of the dead to the living. Hence:

Now each night in the minaret
I lead myself, guide, mad keeper, up the steps
I throw paisleys to clouds.

For the paisley, taken over by Bond Street designers as a mere decorative motif, is originally a Sufi emblem of the cypress tree bent in the wind, symbolic of the Sufi bowing to God's will in which submission is a triumph of the human spirit. The homosexual Hopkins, a tormented Jesuit, does not preface the poem for nothing. The poem ends:

Send your cries to me, live, if only in this way
Be pitiless, lost letters, you whom I could not save.

The reconnection in words is not only with a lost lover but a lost nationhood. The poet is a homeless man longing for a home. The ending is moving yet resolute. He is defeated but not for want of trying. He is heroic but so are the lost, unsaved ones as heroic or more heroic than he is. His is the compassion of the unaccommodated man for other lost souls, of the unfulfillable lover for the lost love.

In an interview with the *Pioneer*, Delhi (16 August 1997), Ali says he does *not* feel exiled (from Kashmir) in the USA and that the best *rasgolla* of Rash Behari Street is only an affordable plane ticket away. He cites the Palestinians, among others, as truly exiled. I would like to recall here my experience in the Ballatta refugee camp outside Nablus in the West Bank.

'I too am homeless,' I began an address to a group of poetry-loving pro-testors, only to be greeted with titters. The Palestinian in a refugee camp is on a piece of terra firma labelled 'Palestine' in his heart: 'Home is a place in the heart/Without it you cannot build out of defiance or out of stone' (Brodsky). The homosexual alone is truly exiled; truly homeless.

He also says that he tells his Creative Writing class at Amherst, 'You are what you are. Obviously you can't write as Martians. So concentrate on craft.' What he means is what one is will obviously come through in one's poems.

The Politics of Translation: Agha Shahid Ali's Translations of Darwish

Edward Said praises Agha Shahid Ali as the poet of exiles. Said should know — he is both an exile and a philosopher. President Bill Clinton reads Ali in the White House on the Kashmir issue. Ali is both Kashmiri and gay. Clinton, an illegitimate kid who made it to the White House, is good to women, Blacks, gays. He has enunciated the 'Don't Ask/Don't Tell' policy for gays in the military. (That's what we were doing in Asia all the time, anyway. America's behind Asia on this one!) Clinton wants to solve the Kashmir and Palestinian issues before he leaves office. (It is the year 2000.) He fails with the Palestinians. They see through him. (He has been nearly impeached over Monica Lewinsky and wants to leave home and concentrate abroad.) Ali becomes the only Indian English poet mentioned in Salman Rushdie's must-read list of Indian English Writers in *The New Yorker*. It creates a storm in a tea cup in India in all the South Indian salons as R. K. Narayan and U. N. Ananthamurthy have been left out. Can Rushdie read Kannada, Telugu, Malayalam? Ali placidly sits translating Darwish at Amherst. His mother is still alive. (Her brain tumor death, the kind that will fell him a few years later, is still in the future.) He has lost the motherland (Kashmir) but 'he still has mother' (the famous *Deewar* (Chopra 1975) line with which the unsuccessful brother taunts the success-ful one). Mother/Motherland. Foreign parts/mistress. Said is in Columbia, away from Palestine, wrecked by cancer, protected by bodyguards against Israel. Rushdie is in hiding in England, protected by the Secret Service given by Mrs Thatcher, a Prime Minister he mocks, against the wrath of a mad Ayotollah. The mad mullah is actually very sane. Ayesha, who is insulted everyday in Shia Iran for opposition to their Shia Imam Ali, has been insulted by Rushdie. With one fatwa the Ayatolla unites Shia and Sunni (parted for 700 years) by calling Rushdie's insult 'an insult to all Islam'. They won't translate *The Satanic Verses* (1988) into Persian and Hindi. The people will know the truth then. Better just ban the book; kill the translators (the Croatian and Japanese translators *were* killed).

Literary politics, genteel snubs in eighteenth century salons, have become murderous. Gayatri Chakravorty Spivak says that translation is not an innocent activity. (Why should literature be asked to be innocent in an evil world; asked to remain profitless in a commercial world?) She deconstructs translation. To say that Ali's translation of Darwish is poetry and not gay exiles' politics is to remain naïve in a knowing world!

Ali, a Kashmiri gay, loves a poet who celebrates Palestinian male martyrs. In his own *The Country without A Post Office: Poems* (1997), Ali has hymned a mythic Kashmiri boy-lover of his who falls to the occupying Indian forces' bullets. He now can sympathise with Darwish's Palestinian male martyrs in the translated poem sequence from the Arabic of Darwish included in his own book *Rooms are Never Finished*. Yes, the revolution is never finished. All revolutionaries are brothers. All poets are brothers. If all this sounds too idealistic; it is! That's the stuff of poetry trying 'to change the world' (Shelley). The gay poet sympathises with other gay populations, fantasises loving them in the face of hate.

Why is the West messing with the East? It's doing so at least since the Crusades. They are careful not to use the word which connotes superiority. They call it 'clash of civilisations' now. Europe invaded the Middle East in the twelfth–thirteenth centuries until the Mamlukes of Egypt stopped Europe's march into Asia. These are culture wars too. Said responds to Macaulay. The Ayatollah answers Rushdie (albeit with half knowledge or no knowledge at all). Writing is a political act as is translation. The East answers the West now, with its own translations. The disparate East — Arabs and Asians — join hands and consolidate flanks in a culture war. It is all done sweetly through poetry. There is no innocent activity, including poetry, gay poetry included.

If Ali and Said are speaking on the Orient's behalf and to that extent shaming the West if not confronting it, what are they doing sitting at Harvard and Cambridge? The British Council cutely calls this 'hybridisation'. They congratulate themselves that colonialism made a new world order where they themselves became possible. But they are never neocolonials; they are all postcolonial, you see. It is as if India's history began for them in 1947.

I used to be very harsh on my colleagues who fought Indian English on behalf of Indian languages while indulging in polemics couched in the English language or an Indian version of English itself. It is only a thorn that takes out a thorn. 'Knowledge is Power' said the Prophet, meaning 'Know your enemy'. It is only from within the West, perhaps, that the West's cultural hegemony can be fought.

All this is happening behind the scenes, behind the beautiful curtain of poetry's 'beautiful words' which are never innocent. Why doesn't the poet man a barricade, get his hands dirty? Well, Said, Darwish, Ali are all exiles. That is the price of political poetry — loss of the homeland. They have only been left the power of speech and they use it. For sure, the resources of libraries of the West are larger than in the East (some of them plundered from the East in colonial times) and the Eastern intellectuals access these resources. Nothing wrong with that. It is politically savvy to do so, indeed.

Gay liberation was born at the barricades when Stonewall occurred. I say it started in India with the naked Sufi, the Green Saint Sarmad's death at Aurangzeb's hands. To theorise the revolution is also revolution. Ali's revolution is couched in poetry. Indeed, he wished to be the first poet laureate of a free Kashmir.

As a poet-translator, Ali problematises the East–West debate. Darwish's poems eulogise the Moors leaving Andalusia. How did the Moors get there? They were colonisers. There was a time when the East colonised the West: the Moors in Andalusia, the Ottoman Turks in Bulgaria. There are no heroes and villains in poetry. Everyone is compromised; even Ali himself. He had allied himself with a pro-Pakistan militant outfit. He could not declare his homosexuality. His 'Indian-ness' was compromised in some eyes. Poetry makes villains of us all (bourgeois sons becoming bohemian artists). Or, could it be the 'gay' betrayal of the mother/motherland, in the end? The last poet-kings of Andalusia and Oudh lost their states because they were too busy singing, dancing and writing poetry rather than governing.

The politics of gays is the politics of sexual love between men as opposed to war between men. 'Make love, not war' is a slogan taking on a different hue when used to separate two brawling men, say, in a gay bar. The gay poetics of translation are a politics of longing. We gay poets do not only see martyrs; we see the loss of manly life in them — of nights of love abandoned, gone unfulfilled. Loss of potential is the sadness of all wars. Simply put, we do not wish to kill men, we wish to make love to them. We are mocked and considered dangerous for that. The gay poet makes love to a young martyr through the language of an elegy.

Translation is a palimpsest: one language on another, one culture on another. Darwish talks of Andalusia; Ali translates old Andalusia into his contemporary Kashmir. Time, cultures, histories unite. Translation is an act of love, finally. Through translation by a gay poet, gay consciousness infuses history.

Kashmiri and Palestinian Exiles: Unaccommodated Sons of Man

Palestine carries an erotic charge for homosexuals. ~ Jean Genet

Gayatri Chakravorty Spivak says that a translator not only has to translate the textuality of a text but also has to free the sexuality of a text. Further, the translator uses the text being translated as a 'textile' to weave a new text. Translation becomes an act of love, which brings us to the problem of love in ethics. What are the ethics of the first world translating the third world? Are you still a third world citizen if you are successful in the West, like Agha Shahid Ali? What are the ethics of a gay reading of a 'straight' poem? If there is justice in translating everything into English, the language of the majority. Spivak reminds us that there is a 'difference between ethnic minorities in the first world and majority populations of the third'. 'The interesting literary text might be… where you do *not* learn what the majority view of majority… self-representation of a nation state might be'. Ali, an Americanised gay from India translating a Palestinian diaspora poet, would be mighty interesting. Against rhetoric, logic and silence we posit social logic, social reasonableness and disruptiveness of figuration in social practises. A gay translating a refugee doubles disruptiveness.

This is a gay reading of Ali's translation of Darwish's 'Eleven Stars over Andalusia.' It is not reductive but reinterpretative.

Arabia/Andalusia. Two countries. Two peoples. One country in another. One culture on another. Synthesis. Syncretism. Hybridisation. Then, a catastrophe. The Arabs expelled from Andalusia. Palestinians expelled from a homeland. The Moslem population of the Kashmir valley under Hindu India's yoke. Ali's exile and Darwish's. One in America, the other in Beirut. All this is history, public knowledge.

But there is a private history, a suppressed truth — Ali is gay. He is as unaccommodated by his private alienation as by the public, political exile. Which loss do you mourn? The political or the personal?

The personal is the political. 'Was Andalusia here or there? On the land or in the poem?' is how the first poem ends. The Andalusia one mourns is a public suffering for Palestine/Kashmir and a private mourning for its gay martyrs, the poet himself being not the least of them.

The third poem makes the poets' poetic lineage most explicit. 'My words of love will fall into Lorca's poems.' Darwish is a modernist martyr like Federico Garcia Lorca. But Ali is more: he is a gay poet-martyr like Lorca. Not only Granada and Republican Spain mourn Lorca but all the world's gays, and by extension, all oppressed peoples mourn the snuffing out of Lorca's young life.

The Arabs in Andalusia left behind a composite culture. So that when the East is conquered by the West, the West colonises the East. Arabs didn't colonise Spain, they gave them culture. 'I was the reconciliation of Athens and Persia, an East embracing a West.' So the confrontation of politics is replaced by a gay aesthetic of reconciliation in the fifth poem. Now 'nothing remains but translations', one epoch translated into another, one language into another, one poet into another, a defeat in politics becomes a private triumph of the artist-lover, the translator. But a single man is powerless before history. 'Our history passed me on the pavement' — the fate of the scorned gay suitor who must live out his privatest defeats in public cruising places.

And who will recite 'the peace accord'? 'O king of dying?' i.e., peace between conqueror and conquered, even in explicitly sexual terms. Man conquers woman. Gays seek a truce from the sex wars by making love to the same sex. If 'dying' here means 'orgasm' as in Donne and Shakespeare, then it is a love-in-death situation that is promised the gay artist in exile.

The seventh poem asks: Who am I after the night of the estranged? And it answers: 'Through others I once walked towards myself, and here I am losing that self, those others.' The end of life is indeed the end of art, the end of self. But in life to have a 'abnormal' you need a 'normal'; to have self, you need other. Not antagonism of politics but interdependence of gay poetics, a philosophically valid position.

The eighth poem posits today's Arab Andalusia against tomorrow's 'under Columbus' banners'. The fascism of Columbus' patrons, Isabella and Ferdinand, rid Spain of a 'different' Spain, of the Arabs. Is my gay fascism any different from historical world fascism? — the poet asks. 'In which Andalusia do I end? Here or there?' 'Old conquerors left, new conquerors arrived.' Egypt, Morocco, Syria — all lightless. The music in the guitar is water. Something ephemeral, flowing. Certainty gone, the gay poet submits to uncertainty.

The ninth poem exalts suffering. It extols 'the golden dagger that makes my heart dance'. 'Kill me then, slowly, so I may say I love you!, Gay masochism turns here into the poetry of love for foreign parts that indeed loving labour had turned into a homeland, a motherland.

The tenth poem harks from motherland to mother. It returns to the first origin in face of loss: 'I want from love only the beginning'. The Arab/Kashmir poets of exile remember themselves as the child 'who left his heart in his mother's cupboard': Are we one at beginning, or two? Plato's myth says we were one egg which split, so we go searching for our twin. The Semitic myth known to Moslems in Arabia and India states Adam was lonely, so he pulled Eve out of his rib. The gay tragedy of alienation. To heal it 'a little land will suffice for us to meet, a little land will be enough for peace'. This is a dream not only for a nation but specifically for a gay nation.

The last poem, 'Violins', plays a recorso. 'Violins weep for a homeland that might return.' 'Violins weep for Arabs leaving Andalusia/Violins weep for gypsies going to Andalusia.' We are all gay gypsies wailing for a return to Eden. Political opposites are reconciled in gay poetry.

I do not wish to impose a gay reading on complex poems. I am merely teasing out one of many suppressed meanings which is usually overlooked by straight critics. There is always a truth of the victims. Therefore, Nietzsche believes that truth is an interpretation.

Behind Ali's translation is Darwish's text. You can say Darwish 'fathers' Ali's text. The homosexual dreams of an eroticised figure of the father as a love object. Ali recognises Darwish as a 'good father' to him textually and to the Palestinians actually (Darwish being Arafat's PRO in Tripoli after the Beirut debacle in 1982). Just as we recognise the possibility of 'the good father' in ourselves, we must also recognise the possibility of 'the bad father' within ourselves (the one who denies love/sex). Ali is a 'good father' to Kashmir in espousing the Kashmir cause but a bad father to 'the enemy' India. So in textual/sexual politics of translation, the gay poet not only subverts normative heterosexuality but also plays out the political drama of love/hate relations between friends/enemies like Kashmiris, Indians, Palestinians and Israelis, Arab Andalusia and Ferdinand's and Isabella's Spain. Darwish and Ali's nationalistic poems are a cry in the name of revolution against the fathers who lost a fatherland and in the name of the mother/land.

The Mother Matrix: Pasolini, Ali, Genet

Pier Paolo Pasolini's 'Prayer to My Mother' (1962) is a verbal cardiogram of an irreversible heartbreak. Mother dead, the son articulates aloud what he dared not tell mother when she was alive; namely, what a mother means to a gay son. He so little resembles his mother, but she holds his heart. She has edged out all love, made him incapable of loving anyone else. She has foisted on him a high mission: a sexless, Platonic love for mother, so that all other human loves became 'a love of bodies without souls'. Mother alone had soul: to love her had become a gay son's religious mission. An impossible mission, really, in a real world. So that this 'lofty', 'immense', 'incurable committment' to mother became 'a bondage'. Mother was life's 'only colour'. And now she's gone. He, the son, has to live on, when really, there's no rational meaning to life without mother. I am reminded of the Iraqi mother who, during bombardment, saved her son's life by embracing him, but left him without hands or legs.

Agha Shahid Ali and the Mother Matrix

Gay poets are mother fixated though gay love is a male bonding and denotes a basic misogyny that cannot be denied. In his last book *Rooms Are Never Finished* (2003) Agha Shahid Ali uses the first part 'From Amherst to Kashmir' to mourn his mother, who died at 'Lennox Hill', the eponymous hospital of the section's epigraph.

But before the epigraph are the haunting lines that are Pasolini's 'Prayer to My Mother':

I pray you, oh, I pray: Do not hope to die.
I'm here, alone, with you, in a future April...

That is the template for all future mother poems by gay poets.

At 'Lennox Hill', his mother feels the New York City sirens are the trumpetings of elephants of the Hun conqueror, Mihiragula, invading Kashmir. They used to throw them off the cliffs just to rudely enjoy their death trumpetings and 'the green valley would be covered with ivory', the baroque poet tells us. Because, finally, what art can embellish death?

And the baroaque imagery multiplies: his mother dreams at Amherst that she is being stoned to death with diamonds; the son wants his mother to be ever young, ever in song in Kashmir when she decked him up as Krishna; he wants the entire universe to be her tomb, Paradise included. And so on. And this is in just one stanza of a five stanza poem. It ends by saying: 'My mother is my poem.'

The pathos multiplies. A baby elephant returns each year to the pit where its mother died to nudge her bones with its trunk. The horror of the Mother's death magnifies: the mother becomes the dying Kashmir.

Save the rights she gave its earth to cover her, Kashmir
has no rights.

And of course, before death, in transpositions the son had become a mother of the helpless, dying mother. So the son/daughter or son/mother wants to gather the dying mother in his/her arms. He becomes the Pieta, Christ's mother: 'How helpless was God's Mother.' He becomes the martyred Christ, martyred mortally by his mother's death. He becomes that baby elephant but he holds in his cries: 'For compared to my grief for you, what are those of Kashmir...?'

The baroque and the heroic modes continue with the story of Karbala, of Hussayn's martyrdom and his sister Zainab's story being told. Agha Shahid Ali's mother, we are told, always felt the story of Zainab as her own. And Kashmir's story is Karbala's: blood, death and doom. So the universalising continues: One person's death becomes the death of all the universe due to the intensity of love for the dead that the bereaved hold; and the poet is now Christ, now Husayn (his mother called him *bhaiya*, brother, for that was what the historic Husayn was to Zainab whom the Mother identified with). The poet suffers a martyrdom with his mother's death: Christ's story is inverted; the son lives. Or the poet is resurrected when the son dies!

But in a very neat and tricky inversion the son, just prior to the mother's burial, becomes her lover. (Oedipus triumphs this time. The entire vale echoes: 'The Beloved is dead.' Now, the Beloved Witness is the meaning of the name 'Shahid' ('Shah<u>e</u>d': witness; 'shaheed': martyr). The son dies with the mother, instead of the mother. And the book is dedicated to the father, Ashraf! 'In no one's name but hers I let the night begin,' the son ends.

So ends this opera of death in Kashmir. Nostalgia pervades the poem. Krishna reappears on a 78 rpm *bhajan*, the dark lord hiding the night: The dark son as Krishna; the dead mother hidden, as if, by a dark night. There are also Ghalib-Faiz translations.

The father has the last words. For consolation he reads the opening line of Hāfez's *Divān*:

Nothing in this World is without terrible barriers
Except love
— But only when it begins...

Let us end with Pasolini's words: 'Living a consummated Love is agonizing.' The son has triumphed as his mother's lover in death, if not in life. Incest makes cowards of us all, except in art.

Only Jean Genet comes near Pasolini and Ali in description of the mother: Genet, a prostitute's son said: 'If I find my mother's grave I'll spit on it.' She had died, orphaning him at the age of one.

Genet and Hamza's Mother

Jean Genet, in his Palestine book *Prisoner of Love* (1986), a very long book about his life, which like life itself keeps circling back upon itself finally ends with his interview with the mother of Hamza, his lover (unseen for 14 years). It is as thrilling as the recognition of Odysseus scene in Homer. Hamza, the Palestinian rebel, had indeed come to visit his mother from the Ruhr where he eked out a living as a coal miner, away from the Israeli Secret Service. She shows him the door behind the bed, from which he had escaped, never to be found again, like Rumi's Shams. Genet is a lover come back to reclaim his lover's love. But he finds himself loved by his son/lover's mother, who loved her son before he did. And she is not jealous: she shares this love for her son with her son's lover. Such is the simplicity of peasant women. She is described as a Madonna, swirls of white linen circling her head. Genet the novelist sees the son's eyes in the mother's. It is as if he has found the son. He goes away, satisfied, to his own old age and death; the staff of their old age snatched from both mother and lover. Ali the poet concentrated on his own feelings; Genet the novelist looks at his character, Hamza's mother. Who says there are no woman in gay literature? There *is* Mother!

Agha Shahid Ali and the Homo-erotic Ghazal

In his article 'Memory's Homeland: Agha Shahid Ali and the Hybrid Ghazal', Malcolm Woodland brilliantly argues that for postcolonial poets nostalgia for home is the content but the style of their English writing is 'hybrid', harking back to writing-styles of their homeland, e.g., the Urdu ghazal as in Ali's case.

> The word ghazal is of Arabic origin, and means 'talk with women' or 'talk of women'. It also means 'the cry of the gazelle'. It is a lyrical poem consisting of three to thirteen *she'r*s or couplets. Originally it used to be the initial section of a qasida called *nasib*, a kind of erotic prelude to the ode. [...]The rhyme scheme of the ghazal is aa, ba, ca, da, ea, fa, ga, etc. The she'rs are not like the stanzas of the usual poem in English which are always connected. They are semantically independent or semi-independent. Each she'r develops its own world of meaning which may or may not be connected with that of

the next. The ghazal as a form does not exist in English poetry. Probably the only well-known example is a song in James Elroy Flecker's play 'Hassan of Baghdad'.

What the couplets of the ghazal have in common with one another are the devices of meter and rhyme. (Sequeira 2008: 133–34)

The ghazal is characterised by a refrain which points to a 'return'. Woodland says this points towards the poet's desire to return home. In my 'queer' reading, I'd push this argument further: since for the queer poet 'home' means mother (cf. Bachelard 1969) the return could only mean a return to the womb. (See Ali's *Rooms Are Never Finished* (2003) where he returns home to bury his mother in Kashmir in the high ecstatic tones of the literature of his homeland.)

As background, then, here is an assortment of ghazals:

At an exhibition of Mughal miniatures, such delicate calligraphy,
Kashmir paisleys tied into the golden hair of Arabic.

(Call me Ishmael 24)

By the Hudson lies Kashmir, brought from Palestine —
It shows the piano, Bach beguiled by exiles.   (28)

Dying to be cast in saffron plaster — the Brahmin's! —
a soul (they mean the Untouchable's?) — in transit shines?   (38)

Hagar, in shards, reflects her shattered Ishmael.
Call her the desert Muslim —or Jew-of-water.   (46)

Go all the way through *jungle* from *aleph* to *zenith*
to see English, like monkeys, swung beyond English.   (68)

They ask me to tell them what 'Shahid' means: Listen, listen:
It means, 'The Beloved' in Persian, 'witness' in Arabia.   (81)

Exile, diaspora, loss, nostalgia and recovery in cultural hybridity. The play in the last couplet is on 'shahid' ('martyr' in Farsi; 'witness' in Arabic). Ali translated 'martyr' as 'beloved'.

But in the Urdu ghazal it is always the male lover that addresses (a female) beloved. The woman, the Beloved, never speaks. But Ali, a passive homosexual, is both lover and beloved. He can speak in a woman's voice.

There is an old tradition of 'Rekhti' in Lucknow. 'Rekhti' is poetry composed by men in women's voices. This way, pre-marital heterosexual love, proscribed in Islam, could be given a voice. It was only in the bawds' 19th-century Lucknow that ghazals were directly addressed by men-poets to female muses.

This female impersonation in poetry suits a passive gay poet perfectly. Urdu itself is supposed to have begun with Wali Dakkhani, in the Deccan and the language itself was called Rektha. Travelling north, around the Delhi of Amir Khussrau, it was called 'ordu' (meaning 'army camp' in Turkish).

Jameela Nishat (2000: 201–9), the Deccan Urdu poet, thinks rekhti started in the harems of the Golkonda kings who married Gujarati, Punjabi, Andhra wives and loan-words crept into the language. One blind poet, Hashmi (probably queer), was allowed to sneak into the harem and speak in a woman's voice! Jameela (without much linguistic support) needles the men critics by saying their language is women's creation.

A similar phenomenon is to be noticed in the literally thousands of Meera bhajans floating around Mathura, Dwarka, Braj. Gay American anthropologists now believe that gay sadhus wrote love-poems and passed them off apocryphally as Meera's!

In the current Bombay film-world Hindi lyrics are written by queens and mimicked by drag-queens. The lyricist Raja Mehdi Ali Khan, the gay grape-vine has it, was a queen. His women's ghazals, say, 'Apki nazaron ne samjha/Pyar ke kabil hamein' (is still sung. There is a curious link between Bollywood and Hindi-speaking gays in India, says Ruth Vanita (2003).

Agha Shahid Ali himself was the ghazal-singer Begum Akhtar's fan. His family knew her personally. Research-scholar Akshaya Rath calls Ali 'The Homecoming Queen' in relation to his Kashmir migrations from USA to bury dead lovers.

It is wickedly also rumored that Gulzar's feminine lyrics are all purloined from the filmstar Meena Kumari's diaries that she entrusted to him.

As for Shahid Ali, a post-modern, post-colonial, neo-romantic, he loads his every rift with ore. The mother-ode is exile. Edward Said (1994) characterises the intellectual as marginal, amateur, 'author of a language that tries to speak the truth to power.' Being a 'witness' has its pathos and ambiguous eloquence. Foucault reminds us that to be a witness we require 'relentless erudition', to scour alternative sources, exhume buried documents, revive forgotten histories.

❦

11

the anxiety of coming out:
Vikram Seth

A favourite book of mine written by Vikram Seth is *The Humble Administrator's Garden* (1985). He is imitating a Chinese analogue (he was a student of Chinese demography, a study he abandoned for writing). The book has a China part, an India part and a California part named after the wutong, neem and live oak trees, respectively. I think the administrator here is his mother, Justice Leila Seth. The title poem talks of Mr Wang:

> He may have got
> The means by somewhat dubious means, but now
> this is the loveliest of all gardens. What
> do scruples know of beauty anyhow.

That is a gay thought! 'What do scruples know of beauty anyhow.' Those with scruples will not know of beauty. The poet's protagonist, like the poet himself, is smug:

> He leans against a willow with a dish
> And throws a dumpling to a passing fish.

Are there no gay men in China? Thirty million unmarried men, thanks to one child norms and female foeticide. And no homosexuality? Seth is in the closet. He's not telling.

Earlier, in a poem in his book *Mappings* (1994), he's told us he's bisexual:

> Some men like Jack
> and some like Jill
> I'm glad I like
> Them both; but still
>
> In the strict ranks
> of Gay and Straight
> What is my status?
> Stray? Or Great?

~ 'Dubious'

My personal favourite in *Mappings* is 'Six Octets'. They go from 'You have the slimmest body' in Octet 1 to 'You don't love me at all' of Octet 3 to 'I will/Keep clear of you' in Octet 5 to the final 'Here are the plums. Take all you can, my friend'; ending

> These plums that we will separately eat.
> For all their sourness, they are wild and sweet

Back to the *Humble Administrator's* (1985) India: 'Neem'. The Comfortable Classes at Work and Play' shows the Seth family perhaps as smug as China's Mr Wang. But Seth is a family man, perhaps a reason he lived so long in the closet (he came out 'like Noah from the Ark after the flood', as I am wont to say!) For all that he is 'Homeless'.

> I envy those
> who have a house of their own

He longs for

> A place on the earth untenured
> To know that I may die as I have slept
> That things will not revert to a stranger's hand;
> That those I lose may keep what I have kept.

He did later share a London home with a British musician lover for 10 years, someone he dedicated *An Equal Music* (1999) to. They've since parted, but he keeps the house still.

The 'Neem' section's (Seth 1985) best poem is 'The Babur Nama'. It recounts in Babur's words the love for his friend Baburi in the poem's opening section and the father Babur's love for his son Humayun for whom he lays down his life in the poem's final section. The Baburi episode is too well-known to be recounted here but one reads it afresh and marvels at its freshness after so many centuries. (In a middle section Babur, a prose stylist, admonishes his son's letter writing style like any middle-class father.)

Seth lives in his affections. He writes an affectionate and affecting poem. Babur says of his son:

> Nothing was dearer
> Than his life save my own. I offered it.

Simple. The father dies, the ill son regains his health.

I entered the chamber where my son was lying
And circled his bed three times, saying each time,
'I take upon myself all you suffer.'
I forthwith felt myself depressed and heavy
.... He rose in perfect health.

Love-sacrifice of a father for a son. But also a father's self-castration so a son may father, so that heir may turn king.

In another sense, the Babur poem is an expatriate poem. The House of Timur were expatriates in India. 'You rule Hissar; let Kamran be in Balkh.' Seth himself was an expatriate in California.

My favourite California poem of Seth's is 'Ceasing upon the Midnight' (1985). It is Keatsian in its title but in the death wish has all of Baudelaire's 'spleen and ennui' that the fullness, comfort and complacency of California thrusts upon one. Seth wishes to die because he's so bored with comfort. Because comfort is killing him. He gets drunk, lies upon the grass as if dead, rises to write a beautiful poem. Weltschmerz. The purple poetry of the post-Romantics. But so right in its ring of Californian truths: 'The phone rings', 'Something hums/The fridge', 'The furniture of days', 'Joy, frenzy, anything/But this meandering.'

He thinks
of other moons he's seen
And creatures he has been,

Life is a game. And dying is a game. Life is a place. And death is a joke. Ah, California!

To cease upon
The midnight under the live-oak
Seems too derisory a joke.

Could gayness be a way out of boredom? Could the gay life's quickness be a way out of suburban deadness?

But Seth enjoys the cornucopia of suburban comforts. See his *The Golden Gate* (1986) for instance. I was too harsh on him once. I now see him in a mellower light.

The Golden Gate (1986)

This section will consider Vikram Seth's poetical works of the variety of forms he uses and his themes and treatment of subject matter.

The Golden Gate has not been included in Seth's *The Collected Poems* (1995), and it is often treated exclusively as a work of fiction or a novel. Nor is the confusion regarding the book's genre anything new. In an interview with *Publisher's Weekly*, Seth recounts the trouble he had trying to find a publisher for this 'novel in verse' when he sent the book to every poetry editor in America, without the aid of an agent: 'It was rejected by everyone — dozens!' And then a fiction editor took it up, someone who had received it from a friend of a friend. Suddenly, within a week, Knopf, Random House and Viking all wanted to publish it. 'Amazing' (quoted in *Contemporary Literary Criticism*, vol. 90, 1996: 356–57). This confusion continued after the book was published as well — libraries and bookstores were (and still are) unsure whether to put *The Golden Gate* in the poetry or fiction shelves. This is apart from the further problem of whether to classify it as Indian or American writing.

All confusion notwithstanding, *The Golden Gate* remains Seth's longest work in verse. It is also the book that first got him noticed as a poet and established his reputation as a technically sound versifier. I shall, therefore, devote an entire chapter to the volume in this study, and in doing so, will also attempt to discuss the book's novelistic features. I shall consider it as a species of narrative verse, so as to include in my scheme both its status as a poem and as a novel.

The book was first published in 1986 by Random House. The story is set in and around San Francisco, and it takes off when John Brown, a 26-year-old yuppie, tells his ex-girlfriend Janet Hayawaka (Jan) of his loneliness. Her diagnosis is: 'You need a lover, John, I think.' (Seth 1986: 14). Without his knowledge, she advertises on his behalf in a personals column. This, at first, angers John, but he decides to consider the responses. In this manner, he meets Elisabeth Dorati (Liz), a Stanford law graduate. The two fall swiftly in love.

The outer half of the plot involves Philip Weiss (Phil), John's college friend, who has lately given up his job in the defence labs to 'save the world', that is, to the anti-nuclear peace movement. He is also recently divorced from his WASP wife, Claire, and is raising their six-year-old son Paul alone. A party at Liz and John's housewarming provides him the opportunity of meeting Ed, Liz's troubled homosexual brother. Phil and Ed embark on a shaky romance, which ends because of Ed's inability to reconcile his Catholic faith with his sexuality. Meanwhile, Liz and John's domestic bliss is marred by conflicts involving Liz's cat Charlemagne, John's temper and lack of tolerance and (what he perceives as) Liz's flightiness.

Phil's involvement in the peace movement reaches its climax in Chapter 7, with a large demonstration outside the Defence Labs. Soon after this, John and Phil fall out when the homophobic John finds out about Phil's (former) relationship with Ed. Not long after this, John and Liz also break up. Then, in a surprising turn of events, Liz ends up marrying Phil, which further angers and alienates John. John and Jan get back into a relationship eventually, and John is becoming less embittered, when Jan dies tragically. John is left even more lonely and bereft than when we first met him.

Upon publication, *The Golden Gate* was extremely well-received by critics, reviewers and the reading public. Reviewers lauded Seth for his use of form: X. J. Kennedy called it a 'mountain of technical virtuosity' (reprinted in *Contemporary Literary Criticism*, vol. 43, 1987, 390), and renowned Movement poet and critic, D. J. Enright praised the author for 'a technical triumph unparalleled in English.' (reprinted in *ibid.*). Other critics like John Hollander praised Seth's sustained use of rhyme, while David Lehman and Allan Holinghurst praised Seth for having revitalised narrative verse meant for social criticism. Most critics were charmed by Seth's wit and humour, with Kennedy comparing him to Pope, and Thomas Disch comparing him favourably with Aleksander Pushkin. Finally, many critics were also pleased with Seth's choice of subject matter: Yuppiedom in 1980s California. Disch praised the book for being accessible to the common reader, for being entertaining about 'people like you and me' (reprinted in *Contemporary Literary Criticism*, vol. 43, 1987: 388–89). Gore Vidal even went as far as to call it 'the Great Californian Novel', as the blurb on the book's cover informs us. On the other hand, Rowena Hill (*Contemporary Literacy Crticism*, vol. 90, 1996: 347–48) found fault with the values the novel presented, as did Marjorie Perloff (*ibid.* 340–47), who also believed that Seth's emphasis on rhyme and metre was at the expense of in-depth characterisation, plot and satiric force.

The novel, it would be fair to say, created quite a stir with its release. The reason for all this attention was, of course, Seth's successful striding of two literary genres — novelistic fiction and verse. For, by our twenty-first century standards, a novel was usually assumed to be fiction in prose. Early novelistic prose writing began in the sixteenth century and the novel was established as a genre only in the eighteenth century with writers like Daniel Defoe, Samuel Richardson and Henry Fielding writing pioneering works. The history of narrative verse, on the other hand, is as old as the history of literature itself. All the earliest narratives, folklore and ballads were in verse set to music (in most cultures). The classical European epics, popular English ballads and folk songs are all in verse. The modern epics of John Milton and Dante Alighieri, and a little later, the comic epics of John Dryden, Alexander Pope and George Gordon Byron were in narrative verse. Long verse narratives continued to be written in the Victorian age too, by writers like Alfred, Lord Tennyson (1902) and Matthew Arnold (n.d.).

In the twntieth century, verse narratives have been used mainly in drama during the early decades by Thomas Hardy (1965), Christopher Fry, W.B. Yeats, Sean O' Casey, etc. There have been some long sequence poems, as for example. Ezra Pound's *Cantos* (1948) and T. S. Eliot's *Wasteland* (1922) and *Four Quartets* (1943), but the fusion of fiction and verse has been rare. Vladimir Nabokov's *Pale Fire* (1962), however, is an exception. Here, the autobiographical verse narrative (by a recently dead author) is supported by an introduction and commentary by his editor and friend. The end product has been described as a do-it-yourself detective story. Another example is *Summoned by Bells* (1960), John Betjeman's verse autobiography. It is written in blank verse and is, typically of Betjeman, hilarious.

The Golden Gate would seem to follow in the tradition of the eighteenth century comic epics by Pope, and Fielding's 'comic epic poem in prose', *Joseph Andrews* (1742). Byron's *Don Juan* (1819), a rambling mock epic poem would also be an important predecessor for Seth's work. It was also the main inspiration for Alexander Pushkin's novel in verse, *Eugene Onegin*, ([1832–33] 1977), and Pushkin is often called Russia's Byron. We shall see, a little later in this chapter, how Seth uses some of the epic and mock epic conventions, which are a throwback to these works.

The most important and direct influence on Seth's work has been the Pushkin's *Eugene Onegin*. It was first published between 1832 and 1833 and is the earliest of the great Russian classics. Seth adopted the stanza form that Pushkin specially invented for *Eugene Onegin*. In an interview, Seth recounts how he discovered and was inspired by Pushkin's great work:

> [...] I came across two different translations of the same book. *Eugene Onegin* by Pushkin. I had no particular interest in Pushkin or in *Eugene Onegin*, but I was interested in the problem of translation — that is, how two different

translations, both of which use the same metre, the same rhyme scheme, basically the same form, could represent or even claim to represent the same poem. I started comparing them stanza by stanza, but after a while I realised that I was just reading one of them; it was carrying me along, and I was reading it as I would read a novel. That was something that intrigued me, because the idea of novel in verse had at first struck me as some curious hybrid, something that would not work. Here was something that *did* work, and amused me and made me want to write something in a similar form set in my time and in a place I knew.

(Quoted in *Contemporary Authors*, vol. 127, 1989: 392)

The translation that inspired *The Golden Gate* was by Sir Charles Johnston; this appeared 1977 and was enthusiastically received. In *The Golden Gate* (1986: 102), Seth acknowledges his debt to the 'original' (translated) masterpiece:

[…] spare me if I think it best,

5.5

[…]

To stake a stanza to suggest
You spend some unfilled day of leisure
By that original spring of pleasure:
Sweet-watered, fluent, clear, light, blithe
(This homage merely pays a tithe
Of what in joy and inspiration
It gave me once and does not cease
To give me) — Pushkin's masterpiece
In Johnston's luminous translation:
Eugene Onegin: like champagne
Its effervescence stirs my brain.

This description of Pushkin's masterpiece may well be used for Seth's own 'effervescent' style.

Sir Charles Johnston, however, is not the only translator of *Eugene Onegin*. The other celebrated translation was by Vladimir Nabokov and it appeared in 1975. Nabokov eschews rhyme in his version, preferring to stick to unrhymed tetrameter lines and aspiring to a literal translation of Pushkin's meaning. Our interest is not in his translated version of *Eugene Onegin*; rather, it is in the important and thorough introductory remarks that he makes regarding the Onegin stanza and the novelistic structure of Pushkin's work, which I shall look at a little later in this chapter. These remarks would serve as a useful tool for analysing Seth's novel in verse.

The *Eugene Onegin* stanza is based loosely on the sonnet form. It is a 14 line stanza in iambic tetrameter, with a regular rhyme scheme — AbAbCCddEffEgg — with the upper-case alphabets denoting the feminine rhymes. Speaking of the movement of the stanza, Nabokov points out that that the AbAb and gg part are 'usually very conspicuous in the meaning, melody and intonation of any given stanza.' (Pushkin [1832–33] 1975, 10) Nabokov then goes on to compare the pattern of the stanza to a spinning top:

> This opening pattern (a clear-cut sonorous elegiac quatrain) and the terminal one (a couplet resembling the code of an octave or a Shakespearian sonnet) can be compared to the patterns on a painted ball or top that are visible at the beginning and at the end of the spin. The main spinning process involves CcddEffEgg where a fluent and variable phrasing blurs the contours of the lines so that they are seldom seen as clearly consisting of two couplets and a closed quatrain.
>
> (ibid.)

To take an example from Pushkin [1832–33] 1977, the fantastic opening stanza of the book looks like this:

'My uncle — high ideals inspire him;	[A]
but when past joking he fell sick,	[b]
he really forced one to admire him	[A]
and never played a shrewder trick.	[b]
Let others learn from his example!	[C]
But God, how deadly to sample	[C]
Sickroom attendance night and day	[d]
and never stir a foot away!	[d]
And the sly baseness, fit to throttle,	[E]
of entertaining the half-dead:	[f]
one smoothes the pillow down in bed.	[f]
and glumly serves the medicine bottle,	[E]
and sighs, and asks oneself all through:	[g]
'When will the devil come for you?'	[g]

(ibid.)

The AbAb quatrain and the final couplets are, as Nabokov points out, conspicuous. We can also clearly see what he means by 'the main spinning process involves...a fluent and variable phrasing [that] blurs the contours of lines....' There are two enjambments or run-on lines (6,7) and frequent caesuras (lines 6, 9, 13) that prevent the sense dividing clearly into 'two couplets and a closed quatrain.'

Seth adopts this basic brick for *The Golden Gate* and its movement remains, more or less, the same. Here is an example from the beginning of Chapter 5, where the narrator intrudes with a personal digression:

5.1

A week ago, when I finished	[A]
Writing the chapter you've just read	[b]
And with avidity undiminished	[A]
Was charting out the course ahead,	[b]
An editor — at a plush party	[C]
(Well wined, provisioned, speechy, hearty)	[C]
Hosted by (long live!) Thomas Cook	[d]
Where my Tibetan travel book	[d]
Was honored — seized my arm: "Dear fellow,	[E]
What's your next work?" "A novel..." "Great!	[f]
We hope that you, dear Mr. Seth –"	[f]
"...In verse," I added. He turned yellow.	[E]
"How marvelously quaint," he said,	[g]
And subsequently cut me dead.	[g]

(Seth 1986: 100)

We can see in this example from Seth, the aptness of Nabokov's spinning top analogy. The AbAb and gg sections stand out more clearly, while the middle spins to the epigrammatically poised end.

However, not all of Seth's stanzas would follow this basic pattern described by Nabokov. The Pushkin stanza is, as we can see, very fluid and frequent enjambments within and between stanzas make it rather difficult to divide the sense into so many couplets and quatrains. Usually, though, the last couplet is like a coda, as, for example, in the following stanza taken from the beginning of Chapter 4:

4.1

"Liz, dear, it's been lovely meeting	[A]
Your friends, and John; what a nice boy	[b]
We hope that soon..." Without completing	[A]
Her exhortation to enjoy	[b]
A copula more sacramental	[C]
(Resulting in the incidental	[d]

Production of grandchildren — three   [d]
Seems best — to dandle on her knee),   [d]
Mrs. Doprati hugs her daughter   [E]
And drives off with rheumatic care.   [f]
Liz stands and breathes the sharp night air,   [f]
While from the house keen squeals of slaughter   [E]
And wrath attest that Liquid Sheep   [g]
Have just commenced to rant and weep!   [g]

(Seth 1986: 72)

Here, the opening quatrain cannot be very conspicuous in meaning or sound, because the end of the fourth line is an enjambment, and therefore, the meaning of the quatrain is incomplete. Nor is this the only example of a run-on line in this stanza: most of the lines (1,3,4,6,7,12,13) in the stanza are run-on. There are also some caesuras within lines: in line 3, there is a full stop; there are long dashes in lines 7 and 8. All this would reinforce the argument that it is difficult to divide the sense of each individual stanza into neat quatrains and couples.

There are also, in *The Golden Gate*, several examples of enjambments between stanzas. This occurs especially during exchanges of dialogue. The following example is taken from Chapter 4; it is a conversation between John and Paul:

4.16

If John sounds blunt and acrimonious,
It's not surprising. What in Phil
Seemed more refreshing than erroneous
Behaviour once, while they were still
At college, now excites causticity.
Phil's amicable eccentricity
Unsettles John now that it's come
To rest a bit too close to home.
Or it may be that, overtaken
By his defensive doubts, he shrinks
Into a quilled attack. Phil thinks:
"John doesn't like his totems shaken.
Before I've threatened him, he fires."
By way of answer, Phil enquires:

4.17

"And your job gives you satisfaction?"
"It's fun — it's well paid — it's a new

Challenge — " "What is it, John?" Compaction
of payloads…Phil, it can't be true
That you — the whiz kid of computers,
Beloved of bosses as of tutors,
The author of that learned tract
On guidance systems — could in fact
Blow your career — and for dumb slogans."
"To save the world — what's dumb in that?
Before you blow our planet flat
With all your payloads and your bowguns,
We interfering, peace-drugged jerks
Might save your skins and jinx your works."

(Seth 1986: 80)

This sort of enjambment would be only natural in a dialogue, and we see
it again in Chapter 8, in a conversation between Phil and Ed. (Seth 1986:
Sections 8.18–8.19).

I believe that the examples quoted sufficiently illustrate the point that
the Pushkin stanza is one that makes for swift and speedy narration.
However, to counterbalance this, there are stanzas of stunning individual
beauty in the book, where the author pauses in his narration to reflect.
One such example is in Chapter 13, where Seth dedicates a stanza to Saint's
Francis, and prays to him:

13.4

Patron of your beloved city,
O San Francisco, saint of love,
Co-sufferer in searing pity
Of all our griefs, whom from above
Birds would alight on, singing feeding
Within your hands — hands pierced and bleeding
With Christ's own signs — who, stigmatised
As dupe and clown, apostrophised
The sun in its white blistering starkness
As brother, and the blistered moon
As sister, and who, blind at noon,
Opened your heart and sang in darkness —
And where it was, sowed light, look down.
Solace the sorrows of your town.

~ (ibid.: 283)

Yet, even this stanza, quiet in tone, slower moving, has frequent enjambments and cannot be divided into quatrains, couplets or an octave or

sestet. The whole stanza up to the 13th line is a single sentence. Much of its slowness is derived from the frequent caesuras, and more importantly from the catalogue of verbs. There are six clauses in this sentence, describing and movingly capturing the entire life of the saint. He invokes the saint thus, and the prayer only occurs at the end of the sonnet, and then it acquires much quiet force.

There is another difference (apart from the sense distinction of three quatrains, one couplet, and octave–sestet) between the above stanza form and other sonnets in the English language. Most English sonnets, of the Petrarchan or Elizabethan variety, have, from the time of Sidney, been written in the iambic pentameter. Indeed, much of English poetry since the early Elizabethan times has been in the iambic pentameter, so much so that it has come to be considered the standard English measure. Sidney's sonnets and Shakespeare's, Shakespeare and Milton's blank verse are all written in iambic pentameter.

Seth disagrees with what he views as the 'tyranny' of the pentameter. In Chapter 5, he has an apologia for his metre:

5.4

Why, asks a friend, attempt tetrameter?
Because it once was noble, yet
Capers before the proud pentameter,
Tyrant of English. I regret
To see this marvelous swift meter
Demean its heritage, and peter
Into mere Hudibrastic tricks,
Unapostolic knacs and knics.
But why take all this so badly?
I would not, had I world and time
To reassert themselves, but sadly
The time is not remote when I
Will not be here to wait. That's why.

~ (Seth (1986: 102)

This stanza can clearly be divided in sense into an octave and a sestet, forming a sort of Petrarchan sonnet. But that apart, it is a stanza rich in reference and allusion. By the nobility and heritage of the tetrameter, Seth is referring to the fact that the tetrameter is the English ballad metre, the hymn metre and is also called the elegiac metre. All these metres have alternating tetrameter and trimester lines (4 and 3 stresses per line; 8 and 6 syllables). Further, Seth points out in line 5, that this is a 'swift' metre, one that is suited for narration. In fact, it is the metre used for most of the old English ballads like 'The Ballad of Sir Patrick Spens.' This metre is also quite a favourite of Seth's and he uses it elsewhere too, for example, in his fables, which are written in rhyming tetrameter couplets. There is, in line 10, an echo of the opening lines of Andrew Marvell's 'To His Coy Mistress' (a poem alluded to at least once more in the book). The reference in lines 10–14 is to the twentieth century fondness for free verse, which sees rhyme, metre and reason as outdated devices in contemporary poetry. Yvor Winters would be glad to see such a defence of reason and form in a young poet like Seth.

In Seth's hands, the tetrameter line is certainly used for swift narration. As Allan Hollinghurst points out, 'the main characters [...] tirelessly fill out short lines with their conveniently monosyllabic names,. (*Contemporary Literary Criticism*, 90, 1996: vol. 338) An example of this sort has already been quoted: the conversation between John and Phil (in 4.17): "[...] What is it John?" "Compaction/of payloads... Phil it can't be true [...]" Most conversational exchanges follow this pattern. In addition there are, as pointed out earlier, several caesuras, especially in the conversational lines. These make the exchanges seem more natural, closer to normal speech with its hesitation, pauses, abruptness and short sentences. It is only occasionally that characters 'wax eloquent.'

The other major feature of the Pushkin stanza, and one that has been much employed and commented on in *The Golden Gate*, is rhyme. As mentioned earlier, the rhyme scheme of the stanza is a complex pattern of masculine and feminine rhyme: AbAbCCddEffEgg. John Bayley, in his introduction to Johnston's translation of *Eugene Onegin*, observes, 'the richness of the language in rhyme is essential to the swift, smooth movement of octosyllabics; and the comparative poverty of rhymes in English has been the despair of translators.' ([1832–33] 1977: 25). Old and Middle English were (and Low Scots still remains) far richer in rhymes as pointed out by G. S. Fraser, which is why it was easier to use a swift ballad metre in those times. Since the advent of modern English, the language has been much deprived of its rhymes, especially due to the consonant clusters at the end of the words. In Middle English, the last vowel used to be pronounced, giving a musical sound to the line. Fraser gives us examples of the present poverty of rhyme — 'God' can only rhyme with 'sod' or 'odd'; 'love' with 'dove' or 'shove'. This hardly gives us scope for great poetry in rhyme or anything more elevated than:

How off
Of God

To choose
The Jews.

John Bayley asserts that this relative poverty of rhymes is the reason that 'the decasyllabic line, or the iambic pentameter has been the standard English measure — as Dryden observed, it gives the thought more room to turn in […]' (Pushkin [1832–33] 1977: 25). Johnston's successful translation of Pushkin's masterpiece has, therefore, been hailed for its brilliant use of rhyme.

Seth, too, might disagree that English is poor in rhymes. He seems to have a natural gift for rhymed verse, which is evident not only in *The Golden Gate* but in all his works (including the poems in his novel *A Suitable Boy*.) In fact, in his 'About the Author' stanza (written in the same form), he tells us that he 'Was heard to utter/First rhymes ("cat", "mat") at age of three.' (–308). Therefore, he seems quite comfortable with his chosen form — rhyming iambic tetrameter — and does not produce too many audacious Byronic rhymes. One exception would be the following passage from Chapter 4, a digression and a protest against editorial intervention:

4.34

Now, just as things were getting tenser,
And Ed and Phil were making love,
The imperial official censor
Officious and imperious — drove
His undiscriminating panzer
Straight through the middle of my stanza.

~ (Seth 1986: 89)

The last couplet with its panzer/stanza rhyme is bound to raise a laugh. Further, as Majorie Perloff points out, he uses the name 'Cobb and Kearny' (Liz's law firm) to rhyme with 'attorney' — this is another audacious feminine rhyme.

Seth, however, does not use only end rhymes to achieve his poetic effects. He uses a variety of other rhyming devices to create an effect. For example, in the 4.34 stanza quoted above, Seth uses internal rhyme in lines 3 and 4: 'imperial and official' and 'imperious and officious.' By reversing the order of the words, he creates a balance and symmetry and prevents a mere monotonous repetition. Whereas, in another example quoted above, 13.4, the prayer to Saint Francis, Seth uses reverse rhyme in the last line: 'Solace the sorrows of your town.' Further, he uses subtle repetitions throughout the stanza with words like, 'of', 'who', 'whom', 'as'. The whole effect of the stanza is euphonious.

Seth also uses alliteration quite often in the book. One example is in Chapter 5, where Rowena is whisking Phil and Ed off for olive picking:

5.25

You'll feel much better once you've headed
My unprofessional advice,
Practical, priceless, and precise.

(1986: 112)

The main motive of these is usually momentary pleasure at discovering such repetitions and the comic effect. An exception is perhaps stanza 5.4, quoted above. Here, the repeated use of the 'r' consonant sound is not extraneous to the argument of the stanza rather, it is germane to it.

In another example quoted above, stanza 4.17, he uses assonance in the last line: 'Might save your skins — and jinx your works.' The opposition of the two phrases in which the two words occur and the assonance divide the line symmetrically in both meaning and sound. Seth also uses consonance, as for instance in stanza 7.1:

Drives back the dark a little while,
A little space, before it gutters.

~ (Seth 1986: 72)

Rhyme and metre are important in poetry because poetry is meant not only to be read, but also (as it originally was) to be spoken aloud and heard. Metre and rhyme please us with their of rhythm and of similar sounds. The above account, I believe, amply demonstrates the variety that Seth displays in his use of rhyme and shows how he uses metre to the best advantage of his narrative purposes.

Having analysed the basic structure of Seth's stanza, we need to now assert that he uses this form to tell a very contemporary, urban story. His diction (as defined by Donald's Davie and in keeping with the ideas discussed in Chapter 2) accordingly, is urbane and of his time. Seth is a well-travelled, cosmopolitan writer and one who has had an urban up-bringing. His writing, as in this case, is usually about urban concerns. Therefore, his diction is naturally urbane. It is also contemporary, in keeping with the California of the 1980s that he is writing about. Therefore, he speaks quite naturally about 'cream duvets', 'the Liquid Sheep' — a rock band, cat psychiatrists — 'psycho-kitty', Tintin comic books, and also uses jargon from law, economics and computers. His tone varies from lofty to banal to reflective, depending on the need of the moment and the immediate subject matter. For example, he is reflective, sombre and scathing by turns in the first three stanzas of Chapter 7 of *The Golden Gate*. This section is meant to preface the Lungless Labs' peace march and a serious digression and reflection by the author is only appropriate for such a sober theme. Elsewhere, in Chapter 6, where Johan and Charlemagne, the 'magnificat', clash, he is playful, even satirical and humourous. His tone is banal when describing the responses to John's ad, and it is lofty in the prayer to Saint Francis.

Seth's diction, however, especially in the early section of the novel, is not always very chaste, in the eighteenth century sense of the term, outlined in Chapter 2. In the very first chapter of *The Golden Gate*, for instance, the conversation between John and Jan over lunch seems hardly plausible:

1.22

[…] and John behaves
At last less stiffly if not sadly.
"How are the cats?" "Just fine." "And you?"
"Great." "And the sculpture?" "Yes that too."
"Your singing group?" "Oh not too badly.
But I came here to hear your song.
Now sing!" "Jan, I don't know what's wrong.

1.23

I'm young, employed, healthy, ambitious,
Sound, solvent, self-made, self-possessed.
But all my symptoms are pernicious.
The Dow-Jones of my heart's depressed.
The sunflower of my youth is wilting.
The tower of my dreams is tilting.
The zoom lens of my zest is blurred.
The drama of my life's absurd.
What is the root of my neurosis?
I jog, eat brewer's yeast each day,
And yet I felt life slip away.
I wait your sapient diagnosis.
I die! I faint! I fail! I sink!"
[…].

~ Seth (1986: 14)

It is a bit surprising, upon re-reading, to hear such echoes from Shelley in John's speech. He is, by accounts of the author and all subsequent dialogue, quite unlikely to break into 'song' on one command by Jan (or anyone). He has been delineated as a reserved man, who does not find it easy to analyse or talk about his own feelings. And one also wonders why he so quaintly calls Jan's rock band a 'singing group.'

Seth does, as the stanzas move along, rectify his carelessness with diction, and by Chapter 3, he is entirely natural with speech — the conversation here is between Phil and Paul, and Mrs. Craven joins in towards the end. Not just conversation, but descriptions also become far more credible than in the first two chapters. Here is an example of the Californian landscape as described by Seth:

3.5

Two brittle oaks in dark rigidity,
Bare-branched and canted, crown the crest.
Above the rock with swift fluidity
A scrub jay flashes to its nest
— A cyan flicker – where the greenery
Of mistletoe revives the scenery
Entangled in the generous boughs
Of its old host; the cattle browse
Along the moister gullies, scattering
As joggers, pulsing with intent,
Strive ridge-wards, hell or heaven-bent,
Stern visaged, gasping, frothing, battering
The patient earth with the curt beat
Of itchy soles and athletes' feet.

~ Seth (1986)

Diction, used in the eighteenth century sense of the word, implies a selection from the language of men. As Davie puts it, then, a good or chaste diction means a careful selection, whereas bad, loose or unchaste diction implies a careless selection. After the beginning of Chapter 3, Seth's diction remains chaste and economical. A compact syntax is natural for a poet who uses a chaste diction. Seth has a variety of syntax in this volume. This would be inevitable considering the variety such a work must embody. His syntax (again, as Davie defines it), is subjective when he embarks upon a personal digression, as in the beginning of Chapters 5 and 7. It is objective in passages describing the landscapes and changes in season. The above quoted stanza, 3.5, is such an example. His syntax is dramatic when we hear Father O' Hare's speech, and also when Seth follows the form of thought of his characters Jan (end of Chapter 1, Chapter 12), Phil (Chapter 3) and John in the following ironic soliloquy:

6.13

John looks about him with enjoyment.
What a man needs, he thinks, is health;
Well-paid, congenial employment;
A house; a modicum of wealth;
Some sunlight; coffee and the papers;
Artichoke hearts adorned with capers;
A Burberry trench coat; a Peugeot;
And in the evening, some Rameau
Or Couperin; a home-cooked dinner;
A Stilton, and a little port;
And so to a duvet. In short,
In life's brief game to be a winner
A man must have…oh yes, above
All else, of course someone to love

~ (Seth 1986: 29)

As *The Golden Gate* is narrative verse, the syntax is most often active and has a number of transitive verbs. These serve to further the action and to keep up the pace of the novel.

Seth's syntax, in all its variety, is 'authentic', in that it is subordinated to the rational framework of his story and vision in the novel. According to Davie, syntax in poetry is musical when it is used for its own sake and when it does not delineate a movement or feeling, but only gives us the 'morphology of feeling'. On the other hand, authentic syntax is one where the syntax is subordinated to the rational structure of the poem. It is used not just for its own sake, but to enhance the effect that the poet wishes to communicate.

Having looked at the form of *The Golden Gate* in terms of metre, rhyme, diction and syntax, we may now turn our attention to the structural form of the entire novel. Here, again Nabokov's remarks on Pushkin's *Eugene Onegin* might be useful as a tool in analysing *The Golden Gate*. In commenting upon the structure of *Eugene Onegin* Nabokov says, 'But it is in the distribution of the subject matter, the balance of the parts, the switchs and swerves of the narrative, the introduction of characters, the digressions, the transitions and so forth that the technique of our artist is fully revealed.' (Pushkin [1832–33] 1975: 16). This is equally applicable to *The Golden Gate*.

The main characters of *The Golden Gate* are all introduced to us by Chapter 4 (where we finally meet Ed). Some minor but important characters are introduced in Chapter 5 — the Lamonts and Rowena Craven. The first two chapters deal exclusively with John, Jan and Liz. Chapter 3 deals almost exclusively with Phil and Paul. After this, after all the characters finally meet at Liz and John's housewarming, there is a regular alternation between the main plots of the novel — Liz and John and Ed and Phil. Later on, after Chapter 11, the alternation is between Liz and Phil and John and Jan.

The novel's 13 chapters are of variable length, ranging from 36 to 57 stanzas. Chapter 7 is the 'dead centre' of the novel. It is also the climax, with the main focus being the Lungless Valley march. There is an almost perfect symmetry in the plot before and after this chapter. The plot, as it were, turns from this point (that is, all the relationships in the novel turn). Phil and Ed, the last couple to fall in love, are the first to break up (Chapter 8). John and Phil's friendship and camaraderie, already strained but still cordial in Chapter 3, is completely broken in Chapter 9. John and Liz, who fell in love in Chapter 2, whose domestic troubles were brewing in Chapter 6, face worse trouble in Chapter 9 and break up at the end of Chapter 11. Finally, John and Jan, whose friendship was the first relationship to be established in the novel in Chapter 1, fall in love again in Chapter 12. Chapter 13, with Jan's death and a hint of reconciliation in the end, brings the work full circle again.

Chapter 7 itself, though, stands apart from the rest of the novel. Seth has chosen a serious theme for his climax. He has also introduced a character, Father O' Hare, who has the longest speech in the work, and who disappears entirely after it. Seth acknowledges in his interview with *Contemporary Authors* that he was well aware of these problems. Yet, the Lungless Valley march is well-integrated into the plot and themes of the novel. The 'peace' theme is central to the character of Phil. And the march has been publicised in the previous chapter. Further, the legal repercussions of the march are seen in the subsequent chapters, till Chapter 11. It helps to bring Phil and Liz together. Yet, in and of itself, the chapter is different. We know this from Seth's opening stanzas — the most serious and reflective in the book. Seth, here, has adopted a tone of high seriousness. He does not, obviously, wish to treat this theme at all lightly and flippantly. This is evident even in his descriptions of the happy, cheerful mob that has gathered for the march.

The other themes and circumstances in the novel are echoed in various chapters. For example, John's loneliness in Chapter 1 is echoed in Jan's loneliness in Chapter 6 and John's failure to help her. In Chapter 11, we once again see John lonely and Jan, once again, coming to his rescue. John and Phil's disagreement over the Peace Movement in Chapter 6 is repeated, rather more vigorously in Chapter 9, over Phil's (former) relationship Ed. Parties also echo one another, in particular John and Liz's housewarming in Chapter 4 and Jan's party in Chapter 12. The happy mob of Chapter 7 has been anticipated in the breakfast meeting of Chapter 5. Chapters 10 and 11 have the exact same opening lines:

10.1/11.1

The clapboard church with the white steeple
On a gray, frozen day extrudes
A complement of cheerful people

~ Seth (1986: 213, 234)

The setting is the parish church of the Doratis, but the scenes are remarkably different. The purpose of these echoes, then, seems to be to juxtapose the two situations, surprise the reader and highlight the recent changes in the plot.

The transitions from one plot to another also take various forms. Nabokov lists two basic types of transitions, 'the narrational, or natural, and the authorial or rhetorical' (although, 'no rigid distinction is possible.') ([Pushkin 1832–33]1975: 18) Seth uses both kinds of transition in *The Golden Gate*. For example, Chapter 4 begins in media res, at John and Liz's housewarming. This is a natural transition, as are some of the transitions in the novel's last chapter, e.g., 13.31 and 13.5. There are also rhetorical transitions as in Chapter 3, where we first meet Phil and Paul:

3.1

As Liz and John move out of focus
Into an amorous mist, let's shift
Our lens, Dear Reader, [...]

(1986:)

The photographic, cinematic analogy is an apt one, as Seth very often 'zooms in' on his characters from a larger picture. This larger picture may be the landscape (Chapter 3), the particular setting (the church in Chapters 10 and 11) or just a reflection (as in Chapter 7).

Seth's narrator as a character is, by and large, unobtrusive. He comes in on a few occasions, and then is usually witty and funny. There is only one true personal digression. This occurs at the beginning of Chapter 5, where Seth describes a meeting with an editor (5.1, quoted above). This is followed by a subtle apologia for this work:

5.2

Professor, publisher and critic
Each voiced his doubts. I felt misplaced.
A writer is a mere arthritic
Among these muscular Gods of Taste.
As for that sad blancmange, a poet —
The world is hard; he ought to know it.
Driveling in rhyme's all very well;
The question is, does spittle sell?
Since staggering home in deep depression,
My will's gown weak. My heart is sore.
My lyre dumb. I have therefore
Convoked a morale-boosting session
With a few kind if doubtful friends
Who've asked me to explain my ends.

5.3

How do I justify this stanza?
These feminine rhymes? My wrinkled muse?
This whole passé extravaganza?
How can I, (careless of time) use
The dusty bread molds of Onegin
In the brave bakery of Reagan?
The loaves will surely fail to rise
Or else go stale before my eyes.
The truth is I can't justify it.
But as no shroud of critical terms
Can save my corpse from boring worms,
I may as well have fun and try it.
If it works, good; and if not, well,
A theory won't postpone its knell.

~ (Seth 1986: 101)

Right after this stanza, Seth presents us with an apologia for using the tetrameter (5.4), and then pays tribute to *Eugene Onegin* (5.5) (both of these are quoted above). What Seth seems to be lamenting here is not a lack of reason for his metre or rhyme (he defends it admirably later), but the lack of a 'theory' that would sell his work to a publisher and make it acceptable to the critics. He cannot and does not claim to be a postmodernist parodist or any other such theoretical phenomenon ('shroud of critical terms...won't postpone its knell'). In the process of saying this, he subtly indicts the 'publisher, professor, critic' who don't see how a novel in verse can be written at all, or at least without firm theoretical backing. It is, therefore useful to reorient oneself away from the 'theory'-based discussions of the present times to a more Augustan, eighteenth century outlook when reading Seth.

Seth's narrator first makes his presence felt at the end of Chapter 2, when he is satirically and enviously describing Liz and John's 'amorous mist'. His most self-reflexive, audacious and funny interventions in the text occur in Chapters 4 (4.3) and Chapter 11 (11.14), where he is about to launch into a flashback to explain Liz and Phil's sudden marriage:

11.4

To link this chapter of the novel
To John's departure, sketched before,
Requires a flashback. (I should grovel
At this cheap stratagem, and, more,
My bard card should be burned.) Dear Reader,
In mitigation, let me plead a
Drainage of brain. Perhaps you'll wait
Till it's recharged?... You indicate
I must continue with the story?
"...Nae man can tether time or tide;
The hour approaches Tam maun ride...."
Well, dinna fidge — I willna bore ye.
(A safe bet: if you've read till here,
You must possess an iron ear.)

- (Seth 1986: 241)

The last we hear from him, however, is in Chapter 13, where he makes a digression on 'How ugly babies are!' at the birth of Liz and Phil's son.

Seth's narrator is also omniscient. This becomes most evident in Chapter 3, where he makes clear (the absent) Claire's intentions in keeping away from her son and her reasons for leaving Phil. But earlier too, Seth describes Jan and Liz before we actually meet them, therefore demonstrating his foreknowledge of them. This is in contrast to Phil and Ed, whom we meet and discover quite naturally as events unfold.

Seth, in this long verse narrative, also uses some minor epic conventions. He begins his story with an invocation to the Muse, 'Hail Muse!' Second, there is the direct address to the reader, 'Dear Reader', which occurs several times in the work, for example, at the beginning of Chapter 1; at the beginning of Chapter 3; in Chapter 5, where Phil and Ed's lovemaking has been marred by the editorial censor; in Chapters 6 and 11, where he is recounting history and giving us a flashback. Autobiographical and personal digressions are a third type of convention for which both Byron and Pushkin, Seth's predecessors, are famous. However, compared to them, Seth's digressions are rare; he is usually too busy with his plot to digress.

The conflict between Charlemagne and John assumes proportions of a mock epic battle. This has echoes of *Henry Fielding's Joseph Andrews* (1742), where Joseph and Parson Adams, armed with cudgels, are forced to do battle with hounds. The use of cats (Charlemagne, Cuff and Link) in the novel is in the tradition of feline poetry in English literature. In fact, in 6.17, Seth recounts Charlemagne's genealogy:

6.17

[…]
In this connection it's germane
To note his psychic genealogy:
The warrior blood of Charlemagne
Brims with — a bonus for a rhymer —
The hunting spirit of Selima,
The wits of Fritz, the fierce élan
Of the exultant Pangur Ban.
The grand Tiberian Atossa
And the electric Cat Jeoffry
Are honoured in a pedigree
Long as your arm and high as Ossa.
I list these but to illustrate

The hybrid vigour of the great.

~ (Seth 1986: 131)

This stanza and its neighbours are a comic rendering of the epic tradition of recounting the warrior's ancestry and his weaponry and armour before he goes into battle. Arnold Schwarznegger, the iguana, is an exotic entry into the list of pets in English poetry.

Finally, Father O'Hare's speech, which occurs in Chapter 7, may be seen as an attempt at the traditional rhetorical, persuasive speeches common in drama and epic. For instance, Brutus and Mark Anthony's speeches in *The Tragedy of Julius Caesar* (1599), or Satan's speech in pandemonium in Book I of *Milton's Paradise Lost* (1667). In this case too, the scene for such serious rhetoric is very carefully set, the audience for the speech has been gathered, and the speech itself is lofty, direct and argumentative. It also goes on for about 19 stanzas, making it the longest speech in the book.

These conventions are, however, applied to a more or less quotidian tale. Seth fills in his story with the minutiae of everyday life: olive picking, story-telling, playing scrabble and chess, grape harvesting, a lazy Thanksgiving afternoon, domestic pets, iguanas' diets, and the landscape of San Franscisco. The book, in short, 'reeks of the human', to use Davie's illuminating phrase. It should be clear from this analysis of Seth's form that it is correct to infer that he wants to tell his tale as directly, effectively and clearly as possible. In short, this tale about ordinary everyday folk, hopes to be, and is, accessible to them. Further, Seth's themes — friendship, sexuality, love, peace, civic society and tolerance — reflect a socially conscious writer who has something morally important to communicate to his readers (without degenerating into more propaganda). The discussion about the role of the poet in society, which has been emphasised by Winters, Davie and Steele, has an important bearing on Seth's poetic practice too. Seth, here, in *The Golden Gate*, shows himself to be concerned with not only clearly communicating with his readers, but also with being morally useful to them.

Seth's novelistic vision calls for a more humane society where due respect is given to all ways of life and all forms of life. John and the computer whizzes at the Lungless Valley Labs represent the intolerance of the American society of the 1980s. On the other hand, Phil with his free-thinking ways and bisexuality is the liberal ideal. The themes of non-violence and peace are presented to us in Phil's character and his involvement with the peace movement and this theme culminates in the Lungless Valley march. Phil and Ed's brief but troubled relationship deals with the theme of homosexuality in a world that is not always very tolerant towards it. Liz and Phil's hasty marriage touches upon another theme that is a favourite with Seth — that of friendship versus love. Liz chooses to marry Phil even though she does not love him because she prefers the calmness of the friendship they share to the tempestuousness of her passion for John. She considers friendship to be a more solid and safe foundation for a relationship and domesticity. This is a choice we see very often in Seth's works. In *A Suitable Boy* (1993), for instance, Lata chooses to marry Haresh Khanna whom she likes, and not Kabir whom she passionately loves. Further, poems like 'A Little Distance' and 'A Style of Loving' also echo similar sentiments.

This said, I must voice my reservations regarding Seth's character-isation and handling of plot. As mentioned earlier, the plot turns after Chapter 7. Things, in fact, seem to take a turn for the worse, as Seth treats his characters rather brusquely. One wonders, for instance, why Ed, who is given so many passionate and troubled speeches with Phil, is completely ignored after their break-up. Or why we are never told if Phil feels anything at all about Ed, who is now his brother-in-law. Or what exactly is behind Jan's sudden change of heart towards Phil, given her early animosity to him. One also chafes a bit at the Hardyesque blows of fate delivered to John and Jan. One cannot help feeling that perhaps Seth has taken on too many characters and is stuck with a complicated plot which he doesn't quite know what to do with. Seth's characters are not, as John Bayley describes Pushkin's, ones about whom there can be only speculation but no verdict. For what, if anything, makes Seth's characters memorable? What doubts can we have about them or their natures? Seth has not really allowed them to live or breathe. He seems to constantly steer them and leaves them little autonomy to become rounded so that they may surprise the reader. They appear to be too wedded to the causes they represent: for instance, Ed is there to enlarge about the homosexuality theme. John's ultimate sorrow seems to be punishment for his intolerance, as pointed out by Rowena Hill. The tolerant, free-thinking, bisexual Phil is the happiest in the end. This too simplistic correspondence between character, cause and plot is to the detriment of the novel's credibility.

To conclude, I would like to reassert the point that Seth, in writing a novel in verse, has created a work that will be memorable for its undeniable technical brilliance, its effervescence, its many details of daily life and some individual poems in it of rare lyrical beauty, and its humour.

Suniti Namjoshi

Early Work

Suniti Namjoshi's first book, *Poems* (1967) contains 24 poems. The first one, in its entirety, reads:

The Head of the Rose
Quietly we said, "My friend, you have talent."
Left unsaid the ordinary things.
A honeysuckle cottage, chequered tablecloths.
And the feelers we put out, just as other people do.
Twisted and met with tough grace.
What creed was it we affirmed or denied?
Oh I think the Mughal emperor
Built that tomb before her death,
Seeing the black holes in the bright summer.
Was it fear or courage that kept us silent
Watching the dragonfly over the water?
Now I give you the head of the rose.

This first book of poems is dedicated to 'Ai, my grandmother' by Namjoshi, 26 at the time, freshly graduated with an MA English from Poona University and recruited by the Indian Administrative Service (IAS). Her grandmother was Laxmi Devi Naik Nimbalkar, Ranisaheb Phaltan; her father a young Maratha Royal Airforce pilot killed in a crash during World War II; her mother the beautiful, young, widowed princess of a Maratha principality. Namjoshi affirms these women and struggles to be her own woman abroad. Her desires came true. But how could she know in 1967 about that?

She wanted to be a writer. A lesbian writer in English living in London, affecting people's lives by her words rather than by administrative diktat. She addresses a foreign (woman) lover. It could be any gay first meeting (gay men go through such wordlessness, too!). She contextualises her love: 'twisted', 'met with tough grace', 'summer/dragonfly', 'Mughal tomb' (for a dead woman who bore 22 children!). Homosexuality exists within a context of man–woman marriages rejected for friendship between women. It exists in a context of home versus abroad ('honeysuckle cottage/chequered tablecloths'). It is a poem at the head of all poems in a book ahead of all her books and she calls it 'The Head of the Rose'. The rose's interior is its head, as a woman's interior is her maidenhead. (The clitoris, too, is a rose with a head.) Dragonflies live a day, or a summer. They copulate and die. What is the monument to their love? They build no Taj Mahals. Namjoshi's monument of her love for her grandmother, mother, (future) girlfriend(s) is her book of poems.

She now lives in Devon, in a thatched cottage, with a rose-briar over the garden-gate with her girlfriend. Oedipus' future was in his past. In poetry, cause and effect exchange places unlike in science. A poet is a seer.

This is Namjoshi's poem about her mother:

In English
Brocade and silk, ambergris, attar and cloves,
My oriental princess listed to the sound of the exotic.
A bullock cart trundled past the window.
An Oriental cock in russet, gold and blue
Is very male and doing nothing outside
You roll a heart-shaped 'paan' for yourself.
More local colour. Oriental princess,
How can I make these foreigners understand you are my mother?

Her mother is beautiful, the author is not; her mother is a princess, the author is not; her mother married a prince ('Oriental cock in gold and blue' [uniform] who 'does nothing outside'), the author will not. She is Suniti (in later children's fictions, Aditi) and her mother is Sarojini. The two together will translate great Gujarati poetry (again, to be published by Writers Workshop). She will fear and revere her mother. She will keep her 'secret' from her mother: how she, Suniti, was raped at five by a man-servant kept to look after her. This story will be told years later in a novel, *Goja* (2000), published in Australia; not distributed in India because her mother, now 80, still must 'never know'. 'Goja', a one-eyed, old woman-servant, is the keeper of the secret. This woman-servant's biography becomes Suniti's autobiography. Shakespeare's Richard II again, before his abdication, trial, martyrdom: 'Down, down I come like glistering Phaeton…!' Again, the last shall be first and the first shall be last, in Suniti's sexual democracy.

Who is the Indian, lesbian girl child's true mother? The answer is in the preceding poem, 'Once I Saw':

Once I saw the Ganges in the morning
And almost knew then why they called her "mother",
Those others come to Kashi to be cleansed.
We played upon the bank with bows and arrows,
We three alone, my brothers and I,
Never thinking that the throng in the temple
Was us, never guessing that the corpse
In the river was us. We played. That was all
Till the boatman ferried us over, where
The weavers lived and worked, and seeing ourselves
In the looms, we knew our kinship then.

Namjoshi, the future fabulist and parable-maker, is baptised 'poet' here. She sees herself 'in the looms', she will speak in the humble but ecstatic genre of the Sufi weaver-poet Kabir, neither Hindu nor Moslem, but both; neither of the east or the west but of both; neither man nor woman but both like Kabir himself. The baptism water is the Ganges. So she begins to speak in parable.

Parable
Seen a greater profligate?
Wasted money?
But I have wasted time.
Come to my Father's house,
The money spent.
So He gives me eternal life.
Profligate, I, say, "Here's a pickle,
How shall I spend eternity?"

The book begins 'Friend, you have talent.' What is a friend's talent? A friend's talent, ideally, is a talent for friendship. A friend's ship is friend-ship as *The Merchant of Venice* (1596–98) finds out, too late. It is not a waste to waste time over (girl) friendships instead of getting married like all good girls. What dower does a prodigal have, anyway, to get married with? The talent, of course, is poetry about friendship, a spiritual talent.

If the world is a rose, it also has a thorn. Man is a thorn in the rose bower of girlish love. There are umpteen poems upon umpteen suitors (Portia in *The Merchant of Venice*, again). And none choose the right casket because all the suitors are dolts and fools (from a young girl's point of view):

Aphrodisiac
Being wedded and bedded

And not being pig-headed
He sought the horn
Of the white unicorn
For the world is on ugly woman.

Or, again:

Courtship
There is sunshine in the garden.
There are flowers in the hall.
At your gate a lovesick beast
Is breaking down the wall.

In all truth, both the above short poems are ambivalent: they could mean either that Namjoshi is escaping men, or that she is escaping into the arms of a dream lesbian lover.

'Apology' is less ambiguous, or is it?

Apology
So I swung my arms blindly
When I groped for true shapes
And I knocked off the framed photograph
And the old China dog, and you
Were very angry with me. My dear,
I do apologize. Are you really sorry?

Here are three unambiguously male-mocking poems:

Old Friend
Two uncertain steps, you stretch out your hand
Towards the friend you had hoped to meet.
Behind the patina of his charm
And your charm, the geiger counter works
To find the heart of gold.
Your minds slide off each other
And he goes his way wondering,
'What was it I missed?'

The suitors are seeking the true casket, the heart of gold, but fall for charms and miss the magic of true interpersonal alchemy. Here is the second unambiguous failure:

Beauty and the Beast
Beauty loved the ugly beast
And thinking 'twas a prince she's wed
Waited for his shape to change
And found there were two beasts in bed.

What would Jean Cocteau say to that?
A third unambiguous failure:

The Flea-Bitten Monkey
Every night I have taken out the old cloth,
Cloth of poetry, cloth of gold.
To tell you the truth, come here,
Sir, nearer, I'll tell it in your ear.
I've a fondness for it, my bit of fur and bone,
My flea-bitten monkey.
But it must be put away.
Old friend, old skeleton, you're really a worm
And you'll eat away the rest of me
Before I'm dead. Farewell worm.

The 'cloth of poetry' is from the young W. B. Yeats:

I'll spread the cloths of Heaven
under your feet
Tread softly, because you tread on my dreams.

In the nursery, the girl only knows male-poets in Suniti's day. For women, there was the saccharine Elizabeth Barrett; 'Goblin Market' was too lesbian, with 'Laura and Lizzie' eating forbidden fruit. Maybe the flea-bitten monkey is a doll. Instead of a girl doll, Namjoshi had a male monkey doll. She must 'put him away'. If not women, for men, then poetry has to be chosen. 'But if fur and bone' could be the pubescent pudenda, the worm of sex has to be denied. Farewell worm.

Namjoshi is no fool. She is no romantic. She does not deny the world its harsh reality. She lives in a world full of policemen:

Various Reasons
A policeman? He raised his hand? So,
He said "Stop". But is that poetry?
Is that life? Now there are no policemen
In my mind, neither traffic, nor otherwise,

> Tho' of course it's natural to assume,
> But stone walls do not a prison make,
> And by upbringing and birth I'm not a citizen
> Of a police state. Not that I hate policemen
> And they don't really remind me of anything;
> But the policeman said, "Stop".
> And, my dear, they do exist.

This is Namjoshi's humorous, chatty style at its best. Serious stuff in flippant language. Quoting male role models (Waller, here) again to overturn them! A first book poet, yet see how she breaks the line and then uses enjambments to surprise and portray psychic twoness. 'By…birth I'm not a citizen' reads the broken line. Read: I'm a lesbian. I cannot be a citizen. This from the grand-daughter of the Ranisaheb Phaltan! Then the complete line comes: 'I'm not a citizen of a police state.' This is the freedom-loving house of Phaltan, like Aundh, a Poona principality that first pledged itself to Gandhi in spite of its love of British airs. But, by a second irony, a state that gives you life-imprisonment for homosexuality (it was 10 years under the British, till Nehru made it for life) is indeed a police state. (Technically lesbians are exempt because the Victorian law only punishes the penetrator!)

Now, a romantic Anais Nin will think in her insomnia that even the police in Provincetown, Massachusetts (circa 1940s) are benign. They give her an aspirin and put her to bed (alone, of course) instead of booking her for night street-walking (see Nin 1964)! No such romance for Namjoshi. Policemen do exist. So does Cain, in every heart.

Cain
Listen, my brother, variation of self
I respect the battles of a schizophrenic.
Two souls lodged in one body,
We could split the hemispheres,
Your share, my share the less.
You sit with a leaf on your lap and say,
There's world enough to explore and no time.
I suspect sophistry.
You have fixed a door
To your room that you may be
Undisturbed in your little kingdom.
Two worlds: unshared, unnatural
I come to you with the surgeon's knife.

She quotes two Biblical brothers: Cain and Abel. One slew the other. We live with the mark of Cain upon our heads. 'Am I my brother's keeper?' the Bible asks us. We shirk the responsibility. The young Lawrence Durrell had such a poem about a twin shadowing him in the twin cities of Budapest.

> I cough in my sleep in Buda
> He turns in his bed in Pest.

Namjoshi quotes Andrew Marvell's 'To a Coy Mistress' only to dismiss him: 'I suspect sophistry.' She will kill her other half and become free.

It is to be noted that Namjoshi uses a male persona throughout the book. She speaks in a male voice, not female except as a little girl. Her twin, even, is a brother not a sister. If she kills the twin brother then she can live as a realised female.

I also think that the gender lines blurred for India's female rulers, especially Maratha ones. Rani Laxmibai of Jhansi comes to mind:

> Woh khub ladi mardani
> Woh to Jhansiwali rani thi

('Bravely fought the Queen', as Mahesh Dattani translates it.) But the key Hindi word is the gendered *mardani* (*mard* = man), i.e., 'like a man'. In her next book, *More Poems* (1971) Namjoshi gives us a poem about her grandmother's sartorial habits. She wore a Maharashtrian nine yard *kashtha* saree (*Kashtha* means that the saree hem-front was lifted and tucked like a man's dhoti at the back. This made work in the kitchen or the field easier and for martial ladies it made horse-riding astride a steed possible.)

Cain and Abel are twins within Namjoshi herself. (Later in life she will take liberties and make Caliban a female in *Sycorax: New Fables and Poems* [2006]). The social self and the anti-social sexual rebel, both within one breast. So too within India's cities are two cities, — the native and the colonial. Hence Mumbai versus Bombay, Pune versus Poona; Hyderabad versus Secunderabad. Budapest is one city. Even our cities are divided. On her dirt track principality Namjoshi's mother lives with colonial bric-a-brac. She has men wooing her just as her daughter is wooed, but unlike Namjoshi she does not dismiss them:

> Being chivalrous, he ignored the stains on her dress,
> Told her politely, "You're a lovely planet.
> All your children are such good-looking youngsters,

Sure to do well." But she didn't answer
And the observer fell asleep on her breast.

Another stupid male! But for 'The Death of Old Adam', Namjoshi has great respect. This is Orlando carrying his old servant Adam, too weak to walk, onto the stage at the end of *As You Like It* (1599–1600). Is 'Adam' here, her father, the absent male, her dead progenitor whom she remembers as 'a smell of damp earth from his nostrils?' Or is it her old manservant who practiced his droit de seigneur of raping the family's daughter, leaving 'a smell of earth in (*her*) nostrils?'

> Now dirt is dead and hurt is dead
> Not getting is dead.
> There's nothing to get.
>
> ~ 'The Death of Old Adam'

One feels Namjoshi is diddled out of her patrimony like so many Hindu women; so many India's gay sons. 'Did Esau like his pottage?' the poet asks.

At the centre lives her lesbianism ('Red Flower') and her poetry ('The Unicorn'). What does she care for patrimony?

> There's a kind of beauty
> In the corpse of love, freshly picked
> And the juice still held in the petals.
> ....
> ....
> Strip the petals one by one
> Till you come to the private parts,
> ....
> ....
> See(s) infidelity only as a symptom
> Of passion............
> ... to tear the petals, "Love me / Not",
> The answer to which..........
> Is the theme.
>
> ~ 'Red Flower'

Significantly, old Adam died in a 'field of tulips'. As a student of the Metaphysical poets, Suniti should know that they read 'tulips' as 'two lips', i.e., the labia majora and the labia minora : The sexual flowers of the feminist American painter, Georgia O'Keefe.

The Unicorn
I rode the wild unicorn;

In the green light of trees,
In the dark light of night,
Past leaves and silver thorn,
In love and foul weather.
Love, will you ride with me?
But my love stayed behind,
Far away behind me,
And I rode the wild unicorn
Past love and foul weather.

~ Namjoshi (1967)

What does she mean? What is a unicorn? I speculate this poem of 10 lines in two parts is about two loves. The love of sexual (lesbian) indulgence and the love of literature (poetry). A unicorn is trapped when the lady stands against a tree to attract him. As he charges at her to gore her with his single horn, she moves away and he gets trapped by his horn in the tree. A unicorn is a symbol for Christ. It has a spiritual value. So does poetry. The unicorn/poet metaphor is transparent. The lesbian lacks a horn (a phallus, hence uses a dildo, a substitute phallus) in bed. Love is 'foul weather' even if its thorns are 'silver'. Love denied, the poet rides 'the wild unicorn (of poetry)/past love and foul weather.'

It is not as if lesbian love is without its strife. The very third poem in this first book is 'Epitaph':

How would you have us think of you
Now that you are gone?...............
....
My friend you live in twisted mazes,
In the back-slapping of the I and Not-I,
In old wounds and little shames,
Integral part of memory and mind

~ ibid.

Buddhism breaks in early here with the dialectics of 'I and Not-I'. I am both I and the not-I. Cain has a little Abel in him.

The penultimate poem is a Hindu or Buddhist giving-back-to-the-earth-what-you-took poem.

When I Die I Might Be Rich.
A lawyer might come to my stately home
....
But the things on which I had a lease-hold,
Trees, grass and blue sky;

> And those I consumed free,
> Clear water and sun, friendship and love,
> Who's to account for them? Midway
> Through my wealth, I acknowledge my debt.

'Midway' is a Dantean word. The *Inferno* (n.d.) begins :

> In the middle of my journey
> I came to a dark wood
> Where the straight way was lost
>
> ~ Dante (n. d.)

Namjoshi practices Vipasana Buddhism of the Goenka School later in life. But as of everything else, we see its glimmerings here.

The last poem is problematic. I give it in its entirety here:

Angler
> In a pool, tracing concentric circles,
> I thought a profound thought must lie
> At the centre, but only retrieved my finger.
> The pitiless search for epithets for life,
> Amusing on the way, leaves you with the carcass,
> Finger, hand and body.
>
> ~ Namjoshi (1967)

Please note that the book's last word is 'body'. Its first premise is also a (female) body in bed with another (female) body. When we see her courage we come near tears. It is not philosophy (Buddhism) but reality, learnt from the body, as in Tantric Buddhism. The finger is the axis mundi of concentric circles in water. Buddha's (or Siva's) undisseminating and firm linga is the reality of truth. Forms (maya) flow away. Siva, Buddha, the poet, truth remain firm, immutable. The finger is as in 'the moving finger writes/And having writ moves on' (*Omar Khayyam*) or as in Keats' epitaph, 'Here lies one whose name was writ on water.' But it is also Krishna's finger, which in *leela* or play lifted Mount Govardhan to shelter men and beasts from inclement weather. Gender is in flux, the truth of poetry lasts.

Later Works: The Lesbian Caliban

Emancipation should make it possible for woman to be human in the truest sense. Everything within her that craves assertion and activity should reach its fullest expression: all artificial barriers should be broken, and the road towards greater freedom cleared of every trace of centuries of submission and slavery.

~ Emma Goldman

Is there queer contribution to literary history? Is there a continuity of queer literary tradition in India? That is to say, can gay and lesbian subjects, who question, criticise, analyse and resist compulsory heterosexuality, which has been the standard norm in our societies — both in the East and the West — contribute to liberal humanism and at the same time create a canon of their own? Focusing on Suniti Namjoshi's rewritings of canonical texts — of ancient stories and myths in the form of poetry and short fiction (fables) — the present chapter seeks to analyse queer contribution to Indian literary history. It highlights the ways Namjoshi, within frameworks of class, gender, race and ethnicity, embraces the discussion of sexuality and sexual identity in Indian societies.

I

Suniti Namjoshi has consistently, at least from the publication of her *The Jackass and the Lady* (1980), attempted to depict queer lives as an alternative to the dominant model of history/literature, in which her modesty of moral obligations such as self-recognition and the genesis of her queer identity are persistently represented from a feminist perspective. Self-recognition, in Namjoshi's works, is a predisposition which comes from a critical analysis of our tradition(s) that has been male-centred and homophobic throughout the ages.

After the publication of *Feminist Fables* in 1981(co-authored with Susan Irangmar), Namjoshi's reputation as a poet and fabulist seemed to be unblemished and secured. Nevertheless, she has recently been included in some anthologies. Her first four collection of poems came out from Writers Workshop, Calcutta, and the later volumes — *The Authentic Lie* (1982) *Feminist Fables* (1981), *From the Bedside Book of Nightmares* (1984), *The Blue Donkey Fables* (1988), *Flesh and Paper*(1986) and later, *Because of India: Selected Poems and Fables* (1989) — were published abroad.

Although her three collections of fables and poems — *Feminist Fables* (1981), *From the Bedside Book of Nightmares* (1984) and *Sycorax: New Poems and Fables*(2006) — brought her critical acclaim and much popularity, particularly among feminists and lesbians, Namjoshi's high esteem seems to have been vested in her *Because of India: Selected Poems and Fables* (1989), which is, by and large, considered to be her autobiographical work.

Namjoshi was born in Bombay in 1941. She received her bachelor's and master's degrees in English Literature from the University of Pune. For a year, she taught at Fergusson College, Pune, and when she was hardly 23 years old, she was selected for the prestigious Indian Administrative Service (IAS). It was during this period, when she held the position of Assistant Collector, that she, along with her mother, translated some Marathi poetry into English. Her first collection of poems came out in 1967. She gratefully acknowledged P. Lal's help, without whose initial effort her earlier works would not have been published: '…how fortunate it was for me that P. Lal of the Writers Workshop was giving Indian poets who wrote in English a chance to get their work into print.' The 24 poems included in this collection, *Poems*, were composed between 1964 to 1966.

In 1968, Namjoshi took a study leave from the Government of India to do a Master's in Public Administration. While at the University of Missouri, she learnt 'the logic of lesbianism,' she states (Namjoshi 1989). It includes works written in four countries: India, Canada, England and the USA; the collection of poems spans 22 years — from 1967 to 1989. In the introductions to the nine collections of poems and fables anthologised in this volume, Namjoshi remarkably articulates her developments as a lesbian feminist poet, and it leads C. Vijayasree to write: 'Namjoshi is the first Indian woman writer to have openly declared her sexual choice as a lesbian…'

Namjoshi resigned from the IAS in 1969, and went to McGill University where she defended her PhD dissertation on the *Cantos* of Ezra Pound (1948). While at McGill University, she was exposed to issues like gender, ethnicity, sexuality, identity politics, cultural politics, anti-Semitism and sexual identity; furthermore, it was a period of her personal development to write poetry from 'an Asian perspective, an alien perspective, later a lesbian perspective.' Moreover, her development as a diasporic lesbian feminist finds it genesis when she was exposed to several radical movements in the West. In 1972, Namjoshi got a teaching job at Scarborough College, University of Toronto. However, she was aware of the fact that she was hired not because she was a poet, but because she had a degree and because of her academic publications. Poems written from 1972 to 1976 found their place in *The Jackass and the Lady*; they were finally published in 1980. As she emphasises, by 1980 she was a feminist and she 'revised some of her poems accordingly.' There was a quick transformation in her personality and also in her writings: 'I boldly turned "he" into "she" even though I had had "he" originally.

Namjoshi's father died in a plane crash when she was 12 years old. She records her love for her dead father in her philosophical work *The Authentic Lie* (1982). It has three sections: 'Discourse with the Dead' deals with the death of her father; 'The Assassins' examines 'gratuitous killing, whether literal or metaphorical'; and 'The Authentic Lie' presents its readers with her much explored topic 'death'. Namjoshi continuously examines 'death' in poem after poem from the publication of her first collection of poems. The dead, according to Namjoshi, go far away from the existing world of perception. Hence, it is difficult to follow the dead beyond a limit 'if one is alive'.

After a formal reading of Kate Millett and Adrienne Rich, Namjoshi published *Feminist Fables* (1981) which brought her critical acclaim as a feminist writer of difference. *The Conversations of Cow* (1985) is a discourse between Suniti, a lesbian separatist, and Bhadravati, a Brahmin lesbian cow. It explores the connections between ethnicity and sexuality. After the publication of *Feminist Fables* and *The Conversations of Cow*, Namjoshi tried rewriting Shakespeare's mature work *The Tempest* (1610-11), which has been, by and large, a central text in postcolonial studies. As is familiar to Namjoshi's readers, Caliban is a female character and she is lesbian; she can read, write and speak, though in fragments, small sentences and 'simple' English. Miranda, Prospero's daughter, is her counterpart; yet she is the 'other'. Namjoshi's collection of poems and fables *Sycorax: New Fables and Poems* (2006) is once again a reworking of Shakespeare's *The Tempest*. In Shakespeare's hand, Sycorax, the old witch, is dead by the time Prospero and his daughter reach the island. In Namjoshi, however, Sycorax returns from an exile once Prospero and the others leave the island. Sycorax is old, and she realises that death is not too far. Namjoshi thus puts forward a set of heterogeneous themes and issues in her writings and articulates her diasporic lesbian identity in the form of 'questions'. The introduction to *From the Bedside Book of Nightmares* (1984) invokes a sense of self-definition to show the queer's existence, anxieties and mental dilemma. She asks several questions regarding her own lesbian identity, which in fact possess no answers, as lesbianism is 'deviant' and uttering the word is a taboo. She writes:

> It is obvious that for some time now I had been asking the question, what was my position in a world that often seemed absurd to me? All right, I was a lesbian, a lesbian feminist. But what was a lesbian? What was her relation to other people? And what about the problem of warring egos? … I had known for some time that identity isn't only a matter of self-definition. It also depends on the identity that other people attribute to one… But the problem still

remains: as a creature, a lesbian creature, how do I deal with all other creatures who have their own identities, or perhaps their own identifications? It's apparent that the components of the core identity change from place to place and period to period. Today the main components seem to be based on gender, skin colour, and sexual choice, as well as other factors such as nationality and religion, which are more or less important in different places. Any threat to the self causes a violent reaction.

Namjoshi, however, writes back; she writes back against an established canon, a canon that is well established by 'straight narratives' (if we can call them so!); she writes poems and fables in which the 'I' is essentially linked to Namjoshi, the lesbian writer, which we shall discuss in the third part of this chapter. She addresses the contradictions in the process of self-identification — the contradictions which formulate ethnic, sexual and national identities of a queer subject. Using the fable form in several of her books, as well as inventing characters such as the dragon, lesbian Caliban, blue goat and blue donkey, she represents identity that is constantly represented, re/produced, structured, and defined. The form of writing seems to be very important in Namjoshi as she claims that the story-telling method is central to understanding Indian people and Indian society. The fables included in several volumes of her writing may be justified as Indians try to answer in the form of story-telling. Moreover, her texts expose the codes that map the queer body, destabilise the complex codes that construct queer identity, and transform everyday language to articulate hopes and aspirations of a queer subject. She, however, constructs a diasporic lesbian literary history in the process of rewriting 'Straight' literature, giving it a lesbian feminist dimension.

The present chapter reads sections *From the Bedside Book of Nightmares* (1984) and *Sycorax: New Fables and Poems* (2006) to explore Namjoshi's contributions to ethnicity, sexuality and queer history. Her much discussed *Feminist Fables* (1981) and *Because of India: Selected Poems and Fables* (1989) will be cited as examples during the course of discussion. Moreover, the biographical notes to several of her books will be taken into consideration so as to show her development as a poet and fabulist.

II

Race, gender, ethnicity, identity politics and sexual identity are some of the common issues which are constantly articulated in Namjoshi's autobiographical *Because of India: Selected Poems and Fables* (1989) and other collections of poems and fables. It is a well-established fact that in most colonial situations, the obvious marker of difference is race. Owing to the nature of her alternative status — as an immigrant in the West, as a person of colour in the Occident and as a lesbian feminist in a patriarchal society — Namjoshi opts for a reformative programme in literature by rewriting canonical literatures and thereby restructuring histories. She, however, after evaluating the real structure of the world, realises that the possibility of constructing a naturalised identity without the influence of elements like race, class, gender and ethnicity is not possible in the real world. These factors become central to categorising and framing people's identities. Therefore, the reformative programme begins in creating a mirror image of the world — in textuality — which would house and voice women, beasts, birds and such 'other' subjects. Early in her publishing career, even before migrating to the West, Namjoshi was aware of the fact that she is a coloured person; not only human beings, but also nations are emerging 'coloured' in the 'humanist universe'. She writes in *Cyclone in Pakistan* (1971 b):

Haven't you heard? They say
the nations are emerging
black, red, brown, white,
green, yellow, purple, blue,
like spinning confetti
on carnival day.

Namjoshi, in the early 1970s, at the time of the publication of *Cyclone in Pakistan*, became a promising poet. She bitterly satirised a subject's identity based on his/her race. Over-categorisation of people of colour is by and large the starting point to question the organisation of the structure of the world; however, Namjoshi was yet to start her significant project, mainly of the historical reorganisation of canonical literatures.

During the 1970s, several theories emerged in the western world, particularly in the USA, which were based on gender, race and sexuality, away from the mainstream traditional art, literature and politics. Namjoshi, being influenced by western feminism and the gay liberation movement, revised some of her earlier works and concentrated more on her diasporic lesbian identity. Writers such as Kate Millet had a strong impact on her works. Lesbianism was still taboo in the West, though. The structural enactment of these issues allowed her to experience a bitter personal transformation. The reworking on ancient fables, poems and on Shakespeare's *The Tempest* is a product of these literary and sociological movements. Accepted notions regarding subject, sex, personal space and narratives were thus violated in literature to bring the writer and the reader a sense of transformation, relief, education and, moreover, atonement and self-realisation. Namjoshi's works thus re-categorise the connections between ethnicity and sexuality. Personal facts about lesbianism and bitter enactment of a racial self in the western world provide her with a quest to explore the structure of our universe. She writes poems and fables where women, birds and beasts are her subjects.

Since the 'invention' of the AIDS crisis in the early 1980s, homosexuality has been seriously put into question. It was at this juncture that a subject's sexual desires for a person of the same sex did not question the taboo associated with it; rather, it invented a psychosexual syndrome that aroused a sense of guilt, shame, negation, and most importantly the 'phobia' associated with it. 'Death,' particularly since the invention of AIDS, has been a central theme in Namjoshi's works. The writer's role as a ritualistic 'healer' is invented and the process of healing and purification is attained through the theme of 'death,' literal and metaphorical, in literature. Namjoshi's much explored theme — the theme of 'death' — undergoes a significant transformation from *Poems* (1967), the first collection of poems to *Sycorax: New Fables and Poems* (2006), the latest one. *Poems*, seeks to find a metaphor for life in order to document a productive meaning in life, finds none, and demonstrates that 'death' is the ultimate reality. This collection tries to find ways for the 'pitiless search for epithets for life,' and it groups together works which examine the boundaries between life and death. 'Stone walls do not a prison make,' claims Namjoshi early in her career as a poet. She breaks the boundaries of family bondage and migrates to the West to search for a meaning in life. However, racism and conflicts among cultures and nations are subjects of her later works. 'Death' is used here as a metaphor that can portray and can be portrayed — as a transition — from this world to an-Other. Hence she composes the story of 'The Death of Old Adam':

> An old man died in a field of tulips,
> . . . .
> . . . .
> Now dirt is dead and hurt is dead
> Not getting is dead.
> There's nothing to get.
> Let him lie, foul old man.

The body of the old man, metaphorically the writer's body, is presented here as a site that decays and leads to 'nothingness.' What is represented

here is the work of/on the site that is literally indicative of social product-
iveness. The writer's body becomes a symbol for 'change' as his/her work
stays. The poems included in this volume raise questions of power, control,
legitimacy, and finally 'death' — the ultimate reality. Namjoshi prepares
for this day:

> Listen fellows, big poets, small poets,
> what you ought to be doing
> is practicing hard
> for the death of the world.
> When it comes
> we'll be ready,
> singing a song,
> proving nothing to one at all,
> but art was ever subjective.

'Culminations,' where the poet realises the emergence of several worlds or
nations based on races and the colour of the skin, proceeds by an appeal to
poets, big and small, to sing 'the death of the world'; Namjoshi then moves
forward preparing her own "Funeral Song":

> Let the red suns bob in the skies,
> bob and curtsy, 12 red suns,
> over my grave and the death of the world.

The theme of death in this collection of poems is examined from the perspective of a poet. As a poet, then, she declares the death of a person, her
own death, and the death of the world; only art can document the event:
Namjoshi celebrates 'death' with a song. Further, death is no mere event
of a subject's life; it is a passage from this world to another. The other
world's passage opens after the completion of this world's work, deeds
and necessities:

> Whatever the lot allotted in life
> it is important to die
> well-dressed.

The fixed boundaries and working lines in identifying people of gender,
sexual preference and ethnicity are closed with the end of people's lives
and with the 'death of the world.' A grand style of death — 'death' being
"well dressed" — is influential to the constructed structure of the universe.
This rebellious spirit of Namjoshi is found quite early in her career and its
maturity lies in creating the untold stories of Caliban and Sycorax.

In *The Authentic Lie* (1982), however, as a philosopher she mourns the death of her father, she immortalises his death through her art and proceeds to have a 'Discourse with the Dead,' where she lives in the real world of imagination; and the dead, her father, takes her to that dreary 'no-place/where loss is no loss.' The physical transformation of a dead person thus becomes:

First a live man,
Then a dead man:
Where is my father?
In the sky, a personal star,
shedding
effulgence.

The influence of her religious heritage, Hindu philosophy of death, remarkably touches this collection of poems. 'The body is gone/but the soul remains.' The world of the 'dead' probably possesses no earthly hierarchies. A discourse with the 'dead' would thus reveal her hopes and aspirations, apathy and enthusiasm, which is indicative of textually creating a universe that has no worldly pain and suffering based on identity categories. The 'living' and the 'dead' create a world far away from issues like gender and ethnicity; and finally 'death' is a passage to 'an-Other' world of poetic 'perfection'.

In her later collections of poems, Namjoshi becomes more critical while evaluating the concept of 'death'. Her writing in the later stage was deeply affected by the deaths of two of her intimate friends: Mary Meigs, the painter and writer, and Anna Mani, the physicist. Our life goes on in vain, death comes and leaves us lie like a stone, all the miseries leave the dead behind; the 'moving' world remains unaffected, though. Yet life is the only alternative to death. Namjoshi writes in 'The Death of Sycorax':

She died in the morning with the lies
still swarming, the birds still singing,
the sun still rising —
all planetary preoccupations
as per normal —
and the Imperial Powers still warring.

This collection of poems and fables, *Sycorax: New Fables and Poems* (2006), is more psychological than fictional. Namjoshi is establishing here a post-colonial history: first, by drafting Caliban's unwritten history, and second, by projecting the return of Sycorax from her exile. Sycorax is old and intelligent; she realises that death is not too far as old age is approaching. She understands the real nature of the world. Namjoshi predominantly captures her psychological ambivalence; yet as time passes on, she understands that though she has ruled and lived in the island for a long time and later has returned from her exile, nothing much is going to happen when she dies. The story of Sycorax does not end here. Namjoshi explores her secrets: 'she is lonely', 'she talks to herself', 'she is self-critical', and 'at night she turns into a witch'.

Namjoshi, therefore, puts forward a heterogeneous set of subjects, which are transgressive and of professional scholarly field. Rewriting Shakespeare's *The Tempest* centralises the critical enterprise of reclaiming the other's position, while empowering his/her desires, emotions and knowledge. Rewriting the story of a fractured colonialist power, in this context Prospero's failure to control Caliban and Miranda, is to enable or empower the reader to handle an oppositional form of reading practice; hence knowledge, which would in turn generate the idea that 'textual control can be fought with textuality.' She projects the real picture of the world: people contest for land, power, nation, race and ethnicity. The death of a person or people leaves the world unaffected; people move on with their colonising mission to occupy property and new territories. 'Snapshots of Caliban' and 'Sycorax' sustain not just as political poems, they talk a lot about our relationships — woman: woman; man: woman; and man: man. People living in our societies, though, mourn; 'mourning' lasts for a specific period. However, the death of a person or people is essential so that another may rise. Here, death is considered as a metaphor. 'When Sycorax died the island did not sink/into the ocean,' mourns Namjoshi, and adds 'mud and rubble did not, at once/dissolve in the sea.' However, in the next moment she realises its after-effect: 'The stage was left empty, till later/somebody else occupied it.' At the end of the poem Namjoshi does not philosophise 'death' but shows us how the whole world contests for power and position, and moves on with its mission of 'occupying' territories.

As indicated in *Because of India: Selected Poems and Fables* (1989), Namjoshi tries to develop a form of rewriting histories and literatures, first, as a diasporic subject, from an 'Asian perspective'; second, as an immigrant, from an 'alien perspective'; and third, as a sexualised person, from a 'lesbian perspective'. She tries to deconstruct the male-centred spaces and sites, both in the West and the East, the West for being a permanent site for racial encounter; and the East, particularly India, for being a site for normative male Hindu discourse. She tries her hand on these sites, challenging gender, race and sexuality. The historiography of literatures in general, and Indian literature in particular, has been dominated by male writers — in pre-colonialist, colonialist and neocolonialist (post-independent) phases of history. They are the historical products of our male-centred society, portraying male psychology and enslaving female psychology as the 'other' of the former. The proposition that thus Namjoshi puts forward is not why 'the other' categories — women, lesbians, birds, beasts — are constructed, structured or repressed, but she moves her hands in the creation of a new world order, a new space, by snatching power, and thereby creating a new world of women, lesbians, beasts and birds which would in turn be a 'mirror image of the humanist universe,' with women at the centre. Literary historiography needs to be reconstructed, restructured and rewritten to enhance the identity construction movement of the 'other'. Her vision to reconstruct the literary canon and the restructure of the new world is motivated by a sense of self-freedom for the 'oppressed'. Harveen S. Mann thus writes:

> As Namjoshi crosses or erases borders — national, cultural, gender, and narratological — and proffers a transgressive, even subversive, commentary on mainstream traditions both Eastern and Western, she unsettles much on both sides. Failing — here constructed as positive — to achieve any idealised sense of belonging to one (essentialised) culture, nation, or group, or, conversely, to arrive at (an even more problematic) 'universal' state, Namjoshi occupies instead a "third space," an interstitial location between nations and cultures, as theorised by Homi Bhabha….

Laura E. Donaldson (1992) for a womanish reading of Jane Eyre (1847), exposes the 'Miranda Complex' and 'Prospero Complex.' The reading indicates, in principle, how Prospero's role as the colonial master is destablilised by Caliban's 'disastrous rehearsals of enforced heterosexuality' — the attempted rape — a phrase Donaldson quotes from Jeffner Allen's *Lesbian Philosophy: Explorations* (1986). The Miranda Complex is thus upset not only by Prospero, the colonial master, but also by Caliban, though black and a slave, an embodiment of patriarchal artistry. Donaldson observes: 'Caliban's over determined participation in imperialism and masculinism as both victim and victimizer radically questions any construction of him as a homogenous colonized Other of the Prospero Complex.' Caliban's attempted rape, as explained in Allen's text, is by and large used as a weapon of revenge against other men. The colonial stability of the Miranda Complex and normative heterosexual discourse are sidelined in Namjoshi's 'Snapshots of Caliban.' Caliban here is portrayed as lesbian; the patriarchal self of Caliban is disintegrated. She is educated, though sometimes she speaks in fragments, and her writing is lucid. Caliban, like Miranda, maintains a journal and documents her hopes and impediments on a daily basis. Given a chance, she would learn to play chess; however, Prospero and Miranda say that it is a game meant for only two. The complexity of not understanding the 'chess culture' is though a flaw. Caliban strongly believes that she can learn how to play chess. However, she understands the island much better than the colonial master. Prospero and Miranda, at the time of their arrival, depend upon Caliban's help to understand the island better. The following is a passage from Caliban's journal:

> These barriers are nice, those are not nice. This water is fresh. That water is salt. I learnt. I learnt all that by myself, and I told it to them. They were so pleased. But one day when I said to myself, 'Miranda is nice,' and told it to her, she didn't like it. She told it to him. I was whipped afterwards.

The 'dependence' that Prospero and Miranda have, of course in the initial process of the colonial encounter, is what Octave Mannoni theorises as the 'dependence complex' in *Prospero and Caliban: The Psychology of Colonisation* (1964). By the stages of Prospero's 'knowing' and 'understanding' the island, Caliban, the native other, is tricked in its after-effect. The creation of the third space then neutralises the process of subjectivism to a significant degree in actuality. The patriarchal hostility works at one level and is neutralised at another. Moreover, though the patriarchal subjugation is more or less destabilised to a significant degree as a Caliban is female and has nothing to do with patriarchal disposition, another form of relationship interferes in the whole process of colonialism: the racial hostility between Caliban and Miranda, which conceptualises the 'Caliban Complex.' The 'heterosexual encounter' of *The Tempest* (Shakespeare 1610–11) becomes the lesbian 'love and hatred' encounter in 'Snapshots of Caliban.' The threat of rape transforms itself to 'the threat of love' and homophobia, which in turn makes the reader understand why Miranda writes: 'I hate Caliban,' and 'I also feel ashamed.'

Constructed largely from a female Caliban's and Miranda's perspectives, 'Snapshots of Caliban' more or less highlights the hegemony of Europe in the form of racial hostility between Caliban and Miranda. No wonder Namjoshi voices Miranda in the following way:

> …I've seen her gaping
> at the blue heavens, or at me,
> and I fear her dream. For there is something

> I dislike so thoroughly about Caliban:
> If she had her way, she would rule the island,
> and I will not have it.

Though one could easily argue here that Miranda and Caliban stand on the same platform resisting the Prospero Complex, it is also important to see the hostility between Miranda and Caliban largely from the perspectives of third world feminism. Gayatri Chakravorty Spivak becomes highly critical when she analyses first world feminism, and criticises first world feminists for imposing and judging third world feminism with the 'high feminist norm' of Euro-centric civilisation and culture. Critical of 'phallologocentric' historical inquiry, she charges 'bourgeois' western feminists of doing a disservice to third world feminism because of their complicity with international capitalism and thereby oppressing and exploiting women of the third world. It is from this point of view that the problem of the Caliban Complex needs to be analysed. Though both Caliban and Miranda resist the colonial master and Miranda seeks comfort in Caliban in Prospero's absence, she still remains as a subject from the first world. The concluding line of the above poem clearly indicates Caliban's ability to rule the island; it shows, in actuality, the racial gap between Caliban and Miranda. The native other is twice subjugated and is mainly confined to the racial and patriarchal power.

Miranda's psychological ambivalence of seeking comfort, whether in Prospero and Caliban, in other words in patriarchal or racial discourse, is well-explored in Miranda's journal. In the opening lines, Prospero has retired to his cell and will speak to no one. Miranda has a psychological complaint. She thinks that her dreams are 'smashed and broken,' and Caliban is responsible. In the absence of Prospero, however, she would like to tell Caliban how much she hated her; and she writes:

> Caliban, this is a hate poem.
> You are squat and ugly.
> You are not the noble
> the beautiful other,
> You are part of me.

But that's wrong, very wrong. Not what I intended to write at all. I shall cross it out.

The closing passage in this sequence unveils Prospero's understanding of the relationship between Caliban and Miranda, which is more symbolic of 'understanding of the colonised self' than the master's ability to control the other. It is even more critical of the colonial self in the process of self-realisation. In the final section, Prospero's authority over the colonised subject is beyond his control. The existing relationship, that of master and slave, is completely displaced. The final poem comes out from Prospero's mouth where he questions his own ability to control the colonised:

> I made them? Maiden and monster
> and then disdained them?
> Was there something in me
> that fed and sustained them?
> And they mine or their own?
> I dare not claim them.

The colonial self hardly holds any power once Caliban and Miranda realise their positions in the island. Highly symbolic about colonial freedom, the final poem indicates that the psychological hegemony of Europe did not end with the rebellion of Caliban. Though the whole process pipes self-freedom and self-consciousness, it also gives rise to another level of hierarchy between the coloniser and the colonised: a sense of neocolonialism. Diasporic, lesbian and postcolonial, 'Snapshots of Caliban' closes with Prospero's lament; the degradation of the colonial authority marks the end a colonial era. However, the postcolonial site is not free from neocolonialism and the markings of the superiority of the white man. The arrival of Ferdinand is probably deliberately eliminated. Namjoshi's recent collection of fables and poems, which is critical of the native's position — of Shakespeare's witch Sycorax — is *Sycorax: New Fables and Poems* (2006). Frantz Fanon reminds us in his *The Wretched of the Earth* (1961) that unless we addressed the issue of the native's survival, the anti-colonial movement/mission would be a failure. The native's 'salvation' and 'escape from the supremacy of the white man's culture' strongly depend upon addressing the native's 'roots' and his/her survival. In his 'Preface' to *The Wretched of the Earth*, Jean-Paul Sartre highlights the creation of the native intellectual: 'The European *elite* undertook to manufacture a native *elite*.' Namjoshi's second project in the sequence thus deals with the issue of Sycorax's 'survival' — her return to the island after the exile. From Sycorax's monologue we understand that Caliban, the 'native intellectual,' in Fanon's terms, leaves the island with the 'white gods' who are not recognised as gods in Sycorax's world. An oppositional form of reading practice is generated in the process of writing *Feminist Fables, From the Bedside Book of Nightmares* and *Sycorax: New Fables and Poems*. In the process of restructuring Shakespeare's *The Tempest*, Namjoshi not only upsets the existing notions of creating a postcolonial history, she also creates a history for the third world native: postcolonial, queer and diasporic. According to the literary background estimated from both Shakespeare's and Namjoshi's texts, in Shakespeare's text, Sycorax is dead by the time Prospero and Miranda arrive; and in Namjoshi's, the native Sycorax returns to the island from the exile after the so-called 'white gods' leave. The return of the native mother and her understanding of Prospero's domination over the island then ought to be a mission, in Namjoshi's 're-construction' project, which articulates the native's 'survival' — that is to say, in Fanon's voice, a political or economic reconstruction movement the postcolonial nation/culture looks forward for:

> Old women do not die easily, nor
> are their deaths timely. They make a habit
> of outliving men, so that, as I'm still here,
> I'm able to say clearly that when Prospero
> said he took over an uninhabited island
> save for Caliban and the enslaved
> Ariel, he lied.
> I LIVED ON THAT ISLAND.

The spatial disorientation of Sycorax and Prospero after the specific periods of mastery is the inability to determine their control over the island and its inhabitants. While Prospero claims it as an 'uninhabited island,' for Sycorax it was her 'property,' or at least 'as much as it was any-body else's.' After her return, however, after the period of exile, Sycorax not only claims her authority over the island, she is also able to 'fantasise.' In the absence of the other natives, Caliban and Ariel, she develops a psych-ological syndrome — here indicated as positive — of speaking to herself, which in turn becomes a mode of self-expression and self-explanation: 'Now that they've gone/I may return, and ask myself, not who/they were, but who I was and what I mourn.' The criticality of self-analysis in the form of monologue by and large becomes central to the creation of a new postcolonial history.

II

The highly personalised lesbian self, i.e., the feminist and postcolonial narrator of *Because of India: Selected Poems and Fables* (1989) and principal character in *The Conversations of Cow* (1985), in the process of creating a third world historical narrative, gets depersonalised in Snapshots of Caliban and 'Sycorax.' The transition of the narrative self from the 'personalised' narrator/speaker to the depersonalised speaker raises questions of whether Namjoshi is creating a postcolonial historicity or documenting the 'survival' of the native after the colonial period. Anyway, the personalised analysis of her lesbian identity takes the form of a lesbian Caliban to deplore any form of injustice done to the self in any given spatial location. Gender and sexuality, though, become major components in the process of creating an identity category; 'high nationalism' of the Indian subcontinent in identifying a subject's 'belonging' becomes another particle in Namjoshi's identifying her 'self' in her matured works. The diasporic elements in her works thus play a major role in identifying her position in queer Indian literature. It is in this sense that Namjoshi is articulating: 'what the colonial nations/cultures are often criticised for in postcolonial discourse' very much exists in India itself. In the previous chapters, we have discussed how gay and lesbian people are subject to judicial action in any given situation — both for the law for criminal entrapment and social acceptance — and how forming a queer identity/community can be dangerous as lesbianism is still a taboo, according to people's perception.

Namjoshi's critique of postcolonial themes works in an internal level as well. While the hegemony of Europe or America is based on a subject's class, gender and ethnicity, in India it is a person's caste, gender, sexual preference, social or political affiliation and geographical location, which in many ways Namjoshi reminds us of (1989). Identifying the diasporic lesbian 'self' with the motherland then not only puts forward questions related to 'Indianising' queer culture and community, it also upsets 'national' perception of homosexuality, needless to mention that it is a criminal act according to the code of law. It is in this sense that Namjoshi, from the diaspora, is Indianising queer community. Moreover, a sense of belonging for a diasporic lesbian subject questions the nature and mode of existence of the person. Given these conditions, Namjoshi's writing becomes seriously critical about the Indian way of understanding a subject's belonging and subjectivity based on his/her gender, sexual preference and caste. She asserts that the basic features of such a diasporic lesbian personality not only depends upon analysing her own consciousness and self-determination in the process of migration and settlement, it also gets strenghtened in creating several images of the native land that is so hostile towards its queer community.

Mann is correct in observing the significance of modern Indian nation's hostility towards its queer community as the basis of the title's irony 'In this Kind Country.' While he explores Namjoshi's attempts to fashion an alternative Indian 'nation,' we shall here examine how she is creating an alternative tradition for the 'other' groups of people housed in India. Exploring the Caliban Complex makes sense when the diaspora is taken into consideration. Caliban leaves the island with Prospero and Miranda. Whether the lesbian Caliban is accommodated in the island still remains a question. For the Indian lesbian, the West definitely seems to be a promising site for the articulation of her 'self'. Namjoshi is of the opinion that destabilising queer accommodationism is a historical error; the error needs to be rectified, mediated and harmonised. While approaching to publish *Because of India: Selected Poems and Fables*, Namjoshi collects fables and poems from her earlier publications and introduces her readers to her personal life and why the poems and fables were written. In personalising these separate collections in this book, she politicises queer identity against the normative heterosexual discourse. In leaving the prestigious IAS, migrating to the West, choosing a career of teaching and writing, she propagates a sense of understanding self-freedom and self-expression among the normative Indian communities. Moving beyond isolation and homophobia, the diasporic personal narratives, from a social constructionist standpoint, thus are put into a category in this book:

Because of India, before and after
what could we uncover?
the history not for taking:
the family not for joining:
the cause not for naming:

Though an oppositional form of reading practice is generated throughout her texts, given the stands of being a diasporic queer feminist is then not to evade 'Indianising' her poems, fables, themes, forms and methods of approaching the reader. Namjoshi is here employing an 'Indianised' way of writing canonical poems and fables. She uses a simple way of story-telling method that suits India and its formally traditional way of explaining a view, standpoint or question in the way of story-telling. Her fables are written in the way Aesop, Vishnu Sharma, the author of the *Panchatantra* (n.d.), and others write; her refusal to be a part of the normative discourse is to 'Indianise' the traditional way of thinking and understanding caste, gender and sexual preferences. Taken together, these positions of becoming a 'lesbian,' 'feminist' and 'diasporic' subject are ways to normalise the identities of the other inside the colonies. Documenting a personal historicity or proposing a change in personalised narratives is then to articulate and understand the internal multicultural selves and to Indianise them or to indicate how 'the personal, political and poetic or intellectual development is interlinked.'

13

Dinyar Godrej: his mother's son

I begin this chapter by quoting his three poems in full with the permission of the publisher since these poems are not easily available.

Desire Brings Sorrow
(for Eunice de Souza)

Cool, no colour,
flawless shell
without even the stench
of your sea
You say
desire brings sorrow
and have done away
with it, pitched
your maw upon
a distant star
and now enjoy
gutless ananda.

It is not
an easy question of preferences
for us unlike you,
not the choice
of sweet over bitter,
but a concession
that I love and lust
though terribly troublesome
are certainly not
without flavour

Under Water

I

Where are the quiet pools, flat and untroubled,
that mirror nothing?

Where are the depths, covered and shaded,
the wet beds of moss?

I have turned around a question
o my lover
till I have become a question
and memory is the noise of the sea
the crash of a wave that breaks upon me.

2

A little creeping grief
grubbing the ocean floor
heart blot of
grim regularity
searching…

little clawing crust
working under pressure
the moss — long settled — swirls

3

The land is alive with rain.

Children playing on the bank
have plunged a volley of stones
into our dull waters.

Forgotten coral uncovered
beauteous blood bloom,
the rising rush bubbles
with distant chords,
wrenched voices that reverberate.

See infant evil's rippling strength,
terror once dropped concentric grows.
The death ship passes, its bristling wake
Glistening like a row of pearls.

4

'I step out pure from my bath,' she said
'It's like a new birth.'
What was it she lost in there
that made her shine reappear?
I had to find out.

I slipped into the bath and it opened beneath me
I sank through the years to the ocean's bed
and looking up I could see no light
save the mockery of a luminous fish.

I tried speaking but my words were bubbles.
I could not rise for the world was over me.
Then I tried to give up trying
and suddenly the waters cleared.
I saw the continents moving
the world I had loved
afloat.

5

The waters bore down the sacrifice
an old man, ashen and dead.
I am sure he did not feel
the scallops kiss
or the lick of currents —
those were beyond his knowing.
He was sent this way for a purpose.
Who knows whether it was fulfilled?
Several beings fed.

6

Feel
the pull
Atlantis was childhood sinking
a precious bubble
the tug
the wreck weighted with bullion
was young love
the persistence
the poet's surrounded isles
were humanity
of memory.

7

The stone I dropped in the pool as a child,
its ripples now overwhelm me.

Walk carefully through these waters
my lover
for you are now within me.

It is the small fish that have taught me
the wisdom of fright.

On the Road to Jata Shankar
Through looming rocks the sky a jagged knife,
Underneath, trees crawled numerous millipede legs,
Between, the dirt road dipped out of sight too soon.
My mother fluttered birdlike,
Trapped in the plummeting cage of the car.
Her arms turned jelly and cold,
Her scant hair wet with sweat.
Passing swaying trees and outsised rocks
She could not bear to look, and said,
'Stop the car. I want to get out.
I am feeling very frightened.' My father,
Unsettled by her shrill despair, hotly said,
'Don't be crazy! This road is quite travelled.
You can't get out here.'
But we did.
Mum and I walked to make the trees stop.
The shapeful rocks bought comments,
Flecked oddly as they were with pastel blue,
'Mum,' I said, 'You've been here before.
You weren't frightened then.' I can't
Explain my fear,' she said and wished
She had worn her walking shoes.
The rustle of dead leaves
Caused by some small scurrying turned
Attention to the overlordship of silence and
The magnitude of the dwarfing rocks,
Each frozen tree grappling roots in subterranean battle,
Heaving stiffly under the impermanent road.
My mother couldn't bear how the sky narrowed
Miserably like some concept or
How the dark, deceptive road seemed so
Untravelled, not stretching cleanly as conscious purpose,
But going oppressively, oppressedly winding on
Like a trick of the mind she thought
She'd overgrown or just forgotten.
Something happened. Did the sky turn blood red
And the leaves crawl over her skin?
The road, perhaps, shook like an old train,

The silence filled her mind with the hollowness of
bone?

When she reached the car parked in the shade
She grew calmer, remarking that it was lucky
There had been space to turn it around.

In my gay canon I put Padamsee where Nissim Ezekiel is in the Indian poetry canon as a modern innovator, and I put Dinyar Godrej where Ranjit Hoskote is as his brilliant descendant. Eunice D'Souza, Dinyar Godrej's teacher at St Xavier's, felt insulted when a student scoffed at Indian English poets with names like Daruwalla and D'Souza. He had a point. English in India is a postcolonial language. We are postcolonial poets. The colonialists ruled by picking the minorities as their executioners (pun intended), e.g., Armenians and Zoroastrians in the Shah's Iran were pro-regime; Parsis, Christians and Jews in colonial India flourished under British patronage. Only the greatest postcolonial poets are anti-colonial, i.e., reversing the cultural damage to the nation caused by colonialism, e.g., Yeats in Ireland with his Gaelic revival and Tagore in India with his Bangla plays, poems and songs.

As already stated (quoting Foucault), the high capitalist, postindustrial, postcolonial society feminises the men (read: homosexuality) and hysterisises the woman (read: nags and fag hags) in bourgeois society. All the poets had remarkable mothers: Padamsee's mother Koulsumbai was an indomitable woman who buried her beloved son without a tear (Jean Bhownagary); Vikram Seth's mother Leila Seth, the first woman judge of the Himachal High Court, has written an autobiography (2003) detailing her son Vikram's gay life. My mother, 40 years after her death, still shadows my life. Dinyar Godrej's mother was no exception to this rule.

In his poem 'Road to Jata Shankar', Godrej tells of his child's observation of a spoilt trip to the poem's eponymous shrine by the mother's hysterical fit. She orders the father to turn around the car because the rocks on the mountainous road are oppressive to her (shades of E. M. Forster's Adela Quested from *A Passage to India* [1924]). And finally, she thanks God that there was enough space to turn around the car on the narrow road. There are echoes, subtle ones, of meanings barely discerned in this simple yet symbolic exercise of a woman's privilege to become hysterical in the poem. 'Oppressiveness', 'turn around' are symptomatic of this post-industrial disease and its cure. More importantly, it is the unspoken lesson learnt by the gay, soon-to-be-poet son that should concern us here. The gay son is imitating his mother in bed with his lovers and he should really learn *not* to imitate his mother outside bed or his lovers will flee. Father is a much put-upon, patient, hag-ridden caricature of a Parsi man.

At college, he learns to shift his incestuous 'mother love' to a more acceptable even if similar (in age) love object: his poetry teacher (Eunice D'Souza). She gives him Buddhism ('Desire Brings Sorrow') instead in her human wisdom and her teacherly decorum on seeing an incipiently gay boy. It bespeaks a human interaction all too common in the Indian classroom whose outcome is not always as sadly happy as it is in Godrej's poem.

The poet persona goes to London and dives into the gay life as a fish to water ('Under Water'). The cliché is appropriate here because the entire love act/sex act happens under water in his poems, in this case, in a shower with the two lovers bathing. But gay love has less chances of surviving than a snowball in Hell, to use a gay cliché. The lover drowns at the bottom of the pool like a stone or a dead fish. The medium of clarity, his poetic all-seeing quality, also makes human love (which entails compromises) impossible.

We never hear from Dinyar Godrej again, which is a shame.

Ian Iqbal Rashid: His Son's Mother (The Diasporic Experience)

Knowing Your Place

I. **Passage from Africa/A Pass to India**

i
I know these places awkwardly
like the bundles I take with me
that soon I hope
will float beside me constantly.

These places are sudden
with absence of metaphor.
Like the absences my parents live with:
an ebbing of fluency
a poverty of words for white
unable to dream in snow.

ii
They were sent to a place without light.
Home is *the dark continent.*
An immovable mass keeping us separate
blocking the view between our stories.

Did they leave
as I leave now
carrying papers
in case they might vanish?

iii
Vanish and merge
emerging as people we've never known, unfinished.
Like stories with disappeared endings
told by old photos and older women
bent by time and disapproval.

Stories fading
at their salt water edges
curling, crisp with hints.

iv
Stories which hold me often
whose endings
like fists are snake-tight
over-eager embraces
that open to caress me, now and again

now, mocking my obsession
this open hand of a story
its teasing misshapen fingertip of a subcontinent.

And I leave
Reading one of two epic poems
governing a struggle
that will not vanish

gripping a line
that zips open a sky of myth
exposing its soft
little boy's belly

leaving stiff vestments behind,
leaving an anger behind
with the buildings we are tunneling by with a roar

leaving for a place that knows me well
as a cell
under attack
knows its virus.

Memories

The heart is a room
Where time stands still

I go round this room
The room goes round with me
I went it to stand still

Like he and I did
In that upper balcony
It was as if we were alone
He invited me home
— But how?

There was work to do

He asked me to stay
I did not know what to say
He was too much like me
What was there for us to do?

He looked like the Hamlet
We'd read about the other day
But I did not see
How could I know
What he wanted to say

So between saying and not saying
Standing and going
Time went away

NOW

He stands still with me
In that upper balcony

There was so much to do!

'Knowing Your Place', I believe, is Rashid's single most important poem. It has all his work in quintessence. It is subtitled 'Passage from Africa/A Pass to India'. 'Africa/pass': two words in parataxis define 'apartheid' in South Africa's 'pass laws' for Blacks. His parents were sent there, he says (indentured labour for South African sugar plantations after 'abolition of slavery' by the West?). These are 'places without metaphor' (suicide for a poet) and then the passage to Canada and 'the inability' to dream in snow.

It is not a story of arrivals but departures. Not 'homecomings' or 'comings out' but flight, escape, evasion, postponement, an unending quest through generations spanning continents. Not faces, places, histories but papers, passes, passports, visa give face value to shifting identities: eastern/western, native/immigrant, gay/straight. Stories defined by a 'dark' (read: black skin) and read by the 'light' (read: western education).

The passage is through a tunnel (the Middle Passage of African slaves; blotted out histories 'with stories keeping on getting in-between', also the R. Raj Rao-like, Thom Gunn-like metaphor of sperm travelling up a rec-tum). This last image is not fanciful because two gay metaphors greet us towards the poem's end: 'The sky of myth' is ripped open like a 'boy's soft underbelly'. And the final metaphor of

leaving for a place that knows me well
as a cell
under attack
knows its virus'

The poet's persona, the 'I' in this meta-narrative, was reading 'the two epics'. Which two epics — The *Iliad* and *The Odyssey*? Or was it the *Mahabharata* and the *Ramayana*? Or was it the story of straights versus gay? Of white versus black? Or of black markets / White boyfriends where the poet persona (prostitute) is an attacked cell that knows its virus (White man's AIDS)?

The shifting struggle here is typically Canadian, as exemplified also by Shani Mootoo. What comes first: the chicken or the egg? Gay or immigrant identity? Identity politics here is sexual politics.

The boy constructs the myth, later, of the silent screen 'Elephant Boy' Sabu in *Song of Sabu* ('Subbu', really short for 'Subramaniam' from Karnataka). He is the gay pin-up immigrants mythicise and dream about. He is the torn sky of myth; his is the soft boy's underbelly, torn open like a mythic sky. (In 1970s California it was Sajid Khan, Mehboob Khan's adopted 'Son of India', that we dreamt about as Sabu.) The real Sabu's western wife said that a hundred (Indian) relatives she'd never seen suddenly materialised at his death. This is the other side of the same story: the straight White side's.

❧

14
the art of Bhupen Khakhar (1935–2005)

Surrealist Poem
It is not my mother in the garden:
It is my father coming out of the sea

And anything I say will be used against me.

Bhupen Khakhar was a Gujarati chartered accountant who, after retirement, distinguished himself as a painter and teacher at the Baroda School. The Baroda School led by Khakhar and Gulam Mohammed and Nilima Sheikh is characterised by cityscapes peopled by men and women engaged in scenes of daily living. This Indian reality is outdoors while being indoors. (We can always peep into our neighbour's houses in a crowded Indian city and in Sheikh's and Khakhar's paintings.) It seems to me the courtyards, half-open doors, roofless homes are hearts and minds opened up for inspection (Indian notions of psychological privacy too are less rigid than western ones). This reality, at once material and psychological, assumes a surreal quality when the canvasses are washed blue or green as in a Chagall; Indian themes/western techniques, e.g., the oneric vision, especially in Khakhar's Indian homosexual themes. Though trained in western techniques and languages, both Gulam Mohammed Sheikh and Bhupen Khakhar write in their native tongue, viz. Gujarati. In art, though its influence is on the wane, the Baroda School was supposed to have ushered in a new renaissance in painting in India. Khakhar and Sheikh hope also to resuscitate Gujarati letters.

When I telephoned Bhupen for a story, his remarkably childlike voice wondered in equally childlike innocence: 'Would just any story do?' The public expects titillation but the artists had to educate their taste. Homosexuals are whole people and homosexual life and letters do not exist in a vacuum from the mainstream.

Poetry holds, unlike science, that A can be A and not-A at the same time (in science A cannot be not-A ever).

F. Scott Fitzgerald defined 'Genius (as) the capacity to hold two contradictory ideas in one's mind at the same time and yet retain the capacity to function. Dag Hammerskjold said, 'Forgiveness is a child's dream that what is broken will be made whole again and what is soiled will be pure again.' By that token, poetry is forgiveness and the poet is a dreamer, a child and a genius.

Jalaluddin Rumi said, 'To the sacred everything is sacred, to the profane everything is profane.' Again, A can be not-A, the sacred is profaned, and the profane made sacred in childhood, in the dream, and the genius of art.

The Oedipal Complex of Freud simply states that the (western) male child wishes to kill (castrate) the father and marry the mother. When this wish is not fulfilled, the son turns homosexual because of the father's immaturity in *not* relinquishing power to the son.

In India, however, we do not have to live out this intense family romance due to the surrogate parents (aunts and uncles, elder siblings) in the Hindu undivided family. What we have is the four ashrams where sons assume responsibilities at the age of 25 just as the father (who married in his time at 25) is ready to retire at 50. So there is no father–son conflict or castration of the son.

The Puranic myth of Yayati used by Khakhar, however, is against the grain, where the son gives new life to the dying father and sacrifices himself. I read this as a homosexual act of son giving life to father in a sex act.

Bhupen Khakhar is India's first openly gay painter. I am India's first openly gay poet. No one has a problem with homosexuality as a sexual act. It is homosexuality as an identity which is frightening.

Khakhar lived in Khetwadi, Mumbai with his widowed mother. He became a chartered accountant but his heart was always in painting. After a few night classes in painting at the J. J. School of Arts in Mumbai, he started painting non-controversial themes. One of his first portraits is of 'Father and Mother Going on Jatra' in the Parsi portrait style of Eos Studios (Fort). Then, as he secretly cruised the city streets, he started painting what critics now call the 'Series on Trades', e.g., the bidiwallah, the watchwallah, the *Phool*wallah and so on. Khakhar of course, was less interested in the bidi and more interested in the anonymous bidi seller. One way to capture a thing is to dream it. One way to keep a dream is to paint it or write a poem about it. Then a forbidden or secret or ugly passion becomes beautiful. It becomes aesthetic. And no blame attaches to it. And the mother will never know what the gay son is up to looking at these innocent looking paintings.

The next big painting Khakhar did was 'You Can't Please All', a depiction of the Indian tale of the 'Man Who Found a Donkey'. He was leading the donkey when someone suggested he should, instead, be led by the beast. Another suggested he ride it. As he was riding the beast, he followed another suggestion and ended up carrying the beast on his head. The beast dies of exhaustion in Khakhar's allegory. A Khakhar character stands naked behind a covered balcony, watching the scene. What does one do with the beast gifted us by nature, viz. our sexualities? This is the allegorical burden of the painting. But more interesting is the parcelling of space on the canvas to depict the various stages of the narrative where we see all of society at work. An antisocial longing is socialised by art or by social living. Leisure is social but pleasure is always antisocial. The antisocial artist is naked behind a covered balcony in a corner of the painting. The world then becomes his dream.

What happens here is two streams of art theory meeting and parting. One stream is from Ajanta; also found in fourteenth century European painting depicting city scenes or a story with, say, Christ (or Buddha's) Passion at the centre, allegorising human suffering elevated to a divine level. This Aristotle calls 'mimesis' or imitation, which means that there is one single, solid reality out there which the artist perfects by depicting on canvas. So it is not a presentation but a re-presentation of what is out there. The other school says that there is no reality; there are no facts, only interpretation. Interpretation goes according to one's own private reality in one's own head. It is the reality created on canvas in a painting or in words on paper in a poem. It depicts the artists' dreams, longings, visions. There is an interesting story about Max Ernst's father objecting to young Max not putting in their cherry tree in his painting of the family's garden. So Max axed the tree saying: 'Now my painting looks more like reality!'

These are large canvases. The draughtsmanship is amateurish. The donkey lies dead in the middle of the canvas. 'Who was it I heard drowning in my sleep?' asks the surrealist poet.

The second canvas done in the West on his first sojourn there (now lost) is called 'Guru Purnima'. We have reproductions of it and don't be surprised if the huge canvas surfaces on the London art black market now that Khakhar is dead and art prices are soaring. The painting depicts nudity for the first time, just like our Naga sadhus and Digamber Jain *munis*, among others, are licensed to display themselves in all their nakedness because *guruji* is always beyond the body. But Khakhar has a *bania* sense of mischief. He is always wryly smiling at Gujarati, and by extension, Indian hypocrisy. The ladies are at the periphery cooking the *bhog* or *prasadam*. The good looking boys, the *chelas*, have to do *seva* by pressing *guruji's* limbs. This, of course, is a metaphor for masturbation. In Ghalib we have the couplet:

My limbs swelled with pride
When he came and said: Press my limbs!

So, 'Guru Purnima' is an elaborate allegory of a teacher's passion for his disciples and vice versa and the transcending of that passion into Hindu *seva* at *Purnima*, the full blossoming of the moon of one's faculties. It is human and funny that to transcend sex, one has mostly to go through sex, whether it be a learned man or a layman (refer to Jeffrey Kripal 1995).

The nudity in the painting is the personal freeing of Khakhar's own self with the death of his very aged mother. The dutiful gay son was freed of his bondage to mother and could now freely express himself in life and in art. He gave up his practice, set up shop in Baroda at the School of Fine Arts and could now openly live with an older man, Ranchod*bhai*, as a lover (an echo of the father whom Bhupen had lost early in life?). There are several portraits of Ranchod*bhai* in gauzy, see-through, very Gujarati dhotis without underwear, I might add. This was an everyday part of Bombay bania life and no one noticed it except curious, naughty growing boys and girls.

An aside. I remember a Gujarati boys' joke from my Bombay boyhood. A fat man sits in a dhoti in the Bombay suburban train. One schoolgirl tells another, 'See! This man is pregnant.' The other, cleverer than the first, says 'not with a human child but with a baby elephant. See! the baby's trunk is already protruding below his belly!'

It is this repressed Gujarati middle-class milieu where sex comes out as a joke that Khakhar comes from.

Around Khakhar, arose at Baroda what is now loosely called the Baroda School. Part of the group were the Gujarati-speaking Memon painter Ghulam Mohammed Sheikh and his wife Nilima Sheikh. A married Moslem male, Ghulam Mohammed Sheikh was attracted, through Khakhar, to the Hindu myth of the Ardhanariswara. Ghulam draws an oddly neutered being, his hands on his neutered private parts, his face a mask taking flight. Art critic Geeta Kapur, painter Vivan Sundaram's wife, sees this taut, expressionless face as the face of an Egyptian boy pharoah, oddly sexless, possibly Amenhotep's. Amenhotep declared the new religion of Amon-Ra, the sun god, and after he died, his stelae were removed from his monuments. What the artist and art critic are saying here is that differentiated sexual identity comes from an amorphous 'polysexual perverse', to use Freud's phrase. The great bisexual Siva is the forerunner of *all* later constructions of masculinities and femininities in Indian culture. We are here dreaming not our personal history but world history.

Another great painting of Khakhar's is 'The Night Journey'. It is a strangely arresting painting. It is now owned by the *Times of India* and hung at its Bori Bunder Office behind the editor because it is too sexual. The visitor who faces the editor is unsettled by it. Bhupen sold it there for Rs 9 lakh because he needed the money and now it is out of public circulation. 'Hung in a rich man's bathroom', as the phrase goes. I'll describe the painting for you. There are naked fishermen out on a night fishing trip netting huge phallic fish, their bodies bare, their fish-like phalluses open to the moon and the night cold. A Khakhar lookalike sits alone, naked and a naked transvestite, a hijra, dances wearing a blue, star-spangled saree over his head. This is the fate of the aging, passive homosexual, the *koti* or the queen who cannot participate in the sexual fun and games of the young. Repression had delayed his coming out, only to find a very youth oriented gay culture riddled with ageism. The cobalt blues in the night scene are so powerful, the dance movements of the figures at play and rest so arresting that we are mesmerised as if we are voyeurs pulled into a private dream. Of course, the pleasure boat is also the ship of death.

This is the surrealist oneric vision or dream vision or night-journey where modern repressed man sees the glimmerings of his true face only in his dreams. Of course, at the centre of French surrealist poetry of the 1930s, is a woman, a female muse, a reaction against all the boys of Jean Cocteau's films like *Orpheus* (1950). But Khakhar is gay and Indian so he puts the Indian bazaar *chakka* firmly at the centre of his image and self-image.

I could make sense of my dreams only in the light of Khakhar's painting. Once I dreamt that a devoted student of mine, now married, with whom I have had a 20 year platonic relationship as a teacher, was naked with me and between our legs on the ground flowed a river-like liquid of urine, semen or blood, I did not know which. It troubled me because I had worked consciously for 20 years not to have any libidinal attachment to a boy 20 years younger to me. The Night Journey' explained the dream. I wrote a poem. I was liberated from a haunting nightmare.

Homage to Bhupen Khakhar

I

A man's trickle of urine
becomes your Yamuna

a free floating world of love
on a boat
where man can grasp man
and be transformed

Transformed like your winged Yayati
Giving youth to an old Puru
on the earth which becomes
your pink bedsheet

Or where doing the Seva
the disciple is subdued by the master's foot
in upstanding love and mastership

II

Last night I dreamt
I touched my married student
who stood upright for me in my dream
Even in dream I withheld orgasm

This morning I read
Your innocent world again
The tear, the urine trickle
Has become the Yamuna
and on this river I float my boat

(for Giri)

What I did here is use art for interpreting life. Of course, art is a totally
useless activity. 'Poetry makes nothing happen', says W. H. Auden. But
poetry gives us wisdom and keeps us from future folly. Hopefully. There
are boys who fall in love with a father figure like a teacher but they
play their love games amongst themselves. The liberator (the teacher)
is not going to taste liberation himself. He is the discarded old man of
Khakhar's painting. But in the dream, in art, in the poem the metaphor
shines through and becomes its own meaning like God's light in that
almond tree in Sinai.

Bhupen Khakhar's paintings are disturbing not only because they
openly display sexual bonding between males, but also because this
bonding is not between social equals. We have teachers loving students,
older men loving younger men, upper classes looking for love among
social inferiors, father loving son. In the last category comes the Puranic
myth of Yayati which Bhupen loves. King Puru is old. He wants his son's
youth. In Bhupen's retelling of the myth, the father copulates with the
son and sucks out his life. This is a parody of the son breathing into the

father's nostrils at the Kshatriya death ritual. In Khakhar's painting, the father grows pink and healthy and rises winged, the son becomes sickly green with a sagging scrotum and dies. The first Indian Freudian psychologist Dr Girindrasekhar Bose says that while in the West the son loses to the father, Indian fathers willingly castrate themselves by going into the *vanaprastha* ashram voluntarily at 50, handing over the keys of their kingdoms to their 25 year-old princelings. Yayati, the exception, in the Purana tells the dissenting story, the story that is artistic and hence interests artists.

The wings of Yayati in Bhupen's painting show another surrealist transformation: from beast to man to angel. This is the ultimate alchemy dreamt of in medieval alchemy books. So what appears to be love is actually power in this Hindu family. The wise son submits to an unreasonably powerful father. Read: He turns gay.

Another surreal shift is a time shift here. The future (son) is eaten up by the past (father). In life, as in the Oedipus myth, the effect (being gay) is seen before we know the cause (psychological Oedipal conflict).

Khakhar himself was dying by then. I'd write him poems and he wouldn't reply. He was the first to give me a short story in Gujarati for my anthology of gay stories from India (1999).

Pages from a Diary

When we left the Garden he was impatient to reach home. I was crossing the road slowly. Jitubhai had already crossed over, weaving his way between the rickshaws with not a worry for himself; then he waited on the other side impatiently. I was halfway to the other side and had just managed to avoid the last cyclist in my way, when he asked, Where is the scooter?

I said, Next to the Acharya Book Depot. So we will have to go round the circle.

Come, walk a little faster.

He was soon standing near the Acharya Book Depot. Immediately he said, Which scooter?

The grey one.

There are three here.

Here, this one.

I had to obey the authority in his commanding voice. I ripped out the scooter key from the back pocket of my trousers and started the scooter.

Which way?

The lane next to the fire-brigade station.

Impatience, curiosity and eagerness to arrive were Jitubhai's. That's why he had been commanding me. I too was aware that this relationship was to last no more than half an hour. Both of us would forget each other within a day. There was no joy nor excitement in my mind. There was a weariness, a monotony in the chain of happenings in such relationships.

I knew what kind of house it would be. A house with a rexine-covered sofa, a mini-swing, a ceiling fan, and walls painted white or grey.... Lost in thought, I reached the third floor. He had already climbed a staircase ahead of me. I saw him press the bell of room number 305. I climbed the stairs and stood behind Jitubhai. He too was breathless. The door opened three inches.

Jithubhai Key.

The door shut. Two minutes later a bunch of keys was held out by the fingers of a child. She wore bangles on her wrist. Jitubhai took the key.

He unlocked the house right opposite. Inside, an office table, under it a mattress gathered into a roll. Jitubhai switched on the fan. The glass window was shut. The typewriter on the table was covered. Since I wasn't certain where to sit, I pulled out the chair that was pushed into the space under the table and sat on it. The lower fringe of his shirt touched my mouth. Once in a while it flapped across my face when the wind blew.

Jitubhai, Wouldn't you like to stay here? :

I shuddered at the thought of spending the night in that room with no ventilation. I lied. I have to catch the morning bus to Ahmedabad at six.

Go from here.

I have to collect some office papers from home. Besides, I haven't told my people at home, either.

We both knew that this first encounter was also the last one. Jitubhai took off his cap and shirt and stood close to the chair. For the first time I looked at his face in the stark tubelight. An illness years ago had scarred it. The shining head, the sweat-drenched and pock-marked face looked ugly. Moreover, the thin lips made it look cruel too.

A hoarse voice emanated from the tall strong body.

The building-gate closes at nine every night, so be quick.

With this he moved the typewriter with a jerk, and sat on the table. Before my eyes now the white vest, the white dhoti and the phallus that sprang from it. I looked up. The pock-marked cheeks had been smiling. Both eyes were shut to a slit, like the eyes of a Chinese.

He said, All well?

I said, Let's skip this today.

Jitubhai, Why?

Some other time.

You know as well as I do that…

What?

We shall never meet again.

He caught my hand. Involvements, allurement, attraction had disappeared from my heart. I was thinking of paintings. A complete canvas full of white vest, the white dhoti and the slight transparency that revealed the phallus. I tried to get up from the chair. He took my hand, made me sit and said,

What's wrong today?

I'm not in the mood.

What happened to your mood. Did I do something?

No, just feeling off.

Jitubhai : Come on, for my sake.

I stayed there till nine for the sake of a man I would never meet again in my life.

~ (Bhupen Khakhar, *Bombay Dost*, vol. 5, 2 and 3)

Now there is only silence. My dreams continued. My letters to him continued. But the silence from his side was deep and disturbing. Because of prostate cancer he had been neutered, his voice had become strangely high-pitched and he joked about finally becoming the eunuch at the centre of his painting, 'The Ship of Death'. He had invited my young Baroda-born colleague Makrand Paranjape on a boat journey down the Yamuna from Delhi, ending up on the Ganga Ghat at Benares where all good Hindus long to go at the end. Makrand, in his squeamishness, had refused. But I got a poem:

Benaras Cycle

At night
The embers glow
In the orange embers glows a phoenix heart

At dawn
The city of Kali
becomes a golden dawn-fairy

Stone has conversations with water
Over the ages
Water wins
A blue death

I have come to this city of dung
And water
To wash away my sins

My sins are dark indeed
Black as the city at night
In which glows my phoenix heart

The Siva linga
At the golden temple
is a brand: glowing red hot

It brands
Sinners
And cools passion

Everything melts like water in water
The rock-solid ghats
The dying, the dead and their quick mourners

Morning
is just a pale white rag
A naked newborn city wears

On its way to sin.

(for Manu Parekh)

Dirge for Bhupen Khakhar

I

A few years before death
Bhupen the painter meets Makrand the poet
'Let us go for a boatride down the Ganges
upto Benares'
says Bhupen.
Makrand tenses up even re-telling this story
'Think again it's a once in a lifetime chance
A historic boattrip with a great painter'....

II

A few months before death
Bhupen gets a letter from Hoshang the poet :
'I couldn't make sense of my dream
of sleeping with my student
Then I saw your Guru-poornima :
The guru orders and gets sex to go ....'

III

A few days before death
Our boat breaks free of its moorings
Bhupen remembers his friends with his last breath
(Makrand and Hoshang among them)
The boat serenely, effortlessly floats to sea
A drop of water has reached the ocean
Both the river banks have caught fire from the mere passage
of a boat

Towards the end, Bhupen often asked his nurse, the feminist Bina, why Hoshang and he had never met. The Hindus believe that it is good karma if a good man remembers you, of all people, on his deathbed.

I include excerpts from Yashodhara Dalmia's review of Khakhar's last show from *Outlook* (25 March 2002). In her article, 'Forlorn Faces, Close-Up: A Post-9/11 Dread Fills Bhupen Khakhar's Poster Faces', Dalmia says that, 'There is no face which is intact. From a distance they look like the scarred and fractured landscape of another planet. At close quarters, the wounded, splintered images are of people. .... Bhupen Khakhar, in his recent show at the Vadehra Art Gallery in New Delhi, conjures up scenes of everyday life with his characteristic irony. ... the humour is dark, almost forbidding.

In one dramatic painting ... only two faces which emerge from the darkness — one shooting, the other shot at. The twist ... fact that the faces are the same, ... the villain and the victim.

In... *Muslims Around the Mosque I and II*, we see them huddled in fear around mosques... seem to be seeking refuge, whispering the day's events, exchanging information, perhaps the only place where they are free of fear. The even flow of the canvas ... broken at many places by insetting smaller ones which create a tension. .... paintings are marked by homo-eroticism where the diminutive copulating figures, rather like those Mughal miniatures, reveal their scurrilous activity only under the microscope. ... grey and black however echo Goya's *Disasters of War* series....

... Khakhar's oeuvre has been on the marginalized in every sense of the term. Beginning with the vulnerabilities and the quirkiness of the ordinary middle-class man, he went on to make paintings depicting homosexuals which often led to his works being confiscated by art institutions. To observe Muslims who exist in large numbers in cities like Baroda and Ahmedabad in Gujarat and who are shunned in paintings .... In observing the mosques in these cities, Khakhar was to come across a whole panorama of life. An alternative culture with its lyrical calligraphy, its single-minded devoutness and its covetous underlife …

… Khakhar who introduced the kitsch, the calendar, the popular into art, questioning its sanctity. He made life into a scum parade and the street into a marvelous theatre of the absurd. His boundaries … expanding and drawing energy from the street. According to him, "Every time you see objects of popular art they change according to the times and introduce some new element. They don't remain stationary but go on changing. That's what I like about them. They are like the Simenon detective novels where under the guise of a suspense thriller he expresses something very existential. Once you are drawn into the book, it's too late to leave it because you've already crossed 30-40 pages."

… Khakhar would have with him large cut-outs of film stars made under his supervision by a hoarding painter who was also a colleague at the art college in Baroda. These looming figures of Amitabh Bachchan and Shah Rukh Khan have now entered the gallery…. Amitabh Bachchan's back has the face of the massacred hero with a bloody stream running across. It could be the face of any man …

Like Khakhar, I have my own poem on Gujarat:

Gujarat

How far does one go into history
to find kindness
When Yezdagird fought and was defeated
the Arab conqueror praised his valour

Then the Knights understood each other…
Under the cover of night sheltering a fire
We stumbled on a stretch of sand
It was India we had gained and after Iran
We called it Sanjan

Our women took to the saree
Our men to the pugree
Our tongues spoke Gujarati
And the Hindus took us to their hearts

When the Mughal conquered
He sowed the local nobles into animal skins
One a stag, another a bear, a third a buffalo
for weren't they heathen?

When they planted 300 hybrids of mango
The tribals toiled in their gardens

Whose wives warmed their beds
in bed, man and beast are indistinguishable

[I am not angry
I am made gentle by history
Do fall into this gentleness…]
How far does one go into history to find kindness?

And then there was Vali
Who came out of the Deccan
To love boys, Hindu and Turk, indiscriminately
For Love does not discriminate

He found God in boys' eyes
And when the man died
His men made him into a god
And built him a mausoleum, for wasn't he Poet?

Then came the suffering
God on the Cross…
He was fair when I was dark
O Lord take away this blackness
How far does one go into history to find kindness?

Let everything burn said the Sufi
Let everything burn said the Saint
Let everything burn said the leaders
So the mob, their heads on fire
Burnt our mothers, mine and yours

The tomb of the Saint is now dust
No bones rest there/only the word
The word is on the wind
And no body hears

The women poets lament their brother
The children are again asking for sweet words
But there is no sweetness here no sweetness

How far does one go into history to find kindness?

For Vali Gujarati

In my dream
a resurrected man:
My lover erect
Christ reborn

Concentration camp victims begging a body
from their liberators....
He sits up in bed by the support of arms
He will walk on his hands
Finally he will be erect
His palms turned upto stars
Begging mercy from his Creator....
In the dark a man walks towards us
His hand bears a lamp
The other cups the flame
It is the poet out of the night coming
towards us/singing the night of the world

(after Jameela Nishat)

In Memoriam: Bhupen Khakhar (1934-2003)

1

Hello, I'm Bhupen
The high-pitched voice
would giggle into the phone
Then cancer took away that voice

2

He had also lost his testicles
to the surgeon's knife
He grew breasts
They wished a male cancer
would disappear
If one became female

3

He painted 'The Man with Five Penises'
And he thought Hanuman sodomised Rama
But no one would hang that on their walls
So they just embrace

4

Hardy plastered the pages
of his *Jude the Obscure*
with pigs' testicles

thrown at Jude by Arabella
to trick him into marriage

5

In India married women wear white sarees
Sing 'Allah tero naam' like Nanda
Then come out of the satsang chanting
Kill! Kill! Kill! in the Moslem bustee

6

Tick tock tick tock
Went the pendulum of Hanuman's tail
Tick tock went the clock at the clockmaker
Bhupen cruised
Tick-tock took Bhupen's mother
Then his lover Then his balls

7

Art is not art s/d Woolf
Unless it is first androgynous

8

Wilhelm Reich had his Orgone Box :
'If you fuck out your fevers
you won't fuck up families and nations...'
(They put him in a strait-jacket)

9

Plastic flowers are sweeter
Yes, because they don't wither

10

Sweet account-keeper, artist brother
Your Yayati grows wings His scrotum greens
As his son fucks him pink into health

11

And when the body went
Your Avolokiteshwaras swim red and gold
in the jism of the mind

12

Bend your boat Lethe-wards
Sweet old siren Eunuch song and singer
Who feared Mother Fare well upon the Flood!

Now we find your Lithium blue
Pumping in our blood.

Appendix
A Note on Bhupen Khakhar's (implicit) Critique of Gandhism

Bhupen Khakhar's was from the Daman coast, the same Gujarat shores where Gandhi made salt.

> Now I know the difference between you and me
> It is the difference between the sky
> and salt of the sea
> — (Rukmini Bhaya Nair's poem on Gandhi

Is 'difference' a critique? Or is it a circuitous similarity, a belonging with interleaving leaves as in a book with two contradictory ideas bound together in it? More on that later.

The 1930s and 1940s when Khakhar was born and raised, saw the heyday of Gandhism in western India (Bombay–Baroda) and generally India (with pockets of resistance among the Moslems, the Marathas and the Maharajas – the nexus beween the last two finally felled Gandhi to Godse's bullets).

The 1950s, 1960s, 1970s saw Nehru and Indira's India undercut Gandhi. Gujaratis still wore the Gandhi cap and the (transparent) dhoti. Women wore khadi. (This was before Dhirubhai Ambani's 'polyester' era.) State repression grew. With it grew personal rebellion — sexual and social. Amitabh's angry young man in Khakhar's cut-outs from Bollywood films bleeds from behind the cut-out which shows an angry mask. Women were called Manibens, from Mani Bhavan, Laburnum Road, Girgaum, where Gandhi stayed while in Bombay. Gays were called 'Mangubhais'. It is the Mangubhais of the khadi *topi* and dhoti variety that Khakhar represents in their sexual and political ambivalence.

Gandhi had a British gay in his ashram, C. F. Andrews. The two had a voluminous correspondence on what to do with one's overriding sex urge. 'Turn it into seva' was Gandhi's prescription. So we have the sexual *guru–seva* in Khakhar's

'Guru-parva' painting which is slyly humorous as well as shocking, the humour undercutting the shock.

In the representational arts, those of the painters' and the film directors', the dress is the man. Then he moves in space and his actions undercut the appearance. Khakhar's 'Gandhian men' are not what they seem. Teacher seduces student, tailor seduces customer right there on the shop floor while taking 'measurements', neighbours and friends of all ages and faces seduce each other. It is Hieronymus Bosch's 'Garden of Delights' transported from thirteenth century Flanders to Indira Gandhi's rudderless ship of the Indian state.

What about the minorities — not just the gays (who are doing very well, thank you) but the Moslems? In a recent documentary on Gujarat lesbian low-life, *Manjuben Truck Driver* (by a Parsi woman film director, Sherna Dastur [2002]) the eponymous lower middle class truck-driving lesbian, a mannish 'butch' or a 'dyke' wishes to wear the latest fashion — a Taliban suit! Does she realise that the first target of the Taliban would be the lesbian or gay woman?

In his post-9/11 paintings Khakhar showed his persona watching gay activity portrayed in miniscule microscopic size against the looming background of a mosque. Where we are (the setting) undercuts what we do; what we wear contradicts what we are, i.e., the eternal artistic and philosophic conflict between appearance and reality. After all, Oscar Wilde was right: identity is style, not substance. The difference or connection between the sky and sea salt.

afterword: my poetry

It is always difficult for a poet to talk about his poetry. He has written a poem. A comparatively easier task for him than speaking about it. My creative writing teacher at Purdue used to quote Eliot to me: 'There is a difference between the heart that suffers and the hand that writes.' What then is gay poetry? Some generalisations can be made from the practice.

Octavio Paz, writing about the gay Spanish poet Luis Cernuda, a contemporary of Federico Garcia Lorca says:

> Cernuda is a love-poet. But one must begin by stressing something he never concealed: his love was homosexual and he never spoke of any other. His sincerity is not a taste for scandal. It is a point of intellectual and moral honesty. One runs the risk of missing the point of his works if one omits or attenuates this homosexuality, not because the poetry can be reduced to one passion — that would be as wrong as to ignore it — but because it is a point of departure for poetic creation. Erotic preferences do not explain poetry but without them his work would be different. This 'different truth' sets him apart from the world at large; and that same truth in a second movement, leads him on to discover a further truth, his and all of ours.

In giving this book the title *Forbidden Sex/Forbidden Texts: New India's Gay Poets*, I merely meant that my kind of pleasure is forbidden. It means I do not consecrate the authorities that condemn me. I do not feel damned; I merely feel excluded. If there is lament, there is also a giving back blow-for-blow in my poetry. In our society, the honour of husbands still resides between the legs of women, and machismo (*maryada* in Hinduism) is dangerous to me. In Zoroastrianism, in Christianity, in Islam, homosexuality is original sin. There is not the slightest trace of guilt in my work. Against religion's values I set up my own. Hence, though not a religious poet, I'm considered a spiritual poet by my critics.

Who knows love wants nothing else. Love reveals reality to us. The body that escapes after lovemaking is a soul, a conscience which reveals our own soul and conscience to us. The beloved is a body that is penetrable and a consciousness that is not. Love reveals to us the liberty of the beloved to move away. Either we chain the beloved which is inhumane, or we have a multiplicity of loves which dooms us to solitude. A way out is the mystical intermingling of the souls of the lover and beloved in poetry as in religion to end the 'egoism' of youth.

This union means that you do not absorb the beloved who is free and different but allow him or her a space to eternally unfold, to perpetually move and change, like a play, like music, like perpetual recapitulation.

Can we speak of a loved person in the case of a gay poet where the beloved is always changing? Homosexual love is narcissistic and depends on the state of childhood, asking for a parent's unconditional love which makes it tyrannical, capricious, jealous. Love, then, becomes a fate. Lovers die, love remains.

When love is exalted, men are debased. A poet loves not souls and consciences but bodies; not the face, but the ass. A young body personifies cosmic force and it is this cosmic force we love in a young body. We all have value in that we die and love alone exalts us. We aspire to eternity. We go from idolatry to veneration, from sadism to masochism; we suffer and delight in the will to preserve that which is destructible, we go from desire into love.

In love, we see the beloved's questioning face returning our own questions. There is no fulfilment of the 'I'. That is the truth of love. In love we lose our 'I', we wish to be the other. Love is possibility to be the other. Homosexuality is not exceptional, love is.

Love is a transgression. Even the love of Krishna is adultery. All love is immoral. Love escapes common sense and morality (see Kapoor 1973). Poetry does not defend gay rights; it exalts man's highest experience, viz. love — unique love for a unique person which does not die though the person dies.

This is a world without a creator though breathed over with a poetic breath. This is religious atheism. My so-called Sufism, my use of Hinduism which lacks a Christian God. Our misery consists in our being in time, a time which runs out. Hence my use of history. Man remembers, knows and works. Works of man avenge time. Poetry can be sudden revelation, or contemplation, or a vision of the work itself. Art meditating on art comprises the last kind. Self-reflectivity of modern art, the quotation of postmodernism, my Pound pastiches. Myth, poetry, history work on our life and on our work and avenge time. Anais Nin used to say: Live in myth to live a larger life. She was talking about seeing oneself in a mythic double from history. 'I am Baudelaire, I'm Rimbaud, I'm Christ', screamed Hart Crane before he leapt into the sea. His work avenged his life.

What about modern India? How does one interlocute the assassinations of Indira Gandhi, Rajiv Gandhi, Benazir Bhutto? How does one live with Hiroshima, Palestine, Buchenwald, Iraq? It is a tall order for a small poem to redress big wrongs. I do not shirk. I submit. I have lived among these people. I articulate what I know and learn. I drag the macrocosm into my microcosm to enlarge the micro-organism which is the poem, the poet's world. Contemplating historical personages, we fall in love with that which resembles us, we know ourselves by loving our double. This is self-knowledge but through an alien object. Dated time becomes archetype. Man can turn time into stone, music, language, make time mean. Make others understand it. Return the past to the present.

The poet not only gives his own truth but the truth of his tribe, of his language. He gives words to the mute many. This is not about majority and minority opinions. It is about the rejection of false tradition and the discovery of a history that does not end with me. The poet can ascribe the reality of the word to the unreality of his life. Hour by hour, year by year a poet builds his work and leaves it to others to inhabit.

postscript: a note on the structure of this book

A new theme summons a new style. This book is a collage or pastiche of styles. As in the books under discussion, so in this book discussing these books. Criticism encompasses today the old fashioned critical essay but also collage, film montage, poetry, a bric-a-brac of information.

The twenty-first century screams for a twenty-first century style. Messrs Seth, Chandra, Mistri, Ghosh *et al.* live in the eighteenth century of Austen writing the 'Novel of Manners' or at best in Dicken's omnibus novel era of Queen Victoria.

Modern physics tells us that energy comes in a small packets called quanta, not in rivers or waves. The roman fleuve is dead. So is classical criticism. What we have instead are the lightning flashes of Roland Barthes in criticism and the Cuban Gabriel Infante in the novel.

Bibliography

Adam, Barry D. 1987. *The Rise of a Gay and Lesbian Movement*. Boston: Twayne Publishers.

Ahmad, Aijaz (ed.). 1971. *Ghazals of Ghalib*. New York: Columbia University Press.

Albee, Edward. (1958) 1997. *The Zoo Story* in idem, *The American Dream and The Zoo Story*. New York: Plume Books.

———. (1962) 1983. *Who's Afraid of Virginia Woolf?* USA: Signet.

———. (1994) 1995. *Three Tall Ladies*. New York: Plume Books.

Alekar, Satish. 1993. *Begum Barve*. Trans. Shanta Gokhale. Lucknow: Eastern Book Company.

Ali, Agha Shahid. 1997. *The Country without a Post Office: Poems*. New York: W. W. Norton and Company.

———. 2003. *Rooms are Never Finished*. W. W. Norton and Company.

Alighieri, Dante. (n.d.) 1994. *The Inferno of Dante: A New Verse Translation*. Trans. Robert Pinsky and Nicole Pinsky. New York: Farrar, Straus and Giroux.

Alkazi, Roshen. 2003. *Ancient Indian Costume*. New Delhi: National Book Trust.

Allen, Charles. 2000. *Plain Tales from the Raj*. London: Abacus.

Allen, Jeffner. 1986. *Lesbian Philosophy: Explorations*. Palo Alto, California: Institute of Lesbian Studies.

Anand, Mulk Raj and Lance Dane. 1982. *Kama Sutra of Vatsyayana*. New Delhi: Sanskrit Pratishthan for Arnold-Heinemann.

Arnold, Matthew. (n.d.) 2005. *Sohrab and Rustum With Other Poems by Matthew Arnold*. London: Kessinger Publishing.

Bachelard, Gaston. 1964. *The Poetics of Space*. Boston: Beacon Press.

Ballhatchet, Kenneth. 1979. *Race, Sex and Class under the Raj: Imperial Attitudes and Policies and their Critics, 1793–1905*. London: St. Martin's Press.

Barth, John. (1957) 1972. *The Floating Opera*. New York: Bantam Books.

———. (1968) 1988. *Lost in the Fun House*. New York: Anchor.

Barthes, Roland. 1975. *The Pleasure of the Text*. New York: Hill and Wang.

Baudelaire, Charles. (1930) 1947. *The Intimate Journals of Charles Baudelaire*. Trans. Christopher Isherwood. Hollywood: Marcel Rodd Co.

———. (1897) 1950. *My Heart Laid Bare and Other Prose Writings*. Trans. Norman Cameron. London: G. Weidenfield and Nicholson.

Benegal, Dev (dir.). 1994. *English, August*.

Bergman, Ingmar (dir.). 1973. *Scenes from a Marriage*.

Betjeman, John. 1960. *Summoned by Bells*. Boston: Houghton Mifflin.

Bhabha, Homi K. 1994. *The Location of Culture*. London and New York: Routledge.

Bhagat, Chetan. 2005. *One Night at the Call Center*. New Delhi: Rupa &Co.

Bhatt, Mahesh (dir.). 1991. *Sadak*.

———. (dir.). 1997. *Tamanna*.

Bhattacharya, Basu (dir.). *Teesri Aankh.*

Bishop, Elizabeth. 1983. *The Complete Poems, 1927-1979.* New York: Farrar, Straus and Giroux.

Blake, William. (1790-93) 2003. *The Marriage of Heaven and Hell.* Oxford: Oxford University Press.

Bowie, Malcolm. 1991. *Lacan (Modern Masters).* London: Fontana Press.

Brant, Berth. 1994. *Writing as Witness: Essay and Talk.* Toronto: Women's Press.

Brontë, Charlotte. 1847. *Jane Eyre.* London: Smith, Elder & Company.

Brontë, Emily. (1847) 1983. *Wuthering Heights.* Bantam Classics.

Byron, Mark. 2007. *Ezra Pound's Cantos: A Compact History of Twentieth-Century Authorship, Publishing and Editing.* Sydney: University of Sydney.

Butler, Judith. 1990. *Gender Trouble: Feminism and the Subversion of Identity.* New York: Routledge.

Byron, George Gordon. (1819) 1958. *Don Juan.* Boston: Houghton Mifflin.

Carne, Marcel (dir.). 1945. *Les Enfants du Paradis.*

Caudwell, Christopher. 1986. *Collected Poems: 1924-1936.* Ed. Alan Young. Manchester: Carcanet.

Chaudhuri, Asha Kuthari. 2005. *Mahesh Dattani: Contemporary Indian Writers in English.* New Delhi: Foundation Books.

Chopra, B. R. (dir.). 1957. *Naya Daur.*

Chopra, Vidhu Vinod (dir.). 1993. *1942: A Love Story.*

Chopra, Yash (dir.). 1975. *Deewar.*

Chughtai, Ismat. 2004. *A Chughtai Collection: The Quilt and Other Stories, The Heart Breaks Free, The Wild One.* Trans. Tahira Naqvi and Syeda Hameed. New Delhi: Kali For Women Unlimited.

Cixous, Hélène. 1981. 'The Laugh of the Medusa', in Elaine Marks and Isabelle de Courtivron (eds), *New French Feminisms.* New York: Schocken.

Clum, John M. 1992. *Acting Gay: Male Homosexuality in Modern Drama.* New York: Columbia University Press.

Cocteau, Jean (dir.). 1950. *Orpheus.*

Das, Gurcharan. (1962) 2001. *9 Jakhoo Hill* in idem, *Three English Plays: Larins Sahib, Mira, 9 Jakhoo Hill.* USA: Oxford University Press.

Dattani, Mahesh. 1998. *On a Muggy Night in Mumbai,* in idem, *Collected Plays.* New Delhi: Penguin Books India.

———. (dir.). 2002. *Mango Soufflé.*

Dasgupta, Probal. 1993. *The Otherness of English: India's Auntie Tongue Syndrome.* New Delhi: Sage Publications.

Dastagir, Sabu (dir.). 1937. *Elephant Boy.*

Dastur, Sherna (dir.). 2002. *Manjuben Truck Driver.*

Deleuze, Gilles and Félix Guattari. 1983. *Anti-Oedipus.* Trans. Robert Hurley, Mark Seem and Helen R. Lane. Minneapolis: University of Minnesota Press.

———. 1986. 'What is a Minor Literature?', in *Kafka: Towards a Minor Literature, Theory and History of Literature* series, vol. 30. Trans. Dana Polan. Minneapolis and London: University of Minnesota Press.

Dhasal, Namdeo. 2007. *Poet of the Underworld: Poems 1972–2006*. Trans. Dilip Chitre. Pondicherry: Navayana Press.

Dharwadker, Vinay. 1996. 'Introduction', in A. K. Ramanjam, *The Collected Poems of A. K. Ramanujam*. New Delhi: Oxford University Press.

Dodds, E. R (ed.). 1977. *Euripides Bacchae*, 2nd edn. Oxford: Clarendon Press.

Donaldson, Laura E. 1992. *Decolonizing Feminisms: Race, Gender and Empire Building*. Chapel Hill: University of North Carolina Press.

Dostoyevsky, Fyodor. 1975. *Crime and Punishment*. New York: Norton.

Doyle, Brian. 1989. *English and Englishness*. London and New York: Routledge.

Dutt, Guru (dir.). 1957. *Pyasaa*.

Dwyer, Rachel. 2005. *100 Bollywood Films*. London: BFI.

———. 2006. *Filming the Gods: Religion and Indian Cinema*. London and New York: Routledge.

Eliot, T. S. (1922) 2003. 'The Wasteland', in *idem*, *The Wasteland and Other Poems*. UK: Penguin Classics.

———. 1943. *Four Quartets*. New York: Harcourt, Brace and Co.

Fanon, Frantz. (1952) 1994. *Black Skin, White Masks*. New York: Grove Press.

———. (1961) 1965. *The Wretched of the Earth*. New York: Grove Press.

Ellison, Ralph. 1952. *Invisible Man*. New York: Random House.

Farooqui, Mehr Afshan (ed.). 2008. *The Oxford India Anthology of Modern Urdu Literature: Fiction*. New Delhi: Oxford University Press.

Fielding, Henry. (1742) 1967. *Joseph Andrews*. Middletown, Connecticut: Wesleyan University Press.

Forster, E. M. 1924. *A Passage to India*. New York: Harcourt, Brace and Co.

Foucault, Michel. 1979. *The History of Sexuality, Volume 1*. Trans. Robert Hurley. London: Penguin.

Freud, Sigmund. (1929) 1989. *Civilization and its Discontents*. New York: W. W. Norton and Company.

Fries, Kenny. 2007. *The History of My Shoes and the Evolution of Darwin's Theory*. New York: Da Capo Press.

Gandhi, Mohandas Karamchand and Rajendra Prasad. 1924. *Young India 1919–1922*. Madras: S. Ganesan.

Gasset, Ortega y. 1957. *On Love: Aspects of a Single Theme*. New York: Meridien Books.

Genet, Jean. (1986) 1992. *Prisoner of Love*. Trans. Barbara Bray. Hanover: Wesleyan University Press.

George, Stefan. 1974. *The Works of Stefan George*. Eds Olga Marx and Ernst Morwitz. Chapel Hill: University of North Carolina Press.

Ghosh, Shohini (dir.). 2002. *Tales of the Night Fairies*.

Ginsberg, Allen. 1996. *Indian Journals*. New York: Grove Press

Gokhale, Namita. 1999. *Dreams of Passion*. New Delhi: Penguin Books India.

Gramsci, Antonio, Quintin Hoare and Geoffrey Nowell–Smith. 1972. *Selections from the Prison Notebooks of Antonio Gramsci*. New York: International Publishers.

Greer, Germaine. (1970) 2002. *The Female Eunuch*. New York: Farrer, Straus and Giroux.

Gunn, Thom. 1992. *The Man with Night Sweats*. New York: Farrar, Straus and Giroux.

Hafez. (n.d) 2007. *Diwâni-Hâfez*. Trans. John Payne. USA: Ibex Publishers.

Hall, Stuart. 1994. 'Cultural Identity and Diaspora', in Patrick Williams and Laura Christman (eds), *Colonial Discourse and Post-colonial Theory: A Reader*, p. 394. New York: Colombia University Press.

Hardy, Thomas. 1965. *The Dynasts: An Epic-Drama of the War with Napoleon*. London: Macmillan.

Hawthorne, Nathaniel. (1850) 1981. *The Scarlet Letter*. New York: Bantam Classics.

Hedayat, Sadegh. (1937) 1994. *The Blind Owl*. Trans. D. P. Costello. USA: Grove Press.

Homer. 1967. *The Odyssey of Homer*. Trans. Richmond Alexander Lattimore. New York: Harper & Row.

Housman, A. E. 1896. *A Shropshire Lad*. London: The Richards Press.

Hyman, Timothy and Bhupen Khakhar. 1998. *Bhupen Khakhar*. Bombay: Mapin Publishers.

Ibsen, Henrik. (1879) 1935. *A Doll's House*, in idem, *Eleven Plays of Henrik Ibsen*. New York: The Modern Library.

Ilaiah, Kancha. 1996. *Why I am Not a Hindu*. New Delhi: Popular Prakashan.

Isherwood, Christopher. 1976. *Christopher and his Kind: 1929–1939*. Ed. Aaron Copland. New York: Farrar, Straus and Giroux.

Jaffrey, Zia. 1996. *The Invisible: A Tale of the Eunuchs of India*. New York: Pantheon Books.

Johnson, Samuel. (1744) 1971. *Life of Savage*. Oxford: Clarendon Press.

Joyce, James. (1922) 1946. *Ulysses*. New York: Random House.

——. 1907. *Chamber Music*. London: Elkin Mathews.

Jussawalla, Adil J. 1976. *Missing Person*. Bombay: Clearing House.

Kakar, Sudhir. 2007. *The Indians*. New Delhi: Penguin Books India.

Kamleshwar. (1957) 2005. *A Street with 57 Lanes*. New Delhi: Hindi Book Centre.

Kanga, Firdaus. 1990. *Trying to Grow*. London: Bloomsbury.

Kapoor, Raj (dir.). 1964. *Sangam*.

——. 1973. *Bobby*.

Kapur, Ratna. 2003. 'Too Hot to Handle: The Cultural Politics of Fire', in Brinda Bose (ed.), *Translating Desire*. New Delhi: Katha.

Keats, John. 1978. *The Poems of John Keats*. Cambridge: Belknap Press of Harvard University Press.

Khan, Mehboob (dir.). 1957. *Mother India*.

Kolatkar, Arun. 1976. 'Jejuri' in idem, *Jejuri* . New York: New York Review Books Classics.

——. 2005. *Kala Ghoda Poems*. Mumbai: Pras.

Kramrisch, Stella. 2002. *The Hindu Temple*, 2 vols. New Delhi: South Asia Books.

Kripal, Jeffrey. 1995. *Kali's Child: The Mystical and the Erotic in the Life and Teachings of Ramakrishna*. Chicago: University of Chicago Press.

Lajmi, Kalpana (dir.). 1997. *Darmiyaan*.

Lal, P. (ed.). 1969. *Modern Indian Poetry in English: An Anthology and a Credo.* Calcutta: Writers Workshop.

Lawrence, D. H. (1920) 1995. *Women in Love.* Signet Classics.

Lipking, Lawrence. 1981. *The Life of the Poet: Beginning and Ending Poetic Careers.* Chicago: University of Chicago Press.

Loomba, Ania. 1992. 'Tangled Histories: Indian Feminism and Anglo-American Feminist Criticism', in Rajeswari Sundar Rajan (ed.), *The Lie of the Land: English Literary Studies in India.* New Delhi: Oxford University Press.

Lorca, Federico Garcia. 1998. *Poet in New York.* Trans. Greg Simon and Steven F. White. New York: The Noonday Press.

Lorde, Audre. 1988. *A Burst of Light.* Ann Arbor, MI: Firebrand Books.

Lutyens, Mary. 1973. *The Penguin Krishnamurti Reader.* UK: Penguin Books.

Maloney, Kathy (dir.). 2005. *Geja Poeto: Mother Hoshang.*

Mannoni, Octave. 1964. *Prospero and Caliban: The Psychology of Colonization.* New York: Praeger.

Manto, Sa'adat Hasan. 2001. *A Wet Afternoon: Stories, Sketches, Reminiscences.* Trans. Khalid Hasan. Islamabad: Alhamra.

Marcuse, Herbert. 1955. *Eros and Civilisation: A Philosophical Inquiry into Freud.* New York: Vintage Books.

Marvell, Andrew. (n.d.) 1919. 'To His Coy Mistress', in Arthur Quiller-Couch (ed.), *The Oxford Book of English Verse: 1250–1900.* London: Oxford University Press.

McLaren, Norman. (dir.). 1968. *Pas de Deux.*

Mehboob (dir.). 1949. *Andaaz.*

Mehra, Prakash (dir.). 1981. *Laawaris.*

Mehta, Deepa (dir.). 1996. *Fire.*

———. (dir.). 1998. *Earth.*

———. (dir.). 2005. *Water.*

Melville, Herman. (1851) 1992. *Moby Dick.* UK: Penguin Classics.

Merchant, Hoshang. 1999. *Yaraana: Gay Stories from India.* New Delhi: Penguin Books.

———. 2006. *Juvenilia.* Calcutta: Writers Workshop.

Milton, John. (1667) 2007. *Paradise Lost: A Poem Written in Ten Books.* Pittsburgh, Pa.: Duquesne University Press.

———. 1901. *Ode: On the Morning of Christ's Nativity.* Chicago: R. F. Seymour.

Mitchell, Juliet. 1974. *Psychoanalysis and Feminism.* Harmondsworth, UK: Penguin Books.

Mootoo, Shani. 1996. *Cereus Blooms at Night.* New York: Grove Press.

Nabokov, Vladimir. 1962. *Pale Fire.* New York: Putnam.

Nair, Rukmini Bhaya. 1999. *The Ayodhya Cantos.* South Asia Books.

Namjoshi, Suniti. 1967. *Poems.* Calcutta: Writers Workshop.

———. 1971a. *More Poems.* Calcutta: Writers Workshop.

———. 1971b. *Cyclone in Pakistan.* Calcutta: Writers Workshop.

———. 1980. *The Jackass and the Lady.* Toronto: The League of Canadian Poets.

———. 1982. *The Authentic Lie.* Fredericton, New Brunswick: Fiddlehead Poetry Books.

Namjoshi, Suniti. 1984. *From the Bedside Book of Nightmares*. Fredericton, New Brunswick: Fiddlehead Poetry Books & Goose Lane Editions.

———. 1985. *The Conversations of Cow*. London: Women's Press.

———. 1986. *Flesh and Paper*. Charlottetown, Prince Edward Island: Ragweed Press.

Namjoshi, Suniti. 1988. *The Blue Donkey Fables*. London: Women's Press.

———. 1989. *Because of India: Selected Poems and Fables*. London: Onlywomen Press.

———. 2000. *Goja: An Autobiographical Myth*. North Melbourne, Vic.: Spinifex.

———. 2006. *Sycorax: New Fables and Poems*. New Delhi and New York: Penguin Books.

Namjoshi, Suniti and Susan Trangmar. 1981. *Feminist Fables*. London: Sheba Feminist Publishers.

Nandy, Ashis. 1989. *The Intimate Enemy: Loss and Recovery of Self under Colonialism*. USA: Oxford University Press.

Neruda, Pablo. 1961. *Selected Poems*. New York: Grove Press.

Nietzsche, Friedrich Wilhelm. 1956. *The Birth of Tragedy and the Genealogy of Morals*. New York: Doubleday.

Nin, Anais. (1931–32) 1990. *Henry and June: From "A Journal of Love": the Diary of Anais Nin*. New York: Harvest Books.

———. (1947) 1959. *Children of the Albatross*. Denver: Swallow Press.

———. 1964. *Collages*. Denver: Swallow Press.

Nishat, Jameela. 2000. 'Dakhni Urdu as a Vehicle of Social Interaction', in Harsh K. Gupta, Aloka Parasher-Sen and D. Balasubramanian (eds), *Deccan Heritage*. Hyderabad: Indian National Science Academy and Universities Press.

———. 2002. 'On Rekhti', *Deccan Heritage*, vol. 1(2), pp. 201–209.

O'Neill, Eugene. (1922) 1998. *Anna Christie* in idem, *Four Plays by Eugene O'Neill: Anna Christie; The Hairy Ape; The Emperor Jones; Beyond the Horizon*. New York: Signet Classics.

Onir (dir.). 2005. *My Brother Nikhil*.

Padamsee, Sultan. 1975. *Poems*. Calcutta: Writers Workshop.

Pandey, Rakesh. 2004. 'Archaic Knowledge, Tradition and Authenticity in Colonial North India, circa 1780–1960'. Unpublished PhD dissertation. University of London.

Paranjape, Makarand (ed.). 1993. *Anthology of New Indian Poetry in English*. New Delhi: Rupa & Co.

Pasolini, Pier Paolo. (1962) 1996. 'Prayer to My Mother', in *Pier Paolo Pasolini: Poems*. Trans. Norman McAfee and Luciano Martinengo. Farrar, Straus and Giroux.

———. 2001. *Roman Poems*. San Francisco: City Lights Books.

Patel, Gieve. 1976. *How Do You Withstand, Body*. Mumbai: Clearing House.

———. 1988. *Mr Behram*. Bombay: Praxis.

Plato. (360 BC) 2000. *The Republic*. New York: Cambridge University Press.

Plummer, Carol A. 1984. *Preventing Sexual Abuse: Activities and Strategies for those Working with Children and Adolescents*. Holmes Beach, Fla.: Learning Publications.

Plummer, Kenneth. 1981. *The Making of the Modern Homosexual*. Totowa, New Jersey: Barnes and Noble Books.

Pound, Ezra. 1948. *The Cantos of Ezra Pound*. New York: New Directions.

Pope, Alexander. 1714. *Rape of the Lock*. London: Bernard Lintot.

Proust, Marcel. (1922) 1999. *Sodom and Gomorrah*. Trans. John Sturrock. New York: Modern Library.

Pushkin, Alexander. (1832–33) 1975. *Eugene Onegin*. Trans. Vladimir Nabokov. Princeton, New Jersey: Priceton University Press.

Pushkin, Alexander. (1832–33) 1977. *Eugene Onegin*. Trans. Charles Johnston. New York: Viking Press.

Rao, R. Raj. 2000. *One Day I Locked My Flat in Soul City*. New Delhi: Rupa & Co.

———. 2003. *The Boyfriend*. New Delhi: Penguin India.

———. 2006. *Bomgay*. New Delhi: Aark Arts.

Ratnam, Mani (dir.). 1995. *Bombay*.

Reddy, Gayatri. 2005. *With Respect to Sex: Negotiating Hijra Identity in South India*. Chicago: University of Chicago Press.

Reich, Wilhelm. 1970. *The Mass Psychology of Fascism*. New York: Farrar, Straus & Giroux.

Rich, Adrienne. 1994. 'Compulsory Heterosexuality and Lesbian Existence', in *idem*, *Blood, Bread, and Poetry*. New York: Norton Paperback.

Rilke, Rainer Maria. 1936. *Sonnets to Orpheus*. London: Hogarth Press.

———. (1931) 1939. *Duino Elegies*. Trans. J. B. Leishman and Stephen Spender. New York: W. W. Norton and Company.

Rimbaud, Arthur. 1995. *A Season in Hell: The Psychological Autobiography of Arthur Rimbaud*. Trans. Patricia Roseberry. Harrogate: Broadwater House.

Rūmī, Maulana Jalāl al-Dīn and Shams-i Tabrīzī. 1973. *Divani Shamsi Tabriz*. Trans. Reynold Alleyne Nicholson. San Franscisco: Rainbow Bridge.

Rushdie, Salman. 1988. *The Satanic Verses*. New York: Viking.

Sade, Marquis de. 1992. *Philosophy in the Bedroom*. San Francisco, CA: Wooley Comics.

Said, Edward W. 1994. *Representations of the Intellectual: The 1993 Reith Lectures*. New York: Pantheon Books.

Sedgwick, Eve Kosofsky. 1993. *Tendencies*. Durham: Duke University Press.

Seidman, Steven. 1996. *Social Construction of Sexual Desire*. S. I.: Blackwell Publishers.

Sen, Sudeep, 1992. *Kali in Ottava Rima*. London: Paramount.

Sen, Sukumar. 1960. *History of Bengali Literature*. New Delhi: Sahitya Akademi.

Seth, Leila. *On Balance: An Autobiography*. New Delhi and New York, NY: Penguin, Viking.

Seth, Vikram. 1985. *The Humble Administrator's Garden*. London: Carcanet Press Ltd.

———. 1986. *The Golden Gate*. New York: Random House Inc.

———. 1993. *A Suitable Boy*. New York, NY: Harper Collins.

———. 1994. *Mappings*. New Delhi: Viking.

———. 1995. *The Collected Poems*. New Delhi: Penguin Books India.

———. 1999. *An Equal Music*. London: Phoenix.

Sequeira, Isaac. 2008. 'The Mystique of the Mushaira' in Syeda Imam, *Untold Charminar*. New Delhi: Penguin Books India.

Shakespeare, William. (1592–98) 1923. *Shakespeare's Sonnets*. New Haven: Yale University Press.

———. (1596–98) 1923. *The Merchant of Venice*. Ed. William Lyon Phelps. New Haven: Yale University Press.

———. (1609) 1925. *Pericles, Prince of Tyre*. New Haven: Yale University Press.

———. (1606) 1947. *King Lear*. New Haven: Yale University Press.

———. (1599–1600) 1954. *As You Like It*. New Haven: Yale University Press.

———. (1603–1604) 1954. *Measure for Measure*. New Haven: Yale University Press.

———. (1623) 1954. *Twelsth Night*. New Haven: Yale University Press.

———. (1595) 1990. *Richard II*. Ed. Andrew Gurr. Cambridge: Cambridge University Press.

Shantideva. (n.d.) 2006. *The Way of the Bodhisattva*. Trans. Padmakara Translation Group. Shambhala Publications.

Sharma, Pandey Bechan ('Ugra'). 2006. 'Chocolate', in Ruth Vanita (ed.), *Chocolate and Other Writings on Male–Male Desire*. New Delhi: Oxford University Press.

Sharma, Vishnu. (n.d.) 1881. *Panchatantra*. Ed. Pandit Jibananda Vidyasagara. Calcutta.

Sholokov, Mikhail. (1934) 1989. *And Quiet Flows the Don*. USA: Vintage Books.

Sinfield, Alan. 1992. 'Politics of English and Subcultures, in *idem*, *Faultlines: Cultural Materialism and the Politics of Dissident Reading*. Berkeley: University of California Press.

———. 1993. *Literature, Politics and Culture in Postwar Britain*. Oxford: Blackwell Publishers.

Sophocies. 1967. *The Complete Plays of Sophocies*. Trans. Sir Richard Claverhouse Jebb and Moses Hadas. New York: Bantam Books.

Spenser, Edmund. (1596) 1978. *The Faerie Queene*. Ed. Thomas P. Roche and C. Patrick O'Donnell. Harmondsworth and New York: Penguin Books.

Spivak, Gayatri Chakravorty. 1987. 'Sex and History in *The Prelude* (1805): Books IX to XIII', in Richard Machin and Christopher Norris (eds), *Post-Structuralist Readings of English Poetry*, pp. 193–226. Cambridge: Cambridge University Press.

———. 1999. 'Translation as Culture', in Isabel Carrera Suarez, Aurora Garcia Fernandez and M. S. Suarez Lafuente (eds), *Translating Culture*. UK: Dangaroo Press.

Strindberg, Johan August. (1907) 1958. *The Father*. UK: Harmondsworth.

Sukthankar, Ashwini (ed.). 1999. *Facing the Mirror: Lesbian Writing from India*. New Delhi: Penguin Books India.

Sunder Rajan, Rajeswari (ed.). 1992. *The Lie of the Land: English Literary Studies in India*. New Delhi: Oxford University Press.

Tagore, Rabindranath. 1913. *Gitanjali*. London: Macmillan.

Tennyson, Alfred, Lord. 1902. *Idylls of the King*. New York: G. P. Putnam and Sons, the Knickerbocker Press.

Tennyson, Alfred, Lord. 1973. *In Memoriam; an Authoritative Text, Backgrounds and Sources, Criticism*. New York: W. W. Norton and Company.

Tharu, Susie and K. Lalitha (eds). 1993. *Women Writing in India*, vol. 1. New Delhi: Oxford University Press.

Trilling, Lionel. 1950. *The Liberal Imagination: Essays on Literature and Society*. New York: Viking Press.

——— (ed.). 1964. *The Experience of Literature*. New York: Harcourt Brace.

Ullman, Liv. 1976. *Changing*. New York: Alfred A. Knopf.

Vaidyanathan, T. G. and Jeffrey John Kripal. (eds). 1999. *Vishnu on Freud's Desk: A Reader in Psychoanalysis and Hinduism*. Delhi and New York: Oxford University Press.

Vanita, Ruth. 2003. 'Same-Sex Love', in Brinda Bose (ed.), *Translating Desire*. New Delhi: Katha.

Vanita, Ruth and Saleem Kidwai. 2000. *Same-Sex Love in India: Readings from Literature and History*. New York: St. Martin's Press.

Wadia, Riyad Vinci and R. Raj Rao. 1996. *Bomgay: A Collection of Six Short Films*. Bombay: Wadia Movietone.

Warton, Thomas. 1824. *The History of English Poetry from the Close of the Eleventh to the Commencement of the Eighteenth Century*, 4 vols. London: Tegg.

Weeks, Jeffrey. 1977. *Coming Out: Homosexual Politics in Britain from the Nineteenth Century to the Present*. London and New York: Quartet Books.

Weinrich, James. 1992. 'Reality or Social Constructions?', in Edward Stein (ed.), *Forms of Desire: Sexual Orientation and the Social Constructionist Controversy*, p. 176. New York: Routledge.

Whitman, Walt. 1982. *Complete Poetry and Collected Prose*. New York: Literary Classics of the United States, distributed by Viking Press.

White, Edmund. 1982. *A Boy's Own Story*. New York: Vintage Books.

———. 1993. *Genet: A Biography*. London: Chatto and Windus.

Wilde, Osca. 1905. *Intentions: The Decay of Lying, Pen, Pencil and Poison, the Critic as Artist, the Truth of Masks*. New York: Brentano.

Wolpert, Stanley. 1996. *Nehru: A Tryst with Destiny*. New York: Oxford University Press.

Woodland, Malcolm. 2005. 'Memorys' Homeland: Agha Shahid Ali and the Hybrid Ghazal', *ESC*, vol. 31(2–3): 249–72.

Woolf, Virginia. (1922) 2004. *Jacob's Room*. London: Vintage Classics.

Yeats, W. B. 1956. *The Collected Poems of W. B. Yeats*. New York: Macmillan.

Zola, Emile. 1997. *Germinal*. Paris: PUF.

Printed in the United Kingdom by
Lightning Source UK Ltd., Milton Keynes
137507UK00004B/4/P

9 780415 484510

Weapons of
Mass Destruction

Opposing Viewpoints®

James D. Torr, *Book Editor*

Bruce Glassman, *Vice President*
Bonnie Szumski, *Publisher*
Helen Cothran, *Managing Editor*

**OPPOSING
VIEWPOINTS®
SERIES**

GREENHAVEN PRESS
An imprint of Thomson Gale, a part of The Thomson Corporation

THOMSON
™
GALE

Detroit • New York • San Francisco • San Diego • New Haven, Conn.
Waterville, Maine • London • Munich

KVCC   KALAMAZOO VALLEY
COMMUNITY COLLEGE
LIBRARY

U
793
.W43277
2005

JAN 1 0 2005

© 2005 Thomson Gale, a part of The Thomson Corporation.

Thomson and Star Logo are trademarks and Gale and Greenhaven Press are registered trademarks used herein under license.

For more information, contact
Greenhaven Press
27500 Drake Rd.
Farmington Hills, MI 48331-3535
Or you can visit our Internet site at http://www.gale.com

ALL RIGHTS RESERVED.
No part of this work covered by the copyright hereon may be reproduced or used in any form or by any means—graphic, electronic, or mechanical, including photocopying, recording, taping, Web distribution or information storage retrieval systems—without the written permission of the publisher.

Every effort has been made to trace the owners of copyrighted material.

Cover credit: © PhotoDisc

LIBRARY OF CONGRESS CATALOGING-IN-PUBLICATION DATA

Weapons of mass destruction : opposing viewpoints / James D. Torr, book editor.
    p. cm. — (Opposing viewpoints series)
Includes bibliographical references and index.
ISBN 0-7377-2250-9 (lib. : alk. paper) — ISBN 0-7377-2251-7 (pbk. : alk. paper)
    1. Weapons of mass destruction. 2. United States—Military policy. 3. Iraq War, 2003. I. Torr, James D., 1974– . II. Opposing viewpoints series (Unnumbered)
U793.W43277 2005
358'.3'0973—dc22   2004047587

Printed in the United States of America

"Congress shall make
no law...abridging the
freedom of speech, or of
the press."

First Amendment to the U.S. Constitution

The basic foundation of our democracy is the First
Amendment guarantee of freedom of expression.
The Opposing Viewpoints Series is dedicated to the
concept of this basic freedom and the idea that it is
more important to practice it than to enshrine it.

Contents

Why Consider
Opposing Viewpoints?

"The only way in which a human being can make some approach to knowing the whole of a subject is by hearing what can be said about it by persons of every variety of opinion and studying all modes in which it can be looked at by every character of mind. No wise man ever acquired his wisdom in any mode but this."

John Stuart Mill

In our media-intensive culture it is not difficult to find differing opinions. Thousands of newspapers and magazines and dozens of radio and television talk shows resound with differing points of view. The difficulty lies in deciding which opinion to agree with and which "experts" seem the most credible. The more inundated we become with differing opinions and claims, the more essential it is to hone critical reading and thinking skills to evaluate these ideas. Opposing Viewpoints books address this problem directly by presenting stimulating debates that can be used to enhance and teach these skills. The varied opinions contained in each book examine many different aspects of a single issue. While examining these conveniently edited opposing views, readers can develop critical thinking skills such as the ability to compare and contrast authors' credibility, facts, argumentation styles, use of persuasive techniques, and other stylistic tools. In short, the Opposing Viewpoints Series is an ideal way to attain the higher-level thinking and reading skills so essential in a culture of diverse and contradictory opinions.

In addition to providing a tool for critical thinking, Opposing Viewpoints books challenge readers to question their own strongly held opinions and assumptions. Most people form their opinions on the basis of upbringing, peer pressure, and personal, cultural, or professional bias. By reading carefully balanced opposing views, readers must directly confront new ideas as well as the opinions of those with whom they disagree. This is not to simplistically argue that everyone who reads opposing views will—or should—change his or her opinion. Instead, the series enhances readers' understanding of their own views by encouraging confrontation with opposing ideas. Careful examination of others' views can lead to the readers' understanding of the logical inconsistencies in their own opinions, perspective on why they hold an opinion, and the consideration of the possibility that their opinion requires further evaluation.

Evaluating Other Opinions

To ensure that this type of examination occurs, Opposing Viewpoints books present all types of opinions. Prominent spokespeople on different sides of each issue as well as well-known professionals from many disciplines challenge the reader. An additional goal of the series is to provide a forum for other, less known, or even unpopular viewpoints. The opinion of an ordinary person who has had to make the decision to cut off life support from a terminally ill relative, for example, may be just as valuable and provide just as much insight as a medical ethicist's professional opinion. The editors have two additional purposes in including these less known views. One, the editors encourage readers to respect others' opinions—even when not enhanced by professional credibility. It is only by reading or listening to and objectively evaluating others' ideas that one can determine whether they are worthy of consideration. Two, the inclusion of such viewpoints encourages the important critical thinking skill of objectively evaluating an author's credentials and bias. This evaluation will illuminate an author's reasons for taking a particular stance on an issue and will aid in readers' evaluation of the author's ideas.

It is our hope that these books will give readers a deeper understanding of the issues debated and an appreciation of the complexity of even seemingly simple issues when good and honest people disagree. This awareness is particularly important in a democratic society such as ours in which people enter into public debate to determine the common good. Those with whom one disagrees should not be regarded as enemies but rather as people whose views deserve careful examination and may shed light on one's own.

Thomas Jefferson once said that "difference of opinion leads to inquiry, and inquiry to truth." Jefferson, a broadly educated man, argued that "if a nation expects to be ignorant and free . . . it expects what never was and never will be." As individuals and as a nation, it is imperative that we consider the opinions of others and examine them with skill and discernment. The Opposing Viewpoints Series is intended to help readers achieve this goal.

David L. Bender and Bruno Leone,
Founders

Greenhaven Press anthologies primarily consist of previously published material taken from a variety of sources, including periodicals, books, scholarly journals, newspapers, government documents, and position papers from private and public organizations. These original sources are often edited for length and to ensure their accessibility for a young adult audience. The anthology editors also change the original titles of these works in order to clearly present the main thesis of each viewpoint and to explicitly indicate the opinion presented in the viewpoint. These alterations are made in consideration of both the reading and comprehension levels of a young adult audience. Every effort is made to ensure that Greenhaven Press accurately reflects the original intent of the authors included in this anthology.

Introduction

> *"Weapons of mass destruction (WMD)—nuclear,*
> *biological, and chemical—in the possession of hostile states*
> *and terrorists represent one of the greatest security*
> *challenges facing the United States."*
>
> —*President George W. Bush*

The term *weapons of mass destruction* has two connotations. In its broader, literal sense, it is used to refer to weapons whose destructive power far surpasses that of guns or conventional explosives. However, the term is more often used in a narrower sense, to refer specifically to nuclear, biological, and chemical (NBC) weapons. Since the September 11, 2001, terrorist attacks, which raised awareness of America's vulnerability, the United States has greatly intensified its efforts to stop the spread of nuclear, biological, and chemical weapons. When the president and other officials refer to "weapons of mass destruction," they usually mean NBC weaponry.

In fact, while September 11 awakened America to the threat of terrorism perpetrated by groups such as al Qaeda, U.S. foreign policy since September 11 has been dominated by concerns about the development of NBC weapons by countries such as North Korea and Iran. President Bush linked the two concerns in his January 29, 2002, State of the Union address: "[We must] prevent regimes that sponsor terror from threatening America or our friends and allies with weapons of mass destruction." He warned:

> North Korea is a regime arming with missiles and weapons of mass destruction, while starving its citizens. Iran aggressively pursues these weapons and exports terror, while an unelected few repress the Iranian people's hope for freedom. Iraq continues to flaunt its hostility toward America and to support terror. . . . States like these, and their terrorist allies, constitute an axis of evil, arming to threaten the peace of the world. By seeking weapons of mass destruction, these regimes pose a grave and growing danger. They could provide these arms to terrorists, giving them the means to match their hatred. . . . The United States will not permit the world's most dangerous regimes to threaten us with the world's most destructive weapons.

In the months that followed, President Bush elaborated on the U.S. strategy to prevent the proliferation of weapons of mass destruction (WMD). *The National Strategy to Combat Weapons of Mass Destruction*, released by the White House in December 2003, formally summarizes three pillars of U.S. policy: 1) WMD consequence management; 2) nonproliferation; and, 3) counterproliferation.

According to the *National Strategy*, consequence management refers to homeland security efforts to "reduce to the extent possible the potentially horrific consequences of WMD attacks at home and abroad." Such efforts include WMD-response training programs for firefighters, medical workers, and other first responders, and stockpiling of vaccines for smallpox and other diseases that might be used as bioweapons. However, because a WMD attack would be so devastating, U.S. strategy places a higher priority on preventing a WMD attack than on reacting to one.

Nonproliferation refers primarily to diplomatic efforts to encourage states with WMD programs to end them, and to dissuade states without WMD programs from starting them. The principal nonproliferation agreement is the Nuclear Nonproliferation Treaty (NPT). Originally signed in 1968 by the United States, the United Kingdom, the Soviet Union, and fifty-nine other countries, the NPT currently includes every member of the United Nations except India, Israel, and Pakistan. The NPT obligates states with nuclear weapons not to transfer their weapons, or the technology to build them, to nonnuclear states, and it obligates nonnuclear states not to acquire or produce nuclear weapons. A similar treaty for chemical weapons, the Chemical Weapons Convention, was ratified by the United States in 1997, while a proposed Biological Weapons Convention is being developed by international committees.

Counterproliferation is the most complicated and most controversial part of *The National Strategy to Combat Weapons of Mass Destruction*. One of the main aspects of counterproliferation is deterrence. Essentially, deterrence is based on the idea that the power of the U.S. military—including both conventional forces and nuclear weapons—will discourage other countries from using WMD. As the *National Strategy* states, "The United States will continue to make clear that it reserves the right to respond with overwhelming force—including through resort to all of our options—to the use of WMD against the United States, our forces abroad, and friends and allies."

Another controversial part of counterproliferation is the United States' declaration that it will preemptively attack nations that threaten to use or develop WMD. The debate over preemption first entered the national mainstream when, in a June 2002 speech, President Bush spoke of the need to strike first against terrorist threats: "If we wait for threats to materialize, we will have waited too long. . . . We must take the battle to the enemy, disrupt his plans and confront the worst threats before they emerge." The *National Strategy* describes preemption as a supplement to deterrence:

> Because deterrence may not succeed, and because of the potentially devastating consequences of WMD use against our forces and civilian population, U.S. military forces and appropriate civilian agencies must have the capability to defend against WMD-armed adversaries, including in appropriate cases through preemptive measures. This requires capabilities to detect and destroy an adversary's WMD assets before these weapons are used.

Preemption is more controversial than deterrence because it means that the United States may use military force against another nation, even if that nation has not used WMD against the United States or its allies.

This was the case with the spring 2003 U.S. invasion of Iraq. In September 2002, President Bush addressed the United Nations, arguing that Iraqi leader Saddam Hussein was not complying with UN resolutions to allow weapons inspectors to determine whether Iraq was building WMD. Bush warned that a military invasion of Iraq might be necessary. The United States maintained throughout 2002 that Iraq was secretly building chemical and biological weapons, as well as slowly expanding its nuclear program. Finally, after several failed attempts to gain UN approval for an invasion of Iraq, the United States and the United Kingdom invaded the nation in March 2003 to bring down the regime of Saddam Hussein. The invasion was successful, but the United States found no actual weapons of mass destruction in Iraq, and unearthed only limited evidence that Iraq was pursuing WMD programs, leading many critics to question whether the invasion was justified.

The controversy over the invasion of Iraq is part of a broader debate about how to deal with other nations believed to be developing WMD. Critics of deterrence maintain that the United States should not threaten war in order to maintain peace, and that by maintaining a large nuclear arsenal, the United States undermines international nonproliferation efforts. Critics of preemption charge that the policy may actually lead other nations to develop WMD in order to deter the United States from invading. The authors in *Opposing Viewpoints: Weapons of Mass Destruction* examine these policies and other issues in the following chapters: How Likely Is an Attack Involving Weapons of Mass Destruction? How Should the United States Deal with Countries That Threaten to Develop Weapons of Mass Destruction? What Policies Should the United States Adopt Toward Nuclear Weapons? How Can the United States Defend Itself Against Weapons of Mass Destruction? Although there is plenty of disagreement about how the United States should deal with weapons of mass destruction, all sides in the debate agree on the need for strategies to prevent their use.

CHAPTER 1

How Likely Is an Attack Involving Weapons of Mass Destruction?

Chapter Preface

Most experts believe that the likelihood of a terrorist attack involving weapons of mass destruction (WMD) is low—at least, lower than the likelihood of a conventional attack. Nuclear, biological, and chemical (NBC) weapons are simply harder to build and use than conventional arms and explosives. There have historically been very few terrorist incidents involving chemical or biological weapons and none involving nuclear weapons, in contrast to scores of bombings, aircraft hijackings, and hostage-takings since the 1970s.

However, while the likelihood of a WMD terrorist attack may be low, if one were to occur, it could be devastating. As a report from the Executive Session on Domestic Preparedness, a task force on homeland security sponsored by Harvard University, puts it,

> The consequences of a successful [WMD] attack would be severe. . . . Relatively small amounts of some chemical and biological agents can create mass casualties, potentially causing large numbers of fatalities and an overwhelming number of injuries. The consequences of a WMD incident could also include economic damage, environmental contamination, international repercussions, increased internal police powers, and deleterious psychological effects on citizens.

Therefore, the task force concludes, "Terrorism with weapons of mass destruction should . . . be seen as a *low-probability* but *high-consequence* threat." Although terrorism with conventional weapons is considered much more likely than a WMD attack, the enormous dangers associated with a major WMD strike are a driving force in U.S. homeland security efforts. The authors in the following chapter examine what types of WMD attack are most likely, and whether the threat from NBC weapons has been exaggerated.

"The United States finds itself at greater risk of an attack by nuclear-based weaponry today than at the height of the Cold War."

The Likelihood of a Nuclear Missile Attack Is Greater than Ever Before

John J. Stanton

John J. Stanton is a member of the professional staff at the National Defense Industrial Association, a trade organization representing America's defense industries. In the following viewpoint he maintains that the threat of terrorists building or stealing a nuclear weapon is serious and growing. He contends that the materials needed to make nuclear weapons are regularly bought and sold on black markets around the world. Stanton discusses some of the measures in place to deal with nuclear threats but argues that much more funding is needed for both homeland security efforts and international initiatives to monitor nuclear trafficking.

As you read, consider the following questions:
1. What is the purpose of U.S. nuclear weapons labs' "Nth Country Experiments," according to Stanton?
2. About how many tactical nuclear weapons are estimated to be in the Russian nuclear arsenal, including those stored or slated for dismantlement, according to the author?
3. What field exercise did DTRA run in Salt Lake City prior to the 2002 Olympics, as described by Stanton?

John J. Stanton, "Is the U.S. Prepared for Nuclear Terrorism?" *Security Management*, vol. 46, March 2002, p. 156. Copyright © 2002 by ASIS International, 1625 Prince St., Alexandria, VA 22314. Reproduced by permission.

In October 2001, in Philadelphia, Pennsylvania, two portable moisture density gauges containing sealed sources of radioactive material were reported stolen off the back of a pickup truck at a worksite, despite being properly chained and locked. The event was disturbing, but not unusual. There are approximately "150,000 licensees for radioactive materials in the U.S. and 2 million devices containing radioactive material in use in the U.S. today," according to Richard Meserve, chairman of the U.S. Nuclear Regulatory Commission (NRC). From these, "an average of approximately 375 sources or devices of all kinds are reported lost or stolen each year in the U.S., that is, roughly one per day," says Meserve.

That chilling statistic illustrates why, in a run of events worthy of Stanley Kubrick's *Dr. Strangelove*, the United States finds itself at greater risk of an attack by nuclear-based weaponry today than at the height of the Cold War. Analysts say that this new nuclear threat will never be eliminated, only minimized. They point to the quantities of lost or stolen (called "orphaned") radioactive waste in the United States and around the world that would be easy for terrorist groups to obtain. They also point to the arsenal of loosely guarded Russian tactical nuclear weapons (TNWs), some of which are also already missing. As Michael Levi of the Nuclear Project at the Federation of American Scientists in Washington, D.C., puts it: "Orphans tend to find parents real fast."

Indeed, there is a lucrative international market for nuclear equipment and radioactive material. Between 1993 and 2001, the Illicit Trafficking Database Programme of the International Atomic Energy Association (IAEA), in which 70 nations participate, recorded instances of trafficking, of which about half involved radioactive sources. The IAEA reports that the number of incidents of trafficking has increased in recent years, mainly involving radioactive sources, such as highly enriched uranium. As recently as December 2001, Russian authorities arrested a group attempting to sell two pounds of weapons-grade uranium.

Bombs and RDDs

Levi suggests that threat assessors think creatively when trying to determine how terrorists might irradiate a population.

"We tend to associate terrorists with things that blow up. The prevailing view is that a radiological dispersion device (RDD) or nuclear bomb will be the preferred method of delivery, but it's equally likely that terrorists will buy radioactive waste and manually disperse it in terminals, subways, or other crowded places," although that might not compare to the psychological damage inflicted by the explosion of an RDD or the detonation of a low-yield nuclear weapon in a U.S. city.

Of course, the successful detonation of a low-yield nuclear device or RDD would far surpass the aftermath of the terrorist attacks on September 11, 2001.

But can an RDD or nuclear device be built? The evidence from the IAEA's Illicit Trafficking Database Programme and the NRC's "orphaned" U.S. materials list indicates that radioactive material could easily find its way into the wrong hands. And although an RDD is likely to emit deadly radiation to its attacker, September 11th proved that the willingness of terrorists to sacrifice their own lives should not be underestimated.

"The Russians believe very strongly that a sophisticated substate group with 30–50 people using off-the-shelf equipment could actually create the bomb-grade materials from low-grade uranium and make several bombs a year," says Dr. Bruce Blair, President of the Center for Defense Information.

It's no secret that a few good physicists can get together and do the math for a rudimentary nuclear weapon. In fact, physicists on track to be employed by U.S. nuclear weapons labs bide their time engaging in "Nth Country Experiments," while awaiting security clearances.

"The labs routinely conduct break-in assignments like Nth Country where they have the new employees do their best to design a nuclear weapon on the cheap. The labs like it because sometimes the results are new and innovative," says Blair.

Tactical Nuclear Weapons

Another concern is that the risk of tactical nuclear weapons [TNWs] is being overlooked in the discussion of new nuclear threats to the United States. "Tactical nuclear weapons pose unique dangers as weapons of terror," says Allistair Millar, vice president and director of the Fourth Freedom

Preventing Nuclear Terrorism: Top Eight Gaps in Defenses

Top 8 gaps	Remarks
Uninspected shipping containers	97%–98% Maritime containers uninspected. "Container security initiative" grossly inadequate. Terrorists have exploited container freight in past.
Flawed ID verification at borders	Antiquated credentials verification easily fooled. Undercover agents demonstrated easy access with fake ID.
Poor terrorist intelligence	U.S. terrorist cells still not identified & located. Global & domestic intelligence sharing highly deficient.
Unsecured nuclear storage facilities	"Loose nukes" are still unsecured. Only 17% of Russian N-sites are known to have comprehensive security. Global situation less defined & possibly worse.
Weakly protected nuclear reactors	Nuclear power industry resists stronger security. Mock attack drills reveal high failure rate of security systems. Little or no protection from airborne attacks.
Unresolved North Korea crisis	North Korea postured to produce fissile materials and nuclear bombs. Sales to rogue states or terrorists feared. Economic sanctions; maritime interdiction; and military strikes not reliable prevention measures.
Flawed export control regime	WMD programs in Iraq. Iran, and North Korea exploited flaws in export control regimes. Terrorists could pursue similar strategy (in addition to black market purchases, theft & smuggling).
Unratified comprehensive test ban treaty (CTBT)	CTBT urgently needed to bolster nuclear nonproliferation treaty (NPT) and halt new warhead development. NPT is the cornerstone of nonproliferation regime and CTBT ratification is essential to assuring continued participation of all NPT signers.

Third Millennium Foundation, July 2003.

Forum's office in Washington, D.C. "Their often-smaller size increases their portability and vulnerability to theft by non-nuclear states and potential nuclear terrorists," he says. "Characteristics of command unique to TNWs, such as pre-delegated launch authorization, and often inadequate safeguards, such as ineffective permissive action links, add to their potential unauthorized, accidental, or illicit use," continues Millar. Yet, he notes, "we don't have a system for accounting for TNWs, which are not monitored or controlled by any existing treaties or formal agreements."

Millar recently authored a report with his colleague Brian Alexander titled "Uncovered Nukes: A fact sheet on tactical nuclear weapons." In it, he noted that the U.S. TNW arsenal is estimated at 1,670 warheads. These are stored mainly in the U.S. mainland, but 150–200 U.S. TNWs are deployed across eight bases in Europe.

Estimating the Russian arsenal is more complicated. There are numerous conflicting accounts and serious doubts about whether the Russians themselves even know the total number of TNWs they have. The most recent estimate of the Russian TNW arsenal is around 3,590 deployed weapons, but when estimates of warheads stored or slated for dismantlement are taken into account, these estimates grow to as high as 15,000.

"This is a very serious problem particularly as it relates to Russia," says Millar. There is no real evidence that TNW demilitarization took place, because the Russian 12th Main Directorate of the Ministry of Defense [responsible for nuclear munitions deployment, testing, security] and Miniatom [oversees deactivation of nuclear weapons and stockpiles of plutonium] don't talk to each other and have poor record-keeping capability."

DTRA and NEST

"How do we talk to America about these types of problems?" asks Defense Threat Reduction Agency (DTRA) spokesperson Captain Robert Bennett (USA). "Our Consequence Management Advisory Team has been looking at ways to improve how we support the civilian sector's response to the detonation of an RDD or other nuclear device. We've held human behavior workshops and have done modeling and simulation to determine blast impact and radioactive fallout. And we've learned a heck of a lot from the response to September 11th."

One of DTRA's signature services is the Hazard Prediction Assessment Capability (HPAC) computer program designed to help first responders predict where a radioactive cloud will move, thereby helping them allocate resources appropriately. "Time delayed effects come into play here, and this particular program considers weather conditions along with the radiological factors. It can show you what will happen in 20 minutes, then 40 minutes, and so on. We provide this to first responders when they ask for it. It was configured to track asbestos particles released from the structures destroyed on September 11th."

DTRA has held many field radiological response exercises [in 2001]. One held [in spring 2001] was Olympic Response IT in Salt Lake City, Utah. In that scenario, radioactive waste was encased and strapped with TNT and detonated, dispersing a deadly cloud. There, says Bennett, DTRA helped the Salt Lake City Olympic Committee "to understand the dangers and how best to deal with them."

Bennett takes pains to point out that there is "the realization that we can't be there first." He notes that when DTRA arrives on the state or local scene, "we [DTRA] work for the mayor or governor."

But the real nuclear gumshoes are the Nuclear Emergency Search Team (NEST), which draws talent from the nation's nuclear weapons labs and volunteers from the Department of Energy. Since 1975, NEST has examined no terrorist nuclear threats. That's according to *Atomic Audit: The Costs and Consequences of U.S. Nuclear Weapons Since 1940* (published by the Brookings Institution). NEST also maintains a massive database that "contains everything publicly available about making a nuclear weapon."

More Needs to Be Done

According to Blair, while these groups are doing useful work, the overall government effort falls short. For example, even though federal funding levels have increased . . . they still do not adequately address homeland defense. In Blair's view, funding priorities are still heavily tilted toward procuring machinery for distant wars rather than funding domestic measures to protect and defend the American populace right here at home. "There's tremendous misallocation. Security and protection of the U.S. mainland has been underfunded and not thought through," he says.

Millar believes that U.S. civilian political leadership is encouraging policies that increase risk to the military. He states that military thinkers in war colleges around the land are a step ahead of their civilian counterparts in pushing for aggressive, codified nonproliferation treaties that include TNWs, for example. They recognize that military action alone cannot minimize these new nuclear threats.

International initiatives to monitor illicit trafficking through the IAEA need further funding by the U.S. government as well. In addition, U.S. government regulators, such as the NRC, must be more aggressive in monitoring the private sector's use, transport, and disposal of radioactive materials. Finally, federal agencies must provide state and local governments with support to manage the consequences of a worst-case nuclear attack.

| *"The ballistic missile threat today is confined, limited and changing relatively slowly."*

The Likelihood of a Nuclear Missile Attack Has Been Exaggerated

Joseph Cirincione

Joseph Cirincione is the director of the Non-Proliferation Project at the Carnegie Endowment for International Peace. In the following viewpoint he argues that government officials have placed too much emphasis on the threat posed to the United States by nuclear ballistic missiles. Cirincione contends that although ballistic missiles are the most dangerous weapons in the world, they pose much less of a threat than they have in the past. The author notes most countries' missiles do not have the range to reach the United States. Many experts worry that Iran or North Korea might develop long-range ballistic missiles in the future, but Cirincione argues that even if they do, in the worst-case scenario a nuclear attack from one of these nations would not be as bad as the catastrophic nuclear threat the Soviet Union posed during the Cold War.

As you read, consider the following questions:

1. What two nations have ballistic missiles capable of reaching the United States, according to the author?
2. What does the author believe is the "most significant proliferation threat"?
3. Why does Cirincione believe that other nations would be deterred from using ballistic missiles against the United States?

Joseph Cirincione, "A Much Less Explosive Trend," *Washington Post*, March 10, 2002, p. B03. Copyright © 2002 by the Washington Post Book World Service/Washington Post Writers Group. Reproduced by permission of the author.

The president says the ballistic missile threat is growing and warns us how much more terrible [the September 11, 2001, terrorist attacks] could have been if the terrorists had missiles. The CIA director says the proliferation of missile designs and technology has "raised the threat to the U.S. . . . to a critical threshold." Congress appropriates $8 billion a year to research missile defense systems—the largest weapons program in the budget. The prevailing wisdom in Washington is that missile threats are mushrooming.

But are they? Ballistic missiles with nuclear warheads are the most dangerous weapons ever invented. Within minutes of launch they can destroy a distant city the size of Washington. However, the threat they pose now is less than in the past and is steadily declining. Today there are many fewer ballistic missiles in the world than 15 years ago, fewer nations trying to develop them, and only four potentially hostile nations trying to develop long-range versions. Moreover, the limited attack we most fear now from a rogue state would be much smaller than the nuclear holocaust we feared during the Cold War.

Of the more than 190 nations in the world, 35 of them, including the United States, have ballistic missiles. These are missiles that, like the V-2s first used by Nazi Germany, have a brief period of powered flight, then coast through space or the upper atmosphere on a ballistic trajectory that brings them back to Earth. Although the number of states with such missiles grew steadily during the Cold War, it is now decreasing. [Since March 2001], for example, Hungary, Poland and the Czech Republic have destroyed their small arsenals of Soviet-supplied Scud missiles; only Bahrain has joined the missile club with the purchase of some short-range missiles from the United States.

The existence of three dozen countries with ballistic missiles would still seem very dangerous but for two factors: Almost all these nations are friends of the United States, and almost all have only short-range missiles that threaten only their neighbors.

Distance Provides Security

The United States is protected from most missile threats by the oceans. Almost any nation wishing to attack America from its own territory must build a missile capable of traveling thousands of miles. Fortunately, it is very difficult and expensive to do that. This is why 21 of the 35 nations possessing missiles have been able to deploy only short-range missiles, much like the V-2s, that can't go farther than 200 miles. Three others have short-range missiles capable of traveling 600 miles. Many of the missiles are old, poorly maintained and unreliable.

Of the other 10 nations besides the United States that have ballistic missiles, most only have medium-range systems that travel about 600 to 1,800 miles. That is far enough for Israel and Iran to hit each other, but not far enough for either to strike the United States.

Only China and Russia are able to attack the United States with nuclear warheads on long-range, land-based intercontinental missiles. This has not changed since Russia and China deployed their first ICBMs in 1959 and 1981, respectively. Even this threat is dwindling. Over the past 15 years, arms control agreements have cut arsenals capable of hitting the United States by 57 percent. The size of the Russian force, because of financial constraints, is expected to shrink further, from 1,022 to about 400 long-range missiles by the end of this decade; China might modernize and add to its 20 long-range missiles, but will probably deploy fewer than 40.

Not only is the American homeland less threatened by ballistic weapons; so are U.S. allies and troops in Europe. Arms control treaties with Moscow eliminated the entire class of intermediate-range ballistic missiles from the arsenal that once threatened Europe. Only three percent of the 680 missiles once in this class remain worldwide: China, with about 20 missiles, is the only nation that still possesses them.

Newly Emerging Nuclear Powers

What about the prevailing anxiety over newly emerging missile powers? The number of countries trying to develop ballistic missiles also has decreased and the nations still attempting to do so are poorer and less technologically advanced than were those trying 15 years ago. In the 1980s, we worried about missile programs in Argentina, Brazil, China, Egypt, Libya, India, Israel, Iraq, Pakistan, the Soviet

Union and South Africa. In 2002, the Soviet Union is long gone; former Soviet republics Ukraine, Belarus and Kazakhstan have given up their missiles. Brazil, Argentina, Egypt and South Africa have abandoned their programs, Libya's is defunct, and Iraq's has been largely shut down. Only North Korea and Iran have started new programs.

Rogue States: Nuclear Red Herrings

The United States and Russia currently possess 96 percent of the world's total inventory of 30,000 nuclear weapons. Most of the rest belong to U.S. allies and friends—Britain, France and Israel. The combined arsenals of Pakistan and India, with whom the United States enjoys reasonable relations, represent a small fraction of 1 percent. That leaves China, hardly an enemy, whose 1 percent of the world total includes 20 long-range missiles that could hit the United States (compared to 6,000-plus U.S. nuclear weapons that could reach China today). Then there is North Korea, which maybe has a couple of weapons but no missiles or planes capable of dropping them on U.S. targets. The other proliferant states of concern—notably Iran—do not yet possess a single nuclear bomb.

Bruce Blair, *CDI Defense Monitor*, January/February 2004.

The most significant proliferation threat today comes from the slow but steady increase in the number of states testing medium-range ballistic missiles. This development is often cited as evidence of a larger proliferation threat. Seven nations—China, India, Iran, Israel, Pakistan, North Korea and Saudi Arabia—now have missiles in this range. Of these, three potentially could come into conflict with the United States—China, Iran and North Korea.

But China is the only potentially hostile nation with both ballistic missiles that can reach the United States and the nuclear warheads to put on them. North Korea might in the next 10 years develop a missile with a nuclear warhead that could reach the United States, but it does not have that capability now. Iran has neither long-range missiles nor nuclear warheads. Iran's effort to import and duplicate North Korean missiles appears in disarray after its Shahab-3 missiles blew up in two of the three tests it conducted in 1998 and 2000. . . . While theoretically possible, it appears unlikely that . . . Iran . . . will have a nuclear-armed long-range missile within the next 10 to 15 years.

Still, even if there are fewer missiles and fewer nations with missiles, if one of these three nations deployed a long-range missile by 2010, wouldn't that mean the missile threat was more acute? Not necessarily. Capability does not necessitate use. Each of these countries would almost surely be deterred from attacking the United States by the certainty that swift retaliation would follow even a failed or thwarted attack. It is also likely that the United States would preemptively destroy a missile as it was being assembled for launch.

Even our worst-case scenarios aren't as bad as they once were. If deterrence or preventive defense failed, the damage that countries such as North Korea, Iran or Iraq could inflict with one or two warheads would be a major catastrophe. But compare that to the nuclear exchange we feared 15 years ago—in which thousands of Soviet warheads would have destroyed our country, or even the planet. The United States and NATO [North Atlantic Treaty Organization] spent hundreds of billions of dollars, fielded dozens of military systems and endured numerous diplomatic crises precisely because we feared those missiles. We lived through decades of anxiety, from civil defense drills in classrooms to dueling deployments of Soviet SS-20s in Eastern Europe and U.S. Pershing and cruise missiles in Western Europe. In no sense can the missile threat today be considered more imminent or lethal than the threat 15, 20 or 40 years ago.

Then why do so many people feel it is?

An Exaggerated Threat

It may be the psychology of threat assessments. Proliferation experts invariably see the future as more threatening than the past. It is, after all, the unknown. In addition, historical revisionism has transformed the Soviet Union to an almost benign, predictable and deterrable foe, in contrast to today's supposedly unpredictable, less easily deterred rogues. This was not how the Soviet threat was viewed at the time, however.

More concretely, the estimates of the ballistic missile threat prepared by the intelligence community over the past few years have focused on Iran, Iraq and North Korea, rather than assessing the entire global picture. This approach distorts the threat. Like a fun-house mirror, it makes objects appear larger than they really are.

This is not primarily the fault of the agencies, which, in fact, have sophisticated and varied opinions on the threat. After the Republican Party won control of Congress in 1994, congressional leaders relentlessly attacked government analysts who presented balanced assessments for understating the missile threat. Congress mandated its own assessment by a hand-picked commission chaired by Donald Rumsfeld. His 1998 report warned that a ballistic missile attack could come from a hostile state "with little or no warning." This fit with preconceived positions for increased defense budgets and a crash program to field a national missile defense system. U.S. intelligence agency analysts fell in line, giving Congress the worst-case scenarios some lawmakers sought. As Richard Perle said at the beginning of the Reagan presidency, "Democracies will not sacrifice to protect their security in the absence of a sense of danger." Exaggerated views of the missile threat provided that sense of danger.

September 11 showed us real danger. And it had nothing to do with missiles. The ballistic missile threat today is confined, limited and changing relatively slowly. There is every reason to believe that it can be addressed through diplomacy and measured military preparedness. If missile defenses prove feasible, particularly those designed to counter the more prevalent short-range missiles, they can be an important part of these efforts. But they should never dominate our policy. The sooner we restore balance to our assessments, budgets and diplomacy, the better prepared the country will be for the genuine threats we face.

> "*Several factors have come together to increase the likelihood of [biological weapon] acquisition and use by subnational groups.*"

Biological Terrorism Poses a Serious Threat

Amy Sands

In the following viewpoint, originally given as testimony before the U.S. Senate Foreign Relations Committee on March 19, 2002, Amy Sands argues that terrorist use of biological weapons against the United States could result in an outbreak of disease, with casualties many times those that resulted from the September 11, 2001, terrorist attacks. Moreover, Sands questions many of the reasons experts cite to argue that a bioterror attack is unlikely. For example, Sands argues against the conventional wisdom that rogue states are unlikely to provide terrorists with bioweapons, and she disputes the widespread belief that terrorists do not have the means to build their own bioweapons. Sands concludes that the United States should reevaluate the bioterror threat and take new steps to counter it. Amy Sands is deputy director of the Monterey Institute's Center for Nonproliferation Studies in Washington, D.C.

As you read, consider the following questions:
1. In the author's view, what particular advantage might terrorists seek to gain from using bioweapons?
2. According to the author, why is the technical workforce needed to manufacture bioweapons more available and inexpensive than it was during the Cold War?

Amy Sands, testimony before the U.S. Senate Foreign Relations Committee, Washington, DC, March 19, 2002.

S ince the end of the Cold War, the acquisition and potential use of chemical and biological technologies and materials by state and sub-state actors have become increasingly real threats. The recent trend towards chemical and biological weapons (CBW) terrorism—most notably the 1995 sarin nerve agent attack in the Tokyo subway and the actual use of anthrax against individuals in the United States, coupled with the state-level proliferation of offensive CBW programs, have created a security environment in which defending against chemical and biological attacks by states as well as sub-national groups must be the top priority.

The anthrax letter attacks that occurred [in fall 2001] only hint at the potential for casualties and widespread panic associated with a BW event. The [September 11, 2001] terrorists were able to plot and train secretly over several years to massacre thousands of people and die in the effort. It is conceivable that terrorists with similar dedication could deliberately obtain, weaponize, and disseminate a contagious pathogen such as smallpox or plague, and the results could make September 11th pale in comparison. In an era where people can literally move anywhere around the world within 36 hours—far less than the incubation period of many diseases of concern—all nations could be affected. In addition, advances in biotechnology, and the proliferation of BW know-how and dual-use equipment, might make it possible for terrorists to engineer highly virulent, antibiotic-resistant "designer" pathogens to suit their needs. . . .

Worrisome Trends

Several factors have come together to increase the likelihood of CBW acquisition and use by sub-national groups. First, terrorists may see CBW as giving them a new advantage. They know we are incredibly worried about such a possibility and may believe such an attack will not only kill many Americans, but also could psychologically "freeze" the United States.

Second, chem-bio materials are available and there is clear evidence of terrorists being interested in obtaining these materials. This supply-demand dynamic could easily be played out at biological research institutions in the FSU [former Soviet Union]. If security is poor or lacking (as many suspect) at these institutions, they would be vulnerable to theft of pathogens, toxins, and other material of potential use by criminals, other countries, or terrorists. Most important, after theft, it would be easy for the perpetrator to hide and transport seed cultures of organisms that could be directly used in biological weapons or to produce toxins.

Third, some terrorist groups exist that are clearly capable of organizing and operationalizing the type of complex long-term effort that would be needed to develop and effectively deliver CBW agents. The planning effort behind the September 11th events was both long term and complex, and it surprised many that terrorists could sustain such an effort. It clearly signaled a level of commitment and operational thoroughness thought to be beyond most terrorist groups.

Fourth, cooperation between groups and with states possessing CBW capabilities may be growing. An example of such cooperation is reflected in Iran's relationship with three terrorist groups, Hamas, Hizbollah, and Islamic Jihad. In April 2001, Iran reiterated its unflinching support for those terrorist groups working against Israel by hosting the International Conference on the Palestinian Intifada in Tehran, which was convened by the Iranian parliament. Those invited included leaders from Hamas, Hizbollah, and Islamic Jihad, presumably to encourage greater cooperation between these groups in their campaigns against Israel. At the conference, Iran's religious leader Ayatollah Khamenei repeated his description of Israel as a "cancerous tumor" ripe for removal.

Finally, the technical workforce needed to develop effective CBW is available and "cheap." This concern about workforce availability deserves more attention. As is well known by now, the Soviet Union established a powerful, well-funded secret program to acquire biological weapons. In 1992, President B. Yeltsin acknowledged the BW program's existence and decreed that it be discontinued and dismantled in Russia. The decree's effect, when combined with the general decrease in public support by the Russian government for science, led to drastic funding cuts for the BW program. Although we do not know the full consequences of these measures, some dedicated BW facilities (such as

Stepnogorsk) were closed down and many others down-sized (including Obolensk and Vektor). Hundreds, perhaps thousands, of scientists, engineers, and technicians were fired or had their wages cut. . . .

A CBW Threat Reality Check

Too often we comfortably reiterate the same threat mantra without examining more closely certain underlying assumptions. Discussed below are several traditionally accepted statements often found in threat assessments that deserve to be challenged.

Assumption: Terrorists don't have physical locations to make/store materials. It is often argued that terrorists may have safe havens, but will still lack a physical infrastructure to develop CBW. Also, it has been assumed that it will be virtually impossible to detect terrorists hunkering down in caves and basements and working on CB agents. However, an often overlooked point is that terrorist groups can and have actually possessed recognizable (and targetable) CBW facilities. While this possibility is not a new concern, the extent of it occurring and its implications may not be fully recognized.

The US government has viewed the subject of terrorist facilities with concern, but little public discussion has developed about terrorists having CBW facilities within their safe havens as well as within established western states. An early, but well publicized, example was the Clinton administration's controversial cruise missile attack on the Al-Shifa pharmaceutical plant in Sudan on August 20, 1998. It argued that the plant was linked to [terrorist Osama] Bin Laden and that it was not a pharmaceutical plant, but a chemical weapons manufacturing complex that was engaged in the production of the nerve agent VX.

At the other extreme of public exposure are the facilities in the former Yugoslavia. On July 8, 1999, the Italian newspaper *Corriere della Serra* indicated that members of the World Islamic Front Against Jews and Crusaders, which was founded by Bin Laden, had purchased three chemical and biological agent production facilities in the former Yugoslavia in early May 1998. According to the article, one such facility was erected in the Bosnian village of Zenica.

The Threat of Smallpox

What is smallpox?

It's a virus. (The scientific name of the most common and deadly form of the disease is *variola major*.) Smallpox is ancient; descriptions of the disease have been found dating from as far back as the 4th century A.D. in China, and less reliable evidence even points to cases as far back as 1200 B.C. . . .

How dangerous is smallpox?

Historically, smallpox killed about 30 percent of those infected. The mortality rate varied with age (with small children and the elderly proving the most vulnerable) and with the strength of a person's immune system (with preexisting illness or malnutrition making one more susceptible). Less frequently, complications such as encephalitis (an inflammation of the brain) and blindness also resulted. Smallpox is one of the most devastating diseases known to humankind, having killed between 300 and 500 million people in the twentieth century alone. . . .

How would a terrorist "weaponize" smallpox?

Smallpox is small enough to be inhaled, so it could be spread in an aerosol. The virus is very stable, which means it isn't easy to destroy, and it retains its potency for days outside a human host. According to the *New York Times* reporters Judith Miller, Stephen Engelberg, and William Broad, smallpox can be freeze-dried and stored at room temperature for months or years, and remain potent when revived with water. American scientists in the 1960s were able to turn dried smallpox into a fine powder and to create tiny aerosol generators that could disseminate the virus.

Could al-Qaeda or other terrorist groups obtain supplies of smallpox?

Smallpox is less readily available than many other agents, such as anthrax or the bacterium that causes plague, and special skills are required to grow the virus in large quantities and to preserve it for dispersion as an aerosol. Thus smallpox would seem an unlikely weapon for small, technically unsophisticated groups of fanatics, bioterrorism experts say—not least because the virus could kill anyone trying to use it. But because it is so dangerous, smallpox may still appeal to ambitious terrorists.

Council on Foreign Relations, Terrorism Questions & Answers Web site, www.terrorismanswers.org/weapons/smallpox.html.

The report also stated that another factory was built near Kandahar, Afghanistan, There was no open investigation or diplomacy, and certainly no cruise missile, directed against these facilities at that time. Allegedly, members of the World Islamic Front for Fighting Jews and Crusaders hired Ukrainian scientists to manufacture unspecified poisons and train Bin Laden's activists in the use of these substances as weapons. The activists would be trained to insert the chemical agents and toxins into explosive devices. Bin Laden planned to send the chemically-trained warriors back to their home countries or to cells in Europe.

During the [2001] war in Afghanistan, US intelligence officials pinpointed two sites that may have been used by al-Qa'ida to produce chemical weapons. The United States believes cyanide was produced at a crude chemical facility in the small village of Derunta (Darunta), near the city of Jalalabad in eastern Afghanistan. The secret laboratory contained bottles of cyanide poison and bomb instruction manuals, and was allegedly run by a man named Abu Khabab. A fertilizer plant in the northern town of Mazar-e-Sharif is also suspected of playing a role in possible chemical weapons production.

Beyond al-Qa'ida there is Aum Shinrikyo, who, through substantial contributions from wealthy members, purchased a wide variety of businesses and facilities including a medical clinic, computer stores, and trading companies. Also, the cult purchased land in Japan, on which they built a compound where they were able to pursue research and development of various dangerous and potentially lethal materials. Using its businesses as a front, the cult could claim some legitimacy for its pursuit of certain chemicals and technology. Although most of the chemicals were obtained from within Japan, Aum purchased some materials from the United States and attempted to buy weapons and technology from Russia. In addition, the cult bought a ranch in a remote area of Australia to carry out testing of nerve agents.

As all these cases demonstrate, terrorists have had access to or possession of facilities. Some of these may even be located outside of safe havens and may appear legitimate, making the task of detecting and identifying them accurately much more difficult. . . .

Assumption: States won't provide terrorists with CBW. Compounding the threat to US national security is the possibility that states with CBW programs or related dual-use technologies could provide sub-national actors with these deadly tools. The issue of state sponsorship of terrorism has been a problem commonly associated with rogue states in the Middle East. States such as Iran, Iraq, Libya, Syria, and Sudan have been linked to numerous terror organizations, providing them with a wide variety of assistance, including financial support, weapons and other equipment and materials, and even specialized training bases. Even though there has been little evidence to indicate that any of these states have transferred CBW material, technology or know-how to such terrorist organizations, the possibility cannot be ruled out. The more states that proliferate and pursue chemical and biological weapons programs, the greater the possibility that sub-national actors will acquire them, either from direct assistance or through other covert means, including theft.

Many of the same states identified as terrorist sponsors are also those accused of attempting to acquire CBW capabilities. Under certain circumstances the leaders of these countries may decide the only practical utility they can derive from their CBW arsenals is by deploying them covertly, using sub-national actors as means of delivery.

Even if a state may not be willing to transfer CBW-related technologies to a sub-national actor, one cannot discount the possibility of rogue elements within a government—such as an extremist clique within the Iranian intelligence apparatus—being prepared to take more risks than the government as a whole. Within national CBW programs, disgruntled or underpaid scientists, or individuals sympathetic to terrorist causes may also be willing to illicitly transfer CBW-related technologies and know-how to terrorist groups. In summary, the threat that a state actor may indirectly or directly transfer CBW-related technologies, equipment and scientific know-how to a sub-national actor is a threat the US government cannot ignore.

Terrorists' Willingness to Resort to Bioweapons

Assumption: Terrorists won't use CBW except in extreme cases.
With the exception of the terrorist group Aum Shinrikyo, the long-held assumption has been that sub-national groups

and terrorists will not use CBW except as a last resort. Many state players perceive a threshold created by international norms that prevents them from openly using CBW. However, non-state players, especially terrorists, do not act under the same restraints as sovereign states. It is possible that these organizations do not perceive such a threshold. Moreover, their assessment of the costs and benefits of using CBW cannot be measured on the same scale as that of nations. Terrorist organizations and religious fanatical groups are not under the same political restrictions as sovereign states. In fact, if the motivation of an organization is to infuse terror, then use of CBW even on a small scale, might be seen as furthering their cause. Omar Bakri Mohammed, an Islamic cleric with ties to Islamic Jihad (and Hamas), advocated the use of biological weapons against "western" forces, saying "if any Muslims are under occupation by a western force, they can use any weapon to survive and that includes biological weapons."

The disparity between Israeli and Palestinian forces may lead to the use of CBW in an effort to balance the scales. This thought was expressed in the Palestinian weekly "Al-Manar":

> While the human-bombs [meaning, suicide bombers] may be followed [and may be stopped by] preventive measures . . . serious thinking has begun for a while about developing a Palestinian weapon of deterrence. This weapon terrifies the Israeli security apparatuses, from time to time, mainly because obtaining its primary components, whether biological or chemical, is possible without too much effort, let alone the fact that there are hundreds of experts who are capable of handling them and use them as weapons of deterrence, thus creating a balance of horror in the equation of the Palestinian-Israeli conflict. A few bombs or death-carrying devices will be enough, once they are deployed in secluded areas and directed at the Israeli water resources or the Israeli beaches, let alone the markets and the residential centers. [This will be carried out] without explosions, noise, blood, or pictures that are used to serve the Israeli propaganda. Anyone who is capable, with complete self-control, of turning his body into shrapnel and scattered organs, is also capable of carrying a small device that cannot be traced and throw it in the targeted location.

Thus, an asymmetric conflict, even where the imbalance

is not so great, can be used as justification for turning to CBW. It would be folly not to recognize and respond to all the trends pointing to the CBW option as one increasingly attractive to terrorists.

Assumption: US must focus efforts on homeland security and defense. While this assumption is not wrong, it may lead to neglecting other venues in which US interests or allies are at risk. A good case in point is US Central Command in the Middle East. It is very much at risk given its location in the heart of some of the most anti-American groups. It would be a mistake to pour so much into enhancing US domestic security when equal attention should be given to those Americans mobilized and deployed to protect us. In addition, planning for responding to CBW terrorism must consider providing assistance to allies. What if Italy is the site of a smallpox attack—we had better have planned some way to have adequate resources available to contain the consequences of such an attack. This means having vaccine available in some international organization or stockpile above and beyond what is needed for the US population.

Reassessing the Bioterror Threat

We have to be prepared to respond to chem-bio events and to do everything we can to prevent them from ever occurring. But, that will require new ways of approaching old, evolving, and emerging perils.

First, what is required is innovative thinking and a re-conceptualization of threats in the 21st century. In past years, when terrorists were unlikely to have the capability to cause or even seek mass casualties, US foreign policy could focus on the more critical and traditional problem of state threats. Even in the aftermath of the collapse of the Soviet Union and subsequent re-making of the world order, it was clear who the enemies were (Iraq, North Korea), and these enemies were defined not only by their antagonism towards the United States and its values, but also by the fact that they were seeking weapons of mass destruction.

Addressing even the "old" threats will require more than just military power. It requires a long term dedication to a multi-dimensional and multi-faceted approach that seeks to prevent WMD acquisition and use, strengthens anti-proliferation norms, develops adequate defenses here and elsewhere, and prepares for effective consequent mitigation and management in the advent of a WMD attack. Specifically, this means not only putting significant money into US military and intelligence capabilities, but also into international organizations and collaborations. It involves finding ways to bridge gaps within the US government as well as between states, communities, and even tribes. It also means forging new partnerships and helping to build trust and cooperation in areas where these have been scarce commodities.

Second, the United States, while recognizing the ongoing threat from proliferant states, also faces a threat from a new type of terrorist. The US appears to be approaching the problem of mass-casualty transnational terrorism, and the possibility of terrorist use of WMD, in a manner consistent with deeply entrenched Cold War assumptions about warfare and deterrence. The terrorists of today do not, by and large, behave like states, nor are they part of the international "system." Addressing those terrorists who seek and obtain WMD will require much of the same effort that has been expended on states in the past, plus a strategy that addresses the root causes and nature of terrorism. Long-term approaches that go beyond the next election must be incorporated into the national counterterrorism strategy. These approaches include investing in states that are in danger of collapse in order to prevent the spiral into statelessness that creates a haven for terrorism; involving allies and partners in regional confidence-building measures that are designed to validate US policy to the publics of other nations rather than just the governments; and creating an international safety net to ensure that the rule of law and social infrastructures remain intact even through conflict.

> *"The probability of a major biological attack by either a state or a sophisticated terrorist group seems remote."*

The Threat of Biological Terrorism Has Been Exaggerated

John Parachini

John Parachini is a policy analyst for RAND, a nonprofit research institution that specializes in national security issues. The following viewpoint is based on testimony that Parachini gave before Congress in October 2001. In it, he argues that the prospect of bioterrorism has garnered more attention from the government and generated more fear among the public than is warranted. Biological weapons are very difficult to develop, Parachini argues; terrorists would likely need the resources of a government to develop bioweapons, and even anti-American governments would be unlikely to provide such dangerous weapons to terrorist groups they cannot fully control. In addition, Parachini believes that there are major disincentives to using biological weapons, including the fact that terrorists can already cause serious damage with conventional explosives.

As you read, consider the following questions:

1. How many significant bioterror attacks have there been since 1983, according to Parachini?
2. In the author's view, what is the major disincentive to state use of biological weapons?
3. In Parachini's opinion, what is the greatest disincentive to terrorist use of biological weapons?

John Parachini, testimony before the House Subcommittee on National Security, Veterans Affairs, and International Relations, Committee on Government Reform, Washington, DC, October 12, 2001.

S ince the [September 11, 2001, terrorist attacks], many Americans have become concerned about the prospect of biological terrorism. After all, it seems plausible that hijackers willing to kill themselves, those aboard commercial airliners, and thousands more in the World Trade Center and the Pentagon might be willing to use biological agents to kill indiscriminately. . . .

Exaggerated Fears

The fear over biological terrorism is greater than the fear inspired by more conventional forms of terrorism. Some of this fear is justified and some of it is exaggerated. Some agents are highly contagious and lethal. Indeed, some biological agents if used in certain ways have the potential to deliver a strategic strike with casualty results similar to nuclear weapons. In fact, simply the fear they evoke imbues them with power. And perhaps the most frightening aspect of biological weapons is how they invade the body without notice. We fear threats we cannot see, hear, or feel.

However, in these uncertain times, it is important to maintain some perspective of the relative dangers. The twentieth-century history of warfare, terrorism, and crime involving biological agents is much less deadly than that of the history with conventional explosives. While history is not a perfect guide to the future, it does provide a context for our thinking about the future. Dramatic advances in the biological sciences could create previously unimaginable opportunities for terrorists bent on using the life sciences for their pernicious purposes. At the same time, biotechnology may provide tools that lessen these dangers. Remedies for enhanced or improvised conventional explosives, such as those used on September 11th, may be equally difficult to handle if not more so. Since the future is impossible to see clearly, we must anticipate a number of possible scenarios. We need to take account of history and hedge against the seeming imponderables of the future.

Given these heightened (and even exaggerated) public fears and given reports that law enforcement and intelligence officials believe that another terrorist attack of some kind is highly likely . . . there is a real need to conduct a thorough and sober assessment of biological terrorism. Such an assessment entails answering two interrelated questions. First, how feasible is it for terrorists groups to use biological and chemical weapons? And second, given the question of feasibility, how likely is it that terrorist groups would conduct attacks using biological or chemical weapons? The answers to both of these questions vary in terms of the actors involved, that is whether the biological is state-sponsored or whether it is the effort of sub-national groups or individuals acting in concert or independently of a state. . . .

How Feasible Is It for Terrorist Groups to Use Biological Weapons?

When it comes to the feasibility of using biological or chemical weapons, states are more likely to have the resources, technical capabilities, and organizational capacity to assemble the people, know-how, material, and equipment to produce such weapons and to be able to clandestinely deliver them to valued targets. Nonetheless, mustering the resources and capabilities to inflict a devastating blow with biological agents has proven to be a formidable task even for states. The United States and the former Soviet Union dedicated considerable national defense resources to their biological weapons programs, and both countries encountered significant difficulties along the way. Iraq also dedicated considerable resources to its biological weapons program; although Iraq's effort was more successful than most experts imagined possible, it still encountered a number of significant challenges. Some of these difficulties are unique and inevitable for state programs that aim to achieve a militarily significant capacity with military-grade agents. Lower standards of achievement are certainly possible. On balance, then, a state's ability to command resources and organize them for certain priority scientific and industrial objectives presents the potential for the greatest threat of bioterrorism.

When it comes to the feasibility of biological terrorism perpetrated by sub-national groups and individuals, the range of capability (and level of consequence) depends on whether the groups or individuals are state-sponsored or not. High-consequence biological attacks would require the assistance of a state sponsor or considerable resources. However, even these conditions do not ensure high-consequence attacks by sub-national groups or individuals. There are no widely agreed upon historical examples in the open source literature of states providing sub-national groups with biological weapons for overt or covert use. Money, arms, logistical support, training, and even training on how to operate in a chemically contaminated environment are all forms of assistance states have provided to terrorists. But historically they have not crossed the threshold and provided biological weapons materials to insurgency groups or terrorist organizations. Even if states sought to perpetrate biological attacks for their own purposes, they would probably not trust such an operation to groups or individuals that they do not completely control. . . .

Auth. © 2002 by *The Philadelphia Inquirer*. Reproduced by permission of Universal Press Syndicate.

What is more likely than a conscious decision by a country's command authority is that an unauthorized faction within a state might take it upon itself to use a sub-national group to do its dirty work. The alleged involvement of the Iranian government security services in the attack on American military personnel in Khobar Towers seems to be an example of this type of involvement. Thus, while the probability of states using sub-national groups or individuals to perpetrate a biological warfare attack on its behalf seems low, it is not zero. In these times of dramatic change, American and allied intelligence services should be attentive to this possibility, even though it is without historical precedent and seems unlikely.

Sub-national groups or individuals can develop or acquire their own biological weapon capabilities for clandestine use, but it is not easy. Terrorist groups and individuals have historically not employed biological weapons because of a combination of formidable barriers to acquisition and use and comparatively readily available alternatives and disincentives. Procurement of materials and recruitment of people with skills and know-how are formidable barriers. Even if some of the materials and production equipment are procurable for legitimate scientific or industrial purposes, handling virulent biological materials and fashioning them into weapons capable of producing mass casualties is beyond the reach of most sub-national groups or individuals.

Few Real-Life Instances of Bioterrorism

In the last twenty years, there are only two significant cases of sub-national groups using or attempting to use biological weapons and a few cases where groups or individuals made efforts to acquire biological materials. In the first of those cases, the Rajneeshees, a religious cult group located in Oregon, sought to win a local election in 1984 by running its own candidates and sickening local townspeople who they expected would vote against them. Using their medical clinics, cult members ordered a variety of bacterial cultures from the American Type Culture Collection located in Maryland. They intentionally and indiscriminately contaminated ten salad bars with a strain of salmonella, sickening at least 751 people. They used commercially available biological agents to incapacitate people clandestinely, because it was important for them to avoid attracting attention. Indeed, the intentional character of the outbreak was not recognized for over a year, when members of the cult revealed details about the attacks to authorities in exchange for lighter sentences stemming from other charges.

The other case occurred more than ten years later, when another religious cult, a Japanese group called the Aum Shinrikyo, sought to develop and deliver biological agents against a number of targets. The Aum's unsuccessful attempts at biological terrorism came to light after it released liquid sarin on the Tokyo subway. While this attack was heralded as a sign that sub-national groups would begin breaking the taboo on use of unconventional weapons, six years have passed since the attack and no other group has done so.

The clearest explanation for this extremely small historical data set is the difficulty of acquiring and delivering biological weapons, as well as a number of disincentives to doing so.

How Likely Is It That Terrorist Groups Would Use Biological Weapons?

The probability of a major biological attack by either a state or a sophisticated terrorist group seems remote. In contrast, smaller acts of biocriminality, such as the [2001] anthrax case in Florida, are much more likely biological terrorist attacks. While states can amass the resources and capabilities to wage biological terrorism, considerable disincentives keep them from doing so. A state that undertook a clandestine attack using biological weapons risks the prospect of the attack being traced back to them. The response to an attack with biological weapons could be devastating, which gives states reason for caution. While different U.S. administrations have articulated American policy on responding to known biological attacks in different ways, the basic position is that the United States reserves the right to respond with the full range of capabilities in the arsenal. Strategic ambiguity provides maximum flexibility while leaving no uncertainty about the potential magnitude of the response—devastating. The threat of retaliation is believed to deter states from using biological weapons clandestinely against other states.

However, there are three circumstances when a state might clandestinely wage biological terrorism. First, a state struggling for its existence might be willing to use biological weapons clandestinely as a means to forestall or to prevent a seemingly imminent defeat. There is no historical example of a state responding with a biological weapon in a moment of desperate struggle for its existence, but it is conceivable.

Second, if a state felt it could attack with biological weapons and be undetected, it might do so. In the twentieth century, there are a few examples of states using biological agents clandestinely except during times of war. For example, in the First World War, Germany sought to disrupt allied logistical capabilities by infecting horses with glanders—a contagious and destructive disease caused by a bacterium. There are a few other alleged wartime cases, but none in times of peace.

The third situation when a state might engage in biological terrorism would be when it sought to perpetrate an attack against its own citizens. In the 1980s, both the Bulgarian and the South African governments used biological materials to kill domestic political opponents. South Africa had a significant clandestine chemical and biological program that supported a major effort against regime opponents. Little is known about the Bulgarian program. Bulgarian operatives are believed to have assassinated a Bulgarian dissident in London with the toxin ricin, which they received from the Soviet KGB. Aside from state assassinations of perceived regime opponents, historically states have been extremely reluctant to use biological weapons overtly or covertly.

Thus, state biological terrorism is a low probability threat, albeit one with potentially catastrophic consequences. During times of war, this threat increases in probability and is highest when a command authority perceives itself in a desperate situation in which using any means necessary may be its only option for survival.

Disincentives to Bioterror

On a more general level, there are incentives and disincentives for using biological weapons, but the disincentives tend to win out. As for the incentives, the acquisition, transfer, production, and delivery of biological weapons make them comparatively easy to conceal if managed by skilled personnel. (Conversely, of course, while they are comparatively easy to conceal, some agents can be extremely contagious and some can be extremely deadly, making them difficult to handle.) Because bacteria and viruses are living microorganisms, small amounts can be used to grow much larger quantities. In addition, some biological agents, such as toxins, can be derived from naturally occurring plants or animals. Thus, the physical properties of some biological agents make them effective strategic weapons that can be assembled covertly.

Indeed, biological agents may appeal to terrorist groups because of what they can do or what they represent. As for what they can do, such agents may be desirable because they affect people indiscriminately, have a delayed impact, can be confused with natural disease outbreaks, and, in some cases, incapacitate rather than kill. As noted earlier, the Rajneeshees chose a biological material that would incapacitate people rather than kill, because they did not want their attack to provoke the scrutiny of authorities. Aum, in contrast, was fascinated with poisons. The cult's leader Shoko Asahara wrote songs about sarin. In addition to this pernicious obsession, Aum leaders had delusions of grandeur that far exceeded reality. They imagined a world they sought to create that was not constrained by the world in which they lived. To bring this imaginary world into being, they sought weapons they believed might trigger an apocalypse from which they would emerge as a dominant power. Since Aum leaders viewed their organization as a government and military in waiting, seeking to acquire some of the most potent weapons it believed states possessed. Instead of seeking lower-grade pathogens, Aum sought pathogens that are generally associated with military biological weapons programs. Aum exhibited this unique combination of obsession, delusions of grandeur, and belief in an apocalypse they could launch that would enable them to reign like leaders of a state.

Despite the incentives for seeking and using biological weapons, there are a number of even more compelling disincentives. As noted earlier, terrorists may hesitate in using biological weapons specifically because breaking the taboo on their use may evoke considerable retaliation. In addition, state sponsors of terrorist groups may exert restraint on the weapons the group uses. State sponsors have a great incentive to control the activities of the groups they support, because they fear that retaliation may be directed against them if they are connected to a group that used biological weapons. Moreover, terrorists may be drawn to explosives like arsonists are drawn to fire. The immediate gratification of explosives and the thrill of the blast may meet a psychological need of terrorists that the delayed effects of biological weapons do not.

However, perhaps the greatest disincentive to using biological weapons is that terrorists can inflict (and have inflicted) many more fatalities and casualties with conventional explosives than with unconventional weapons. Putting aside the spectacular quality of the Aum subway attack with liquid sarin, far fewer people died or were injured than in similarly spectacular attacks with conventional explosives. In comparison to the bombings of the Murrah federal building in Oklahoma City, the Khobar Towers military barracks in Saudi Arabia, and the U.S. embassies in Kenya and Tanzania, fewer people died as a result of the sarin release. In comparison with the recent attacks on the World Trade Center and the Pentagon, the Tokyo subway incident, though clearly tragic, was simply an event of much smaller scale.

Periodical Bibliography

The following articles have been selected to supplement the diverse views presented in this chapter.

Michael Duffy	"Could It Happen Again?" *Time*, August 4, 2003.
Gregg Easterbrook	"The Big One: The Real Danger Is Nuclear," *New Republic*, November 5, 2001.
Economist	"The Spores of War," November 30, 2002.
Sarah Estabrooks	"Nuclear Terrorism," *Ploughshares Monitor*, December 2001.
Sydney J. Freedberg Jr.	"Beyond the Blue Canaries," *National Journal*, March 10, 2001.
Laurie Garrett	"The Nightmare of Bioterrorism," *Foreign Affairs*, January/February 2001.
Richard L. Garwin	"The Technology of Mega Terror," *Technology Review*, September 2002.
Siobhan Gorman and Sydney J. Freedberg Jr.	"A Burnt-Orange Nation," *National Journal*, March 1, 2003.
Richard Lacayo	"Will We Be Safer?" *Time*, September 8, 2003.
John Newhouse	"The Threats America Faces," *World Policy Journal*, Summer 2002.
John Parachini	"Putting WMD Terrorism into Perspective," *Washington Quarterly*, Autumn 2003.
Douglas Pasternak	"A Nuclear Nightmare," *U.S. News & World Report*, September 17, 2001.
John L. Scherer	"Awaiting Armageddon: Is the Paranoia Justified?" *USA Today Magazine*, January 2004.
Jonathan B. Tucker and Amy Sands	"An Unlikely Threat," *Bulletin of the Atomic Scientists*, July 1999.
World Watch	"Weapons of Mass Distraction," July/August 2003.

How Should the United States Deal with Countries That Threaten to Develop Weapons of Mass Destruction?

Chapter Preface

"Is Iran next after Iraq?" asked BBC correspondent Justin Webb in a May 2003 report. Many journalists and political observers have asked the same thing about North Korea. President George W. Bush declared in January 2002 that all three nations were developing weapons of mass destruction (WMD) and therefore constituted an "axis of evil," so when the United States invaded Iraq in spring 2003, Webb and other political observers questioned whether Iran and North Korea might also become military targets.

Iraq had previously flouted international law in August 1990, when it invaded neighboring Kuwait. The United States, as part of a coalition of nations chartered by the United Nations, quickly drove the Iraqi occupation army out of Kuwait in February 1991. Soon after, Iraqi leader Saddam Hussein accepted the terms of a UN resolution requiring it to end its WMD programs. For the rest of the 1990s, the Iraqi government walked a fine line, alternately agreeing and refusing to cooperate with UN weapons inspectors.

After the September 11, 2001, terrorist attacks on America, President George W. Bush and other U.S. officials began arguing that Iraq was moving forward with its WMD programs and therefore constituted a threat to the United States. In consequence,White House officials claimed, Saddam Hussein must be removed from power. However, the UN Security Council refused to pass a resolution authorizing military action against Iraq. France, Germany, and other nations argued that UN weapons inspectors in Iraq should be given more time to find concrete evidence of Iraq's WMD programs. The United States invaded Iraq without UN approval on March 20, 2003.

A continuing controversy over Iraq is whether the U.S. invasion was indeed necessary, or whether further inspections could have kept Saddam Hussein in check. The debate over how to keep Iran and North Korea from pursuing their own WMD programs also comes down to a choice between diplomacy and the use of force. The authors in the following chapter offer their opinions about how the United States should deal with the "axis of evil."

*"The [Bush] administration's refusal to sit
down and talk [with] North Korea . . .
makes no sense."*

Negotiation Can Reduce the Nuclear Threat Posed by North Korea

Leon V. Sigal

Leon V. Sigal is director of the Northeast Asia Cooperative Security Project at the Social Science Research Council in New York and the author of *Disarming Strangers: Nuclear Diplomacy with North Korea*. In the following viewpoint he discusses the diplomatic standoff that arose in late 2002 between North Korea and the United States over North Korea's decision to move forward with its nuclear weapons program. Writing in February 2003, Sigal warns that the United States should not be too aggressive in its dealings with North Korea. Sigal believes that trying to coerce North Korea into dismantling its nuclear program will only worsen the crisis; instead, the United States should negotiate with North Korea and grant it some concessions, such as a pledge that the United States will not attack it.

As you read, consider the following questions:
1. What is North Korea's "basic stance," as described by Sigal?
2. How did President George W. Bush repudiate the U.S. pledge of "no hostile intent" toward North Korea, in Sigal's view?
3. In the author's opinion, what are the four options that the United States has in dealing with North Korea?

Leon V. Sigal, "The North Korean Crisis: A Humanitarian Perspective," *Asian Social Issues Program* (ASIP) on AsiaSource.Org, a research site of the Asia Society, February 12, 2003. Copyright © 2003 by the Asia Society. All rights reserved. Reproduced by permission.

[A]s of February 2003,] North Korea has . . . lit three nu-clear fuses, all of them long ones. North Korea could soon light a short nuclear fuse as well.

It is seeking equipment to enrich uranium. [According to] U.S. intelligence estimates, and I quote, North Korea "is constructing a plant that could produce enough weapons-grade uranium for two or more nuclear weapons per year when fully operational, which could be as soon as mid-decade." The uranium enrichment fuse, in other words, is more than three years long.

North Korea is preparing to restart production of pluto-nium by refueling its reactor at Yongbyon, which had been frozen under the 1994 Agreed Framework. Once refueled—the North told the IAEA [International Atomic Energy Agency] that would take one or two months—the reactor could generate a bomb's worth of plutonium in a year. Allow-ing at least another six months to reprocess and weaponize the plutonium, it could have a nuclear device in a year and a half, another device a year or so later, or five to six in five years.

Pyongyang [the capital and government of North Korea] also says it will resume construction of two reactors frozen under the 1994 accord. It will take at least two years to com-plete the first, longer to complete the second. Were they up and running, the three reactors could generate 30 bombs' worth of plutonium a year. Again, that fuse is quite long.

North Korea has yet to light a short fuse by removing the spent fuel now stored in casks in Yongbyon and reprocessing it. It could soon do so. If it does, within a year it could have five or six bombs' worth of plutonium fabricated into nu-clear devices.

These nuclear fuses are real. By contrast, whether or not North Korea already has one or two bombs is not known for sure. A divided U.S. intelligence community estimated in November 1993, nearly a year before the Agreed Frame-work was signed, that "it was more likely than not" it had "one, possibly two" nuclear devices, which was later lowered to one. Why the administration is now treating that possi-bility as a certainty is worth asking.

By its actions Pyongyang has convinced many in Wash-ington it is determined to arm and should be punished for brazenly breaking its commitments. Both that assessment and the policy that flows from it are wrong.

North Korea is no Iraq. It says it is ready to give up its nuclear, missile, and other weapons programs. In return it wants the United States to stop treating it like an enemy. The North's willingness to cut its nuclear fuses before they detonate a grave crisis is worth probing in direct negotiations.

That is what Pyongyang is seeking by renouncing the nuclear Nonproliferation Treaty. Renunciation not only leaves it no longer lawfully bound not to make nuclear arms, although it says it does not intend to do so "at this stage." It also leaves the 1994 Agreed Framework in effect as the only basis for negotiating inspections directly with the United States. This is intended to underscore North Korea's basic stance that if the United States remains its foe, it feels threatened and will seek nuclear arms and missiles to counter that threat, but if the United States is no longer its foe, it says it will not.

A Decade of Distrust

To understand why the North is acting this way, it is essential to recall how we got here. In the early 1990s Pyongyang decided to trade in its plutonium program in return for an end to enmity. At the same time it kept its nuclear option open as leverage on Washington to live up to its end of the bargain.

That became the basis of the October 1994 Agreed Framework, whereby North Korea agreed to freeze and eventually dismantle its plutonium program in return for two new light-water reactors for generating electricity, an interim supply of heavy fuel oil, gradual relaxation of U.S. economic sanctions, and, above all, improved relations.

Washington got what it most wanted up front, but it did not live up to its end of the bargain. When Republicans won control of Congress in elections just weeks later, they denounced the deal as appeasement. The Clinton administration, unwilling to challenge Congress, back-pedaled on implementation. It did little easing of sanctions until 1999. Reactor construction did not get under way until 1999. It did not always deliver heavy fuel oil on schedule. Above all, it did [not] live up to the pledge made in Article II to "move toward full normalization of political and economic relations"—in other words, end enmity. When Washington was slow to fulfill the terms of the accord, Pyongyang threatened to break it in 1997. Its effort to acquire technology to enrich uranium began soon thereafter.

Don't Try Regime Change in North Korea

Is it time for Operation Korean Freedom? The regime change in Iraq [in 2003] has prompted some to urge regime change in the other two members of the President George W. Bush's "axis of evil"—North Korea and Iran. . . .

What unintended consequences might result if the United States now ousts the brutal dictator of North Korea? . . .

War. North Korea takes military action to avert regime collapse or to coerce an end to the international pressure. South Koreans fear this outcome the most, because their country could be ravaged in the process. If North Korea indeed has nuclear weapons, it might use them. . . .

Civil War. Kim Jong-il's government collapses into factions and civil war breaks out. The loss of central control would leave North Korean weapons of mass destruction in the hands of domestic factions, which could try to sell them to third parties. . . .

A Worse Regime. A new regime takes over in North Korea that is weaker than Kim Jong-il's and even more nationalistic. . . .

These grim prospects, coupled with the lack of preparation for regime change, explain the reluctance of South Korea, China and Japan to support a policy of toppling Kim Jong-il.

This also explains why the United States has chosen the path of negotiation instead of launching an "Operation Korean Freedom." The likely dangerous consequences of regime change should also affect the willingness of the United States to accept a compromise in talks. Our tough stance may have been a good opening position, but only compromise can put this crisis behind us.

Bruce Bennett and Nina Hachigan, "Don't Try Regime Change in North Korea," *International Herald Tribune*, January 30, 2004.

At the same time the North tried again to improve relations, this time using its missile program as inducement. On June 16, 1998, it publicly offered to negotiate an end to its development as well as exports of ballistic missiles in return for a declared end to enmity. It coupled that offer with a threat to resume missile tests, a threat it carried out on August 31 when it launched a three-stage rocket, the Taepodong I, over Japan in an unsuccessful attempt to put a satellite into orbit.

Pyongyang's tactics led many to conclude it was engaging in blackmail in an attempt to extort economic aid without giving up anything in return. It was not. It was playing tit for tat, cooperating whenever Washington cooperated and retaliating when Washington reneged, in an effort to end hostile relations.

Thanks to [South Korean president] Kim Dae Jung and [former U.S. defense secretary] Bill Perry, Washington got back on the road to reconciliation in 1999. That policy paid off that September when Pyongyang agreed to suspend its test launching of missiles while negotiations proceeded. In return, Washington promised to end sanctions under the Trading with the Enemy Act, a pledge it carried out after the June 2000 North-South summit.

High-level talks in October 2000 yielded a pledge that "neither government would have hostile intent toward the other." In plain English, we are not enemies.

The declared end to enmity opened the way to a missile deal. In negotiations with Secretary of State Madeleine Albright in Pyongyang, North Korean ruler Kim Jong Il offered to end exports of all missile technology and to freeze testing, production, and deployment of all missiles with a range of 300 miles. Kim wanted President [Bill] Clinton to come to Pyongyang to seal the deal, consummation of a ten-year campaign to end enmity with the United States. Without his commitment to come, negotiations stalled.

The Bush Administration's Hardline Stance

Instead of picking up the ball where Clinton had dropped it, [President George W.] Bush moved the goalposts. Although it was aware of North Korea's ongoing nuclear and missile activities, the administration did not resume negotiations. Instead, it tried to reinterpret the Agreed Framework unilaterally, demanding prompt inspections to get at the North's nuclear past. In response, the North expressed willingness to renegotiate the 1994 nuclear accord, trading expedited inspections for electricity, which it regards as compensation for the delay in reactor construction, but without a deal it warned it could "no longer keep its nuclear activities in a state of freeze and implement the Agreed Framework." The North accelerated efforts to acquire the means to enrich uranium. Then in 2002 President Bush repudiated the U.S. pledge of no "hostile intent" by naming North Korea to the so-called "axis of evil" and announcing a new doctrine of waging preventive war—without allies, without U.N. sanction, in violation of international law. The North in turn began acquiring an operational capability to enrich uranium.

North Korea wants direct negotiations with the United States. It says it is willing to refreeze the plutonium program that it has unfrozen and to negotiate verifiable elimination of its uranium enrichment program. It has also offered to discuss its chemical and biological programs.

In return it says it wants a written pledge that the United States will not attack it, impede its economic development, or seek to overthrow its government—not a reward for bad behavior but nothing more than the commitments Washington made in 1994 and did not keep. If Washington refuses, Pyongyang will proceed with nuclear arming. And until it is sure the political relationship is improved, it will keep its nuclear option open as a hedge by refusing to dismantle its plutonium facilities for now.

Negotiations with North Korea can avoid a replay of the 1994 nuclear crisis. Then, as now, Washington had four options: compel the collapse of North Korea, which was thought likely to provoke the North to nuclear arm sooner than collapse; impose sanctions, which were rightly deemed unlikely to be effective; attack its nuclear facilities, which was not certain to eliminate all the nuclear material and sites in the North but sure to risk war and raise a political storm in the South; or negotiate.

The administration's refusal to sit down and talk until North Korea dismantles its uranium enrichment program makes no sense. Do we really want the North to dismantle it without U.S. inspectors present? And how do we get inspectors into North Korea without negotiating with Pyongyang?

Pyongyang seems willing to cut its nuclear fuses while negotiations proceed. Negotiations can begin now before the North gets closer to making bombs or later after the North has some. By refusing to deal, President Bush may have to live with a nuclear-arming North Korea. Why would North Korea give up its nuclear and missile programs if the United States remains its foe?

This administration began, like its predecessors, by demonizing North Korea as a rogue state. A rogue is a criminal and the way to treat criminals is to punish them, not negotiate.

The administration's approach has put the United States in the way of reconciliation between North and South Korea, which is political dynamite in the South. The Bush administration is also alienating Japan and antagonizing China. An attempt to rein in the United States has been the catalyst for unprecedented cooperation among the other five powers in Northeast Asia. The Japan-D.P.R.K. [Democratic People's Republic of Korea, the official name of North Korea] summit meeting last September [2002] and the recent Japan-Russian summit should be seen in this light. So should the warming between South Korea and China. Hardline unilateralists are putting Washington on a collision course with its own allies, undermining political support in South Korea and Japan for the alliance and jeopardizing the U.S. troop presence in the region.

Diplomacy vs. Coercion

There is a better way: diplomatic give-and-take. That was the strategy pursued in tandem by South Korea and the United States in 1991 and again in 2000, the most fruitful years of dealing with North Korea.

The great divide in American foreign policy thinking is between those who believe that to get our way in the world we have to push other countries around and those who think that cooperation can sometimes reduce threats to our security.

In closing, it is worth reminding ourselves, what U.S. interests are at stake with North Korea.

First, the United States wants to assure that, whatever happens internally in North Korea, the artillery Pyongyang has emplaced within range of Seoul [South Korea, America's ally] is never fired in anger.

Second, it wants to stop the North from nuclear arming.

Third, it wants to prevent the North from developing, testing, deploying and selling any more ballistic missiles.

Fourth, it wants a ban on biological and chemical weapons.

Fifth, it seeks reconciliation between the two Koreas.

The only way to achieve these aims is to test whether North Korea is willing to cooperate with the United States. Coercion will not work; it will only ensure that North Korea deploys more artillery near the demilitarized zone, seeks more aggressively to acquire nuclear arms, and tests, deploys and sells more missiles. It will further alienate allies South Korea and Japan and antagonize China.

The crime-and-punishment approach has never worked before with North Korea and there is no reason to believe it will work now. It will only impede efforts to ease the humanitarian crisis in North Korea. Whenever tensions have risen in the past, both the United States and the D.P.R.K. have made it more difficult for humanitarian agencies and NGOs [nongovernmental organizations] to do their work there.

"[North Korea] has absolutely no intention of ever giving up its nuclear capability."

Negotiation Cannot Reduce the Nuclear Threat Posed by North Korea

Nicholas Eberstadt

In the following viewpoint Nicholas Eberstadt argues that the United States should not make any concessions to North Korea in the hope of encouraging that nation to end its nuclear weapons program. Eberstadt maintains that for years North Korea has engaged in nuclear blackmail, alternately threatening to develop nuclear missiles, then making promises not to once it secures promises of oil, food aid, and other benefits from the United States and its allies. Instead of granting North Korea more concessions, he concludes, the United States must recognize that North Korea has no intention of ever willingly abandoning its nuclear program. Nicholas Eberstadt holds the Henry Wendt Chair in Political Economy at the American Enterprise Institute.

As you read, consider the following questions:

1. What is the name of the bargain that the Clinton administration forged with North Korea in 1994, according to Eberstadt?
2. What "bold solution" for ending the nuclear crisis did North Korea pitch in February 2004, as described by Eberstadt?

Nicholas Eberstadt, "La Grand Illusion, Korean Style," *The American Enterprise*, February 13, 2004. Copyright © 2004 by the American Enterprise Institute for Public Policy Research. Reproduced by permission of the author and *The American Enterprise*, a magazine of Politics, Business, and Culture. On the Web at www.TAEmag.com.

How many times can someone sell the same dead puppy to the same bunch of suckers? In effect, North Korea's Kim Jong Il is currently conducting an international experiment to determine the precise answer to this question.

The goods "the Dear Leader" has been hawking, of course aren't really non-performing pets—they're phony nuclear deals. And the designated "marks" in this scam aren't school-children, or simpletons at a county fair—they're top Western and Asian statesmen.

Today, once again, Pyongyang [the capital and government of North Korea] is asking the United States and its Northeast Asian allies and associates to pony up to buy a this-time-we-really-mean-it shutdown of the DPRK's [the Democratic People's Republic of Korea] nuclear weapons program.

Given the high stakes in this North Korean sting, and the sophistication of the intended victims, you'd think the game would have been shut down early. But you'd be wrong. The latest hapless steps toward another session of "Six Party talks" on the North Korean nuclear drama, in fact, suggest that the usual dupes are assuming position for another round of North Korean atomic bait-and-switch.

A Long-Running Scam

A little background may elucidate the present state of play. The dynastic enterprise known as the DPRK has been open for business since 1948, and for most of that time it has been building, and gaming, its nuclear program. Long ago, Kim & Son figured out a shakedown formula for extracting protection money from abroad in return for promising to scrap the nuke program.

It works like this: Make a Deal. Break the deal. Then demand a new deal for more, issuing dark threats until you get what you want.

That gambit, to be sure, could be dismissed as little more than basic coursework for Mafia 101. But any Goodfella would have to admit: so far, the formula's worked pretty well for Pyongyang.

Just look at the record. In the early 1990s, Pyongyang got the previous President [George] Bush to remove all US nuclear weapons from South Korea to grease a 1991 North-

South deal for the "de-nuclearization" of the Korean peninsula. Soon Pyongyang was caught cheating on that particular understanding—so it threatened to turn Seoul [South Korea, America's ally] into a "sea of fire," and got an improved bargain from the Clinton Administration (the "Agreed Framework" of 1994, with free oil shipped and free nuclear reactors in exchange for a freeze on then-extant DPRK nuclear sites). And when Kim & Co. seemed to be cheating on the "Agreed Framework" in 1999, Washington paid 500,000 tons in food aid—Pyongyang actually called it an "inspection fee"—to check out a single suspect nuclear site. (In the course of those negotiations, incidentally, North Korea warned Washington about a possible "pre-emptive strike" on the US if the talks didn't work out.)

In October 2002, once again, North Korea was caught cheating on its nuclear freeze arrangements—this time, with its now-notorious secret highly enriched uranium (HEU) program. So what did Pyongyang do? Naturally, it upped the ante.

It kicked out all the "Framework's" inspectors, unsealed the 8000 "Framework" plutonium fuel rods, tore up its copy of the Nuclear Nonproliferation Treaty, and announced that it was reprocessing the fissile material for a "peace deterrent." It started saying it possessed nuclear weapons, and that it was time to test, or sell, one of them. And it began asking its "negotiating partners" for a whole lot more money to keep things quiet in the neighborhood. To prove it was serious about its new proposed terms of trade, North Korea blew off Beijing and Washington in the "Three Party Talks" of April 2003, and then dissed them both again—plus Seoul, Tokyo and Moscow—in the expanded "Six Party Talks" of August 2003.

A New Round of Nuclear Appeasement

So here we are. And as 2004 commences, it looks as if Pyongyang's blackmail entrepreneurs have judged their international market correctly. Far from fashioning real-time penalties for the world's most naked and provocative violator of proliferation strictures, Western and Asian diplomatists are whipping out their calculators to figure the new price for postponing a North Korean nuclear breakout.

For the moment, the primary obstacle to nuclear appeasement bonuses for Pyongyang is the United States—or more specifically, the President [George W. Bush] and certain limited circles within his government. [In February 2004], however, Pyongyang executed a deft end-run around W., using US minions to do the blocking.

LURIE'S WORLD

"Now, if you'll just put it down carefully. . . ."

Lurie. © 1995 by Cartoonews International Syndicate. Reproduced by permission.

North Korea's play was to invite an unofficial delegation of Americans (all would-be dealmakers) for a pilgrimage to Pyongyang—and then, with the international media trained on the event, to rush past the White House with a highly-publicized "bold solution" for ending the nuclear impasse.

As the US stage props settled into their hotel rooms, North Korea's news agency pitched the package: in return for an end to Washington's sanctions and a resumption of free supplies for oil, power and energy from the US and its allies, Pyongyang would "refrain from [the] test and production of nuclear weapons and stop even operating nuclear power industry for a peaceful purposes."

Some deal, huh? North Korea gets the status quo ante "Framework" fuel aid, plus new money from the World Bank and other institutions ("ending sanctions" is code language for Washington's unlocking the door to multilateral aid). And for all this, America gets a promise—from Kim Jong Il, no less—that he won't blow off a bomb, or build any new ones—at least for now.

The Illusion of Progress

So how did North Korea's interlocutors react to this awful proposal? By falling all over themselves. "An important and serious step," enthused Moscow. "Helpful in creating the atmosphere for a second round of talks," chirped Seoul. Beijing "welcomed" North Korea's "further willingness" to "stop nuclear activities." And in Washington, an upbeat [Secretary of State] Colin Powell hailed the offer as "an interesting step," "a positive step" for "the next round of six party framework talks." Lost in this feel-good chorus was any apparent recollection of the original objective of those framework talks: namely, to hold Pyongyang to its previous promises to scrap its nuke program completely and forever.

As North Korea's neighbors get ready to shuffle off to their next obligatory fleecing in this ongoing hustle, one may wonder: what keeps this con going? It's not that American and Asian leadership is invincibly ignorant—not at all. Rather, it's that they've bought into a variant of La Grande Illusion (as such thinking was called in France in the late 1930s). The notion that the Kim regime has absolutely no intention of ever giving up its nuclear capability—at any price, for any reason—is too terrible to face. Better to play pretend—even if this means being bilked without cease for fake "breakthroughs" and bogus "accords."

> *"Rogue states such as Iran . . . whose pursuit of weapons of mass destruction makes them hostile to U.S. interests, will learn that their covert programs will not escape either detection or consequences.*

The United States Must Prevent Iran from Developing Nuclear Weapons

John R. Bolton

John R. Bolton is the U.S. Department of State undersecretary for arms control and international security. In the following viewpoint he argues that the United States must prevent rogue nations such as Iran from developing nuclear weapons. Iran claims it is pursuing a nuclear energy program, but Bolton maintains that Iran's pursuit of nuclear technologies is part of a covert nuclear weapons program. Bolton explains that U.S. strategy in Iran is to work with the international community to end Iran's nuclear program. He urges the United States to continue its efforts to prevent the transfer of nuclear materials to Iran. Bolton hopes for a diplomatic solution in Iran, but also warns that when it comes to rogue states developing WMD, "no option is off the table."

As you read, consider the following questions:

1. What is the "management" of spent nuclear fuel a euphemism for, according to the author?
2. What statement from Iranian official Hasan Rowhani makes Bolton doubt Iran's commitment to ending its nuclear program?

John R. Bolton, remarks to the Conference of the Institute for Foreign Policy Analysis and the Fletcher School's International Security Studies Program, Washington, DC, December 2, 2003.

P rogress by terrorist states towards a nuclear weapons capability, while often slow and uncertain, concealed and camouflaged, must nonetheless engage American attention in a sustained and systematic fashion. Often undertaken in conjunction with ambitious ballistic missile programs, efforts to attain nuclear weapons pose a direct and undeniable threat to the United States and its friends and allies around the world. Whether the nuclear capabilities of states like Iran, North Korea and others are threats today, or "only" threats "tomorrow," there can be no dispute that our attention is required now before the threats become reality, and tens of thousands of innocent civilians, or more, have been vaporized.

This is not to say by any means that we should not also be gravely concerned about chemical and biological weapons programs. We are, and many of the steps that we take internationally against nuclear weapons are applicable to chemical and biological threats as well. In fact, states around the world are closely scrutinizing the way we deal with the proliferation of nuclear weapons, and you can be sure that they will draw the appropriate conclusions about the utility of other weapons of mass destruction (WMD) based on our performance in the nuclear field.

The Need to Confront Rogue States

Of course, our information about WMD programs in other countries is not perfect. No one is more aware of the uncertainties that we face than the senior American intelligence officials and policy makers who deal with these life-and-death issues. Some analysts have said that not finding WMD in Iraq—to date—proves that [Iraqi leader Saddam Hussein] was not an imminent threat, and that our Coalition military action [in 2003] was therefore not justified. These criticisms miss the mark that our concern was not the imminence of Saddam's threat, but the very existence of his regime, given its heinous and undeniable record, capabilities, intentions, and long-standing defiance of the international community. President [George W.] Bush specifically and unambiguously addressed this issue in his January 2003, State of the Union message when he said: "Some have said we must not act until the threat is imminent. Since when have terrorists and tyrants announced their intentions, politely putting us on notice before they strike? If this threat is permitted to fully and suddenly emerge, all actions, all words, and all recriminations would come too late. Trusting in the sanity and restraint of Saddam Hussein is not a strategy, and it is not an option."

Given the right opportunity or incentive, Saddam could have easily transferred WMD capabilities to terrorist groups or others for their use against us, with potentially catastrophic results. State sponsors of terrorism are aggressively working to acquire weapons of mass destruction and their missile delivery systems. While Saddam's removal from power has unquestionably improved the international security situation, we face significant challenges in other parts of the world. Rogue states such as Iran, North Korea, Syria, Libya and Cuba, whose pursuit of weapons of mass destruction makes them hostile to U.S. interests, will learn that their covert programs will not escape either detection or consequences. While we will pursue diplomatic solutions whenever possible, the United States and its allies are also willing to deploy more robust techniques, such as the interdiction and seizure of illicit goods. If rogue states are not willing to follow the logic of nonproliferation norms, they must be prepared to face the logic of adverse consequences. It is why we repeatedly caution that no option is off the table.

Iran's Nuclear Ambitions

Let me discuss [one problem] in particular: Iran. . . . Although Iran has biological, chemical and missile programs, I will focus today on their nuclear weapons program, which Iran itself has acknowledged has been underway for at least eighteen years—all in violation of Iran's obligations under the Nuclear Nonproliferation Treaty ("NPT"). Our strategy for nearly three years has been to use bilateral and multilateral pressure to end that program, and to secure international consensus against Iran's pursuit of a nuclear weapons capability. On November 26, [2003] the International Atomic Energy Agency ("IAEA") Board of Governors unanimously adopted a resolution that "strongly deplores Iran's past failures and breaches of its obligations to comply with the provisions of its Safeguards Agreement. . . ." There was also unanimous agreement that "should any further serious Iranian failures come to light, the Board of Governors would meet immediately to consider . . . all options at its disposal, in accordance with the IAEA Statute and Iran's Safeguards Agreement."

The Possibility of Military Action Against Iran

Whether the [Iranian] regime is prepared to alter its long-term nuclear strategy is still an open question. In nuclear policy, the Iranian leadership is facing its toughest dilemma in more than 20 years. On one hand, there is a strong desire to develop an arsenal of nuclear weapons as a national deterrent: Iran is located in a rough neighborhood that includes at least five states with nuclear weapons. On the other hand, pursuing a nuclear program will isolate Iran, lead to new sanctions, and give the United States a pretext not only to destroy Iran's nuclear centers, but even to use a mixture of military and political pressure to topple the regime itself.

That fear is well grounded: Reports suggest that covert action could be used against Iran's nuclear installations. The U.S. has already recruited a number of Mujahedin Khalq [Iranian opposition group] elements in Iraq and won a pledge from their leader, Massoud Rajavi, to help with sabotage attacks inside Iran if necessary. If the U.S. and/or Israel were to strike areas in Iran, Tehran would be unable to retaliate except through Lebanese and Palestinian radical groups. The regime would appear weak and vulnerable, thus encouraging domestic opponents who dream of its overthrow.

Amir Taheri, *National Review*, November 10, 2003.

This decisive action followed three successive reports by the IAEA's Director General, which established beyond doubt Iran's multiple violations. While Iran has consistently denied any program to develop nuclear weapons, the IAEA has amassed an enormous amount of evidence to the contrary that makes this denial increasingly implausible.

In what can only be an attempt to build a capacity to develop nuclear materials for nuclear weapons, Iran has enriched uranium with both centrifuges and lasers, and produced and reprocessed plutonium. It attempted to cover its tracks by repeatedly and over many years neglecting to report its activities, and in many instances providing false declarations to the IAEA. For example, the IAEA Director General reports that Iran conducted uranium enrichment experiments with centrifuges using uranium Iran told the IAEA was "lost" due to its leaking valves. Iran conducted unreported uranium conversion experiments with uranium Iran declared to the IAEA as process loss. And Iran delayed IAEA inspectors until key facilities had been sanitized.

I repeat: The United States believes that the long-standing, massive and covert Iranian effort to acquire sensitive nuclear capabilities make sense only as part of a nuclear weapons program. Iran is trying to legitimize as "peaceful and transparent" its pursuit of nuclear fuel cycle capabilities that would give it the ability to produce fissile material for nuclear weapons. This includes uranium mining and extraction, uranium conversion and enrichment, reactor fuel fabrication, heavy water production, a heavy water reactor well-suited for plutonium production, and the "management" of spent fuel—a euphemism for reprocessing spent fuel to recover plutonium. The IAEA Director General's report confirms that Iran has been engaged in all of these activities over many years, and that it deliberately and repeatedly lied to the IAEA about it.

The International Community Must Act

The international community now needs to decide over time whether Iran has come clean on this program and how to react to the large number of serious violations to which Iran has admitted. Unfortunately, Iran itself has already indicated that it has mixed feelings about its obligations to adhere to the IAEA's resolutions. [In October 2003] Hasan Rowhani, head of Iran's Supreme National Security Council and the man who concluded the October deal in Tehran with the three European foreign ministers, gave Iran's most recent interpretation of the IAEA's actions. He said, "our decision to suspend uranium enrichment is voluntary and temporary. Uranium enrichment is Iran's natural right and [Iran] will reserve for itself this right. . . . There has been and there will be no question of a permanent suspension or halt at all." Rowhani went on to say, "We want to control the whole fuel cycle. Since we are planning to build seven nuclear fuel plants in the future, we want to provide fuel for at least one of the plants ourselves."

The IAEA's November 26 resolution should leave no doubt that one more transgression by Iran will mean that the IAEA is obligated to report Iran's noncompliance to the Security Council and General Assembly of the United Nations, in accordance with Article XII.C of the IAEA Statute. This Statute explicitly states that when non-compliance is found, the "Board shall report the non-compliance to all members and to the Security Council." Iran's Safeguards Agreement similarly provides that if the Board finds "the Agency is not able to verify there has been no diversion of nuclear material required to be safeguarded," the Board may report to the Security Council. The real issue now is whether the Board of Governors will remain together in its insistence that Iran's pursuit of nuclear weapons is illegitimate, or whether Iranian efforts to split the Board through economic incentives and aggressive propaganda will succeed. For our part, the United States will continue its efforts to prevent the transfer of sensitive nuclear and ballistic missile technology to Iran, from whatever source, and will monitor the situation there with great care.

"A U.S. or Israeli attempt to strike Iran's nuclear facilities . . . could well have the unintended consequence of antagonizing a highly nationalistic and largely pro-Western populace."

The United States Should Not Take an Aggressive Stand over Iran's Nuclear Program

Karim Sadjadpour

Karim Sadjadpour argues in the following viewpoint that, despite its government's past hostility to the United States, Iranians under thirty are one of the most pro-American groups in the Middle East. Most Iranians, according to the author, do not want their government to develop nuclear weapons for fear that such an action would worsen relations with the United States and enable Iran's hard-line government to stay in power. However, the author warns that a military strike or other aggressive action on the part of the United States could alienate Iranians and convince them to support a nuclear program. Karim Sadjadpour is an analyst with the International Crisis Group and a visiting fellow at the American University of Beirut.

As you read, consider the following questions:

1. What effect has the Iran-Iraq war had on Iranians, in the author's opinion?
2. What proportion of Iranians are under thirty, according to the author?

Karim Sadjadpour, "Iranians Don't Want to Go Nuclear," *Washington Post*, February 3, 2004. Copyright © 2004 by the Washington Post Book World Service/ Washington Post Writers Group. Reproduced by permission of the author.

D o the people of Iran want the bomb? Iran's [October 2003] decision to allow for tighter inspection of its nuclear facilities—which Iran says are for civilian purposes— was hailed by Iranian and European officials as a diplomatic victory, while analysts and officials in Washington and Tel Aviv continue to be wary of Tehran's intentions. But despite the attention given to Iran's nuclear aspirations in recent months, one important question has scarcely been touched on: How do the Iranian people feel about having nuclear weapons?

Iranian officials have suggested that the country's nuclear program is an issue that resonates on the Iranian street and is a great source of national pride. But months of interviews I have done in Iran reveal a somewhat different picture. Whereas few Iranians are opposed to the development of a nuclear energy facility, most do not see it as a solution to their primary concerns: economic malaise and political and social repression. What's more, most of the Iranians surveyed said they oppose the pursuit of a nuclear weapons program because it runs counter to their desire for "peace and tranquility." Three reasons were commonly cited.

Most Iranians Want Peace and Greater Freedom

First, having experienced a devastating eight-year war with Saddam Hussein's Iraq that took the lives of hundreds of thousands of their compatriots, Iranians are opposed to reliving war or violence. Many Iranians said the pursuit of nuclear weapons would lead the country down a path no one wanted to travel.

Two decades ago revolutionary euphoria was strong, and millions of young men volunteered to defend their country against an Iraqi onslaught. Today few Iranians have illusions about the realities of conflict. The argument that a nuclear weapon could help serve as a deterrent to ensure peace in Iran seemed incongruous to most. "If we want peace, why would we want a bomb?" asked a middle-aged Iranian woman, seemingly concurring with an influential Iranian diplomat who contends that a nuclear weapon "would not augment Iran's security but rather heighten its vulnerabilities."

Second, while a central premise of Iran's Islamic government from the time of its inception has been its steadfast opposition to the United States and Israel, for most Iranians no such nemeses exist. Iran's young populace—more than two-thirds of the country is younger than 30—is among the most pro-American in the Middle East, and tend not to share the impassioned anti-Israel sentiment of their Arab neighbors. While the excitement generated on the Indian and Pakistani streets as a result of their nuclear detonations is commonly cited to show the correlation between nuclear weapons and national pride, such a reaction is best understood in the context of the rivalry between the two countries. The majority of Iranians surveyed claimed to have little desire to show off their military or nuclear prowess to anyone. "Whom would we attack?" asked a 31-year-old laborer, echoing a commonly heard sentiment in Tehran. "We don't want war with anyone."

Building a Better Relationship with Iran

A new and candid, if not necessarily congenial, relationship would be mutually beneficial to [the United States and Iran] in several strategic respects, ranging from stability in Iraq to the fight against nuclear proliferation and terrorism to Iran's own desire to end its international isolation. . . .

Many hurdles stand in the way of a genuine rapprochement between the United States and Iran, including complex legal problems dating from the 1979 embassy takeover. Yet the beginnings of a strategic course correction are in place; to make it real, what is now needed is bold, consistent and creative diplomacy.

At a time when the Bush administration needs to stabilize Iraq [after the 2003 war] and turn over sovereignty to an untested government, to put new life into the Middle East peace process, and to make progress in the war against terrorism, what better way than to deal directly with a conflicted but proud nation that also will have a great deal to say about what happens in the region for a long time to come?

James E. Goodby and Fred Hill, "America and Iran Need to Talk," *International Herald Tribune*, February 13, 2004.

Finally, many Iranians, youth in particular, are opposed to the Islamic republic's becoming a nuclear power because they believe it would further entrench the hard-liners in the government. "I fear that if these guys get the bomb they will be able to hold on to power for another 25 years," said a 30-

year-old Iranian professional. "Nobody wants that." In particular some expressed a concern that a nuclear Iran would be immune to U.S. and European diplomatic pressure and could continue to repress popular demands for reform without fear of repercussion.

At the same time, most Iranians—including harsh critics of the Islamic regime—remain unconvinced by the allegations that their government is secretly pursuing a nuclear weapons program. Many dismiss it as another bogeyman manufactured by the United States and Israel to further antagonize and isolate the Islamic regime. "I don't believe we're after a bomb," said a 25-year-old Tehran University student. "The U.S. is always looking for an excuse to harass these mullahs." A recently retired Iranian diplomat who said he is "strongly critical" of the Islamic government agreed with this assessment, saying Iran's nuclear program "is neither for defensive nor offensive purposes. . . . It's only for energy purposes."

I draw two lessons from this. First, the European-brokered compromise on Iran's nuclear program, which appealed to reformists and pragmatists within the Iranian government, was also a victory of sorts for the Iranian people, who are eager to emerge from the political and economic isolation of the past two decades and are strongly in favor of increasing ties with the West. A blatant lack of cooperation with the international community would not have been well-received domestically.

Second, a more aggressive reaction by the international community—a U.S. or Israeli attempt to strike Iran's nuclear facilities—could well have the unintended consequence of antagonizing a highly nationalistic and largely pro-Western populace and convincing Iranians that a nuclear weapon is indeed in their national interests. Such a reaction would be disastrous for U.S. interests in the region, especially given Iran's key location between Iraq and Afghanistan.

Western and Israeli diplomats and analysts should know that the ability to solve the Iranian nuclear predicament diplomatically has broad implications for the future of democracy and nonproliferation in Iran and the rest of the Middle East. The goal is to bring the Iranian regime on the same page with the Iranian people. A non-diplomatic attempt to destroy Iran's nuclear facilities could do precisely the opposite.

"The Bush administration continually hyped unproven but sensational allegations [about Iraq]."

The U.S. Invasion of Iraq Was Based on False Pretenses

Thomas R. Eddlem

Thomas R. Eddlem argues in the following viewpoint that the Bush administration used inflammatory rhetoric to lure the American public into supporting the spring 2003 U.S. invasion of Iraq. According to Eddlem, President Bush and other senior U.S. officials justified going to war by claiming that Iraq possessed biological and chemical weapons, and was seeking to build nuclear weapons. However, writes Eddlem, David Kay—the CIA official appointed to lead the U.S. effort to find Iraq's weapons of mass destruction in the wake of the invasion—submitted a report in October 2003 stating that search teams had found no weapons of mass destruction. Eddlem contrasts the claims of the Bush administration with the findings of the Kay report to support his view that America was deceived about Iraq's weapons of mass destruction. Thomas R. Eddlem is the editor of the *Hanson Express* in Hanson, Massachusetts, and is a regular contributor to the *New American* and *Point South* magazines.

As you read, consider the following questions:

1. According to the author, what false claim did President George W. Bush make in his January 28, 2003, State of the Union address?
2. What does the discovery of Botulinum type B in Iraq prove, according to David Kay?

Thomas R. Eddlem, "Deceiving Us into War," *New American*, vol. 19, November 17, 2003, p. 10. Copyright © 2003 by American Opinion Publishing Incorporated. Reproduced by permission.

"Facing growing doubts at home about the wisdom of attacking [Iraq in 2003], President [George W.] Bush ... will launch a campaign to defend the U.S. invasion," began a Reuters wire dispatch on October 8 [2003]. President Bush is going to need a public relations campaign of unprecedented proportions.

Bush initially persuaded the American people to accept the war because of the alleged imminent threat of chemical and biological attacks against the U.S. from Iraq. In addition, he warned, there was the looming danger of Iraqi nuclear terrorism. In an October 7, 2002, speech, President Bush summarized the justification for war against Saddam Hussein: "America must not ignore the threat gathering against us. Facing clear evidence of peril, we cannot wait for the final proof—the smoking gun—that could come in the form of a mushroom cloud."

It's hard to invoke an image more frightening than that. But mushroom cloud talk aside, the only cloud of smoke that emerged from the war debate was the evaporating smoke and mirrors campaign used by Bush administration officials to exaggerate—and perhaps falsify—intelligence to support launching the war against Iraq.

Bait and Switch

Most Americans thought that the Iraq War was fought for the limited objective of removing the putative threat—Saddam Hussein. Administration spokesmen repeatedly suggested it would be a "cakewalk." The general impression given was that we would be out in a relatively short time. But that war quickly mutated into an occupation and reconstruction projected to last for years (or decades), at an enormous cost of blood and treasure.

It is beyond doubt that Iraq pursued an active chemical and biological weapons program for more than two decades. Saddam also at one point had a primitive nuclear program. However, the charge that Iraq's nuclear program was advanced was far-fetched. The claim that Iraq still had vast stockpiles of chemical and biological weapons at the time of our Operation Iraqi Freedom invasion was also dubious and remains unproven. It was an obvious, calculated ploy to win public support for launching an aggressive war.

The new Bush public relations campaign is a classic bait-and-switch operation. The White House spinmeisters are laboring to divert public attention from past administration hoaxes and locus it instead upon the new freedom experienced by the Iraqi people, now that Saddam Hussein is no longer running the country. But freeing the Iraqi people from tyranny, no matter how desirable, was never a justification for war. If it were, we would soon be sending U.S. troops to overturn dozens or equally despotic regimes.

The administration already appears to be backing down from pre-war claims made by senior officials that there were huge stockpiles of chemical and biological weapons and an advanced nuclear program. The Bush administration, recall, did not merely claim that Saddam Hussein had weapons of mass destruction [WMDs]. Iraq was bulging with such weapons, we were told, and the direct threat those weapons presented to the United States was supposedly so great and so imminent that we had no choice but to act quickly.

"There are a number of terrorist states pursuing weapons of mass destruction—Iran, Libya, North Korea, Syria, just to name a few—but no terrorist state poses a greater or more immediate threat to the security of our people than the regime of Saddam Hussein and Iraq," Secretary of Defense Donald Rumsfeld told the Senate Armed Services Committee on September 19, 2002. "The goals of our coalition are clear and limited. We will end a brutal regime, whose aggression and weapons of mass destruction make it a unique threat to the world," President Bush said in a message to the Iraqi people on April 10 of [2003].

National Security Adviser Condoleezza Rice told NBC's *Meet the Press* on September 28: "Let's remember that the intelligence going into the war—it's quite separable from what [arms inspector] David Kay now finds. . . ." Rice would be correct if U.S. intelligence agencies were giving the White House different intelligence before the war from what U.S. inspector David Kay has found. But this has not been the case. The intelligence going into the war actually coincides with the virtually nonexistent threat Kay has thus far uncovered.

Following are some examples of how the Bush administration deceptively used (or flat-out ignored) intelligence from its own agencies to manipulate popular support toward the war against Iraq.

Saddam and September 11

> We've had no evidence that Saddam Hussein was involved with the September 11th [attacks].
>
> —President George Bush, after meeting with members of the Congressional Conference Committee on Energy Legislation, September 17, 2003

Huh? Most Americans would probably be somewhat startled to hear the president's remark above. According to opinion polls, a majority of Americans believe that Saddam Hussein was behind the September 11 [2001] terrorist attacks on the U.S. That's the main reason we went to war, right? Much of the popular support for attacking Iraq was based on this presumption of guilt and the need for a just response. The Bush administration and its media allies have done everything possible to create that impression. They have done this primarily through clever inference and insinuation, constantly juxtaposing Saddam's crimes and villainy with the 9-11 atrocity. But they have provided no hard evidence of Iraqi ties to the attacks. This is one of the biggest bait-and-switches in the "War on Terror.". . .

Significant Quantities of Uranium

> The British government has learned that Saddam Hussein recently sought significant quantities of uranium from Africa.
>
> —President George W. Bush, State of the Union address, January 28, 2003

This statement is now widely known to be based upon a forgery. Recently, the Bush administration's own chief investigator for weapons of mass destruction, David Kay, concluded: "We have not uncovered evidence that Iraq undertook significant post-1998 steps to actually build nuclear weapons or produce fissile material." In other words, Kay says there's no evidence that Bush's "mushroom cloud" was anything but a figment of overheated war propaganda.

That Bush's statement about uranium was false is now

common knowledge; that Bush made the claim against the advice of his own intelligence agencies needs to be more widely known. According to CIA Director George Tenet, the CIA twice warned the Bush administration that the evidence supporting the claim was unreliable.

Iraq and the Future of Preemption

The Bush Administration's rationale for regime change in Baghdad hinged on the danger posed by Saddam Hussein's quest for weapons of mass destruction, and on the frightening possibility that a confluence of objectives could prompt the transfer of such tools of destruction to terrorists. The need for a preventive response, in turn, served as the guiding principle behind Washington's subsequent decision to resort to military action [in 2003]. . . .

The course of events in Iraq has profound consequence for the future of pre-emption. The postwar difficulty experienced by the United States in uncovering Iraq's weapons of mass destruction programs has increasingly called into question the rationale for preemptive action: the notion that Iraq was an imminent threat to U.S. and regional security. Over time, this situation could prove seriously damaging to the viability of the Bush strategy. An unambiguous, post-facto demonstration of the global threat posed by Saddam Hussein's regime remains essential to shoring up legitimacy for the Bush Administration's pre-emption strategy among already skeptical members of the international community. That American efforts—spearheaded by Dr. David Kay's Iraq Survey Group—have, despite some successes, so far fallen short of accomplishing this goal does not bode well, either for preemption's popular appeal or its international acceptance.

Ilan Berman, *National Interest*, Winter 2003.

Other intelligence reports reached the White House revealing the same conclusion. Former U.S. Ambassador Joseph Wilson explained to NBC's *Meet the Press* on October 3 [2003]:

When the State Department said, "We were duped by that information," that was a misstatement of fact because I knew that there were at least three reports pertaining to this particular case: mine, but also the report of our ambassador on the scene and, also, the report of the deputy commander in chief of U.S. Armed Forces Europe, a four star Marine

Corps general, all of whom had gone down to take a look at this allegation and all of whom had reported that it was not true. There was one report, which turned out to be a forged document, which was so dicey that even an Italian weekly tabloid magazine would not use it. And yet it was that report that formed the basis for the 16 words in the State of the Union address.

Tenet explained in a July 11 [2003] press release . . . : "[CIA] officials who were reviewing the draft remarks [in the State of the Union speech] on uranium raised several concerns about the fragmentary nature of the intelligence with National Security Council colleagues. Some of the language was changed. From what we know now, Agency officials in the end concurred that the text in the speech was factually correct—i.e. that the British government report said that Iraq sought uranium from Africa." Despite CIA concerns, the administration resorted to using the dubious—and now discredited—British report to alarm the American people.

Why? If President Bush did not know that the evidence supporting the allegation was fragmentary and unreliable, certainly his advisers did. Yet his advisers allowed him to use it anyway to make the case for war. Considering this example alone, a neutral observer might conclude that this case of exaggerating the evidence was an honest mistake.

But this was hardly a lone example of exaggeration or tinkering with the truth. . . .

Trailer Trash

We found the weapons of mass destruction. We found biological laboratories. You remember when Colin Powell stood up in front of the world, and he said, Iraq has got laboratories, mobile labs to build biological weapons. . . . [W]e've so far discovered two. And we'll find more weapons as time goes on. But for those who say we haven't found the banned manufacturing devices or banned weapons, they're wrong. We found them.

—President Bush, in remarks broadcast by Polish television, after the discovery of two tractor trailers alleged to have been designed for producing biological weapons, May 30, 2003

The first thing that needs to be pointed out is that this statement contains both a major falsehood and a major sleight-of-hand. The falsehood is that the trailers were weapons of mass destruction—which they definitely were not. The sleight-of-hand concerns the administration's conspicuous switch from charges about actual weapons to weapons programs. Before the war, and up until June 9 [2003], Bush and his top administration officials spoke not about WMD weapons programs but actual stockpiled weapons.

A huge sea-change in the administration's claims of Iraq's on-the-ground threat occurred on June 9. When questioned at a photo-op on that date about the failure to find WMDs, Bush responded: ". . . I mean, Iraq had a weapons program. Intelligence throughout the decade showed they had a weapons program. I am absolutely convinced with time we'll find out that they did have a weapons program."

President Bush said on the eve of war that "Intelligence gathered by this and other governments leaves no doubt that the Iraq regime continues to possess and conceal some of the most lethal weapons ever devised. . . . The danger is clear: using chemical, biological or, one day, nuclear weapons, obtained with the help of Iraq, the terrorists could fulfill their stated ambitions and kill thousands or hundreds of thousands of innocent people in our country, or any other. . . . We cannot live under the threat of blackmail." To go from talk about actual chemical and biological weapons already produced, to tractor trailers that may be capable of producing such weapons, constitutes a huge quantum leap downward in threat assessment.

But there is no reason to believe even this downgraded assessment. President Bush's own WMD inspector for Iraq, David Kay, concluded there was no evidence the two tractor trailers had ever been used to produce biological weapons. Kay reported that his investigation into "the two trailers found in northern Iraq in April has yielded a number of explanations, including hydrogen, missile propellant, and BW (biological weapons) production, but technical limitations would prevent any of these processes from being ideally suited to these trailers.". . .

Aluminum Tubes: A Hole in the Story

Most U.S. experts think they [aluminum tubes] are intended to serve as rotors and centrifuges used to enrich uranium.

—Secretary of State Colin Powell in an address before the UN Security Council, February 5, 2003

Administration supporters now frequently cite Colin Powell's remarks before the United Nations Security Council as evidence of a strong case that Saddam Hussein was building a nuclear program, especially because Powell did not use the now infamous "16 words" about the supposed attempt to purchase uranium from Africa.

But Powell's story is likewise proven false by the evidence. Bush administration investigator David Kay concluded "the evidence does not tie any activity directly to centrifuge research or development." In other words, Kay's report flatly contradicts Powell's sensational charges.

Former State Department intelligence official Greg Thielmann explained that Kay's conclusions constituted the consensus of some U.S. intelligence officials long before the Kay Report. Thielmann told PBS's *Frontline* for October 9, 2003: "We started out being agnostic on this but the more we got into it, it was not a difficult assessment for us to arrive at, ultimately, that the Department of Energy experts were correct in seeing that these tubes were not well suited for uranium enrichment centrifuge rotors but were in fact for something else." Thielmann had completed his work and left State Department service in October 2002, four months before Powell's address to the Security Council.

Bogus Botox Boast

Let me tell you what the report said. It states that Saddam Hussein's regime had a clandestine network of biological laboratories. They had a live strain of deadly agent called botulinum.

—President Bush, remarks in Milwaukee, October 3, 2003

London's *Independent* newspaper provided an analysis that exposed President Bush's insinuation. "Botulinum type A is one of the most poisonous substances known, and was developed in weaponized form by Iraq before 1991. However, type B—the form found at the biologist's home—is less lethal," the *Independent* noted. "Botulinum type B could also be used for making an antidote to common botulinum poisoning. That is one of the reasons why many military laboratories around the world keep reference strains of C botulinum Okra B. The UK keeps such substances, for example, and calls them 'seed banks.'"

Both strains of botulinum have wide commercial uses worldwide for less than insidious purposes. A form of Botulinum A is commonly marketed in the United States as an anti-wrinkle injection under the well-known brand name "Botox." Botulinum B, which was found in the scientist's refrigerator, is also used to create a muscle pain reliever in the United States under the name "Myobloc."

The Kay Interim report did say the botulinum "can be used to produce biological weapons," but the *Independent* pointed out that Kay did not allege that the botulinum samples found had been formed into anything resembling a weapon: "Note what that sentence does not say: these facilities were suitable for chemical and biological weapons research (as almost any modern lab would be), not that they had engaged in such research. The reference to UN monitoring is also spurious: under the terms of UN resolutions, all of Iraq's chemical and biological facilities are subject to monitoring. So all this tells us is that Iraq had modern laboratories.". . .

The evidence is overwhelming: The Bush administration continually hyped unproven but sensational allegations to get the American people to agree to a war against a regime that was not a direct or imminent threat to the United States. The administration's ongoing public relations campaign to justify transforming the war into an indefinite occupation of Iraq portends more of the same.

6

"The war to remove Saddam was, in the broad strategic sense, in the sense relevant to serious international politics, necessary."

The U.S. Invasion of Iraq Was Justified

Robert Kagan and William Kristol

Robert Kagan is a contributing editor, and William Kristol is editor, of the *Weekly Standard*, a conservative weekly political magazine. In the following viewpoint they defend the U.S. decision to invade Iraq in 2003. That decision has come under intense scrutiny since David Kay, the official in charge of U.S. efforts to find Iraq's weapons of mass destruction in the wake of the invasion, submitted a report in October 2003 stating that search teams had found no weapons of mass destruction. Kristol and Kagan, however, contend that the Iraq war was not waged because Saddam Hussein was believed to have weapons of mass destruction, but because he was intent on building such weapons and adamantly refused to comply with UN inspectors sent to verify that Iraq did not have illegal weapons programs. In the authors' view, the Iraq war was justified because Saddam Hussein, left unchecked, would have eventually been successful in building weapons of mass destruction.

As you read, consider the following questions:
1. Why did Saddam Hussein expel UN weapons inspectors in December 1998, according to the authors?
2. In the authors' view, what was the primary purpose of UN Security Council resolution 1441?

Robert Kagan and William Kristol, "The Right War for the Right Reasons," *The Weekly Standard*, February 23, 2004. Copyright © 2004 by News Corporation, Weekly Standard. All rights reserved. Reproduced by permission.

With all the turmoil surrounding [weapons inspector] David Kay's comments on the failure to find stockpiles of biological and chemical weapons in Iraq [after the 2003 war], it is time to return to first principles, and to ask the question: Was it right to go to war?

Critics of the war, and of the Bush administration, have seized on the failure to find stockpiles of weapons of mass destruction in Iraq. But while his weapons were a key part of the case for removing [Iraqi leader Saddam Hussein], that case was always broader. Saddam's pursuit of weapons of mass destruction was inextricably intertwined with the nature of his tyrannical rule, his serial aggression, his defiance of international obligations, and his undeniable ties to a variety of terrorists, from Abu Nidal to al Qaeda. . . . Together, this pattern of behavior made the removal of Saddam desirable and necessary, in the judgment of both the Clinton and Bush administrations. That judgment was and remains correct.

It is fashionable to sneer at the moral case for liberating an Iraqi people long brutalized by Saddam's rule. Critics insist mere oppression was not sufficient reason for war, and in any case that it was not Bush's reason. In fact, of course, it was one of Bush's reasons, and the moral and humanitarian purpose provided a compelling reason for a war to remove Saddam. . . .

Such a rationale is not "merely" moral. As is so often the case in international affairs, there was no separating the nature of Saddam's rule at home from the kinds of policies he conducted abroad. Saddam's regime terrorized his own people, but it also posed a threat to the region, and to us. The moral case for war was linked to strategic considerations related to the peace and security of the Middle East.

Saddam was not a "madman." He was a predator and an aggressor. He achieved through brute force total dominance at home, and it was through force and the threat of force that he sought dominance in his region, as well. He waged war against Iran throughout the 1980s. He invaded Kuwait in 1990. He spent tens of billions of dollars on weapons, both conventional and unconventional. His clear and unwavering ambition, an ambition nurtured and acted upon across three decades, was to dominate the Middle East, both economically and militarily, by attempting to acquire the lion's share of the region's oil and by intimidating or destroying anyone who stood in his way. This, too, was a sufficient reason to remove him from power. . . .

Saddam's Weapons of Mass Destruction Programs

The threat of Saddam's weapons of mass destruction was related to the overall political and strategic threat his regime posed to the Middle East. Still, there is no question that Saddam's history with and interest in weapons of mass destruction made his threat distinctive. The danger was not, however, that Iraq would present a direct threat to the physical security of the United States or, in the current popular phrase, pose an "imminent" threat to the American homeland. Our chief concern in 1998 . . . was the threat Saddam posed to regional security and stability, the maintenance of which was in large part the responsibility of the United States. If Saddam "does acquire the capability to deliver weapons of mass destruction," we argued, which eventually he was "almost certain to do if we continue along the present course," American troops in the region, American allies, the stability of the Middle East, and the world's supply of oil would all be put at risk. The threat to the United States was that we would be compelled to defend our allies and our interests in circumstances made much more difficult and dangerous by Saddam's increasingly lethal arsenal.

That was why Saddam's weapons of mass destruction programs, both what we knew about them and what we did not know about them, gave the situation a special urgency. It was urgent in 1998, and it was urgent four years later. There was no doubt in 1998—and there is no doubt today, based on David Kay's findings—that Saddam was seeking both to pursue WMD programs and to conceal his efforts from U.N. weapons inspectors. After 1995, when the defection of Saddam Hussein's son-in-law and chief organizer of the weapons programs, Hussein Kamal, produced a wealth of new information about Iraqi weapons programs and stockpiles—information the Iraqis were forced to acknowledge was accurate—the U.N. weapons inspections process had become an elaborate cat-and-mouse game. As President [Bill] Clinton recalled in his speech three years later, Kamal had "revealed that Iraq was continuing to conceal weapons and missiles and the capacity to build many more." The inspectors intensified their search. And they must have been having some success, for as they drew closer to uncovering what the Iraqis were hiding, Saddam grew less and less cooperative and began to block their access to certain facilities. . . .

President Clinton declared in early 1998 that Saddam was clearly attempting "to protect whatever remains of his capacity to produce weapons of mass destruction, the missiles to deliver them, and the feed stocks necessary to produce them." The U.N. inspectors believed, Clinton continued, that "Iraq still has stockpiles of chemical and biological munitions . . . and the capacity to restart quickly its production program and build many, many more weapons." Meanwhile, a February 13, 1998, U.S. government White Paper on Iraq's weapons of mass destruction stated that "in the absence of [United Nations] inspectors, Iraq could restart limited mustard agent production within a few weeks, full-production of sarin within a few months, and pro–Gulf War production levels—including VX—within two or three years."

It was President Clinton who, in February 1998, posed the critical question: "What if [Saddam] fails to comply and we fail to act, or we take some ambiguous third route, which gives him yet more opportunities to develop this program of weapons of mass destruction. . . . Well, he will conclude that the international community has lost its will. He will then conclude that he can go right on and do more to rebuild an arsenal of devastating destruction. And some day, some way, I guarantee you he'll use this arsenal." "In the next century," Clinton predicted, "the community of nations may see more and more of the very kind of threat Iraq poses now—a rogue state with weapons of mass destruction, ready to use them or provide them to terrorists . . . who travel the world among us unnoticed."

Over the course of 1998, the U.N. inspections process collapsed. Attempts to break the stalemate with Saddam and allow the U.N. inspectors access to the prohibited sites came to naught. . . . [In December 1998], the Clinton administration launched Operation Desert Fox, a four-day missile and bombing strike on Iraq aimed at destroying as much of Saddam's weapons capabilities as possible. Based on American intelligence, the Clinton administration targeted suspected weapons production facilities throughout Iraq. The Air Force and intelligence agencies believed the bombing had destroyed or degraded a number of Iraqi weapons of mass destruction facilities, but they never knew the extent of the damage, because, of course, there were no inspectors left to investigate.

Saddam expelled the U.N. inspectors in response to the attack, and they did not return until November 2002. As Clinton . . . recalled, "We might have gotten it all; we might have gotten half of it; we might have gotten none of it. But we didn't know." Clinton went on to say about President [George W.] Bush's actions in the fall of 2002, "So I thought it was prudent for the president to go to the U.N. and for the U.N. to say you got to let these inspectors in, and this time if you don't cooperate the penalty could be regime change, not just continued sanctions.". . .

The inspectors left, and for the next four years, Saddam's activities were shrouded in darkness. After all, many prohibited Iraqi activities had escaped detection even while the inspectors were trying to monitor them. Without the inspectors, the task of keeping track of Saddam's programs was well-nigh impossible.

When the Bush administration came to office, therefore, it had no less reason to worry about Saddam's potential capabilities than the Clinton administration. . . .

A Renewed Urgency

Then came the terrorist attacks of September 11, 2001. September 11 shocked the nation, and it shocked the president. Its effect was to make many both inside and outside the administration take a closer look at international threats, because it was clear that all of us had been too sanguine about such threats prior to September 11. Nor was it in the least surprising that the issue of Iraq arose immediately. . . . After all, we had a decade-long history of confrontation with Iraq, we were flying military missions in Iraqi air space, President Clinton had declared Saddam the greatest threat to our security in the 21st century, Clinton officials like [National Security Adviser] Sandy Berger and [Secretary of State]

Madeleine Albright had concluded that Saddam must eventually be removed, and U.N. weapons inspectors had written one alarming report after another about Saddam's current and potential weapons capabilities.

Dealing with the Hard Cases

Coercive diplomacy, the alternative to war, requires political judgment under conditions of uncertainty, a fact lost in the increasingly rancorous partisan debate. The critics who are bashing President [George W.] Bush for pushing a hard line on Iraq [by going to war with that nation in 2003] are also bashing President Bush for not pushing a hard enough line on North Korea. Ironically, the president is doing everything in North Korea that he was accused of not doing in Iraq: building an international coalition to support pressure on North Korea; not taking North Korean claims at face value; weighing carefully the costs of military action; and so on. The bottom line is that the hard cases—North Korea, Iran and, yes, Iraq—are hard cases precisely because the easy options have been tried and proved wanting.

If the [January 2004 Kay testimony claiming that no weapons of mass destruction were found in Iraq] had been available in March 2003, it's unlikely that the administration would have pressed for war. But since the war case rested on multiple pillars—dealing with a problem now before it became an unmanageable problem later, recognizing that [Iraqi leader Saddam Hussein] could not be trusted in the long run, recognizing that the war on terrorists involved getting tough on the causes of terrorism (stunted political development in the Middle East), recognizing that the status quo policy on Iraq was responsible for creating the conditions that gave rise to [the terrorist group] al Qaeda in the first place—it is possible that reasonable people would have still advocated war.

Peter D. Feaver, "The Fog of WMD," *Washington Post*, January 28, 2004.

So the Bush administration concluded that it had to remove the Saddam Hussein regime once and for all, just as Clinton and Berger had suggested might someday be necessary. . . . Saddam's regime itself was the problem, above and beyond his weapons capabilities. It was an obstacle to progress in the Middle East and the Arab world. It was a threat to the Iraqi people and to Iraq's neighbors. But a big part of the threat involved Saddam's absolute determination to arm himself with both conventional and unconventional weapons. . . .

The Bush administration's approach to Iraq was fundamentally in keeping with that of the Clinton administration, except that after September 11, inaction seemed even less acceptable. The majority of the Democratic party foreign policy establishment supported the war, and not because they were misled by the Bush administration's rhetorical hype leading up to the war. . . . Nor did they support the war because they were fundamentally misled by American intelligence about the nature and extent of Saddam's weapons programs. Most of what they and everyone else knew about those programs we had learned from the U.N. inspectors, not from U.S. intelligence.

Some of that intelligence has now turned out to be wrong. Some of it has turned out to be right. And it is simply too soon to tell about the rest. The press has focused attention almost entirely on David Kay's assertion that there were no stockpiles of chemical and biological weapons when the United States and its allies invaded Iraq last March [2003]. We'll address that assertion in a moment. But what about the rest of Kay's testimony?

The key question for more than a decade, for both the Clinton and the Bush administrations, was not only what weapons Saddam had but what weapons he was trying to obtain, and how long it might be before containment failed and he was able to obtain them. The goal of American policy, and indeed of the U.N. Security Council over the course of the dozen years after the end of the Gulf War in 1991, was not primarily to find Saddam's existing stockpiles. That was subsidiary to the larger goal, which was to achieve Iraq's disarmament, including the elimination not only of existing prohibited weapons but of all such weapons programs, to ensure that Iraq would not possess weapons of mass destruction now or in the future. . . .

It is important to recall that the primary purpose of Security Council Resolution 1441, passed on November 8, 2002, was not to discover whether Saddam had weapons and programs. There was little doubt that Saddam had them. The real question was whether he was ready to make a clean breast of everything and give up not only his forbidden weapons but also his efforts to acquire them once and for all. The purpose was to give Saddam "one final chance" to change his stripes, to offer full cooperation by revealing and dismantling all his programs and to forswear all such efforts in the future. . . .

Resolution 1441 demanded that, within 30 days, Iraq provide "a currently accurate, full, and complete declaration of all aspects of its programs to develop chemical, biological, and nuclear weapons, ballistic missiles, and other delivery systems such as unmanned aerial vehicles and dispersal systems designed for use on aircraft, including any holdings and precise locations of such weapons, components, sub-components, stocks of agents, and related material and equipment, the locations and work of its research, development and production facilities, as well as all other chemical, biological, and nuclear programs, including any which it claims are for purposes not related to weapon production or material." Administration officials doubted Saddam would do this. They hoped only that, once Saddam's noncompliance became clear, they would win unanimous support for war at the U.N. Security Council. . . .

Kay's Findings of Illegal Activity

Now, of course, we know more definitively that Saddam did not comply with Resolution 1441. That is a part of Kay's testimony that has been widely ignored. What Kay discovered in the course of his eight-month-long investigation was that Iraq had failed to answer outstanding questions about its arsenal and programs. Indeed, it had continued to engage in an elaborate campaign of deception and concealment of weapons activities throughout the time when . . . inspectors were in the country, and right up until the day of the invasion, and beyond.

As Kay told the Senate Armed Services Committee [in January 2004], the Iraq Survey Group "discovered hundreds of cases, based on both documents, physical evidence and the testimony of Iraqis, of activities that were prohibited under the initial U.N. Resolution 687 and that should have been reported under 1441, with Iraqi testimony that not only did they not tell the U.N. about this, they were instructed not to do it and they hid material." Kay reported, "We have had a number of Iraqis who have come forward and said, 'We did not tell the U.N. about what we were hiding, nor would we have told the U.N.,'" because the risks were too great. And what were the Iraqis hiding? As Kay reports, "They maintained programs and activities, and they certainly had the intentions at a point to resume their programs. So there was a lot they wanted to hide because it showed what they were doing was illegal." As Kay reported [in] October [2003], his survey team uncovered "dozens of WMD-related program activities and significant amounts of equipment that Iraq concealed from the U.N. during the inspections that began in late 2002." Specifically, Kay reported:

- A clandestine network of laboratories and safehouses within the Iraqi Intelligence Service that contained equipment suitable for research in the production of chemical and biological weapons. . . .
- A prison laboratory complex, which may have been used in human testing of biological weapons agents. Iraqi officials working to prepare for U.N. inspections in 2002 and 2003 were explicitly ordered not to acknowledge the existence of the prison complex.
- So-called "reference strains" of biological organisms, which can be used to produce biological weapons. The strains were found in a scientist's home.
- New research on agents applicable to biological weapons, including Congo Crimean Hemorrhagic Fever, and continuing research on ricin and aflatoxin—all of which was, again, concealed from [inspectors].
- Plans and advanced design work on new missiles with ranges up to at least 1,000 kilometers—well beyond the 150-kilometer limit imposed on Iraq by the U.N. Security Council. These missiles would have allowed Saddam to threaten targets from Ankara to Cairo.

Kay also reported that Iraq "was in the early stages of renovating the [nuclear] program, building new buildings.". . .

We believe that war would have come eventually because of the trajectory that Saddam was on—assuming the United States intended to continue to play its role as guarantor of peace and security in the Middle East. The question was whether it was safer to act sooner or later. The president argued, convincingly, that it was safer—it was necessary—to act sooner. Sanctions could not have been maintained; containment, already dubious, was far less persuasive after September 11; and so the war to remove Saddam was, in the broad strategic sense, in the sense relevant to serious international politics, necessary. This is of course a legitimate subject of debate—but it would be almost as much so even if large stockpiles of weapons had already been recovered.

So what about those stockpiles? The failure to find them, and now David Kay's claim that they did not exist at the time of the invasion last year (a claim reported by an astonishing number of journalists as meaning they never existed at all), has led many to maintain that the entire war was fought on false pretenses. We have addressed that claim. But we also want to address Kay's assertion.

We are prepared to believe that the large stockpiles of anthrax, ricin, VX, and other biological and chemical weapons that once existed were at some point destroyed by the Iraqis. But we do not understand why Kay is so confident he knows what happened to those stockpiles, or to other parts of Saddam's weapons programs that have not been found.

According to Kay's [January 2004] testimony before the Senate (and since he has provided no written report and no documentation to support his recent claims, this is all anyone has to go on), Kay and his team "went after this not in the way of trying to find where the weapons are hidden." When the Survey Group did not find the weapons in "the obvious places," presumably meaning the places that had been identified by intelligence and other sources, Kay explains, he tried other means of discovering the truth. His principal method appears to have been interviews with scientists who would have known what was produced and where it might be stored, as well as a search through a portion of the documents uncovered after the war. Kay acknowledges that stockpiles may, in fact, still be hidden somewhere. But he does not believe they are. . . .

The truth is, neither Kay nor anyone else knows what happened to the weapons stockpiles that we know Iraq once had—because the Iraqis admitted having them. Again, we are willing to be persuaded that Saddam had no weapons stockpiles last year when the war began. But it is too soon, we believe, to come firmly to that conclusion. Nor do we find particularly persuasive the argument that Saddam was only pretending to have weapons of mass destruction, or that he was delusional and being deceived by all around him. These hypotheses are possible. It is also possible we will find stockpiles of weapons, or evidence of their destruction or removal just before the war. . . .

It remains possible that new evidence will be found. We understand why some now want to declare the search over. But we can hardly see how it benefits the people of the United States or the world to declare it over prematurely.

A Just War

Whatever the results of that search, it will continue to be the case that the war was worth fighting, and that it was necessary. For the people of Iraq, the war put an end to three decades of terror and suffering. The mass graves uncovered since the end of the war are alone sufficient justification for it. Assuming the United States remains committed to helping establish a democratic government in Iraq, that will be a blessing both to the Iraqi people and to their neighbors. As for those neighbors, the threat of Saddam's aggression, which hung over the region for more than two decades, has finally been eliminated. The prospects for war in the region have been substantially diminished by our action.

It is also becoming clear that the battle of Iraq has been an important victory in the broader war in which we are engaged, a war against terror, against weapons proliferation, and for a new Middle East. Already, other terror-implicated regimes in the region that were developing weapons of mass destruction are feeling pressure, and some are beginning to move in the right direction. Libya has given up its weapons of mass destruction program. Iran has at least gestured toward opening its nuclear program to inspection. The clandestine international network organized by Pakistan's A.Q. Khan that has been so central to nuclear proliferation to rogue states has been exposed. From Iran to Saudi Arabia, liberal forces seem to have been encouraged. We are paying a real price in blood and treasure in Iraq. But we believe that it is already clear—as clear as such things get in the real world—that the price of the liberation of Iraq has been worth it.

Periodical Bibliography

The following articles have been selected to supplement the diverse views presented in this chapter.

David Albright and Corey Hinderstein — "Iran: Player or Rogue?" *Bulletin of the Atomic Scientists*, September/October 2003.

Jahangir Amuzegar — "Iran's Crumbling Revolution," *Foreign Affairs*, January/February 2003.

Michael Barone — "Stopping Rogue Nukes," *U.S. News & World Report*, November 3, 2003.

Massimo Calabresi — "The Next WMD Crisis: New Evidence Suggests North Korea Is Advancing Its Nuclear-Weapons Plans. What Can the U.S. Do?" *Time*, July 28, 2003.

Michael Duffy — "So Much for the WMD: America's Top Weapons Sleuth Says the Intelligence on Iraq's Arms Was All Wrong," *Time*, February 9, 2004.

Craig Eisendrath — "U.S. Foreign Policy After September 11," *USA Today*, May 2002.

Peter Huessy and Paul Craig Roberts — "Symposium: Will Pre-Emptive War, Such as in Iraq, Make the United States Safer in the Long Term?" *Insight on the News*, April 29, 2003.

Robert Kagan and William Kristol — "Why We Went to War," *Weekly Standard*, October 20, 2003.

James T. Laney and Jason T. Shaplen — "How to Deal with North Korea," *Foreign Affairs*, March/April 2003.

John J. Mearsheimer and Stephen M. Walt — "An Unnecessary War," *Foreign Policy*, January/February 2003.

Alexander V. Nemets and John L. Scherer — "Seeds of North Korea's Contentiousness," *World & I*, June 2003.

Kenneth M. Pollack — "Spies, Lies, and Weapons," *Atlantic Monthly*, January/February 2004.

Jack Spenser — "Do Iraq, Iran, and North Korea Truly Constitute an Axis of Evil?" *USA Today Magazine*, May 2002.

Time — "How Dangerous Is North Korea?" January 13, 2003.

Scott L. Wheeler — "The Link Between Iraq and Al-Qaeda," *Insight on the News*, October 14, 2003.

Kevin Whitelaw et al. — "'We Were All Wrong,'" *U.S. News & World Report*, February 9, 2004.

CHAPTER 3

What Policies Should the United States Adopt Toward Nuclear Weapons?

Chapter Preface

A fundamental controversy in U.S. nuclear policy is the tension between nonproliferation and deterrence. Since the Cold War, the United States has promoted nonproliferation, encouraging nations without nuclear weapons not to build them and countries with nuclear weapons to reduce or limit the size of their nuclear arsenals. The ultimate goal of many advocates of nonproliferation is a world without nuclear weapons.

However, the United States also pursues a policy of deterrence, essentially trying to keep the nuclear peace with the implicit threat that any nation that uses nuclear weapons will become the target of a U.S. nuclear attack. A key part of U.S. nuclear policy is to maintain a nuclear arsenal large enough to be a credible deterrent threat.

The tension between nonproliferation and deterrence is particularly clear in the debate over nuclear testing. As part of its nonproliferation efforts, in 1996 the United States, along with 152 other nations, signed the Comprehensive Nuclear Test Ban Treaty (CTBT), which prohibits all signatories from testing nuclear weapons. Proponents of the CTBT argue that by keeping other nations from conducting nuclear tests, the United States can be assured that its nuclear arsenal will remain the most advanced in the world.

However, the treaty does not take effect until it is approved by the governments of the United States and other signing nations, and in 1999 the Republican-controlled Senate refused to ratify the CTBT. The Bush administration's Nuclear Posture Review (NPR), a congressionally mandated examination of U.S. nuclear policy, also indicates a reluctance to ban nuclear testing. In language that has alarmed antinuclear groups, the NPR states that the United States should be ready "to design, develop, manufacture, and certify new warheads in response to new national requirements; and maintain readiness to resume underground nuclear testing if required."

Whether or not to ban nuclear testing is just one of the issues in the debate over U.S. nuclear policy. The authors in the following chapter offer their viewpoints on nuclear abolition, testing, and deterrence.

*"Safety from nuclear destruction must be
our goal. We can reach it only by reducing
and then eliminating nuclear arms."*

The United States Should Eliminate Its Nuclear Arsenal

Jonathan Schell

In the following viewpoint *Nation* writer Jonathan Schell calls
on the American public to help revitalize the movement to
abolish nuclear weapons. Schell argues that America's need to
maintain a huge nuclear arsenal ended with the Cold War. But
he notes that the Bush administration abandoned the goal of
nuclear arms reduction in 2002 when the United States signed
the toothless Moscow treaty with Russia and then formally
withdrew from the Anti-Ballistic Missile treaty, a more stringent arms control treaty dating back to 1972. Schell believes
that the new U.S. stance on nuclear deterrence will worsen
the threat of terrorism, as more nations develop nuclear
weapons of their own, making it more likely that nuclear
weapons or materials might be stolen by terrorist groups.
Jonathan Schell is the Harold Willens Peace Fellow at the
Nation Institute, and the author of several books, including
The Fate of the Earth and *The Unfinished Twentieth Century*.

As you read, consider the following questions:
1. How many nuclear weapons will be dismantled under
   the Moscow treaty, according to the author?
2. Between what two countries is nuclear war most
   imminent, in Schell's view?
3. What three developments does the author call signs of
   "the second nuclear age"?

Jonathan Schell, "The Growing Nuclear Peril," *The Nation*, vol. 274, June 24,
2002, p. 11. Copyright © 2002 by The Nation Magazine/The Nation Company,
Inc. Reproduced by permission.

KVCC KALAMAZOO VALLEY
COMMUNITY COLLEGE
LIBRARY

On June 12, 1982, 1 million people assembled in Central Park in New York City to call for a freeze of the nuclear arms race. In the years that followed, the cold war waned and then ended, and the strategic nuclear arsenals of the United States and the Soviet Union were not only frozen but cut to about half of their peak. In the early post–cold war years, it seemed conceivable that nuclear arms might be on their way to obsolescence, and nuclear danger pretty much dropped out of the public mind.

A New Nuclear Era?

It's now clear that these hopes were ill founded. The nuclear dilemma was not going away; it was changing shape. Four years ago [in 1998], I asked in a special issue of this magazine [the *Nation*] whether the nuclear arsenals of the cold war were "merely a monstrous leftover from a frightful era that has ended, and will soon follow it into history, or whether, on the contrary, they are the seeds of a new, more virulent nuclear era." The seeds have now sprouted, and that new era is upon us in South Asia and elsewhere.

Today, twenty years after the June 12 demonstration, some of us who were present at the event believe that the time has come again for the public to make its voice heard in protest against the direction of nuclear policies, and we are therefore issuing the Urgent Call on the following page. As one of its signatories, I wish to explain why I think this is necessary. Passages from the Call are in [italics]; the commentary is in ordinary type.

"*Despite the end of the cold war, the United States plans to keep large numbers of nuclear weapons indefinitely.*"

According to President George W. Bush, the recently signed Moscow Treaty, under which the United States and Russia have agreed to a limit on deployed strategic weapons of no more than 2,200 each, "liquidates the legacy of the cold war." Rarely has more contradiction, misdirection and confusion been compacted into a single phrase. Let us count the ways.

(1) The cold war—the global ideological struggle between the United States and the Soviet Union—in fact ended definitively in 1991 with the disappearance of the Soviet Union

from the face of the earth. The President at the time, Bush's father, told us so. As one Russian wag recently commented, "I'm tired of attending funerals for the cold war." The cold war is over. Long live the cold war.

(2) Does liquidating the legacy of the cold war then perhaps mean liquidating the nuclear arsenals that were built up in the name of that struggle? No. Not a single nuclear warhead will be dismantled under the treaty. Even the deployed weapons will, when the reductions are complete, be quite sufficient for either country to blow up the other many times over. It is better that the excess warheads will be in storage than on hairtrigger alert, but the move only reduces the overkill. All the kill remains. In other words, at the treaty's expiration, in 2012, more than two decades after the disappearance of the Soviet Union, the nuclear policies—as distinct from the active and alert force levels—of the two nations will not have changed in the slightest particular.

(3) If neither the cold war nor its nuclear arsenals are being liquidated, does the treaty at least consolidate a postwar friendship between Russia and the United States? On the contrary, the United States has introduced a fresh note of suspicion into the relationship by insisting on storing rather than dismantling the "reduced" weapons in order to "hedge" against some undefined deterioration in relations with Russia—notwithstanding the new consultative relationship of Russia with NATO [North Atlantic Treaty Organization]. One day, the United States thus declares to Russia, 2,200 nuclear weapons may not be enough for dealing with you; we may again need 10,000. That message is reinforced by a shortening of the usual six-month withdrawal time in treaties to three months.

(4) Does the treaty liquidate anything, then? Yes—nuclear arms control. The Bush Administration, which resisted putting even the Moscow agreement in treaty form, has let it be known that it intends no further arms control treaties with Russia. On June 13, [2002] the United States will formally withdraw from the Anti-Ballistic Missile treaty. The world, President Bush is saying, has had all the nuclear disarmament it is going to get out of the end of the cold war. But if the twice-announced end of that conflict cannot get

Russia and the United States out of the trap of "mutual assured destruction," what can? Nothing is on the horizon. Woodrow Wilson fought the "war to end all wars." George Bush has signed an arms control treaty to end all arms control treaties.

Nuclear Proliferation Fuels the Terrorist Threat

"The dangers posed by huge arsenals, threats of use, proliferation and terrorism are linked. . . ."

It's all a matter, as we've learned to say of the pre–September 11 [2001 terrorist attacks] intelligence failures, of connect-

---

End the Nuclear Danger: An Urgent Call

A decade after the end of the cold war, the peril of nuclear destruction is mounting. The great powers have refused to give up nuclear arms, other countries are producing them and terrorist groups are trying to acquire them.

Poorly guarded warheads and nuclear material in the former Soviet Union may fall into the hands of terrorists. The Bush Administration is developing nuclear "bunker busters" and threatening to use them against nonnuclear countries. The risk of nuclear war between India and Pakistan is grave.

Despite the end of the cold war, the United States plans to keep large numbers of nuclear weapons indefinitely. The latest US-Russian treaty, which will cut deployed strategic warheads to 2,200, leaves both nations facing "assured destruction" and lets them keep total arsenals (active and inactive, strategic and tactical) of more than 10,000 warheads each.

The dangers posed by huge arsenals, threats of use, proliferation and terrorism are linked: The nuclear powers' refusal to disarm fuels proliferation, and proliferation makes nuclear materials more accessible to terrorists.

The [September 11, 2001, terrorist attacks] brought home to Americans what it means to experience a catastrophic attack. Yet the horrifying losses that day were only a fraction of what any nation would suffer if a single nuclear weapon were used on a city.

The drift toward catastrophe must be reversed. Safety from nuclear destruction must be our goal. We can reach it only by reducing and then eliminating nuclear arms under binding agreements.

We therefore call on the United States and Russia to fulfill

---

ing the dots. The failure of the end of the cold war's political hostilities to bring with it the end of the cold war's nuclear arsenals is a fact of prime importance for the era that is beginning. No longer justified as a remnant of the old era, they have now become the foundation stone of the new one. They relegitimize nuclear arsenals at lower levels. The plain message for the future is that in the twenty-first century, countries that want to be safe need large nuclear arsenals, even in the absence of present enemies. This of course is a formula for nuclear proliferation.

The place in the world to look today for a portrait of pro-

---

their Commitments under the Nonproliferation Treaty to move together with the other nuclear powers, step by carefully inspected and verified step, to the abolition of nuclear weapons. As key steps toward this goal, we call on the United States to:

- *Renounce* the first use of nuclear weapons.
- Permanently *end* the development, testing and production of nuclear warheads.
- *Seek agreement* with Russia on the mutual and verified destruction of nuclear weapons withdrawn under treaties, and increase the resources available here and in the former Soviet Union to secure nuclear warheads and material and to implement destruction.
- *Strengthen* nonproliferation efforts by ratifying the Comprehensive Test Ban Treaty, finalizing a missile ban in North Korea, supporting UN inspections in Iraq, locating and reducing fissile material worldwide and negotiating a ban on its production.
- *Take* nuclear weapons off hairtrigger alert in concert with the other nuclear powers (the UK, France, Russia, China, India, Pakistan and Israel) in order to reduce the risk of accidental or unauthorized use.
- *Initiate* talks on further nuclear cuts, beginning with US and Russian reductions to 1,000 warheads each.

To sign the statement, go to urgentcall.org or send name, organization/profession (for id only) and contact information to Urgent Call, c/o Fourth Freedom Forum, 11 Dupont Circle NW, 9th Floor, Washington, DC 20036.

Jonathan Schell et al., *Nation*, June 24, 2002, p. 12.

---

liferation is South Asia, where India and Pakistan are closer to nuclear war than any two countries have been since the Cuban missile crisis, or perhaps ever. According to a recent government study, 12 million lives are at immediate risk. A multiple of that could be the eventual total. The world has scarcely begun to absorb the meaning of these figures. It is a crisis in which almost every conceivable form of violence and threat of violence is tied into a single knot. Up to a million men facing each other across an 1,800-mile border are primed for a World War I–style conventional war. Between them is a disputed territory, Kashmir. On that territory a liberation movement pits an indigenous Muslim minority against Indian repression in the part of Kashmir under its control. Extremist groups in Kashmir and supporters who cross the border from Pakistan to aid them add the incendiary ingredient of terrorism. In a deadly new combination, terrorism threatens to unbalance the balance of terror. The leaders of both countries—the dictator Pervez Musharraf of Pakistan and the head of the Hindu fundamentalist Bharatiya Janata Party, Prime Minister Atal Behari Vajpayee of India—have taken "tough" stands from which they can withdraw only at high political cost. In a groggy atmosphere of global inattention and inaction, the two nations drift toward nuclear war. Its outbreak would change history forever.

Even as the great powers' fresh embrace of their nuclear arsenals incites proliferation, proliferation (to further connect the dots) fuels the terrorist danger. A world of multiplying nuclear powers will be a world awash in nuclear materials. To give just one instance, it is known that the Pakistani nuclear-weapon scientist and Muslim fanatic Sultan Bashiruddin Mahmood had visited [terrorist] Osama bin Laden to talk over nuclear matters. [In early 2002], bin Laden announced—falsely, we can only hope—that he possessed nuclear arms, and it is known that the Al Qaeda network has sought them. In a May article in the *New York Times Magazine*, complete with washed-out, vaguely post-apocalyptic photographs of New York, Bill Keller reported that forestalling such an attack is now one of the highest priorities of the federal government.

The relegitimation of nuclear weapons in the toothless

Moscow Treaty, the rising danger of nuclear war in South Asia and the spreading fear of nuclear terrorism in the United States and elsewhere are only the most recent harvest of danger—three new dots on the single, terrifying emerging map of the second nuclear age.

A World Without Nuclear Weapons

"Safety from nuclear destruction must be our goal. We can reach it only by reducing and then eliminating nuclear arms under binding agreements."

The Bush Administration, which is acutely aware of the dangers of both nuclear terrorism and nuclear proliferation (Secretary of Defense Donald Rumsfeld has called the use of a weapon of mass destruction on American soil "inevitable"), has consistently turned to military force as its chosen remedy. Its formula for dealing with terrorism is to overthrow states that harbor terrorists. Its program for stopping proliferation is likewise overthrowing some states—beginning with the government of Iraq—that seek to engage in it. The new strategy has been codified in a new Nuclear Posture Review, which proposes a policy of "offensive deterrence," under which the United States threatens pre-emptive attack, including possible nuclear attack, against nations that acquire or threaten to use weapons of mass destruction. Disarmament has become an occasion for war. But force is more likely to incite proliferation than to end it. In a world whose great powers were committed to nuclear disarmament, the decision by other nations to forgo these weapons would be consistent with national self-respect. But in a world in which one self-designated enforcer of a two-tier nuclear system sits atop a mountain of nuclear bombs and threatens destruction of any regime that itself seeks to acquire them, such forbearance becomes national humiliation—a continuation of the hated colonial system of the past, or "nuclear apartheid," as the Indian government put it.

The Urgent Call, by contrast, proposes a return to the tested and proven path of negotiation, through which 182 countries have already agreed, under the terms of the Nuclear Nonproliferation Treaty, to stay out of the nuclear weapons business. The call raises the banner of a single standard: a world without nuclear weapons.

"We therefore call on the United States and Russia . . . to move together with the other nuclear powers, step by carefully inspected and verified step, to the abolition of nuclear weapons."

The goal of nuclear abolition, it is true, is ambitious, and the difficulties are mountainous. Many will say, as they have throughout the nuclear age, that it is unrealistic. They would perhaps be right if we lived in a static world. But events—in South Asia, in Central Asia, in the Middle East, in New York—are moving at breakneck pace, and the avenues to disaster are multiplying. A nuclear revival is under way. A revival of nuclear protest is needed to stop it.

> "*For the foreseeable future we have no
> alternative but to continue to depend on
> nuclear weapons and the deterrence they
> provide.*"

The United States Should Not Eliminate Its Nuclear Arsenal

C. Paul Robinson, interviewed by James Kitfield

C. Paul Robinson is director of Sandia National Laboratories, a government-owned, privately operated facility that develops technologies to enhance U.S. national security. In 2001 Robinson wrote an influential paper supporting the inclusion of nuclear weapons in U.S. defense policy. The following viewpoint is excerpted from an interview Robinson gave to *National Journal* in September 2001. In it he argues that the abolition of nuclear weapons would severely undermine U.S. national security. Robinson supports reductions in the U.S. nuclear stockpile but believes that America must maintain an arsenal sizable enough to deter other nations from threatening the United States with their own weapons of mass destruction. He also supports the use of smaller nuclear weapons that might be used against rogue nations without inflicting extremely massive casualties.

As you read, consider the following questions:

1. Roughly speaking, about how many nuclear weapons does the author believe the United States must maintain?
2. According to Robinson, why did Iraq refrain from using more of its chemical and biological weapons in the 1991 Gulf War?

James Kitfield, "Ban the Bomb? Heck No, It's Too Useful," *National Journal*, vol. 33, September 8, 2001, p. 36. Copyright © 2001 by the National Journal Group, Inc. All rights reserved. Reproduced by permission.

To his critics, C. Paul Robinson is Dr. Strangelove incarnate, a Cold Warrior who after nearly four decades working in the U.S. nuclear weapons complex learned to love the bomb. While even hardliners in the Bush Administration are today trumpeting "deep cuts" in the U.S. nuclear arsenal, Robinson, director of Sandia National Laboratories, argues for new types of nuclear weapons to deter new kinds of threats. Although most of the globe embraces the dream inherent in the Nuclear Nonproliferation Treaty of a future world without nukes, Robinson—with unusual, to-the-point frankness—decries this "delegitimization" of nuclear weapons.

Not even his critics, however, question Robinson's credentials as an articulate advocate for the continued value of the United States' nuclear deterrent. A physicist by trade, Robinson spent nearly 20 years at Los Alamos National Laboratory, eventually heading its nuclear weapons programs. With the title of ambassador, he also served as Ronald Reagan's chief negotiator and head of the U.S. delegation to the Nuclear Testing Talks in Geneva in the 1980s. He is presently chairman of the policy subcommittee of the Strategic Advisory Group, a panel that advises the four-star commander of U.S. Strategic Command, which is in charge of U.S. nuclear weapons. Many of Robinson's ideas for reshaping America's nuclear arsenal—contained in his white paper "Pursuing a New Nuclear Weapons Policy for the 21st Century"—have been embraced by senior Bush Administration officials. *National Journal* correspondent James Kitfield recently interviewed Robinson in Washington.

The Importance of Deterrence

James Kitfield: In a post–Cold War era when most policy makers are focusing on reducing nuclear arsenals, you argue in your paper that nuclear weapons not only "have an abiding place on the international scene," but also that new ones should be tailored for new kinds of deterrence.

C. Paul Robinson: As I wrote this paper, it felt like putting my head in a guillotine, because I knew that some people were going to try and chop it off for making these arguments. A lot has been done in recent years to delegitimize nuclear weapons to the point that I find people are lulled into a belief that nuclear weapons are going to go away soon, and thus we needn't worry about them anymore. But it's ridiculous to think that we can "uninvent" nuclear weapons.

I also happen to think that nuclear weapons have not only been vital to U.S. national security, but also that history has turned out better for our having nuclear weapons. U.S. nuclear weapons help maintain peace, and a lot of other nations depend on our nuclear umbrella. So, like it or not, for the foreseeable future we have no alternative but to continue to depend upon nuclear weapons and the deterrence they provide.

Are there no compelling strategic and moral arguments for, as you say, "delegitimizing" weapons of such horrific destructive potential? For instance, the United States signed the Nuclear Nonproliferation Treaty, which calls for nonnuclear states to forgo nuclear weapons, and for nuclear weapons states to work to reduce their arsenals eventually to zero.

The NPT Treaty, the arguments surrounding the Comprehensive Test Ban Treaty, and a lot of the rhetoric we heard from the Clinton White House all suggested that sooner or later nuclear weapons are going to go away. I simply don't believe that is true. I think it's important that people wake up and realize that nuclear weapons have meant a lot to our security, and we'd better make sure that our arsenal doesn't erode if our future depends on it.

And you've taken on the mission of sounding the alarm?

No one likes thinking the unthinkable, because it's a tough business. But someone's got to do it. I guess after spending my entire career in this field, I don't think anyone else knows more about the subject than me.

Arms control advocates would argue that the NPT is largely responsible for many nuclear have-nots doing without nuclear weapons.

Yes and no. I believe the establishment of NATO [the North Atlantic Treaty Organization] did more to prevent proliferation than the NPT, because it extended our nuclear umbrella over the nations of Western Europe that could relatively easily have developed their own nuclear weapons. I think there's a lesson in that example which applies today to South Asia.

The Bush Administration has proposed deep reductions in our offensive nuclear arsenal as a sweetener in selling its proposed na-

U.S. Nuclear Forces, 2003

Type	Name	Launchers	Year deployed	Warheads x yield (kiloton)	Warheads active/spares
Intercontinental Ballistic Missiles					
LGM-30G	Minuteman III				
	Mk-12	150	1970	1 W62 × 170	150
	Mk-12	50	1970	3 W62 × 170 (MIRV)	150/15
	Mk-12A	300	1979	3 W78 × 335 (MIRV)	900/20
LGM-118A	MX/Peacekeeper	40	1986	10 W87 × 300 (MIRV)	400/50
Total		**540**			**1,600/85**
Submarine-Launched Ballistic Missiles					
UGM-96A	Trident I C4	96/4	1979	6 W76 × 100 (MIRV)	576
UGM-133A	Trident II D5	288/12			
	Mk-4		1992	8 W76 × 100 (MIRV)	1,920/156
	Mk-5		1990	8 W88 × 475 (MIRV)	384/16
Total		**384/16**			**2,880/172**
Bombers					
B-52	Stratofortress	94/56*	1961	ALCM/W80-1 × 5–150	430/20
				ACM/W80-1 × 5–150	430/20
B-2	Spirit	21/16	1994	B61-7, -11, B83-1 bombs	800/45
Total		**115/72**			**1,660/85**
Nonstrategic forces					
	Tomahawk Ship-Launched	325	1984	1 W80-0 × 5–150	320
	Cruise Missiles	n/a	1979	0.3–170	800/40
	B61-3, -4, -10 bombs				
Total		**325**			**1,120/40**
Grand total**					**~7,650**

ACM: advanced cruise missile; ALCM: air-launched cruise missile; ICBM: intercontinental ballistic missile (range greater than 5,500 kilometers); MIRV: multiple independently targetable reentry vehicles; SLCM: sea-launched cruise missile; SLBM: submarine-launched ballistic missile.
* The first figure is the total inventory, including those used for training, testing, and backup; the second figure is the primary mission inventory: the number of operational aircraft assigned for nuclear or conventional missions.
** Nearly 3,000 additional intact warheads are retained in reserve or inactive stockpiles.

Robert S. Norris, Hans M. Kristensen, and Joshua Handler, "Nuclear Notebook," *Bulletin of the Atomic Scientists*, May/June 2003.

tional missile defense shield. At some point, might such reductions erode the United States' ability to extend its nuclear umbrella?

I support deep reductions, but at some point [those cuts] would call our umbrella into question. I worked on a report on that subject for the commander in chief of U.S. Strategic Command as a member of the Strategic Advisory Group. Essentially, our blueprint concluded that at some point between 2,000 and 1,000 nuclear weapons, we will run into speed bumps and probably a stop sign on reductions. It's not an exact science, and that level would still represent a dramatic reduction from today's massive U.S. and Russian nuclear arsenals.

At some point in reducing our arsenal, we also have to switch from bilateral to multilateral negotiations, because our nuclear arsenal has to deter a potential threat from unforeseen alliances that might develop in the future between other nuclear states. Stranger things have happened throughout history. Somewhat counterintuitively, a world in which there are just a few nuclear weapons would also be very dangerous, because the possibility that one side would "break out," and secretly construct a dominant nuclear force of a hundred or so weapons, would be quite high.

Do you think the Bush Administration's proposed missile defense system will lessen the need for some offensive nuclear weapons in the deterrence equation?

I believe both offensive and defensive systems can coexist as part of an overall national security policy, though I have yet to hear that policy articulated. You'll never have a defense, however, that is dominant against offensive nuclear weapons. When I speak publicly on the subject, I also ask audiences to consider that the United States or one of its allies were attacked with nuclear weapons one day, and our proposed missile defense system worked as advertised. Say only 5 or 10 percent, or whatever number you pick, of the attacking nuclear missiles got through. Do you really think the war is then over? . . .

In your paper, you argue that the United States needs to tailor its nuclear arsenal to deter new types of threats, especially chemical and biological weapons. Do we really need to find new uses for nuclear weapons?

Not necessarily new. We had a pretty good test case with Iraq during the Persian Gulf War. If you look at the volumes of chemical and biological weapons later reported by United Nations weapons inspectors, it was astounding what Iraq possessed. Why weren't those weapons of mass destruction used? Many military experts I've talked to are absolutely convinced it was because of a secret letter sent by President [George] Bush threatening the gravest consequences if such weapons were released. President Clinton made a similar threat against North Korea during a crisis in 1994.

The Need for Smaller Tactical Weapons

If our implicit threat of nuclear retaliation deterred rogue states such as Iraq and North Korea, why do we need new nuclear weapons?

The problem is, the strategic nuclear policy we developed during the Cold War has been stretched about as far as possible to fit a changing post–Cold War era. Today, we are threatened not only by nuclear weapons in the arsenal of peer nuclear competitors like Russia, but increasingly by biological, chemical, and radiological weapons that could kill huge numbers of people in a flash. Yet it's pretty incredible to think that the United States would respond to such an attack by vaporizing 11 million people in a rogue state just because they were poorly led. Where the hell are we going to use missiles with four to eight warheads, or half-megaton yields? Even the few "tactical" nuclear weapons that we have left have high yields of above 100 kilotons. I would hope a U.S. President would think it was crazy to use such weapons in response to a rogue-state attack.

After a decade of trying to sort out what we learned from the Cold War and how we might tailor our nuclear deterrence and deterrent message to fit the future, I now argue that we need lower-yield nuclear weapons that could hold at risk only a rogue state's leadership and tools of aggression with some level of confidence.

Isn't the United States' vaunted conventional military superiority—based in large part on our increasingly accurate precision-guided weapons—enough of a deterrent?

No. We've seen examples as recently as the [1999] air war

with Serbia, when we attacked underground targets with conventional weapons with very little effect. It just takes far too many aircraft sorties and conventional weapons to give you any confidence that you can take out underground bunkers. By putting a nuclear warhead on one of those weapons instead of high explosives, you would multiply the explosive power by a factor of more than a million.

Wouldn't fielding new, low-yield nuclear weapons capable of penetrating underground bunkers require new designs and a return to nuclear testing?

In my paper, I conclude that we would neither have to conduct testing nor redesign for such a weapon, because we have them already. Right now, all of our weapons have primary and secondary stages. Through a process known as "boosting," you get a thermonuclear reaction. The primary alone, however, has a yield of 10 kilotons or less, or basically what you would want for a bunker-buster or a weapon that would cause relatively low collateral damage. All we have to do is send these weapons back to the factory and replace the secondary stage with a dummy. The beauty of that approach is that we are already very good at building dummy secondary stages. For safety and costs reasons, most of the weapons we have flown and tested in the past have had dummy secondary stages. So we could develop these lower-yield weapons without forcing the nuclear testing issue back onto the table, with a richer database of past tests, and at relatively low cost. . . .

How do you respond to critics who believe that by tailoring new nuclear weapons for new types of deterrence, you would make their eventual use in a crisis more likely?

My response is that for God's sake, then, let's think this through in advance rather than doing it on the fly. Say Iraq had instigated the first use of biological or chemical weapons during the Persian Gulf War, causing huge numbers of casualties. How would we have retaliated to make good on President Bush's threat? By vaporizing 11 million people? Because I can tell you, we haven't given a lot of thought to this issue. We need to carefully think through our posture of nuclear deterrence, because whatever decision is made during the next crisis will leave a message to all of history.

Preserving the Peace

Why not send a message that the United States will not be the first to use nuclear weapons?

The burden is on those who believe it is immoral to threaten nuclear retaliation for the use of chemical or biological weapons to propose an alternative. I subscribe to the advice of [former British prime minister] Winston Churchill: "Be careful above all things not to let go of the atomic weapon until you are sure, and more sure than sure, that other means of preserving the peace are in your hands." Those words reflect my thinking on the subject very well.

"Without a low-yield penetrator, rogue-state leaders are able to have, in effect, a safe haven for themselves and their weapons of mass destruction."

The United States Should Modernize Its Nuclear Arsenal

Richard Lowry

In the following viewpoint Richard Lowry argues that the United States needs to build new, smaller-yield nuclear weapons. Lowry maintains that the current U.S. nuclear arsenal is made up of high-yield nuclear weapons that during the Cold War were intended to convince the Soviet Union that it would face annihilation if it started a nuclear war with the United States. Today, maintains Lowry, the idea that America would use these incredibly destructive weapons—which would kill massive numbers of civilians—simply is not credible. He contends that the United States needs smaller nuclear weapons both to provide credible deterrence and to provide a means of destroying deeply buried underground bunkers in which terrorists and rogue nations build and store weapons of mass destruction. Richard Lowry is editor of the *National Review*, a conservative weekly magazine.

As you read, consider the following questions:

1. As stated by the author, what countries have tested nuclear weapons since the United States voluntarily stopped testing in 1992?
2. Why does the Federation of American Scientists oppose low-yield nuclear weapons, as quoted by Lowry?

Richard Lowry, "The Nukes We Need: Adapting Our Arsenal to Today," *National Review*, vol. 54, March 25, 2002. Copyright © 2002 by National Review, Inc., 215 Lexington Ave., New York, NY 10016. Reproduced by permission.

When President [George W.] Bush peered across the DMZ [demilitarization zone] into North Korea [during his visit to South Korea in February 2002], the most important things to see were out of sight. The North Koreans have two related proficiencies: weapons production and tunneling. They built an underground city to conceal work on the No Dong ballistic missile, tested in 1993. In 1998, a tunnel complex big enough to house a plutonium production plant was discovered near a nuclear research center supposedly shut down under the 1994 U.S.–North Korean Agreed Framework. Meanwhile, the North Korea forward staging areas near the DMZ have more than 4,000 tunnels and bunkers.

The Underground Threat

The North Koreans may specialize mainly in backwardness, but in this they are on the cutting edge. Russia, China, Iraq, and other countries all have a new appreciation for the bunker mentality. The Chinese learned from NATO [North Atlantic Treaty Organization] air campaigns in the Gulf and the Balkans that digging is the best way to counteract NATO's mastery of the air. As for the Russians, they have a tradition of digging going back to the Cold War, with some bunkers in Moscow estimated to be 1,000 feet deep, and one facility under Yamantau Mountain in the Urals reportedly as large as the area inside the Washington Beltway.

As the war on terrorism has now also become—at least in the president's rhetoric—a war on weapons of mass destruction (WMD), this drive underground cannot be ignored, especially in U.S. nuclear policy. The U.S. is finally—a decade late—taking account of the end of the Cold War by drastically reducing its operational strategic nuclear force from roughly 6,000 warheads to 2,000. But it makes no sense to react to the changed international environment only by scrapping the old force. The arsenal should also be updated to deal with new realities, most importantly by developing an earth-penetrating nuke, designed to target deeply buried WMD [weapons of mass destruction] sites.

William Schneider, chairman of the Pentagon's Defense Science Board, explains that there has been a revolution in the economics of digging in recent years, thanks mostly to work on the Channel Tunnel. Run as a commercial venture, the Chunnel project emphasized innovation, producing technologies cheaper and more efficient than the traditional blast-and-cut methods. Now, according to Schneider, for a few million dollars a country can buy a Japanese, Finnish, or German machine that can dig an 18-meter-wide hole at a rate of 70 meters a day.

The Robust Nuclear Earth Penetrator

Our potential enemies are burrowing in their chemical weapons capability, their conventional capability, their command and control, biological and nuclear weapons programs. Our current weapons systems cannot destroy targets that are deeply buried in tunnels. They were not designed to do so.

In the 2001 Defense Authorization Bill, the Congress directed NNSA [the National Nuclear Security Administration] to study whether we can take an existing nuclear weapon and encase it in such a way so that it will penetrate the earth before it explodes. The intent is to hold at risk hard and deeply buried targets.

Having a Robust Nuclear Earth Penetrator (RNEP) does not make it more likely that the President would use such a weapon. The use of nuclear weapons is one of the gravest decisions any President can contemplate. It does make it more probable that that weapon would destroy a deeply buried target if he had to use it, and, hence, more likely that we could deter the use of weapons of mass destruction by an enemy.

The President should have options—the options of conventional forces, of precision conventional weapons, and of nuclear weapons that are capable of holding all targets at risk.

U.S. House of Representatives Policy Committee, Subcommittee on National Security and Foreign Affairs, *Differentiation and Defense: An Agenda for the Nuclear Weapons Program*, February 2003.

The U.S. has been working to counteract this new underground capability with conventional weapons. The GBU-28 "Bunker Buster"—a 5,000-lb. laser-guided bomb rushed into production for the Gulf War—has penetrated over 20 feet of concrete and more than 100 feet of earth in tests. Even bigger and better weapons are in the works. One is called "Big BLU," a sort of plus-size daisy cutter (the 15,000-lb. bomb designed to blast clear a 600-meter area that has had a starring role in [the 2001 war in] Afghanistan).

With these bombs, the military is essentially attempting to create something that has the power of a nuclear weapon without actually being nuclear. But the explosive force of conventional weapons can be pushed only so far. In addition, some bunkers are simply too deep and too hard. A recent Pentagon study concluded, "Even with the current strategy and acquisition initiatives, the United States will still not be able to hold all known or suspected Hard and Deeply Buried Targets at risk for destruction, especially the deep underground facilities."

This means that the only conventional force to which some targets will be vulnerable is an invasion or special-forces raid. But not all future conflicts will resemble Afghanistan or the Persian Gulf War, when the U.S. had total control of the skies and could operate almost at will. The ground-force option, in addition to risking American lives, would almost always fail what Keith Payne, head of the influential National Institute for Public Policy (NIPP), says should be a three-pronged test for taking out a dangerous WMD site in a crisis: It should be prompt, predictable (for our leaders, not the enemy), and definitive. A conventional raid might well be none of the above.

The Need for Smaller, More Accurate Nukes

Which leaves nuclear weapons. "From the public record, I don't know of any non-nuclear way of dealing with this underground threat promptly and conclusively," says Payne, whose work has been the basis of the Bush administration's recent reevaluation of U.S. nuclear strategy. A nuke would have several advantages. It passes the prompt-predictable-definitive test. It also might not require intelligence as precise as that necessary for a conventional weapon—the explosive force provides room for error.

And it would destroy the targeted WMD agents rather than spread them as a conventional blast might. As a report from NIPP recently put it, chemical and biological agents "are extremely difficult to destroy (or sterilize) definitely, as opposed merely to disperse, except by means of the extraordinary heat and neutron flux generated by nuclear explosives." A nuke, of course, would create another hazard—radioactive fallout—but a low-yield weapon could be designed to minimize it.

The problem is that we don't have this kind of weapon. Given that we have been in the nuclear business for 50 years, how is that possible? A host of strategic and technical reasons account for it, together with a perverse arms-control orthodoxy that has attempted to keep the U.S. arsenal as massive, inaccurate, and potentially horrific in its effects as possible.

Mutual Assured Destruction relied on the "balance of terror," on the willingness of the U.S. and the Soviet Union to hold their populations hostage. Any highly accurate or earth-penetrating weapon that instead would have been effective against specific military targets was considered "destabilizing"—a "war-fighting" weapon rather than a weapon of generalized terror. So, U.S. nukes tended to be designed for killing lots of Russians rather than destroying narrow military targets.

This was also simply easier as a technical matter. Getting a warhead to drive into the ground, then explode, is a technical challenge on the order of getting a car to drive through a wall, then have its left-turn signal flash. As nuclear expert Robert Barker explains, the weapon has to be fast enough to enter the ground, but not so fast as to destroy the warhead and the mechanism that triggers it. The warhead design, needless to say, must be very rugged. These difficulties, however, are probably surmountable. We dealt with some of them in creating nuclear artillery shells, which had to withstand enormous G-forces.

But arms-controllers aren't interested in having these problems surmounted. In fact, [many] . . . want U.S. nuclear weapons to be as indiscriminate as possible. In their 1983 letter on nuclear weapons, the U.S. Catholic bishops opposed making nukes more accurate. This would seem to be in direct contradiction to Just War Theory, which emphasizes "discrimination" in order to minimize civilian casualties. The bishops' spirit lives on in 1994 congressional language prohibiting the U.S. from "research and development which could lead to the production by the United States of a new low-yield nuclear weapon, including a precision low-yield warhead."

There have, nonetheless, been attempts to update the U.S. arsenal. The Clinton administration worked to develop a penetrator without actually creating a "new" weapon. It gave an existing nuke, the B-61, a new needle-shaped hardened case. But the re-jiggered B-61 relies only on its terminal velocity—it is dropped, unpowered, from the air—to drive it into the earth. A true earth-penetrator would be powered so that it could hit the ground at much higher speeds. (The B-61 burrows about 20 feet deep into dry earth, whereas a true penetrator might need to go through 100 feet of granite.)

One advantage of the B-61 is that its yield can be adjusted downward from its high of 340 kilotons. A low-yield penetrator would probably be 10 kilotons or less (the Hiroshima bomb was 15 kilotons). The issue of size is so important because the U.S. wants a weapon that can be used in a crisis without the sort of massive collateral damage that would be simply unacceptable. As Stephen Younger, then an associate lab director at Los Alamos [nuclear arms facility], wrote in a controversial June 2000 paper, "A reliance on high-yield strategic weapons could lead to 'self-deterrence'"—in other words, an unwillingness on the part of the U.S. to use its own weapons.

The Testing Taboo

If the U.S. wants to develop a useful new nuke it will have to cross another arms-control taboo—against nuclear testing. In theory, it might be possible to jerry-rig a new weapon without testing, but that would be far from ideal as a technical matter. In any case, the "stockpile stewardship program," which was supposed to supplant testing with computer models, was drastically underfunded in the Clinton administration, limiting its usefulness. It is questionable whether we can retain confidence even in our current arsenal without testing, since our warheads were designed to last only 15 to 20 years.

In 1992, the first President Bush signed a bill instituting a voluntary moratorium on testing, although he made clear that he opposed it, and the Senate declined to make it permanent in 1999 by refusing to ratify the Comprehensive Test Ban Treaty. Arms-controllers argue that if the U.S. eschews testing, it will create a new anti-nuclear "norm" around the world. But the Chinese, French, Indians, Pakistanis, and perhaps the Russians have tested subsequent to the U.S. moratorium.

For arms-controllers, the underlying rationale for the taboo against testing seems obvious: to prevent the U.S. from developing a new weapon, and ultimately to force the existing arsenal to die on the vine. It ensures that the U.S. has an aging, less and less reliable arsenal, built for a long-past strategic threat that bears little resemblance to the present one. The last new U.S. nuclear weapon was fielded in the 1980s, which means that it was designed in the 1970s. The longer the U.S. goes without designing and manufacturing a new weapon, the less capable it will be of doing so, as the expertise and manufacturing base wither away.

Credible Deterrence

The thrust of the arms-controllers seems to come down to limiting U.S. power. Consider: Arms-controllers oppose American missile defenses because it is supposedly destabilizing for the U.S. to have sites that can be protected from rogue-state (or Russian or Chinese) attack. On the other hand, arms-controllers apparently don't mind rogue states' having sites that can be protected from U.S. attack. There is no effort to create an international treaty keeping rogues from digging deep bunkers. And arms-controllers oppose a new U.S. weapon that would be capable of holding these sites at risk. Assured destruction apparently looks much better when it applies only to the U.S.

During the debate over missile defense [in 2001], arms-controllers made nice sounds about deterrence (who needs missile defense when you have deterrence?). But deterrence depends on credibility. As long as the U.S. arsenal is chock-full of weapons that can only cause indiscriminate damage—and mass civilian casualties—it doesn't seem credible that we will use them, and so their deterrent value is lost. Which is exactly the way arms-controllers like it—the U.S. arsenal becomes, in effect, irrelevant.

Their complaint about a low-yield nuke is exactly that, in the words of Congress in 1994, it would "blur the distinction between nuclear and conventional war." Or, as a Federation of American Scientists report puts it, "adding low-yield warheads to the world's nuclear inventory simply makes their eventual use more likely." Actually, that's not quite true: It makes their use seem more plausible, which in turn makes their use less likely.

Without a low-yield penetrator, rogue-state leaders are able to have, in effect, a safe haven for themselves and their weapons of mass destruction. If they knew they didn't have any such protection, it might deter them from threatening or attacking the U.S. in the first place. This is how deterrence works. But deterrence also fails, in which case a low-yield penetrator might be necessary to preempt an imminent attack or to retaliate against one—and keep more from coming—by, say, hitting all of [a rogue government's] . . . command bunkers.

The Bush administration is at least making moves toward updating the arsenal. The Minuteman missile is having its 1970s-era guidance system overhauled, so some attention is being paid to applying the benefits of new precision technology to existing nukes. The administration has also undertaken a study of the need for a new earth-penetrating low-yield nuke. Developing one would mean running into the teeth of congressional and international opposition, and it is, of course, extremely unlikely that such a weapon would ever be used. Conventional options would almost always be preferable.

The key word, however, is "almost." Nuclear weapons have always been available as a bad option that might be necessary only if every other option is worse. The world, unfortunately, didn't stop offering us bad options back in 1989. We should stop pretending otherwise.

"These [low-yield tactical nuclear weapons] have not only political but military liabilities."

The United States Should Not Modernize Its Nuclear Arsenal

Michael A. Levi

Michael A. Levi is director of the Strategic Security Project at the Federation of American Scientists in Washington, D.C. In the following viewpoint he argues that the United States should not build new types of nuclear weapons. The rationale for such weapons is that they are necessary to destroy deeply buried targets—underground bunkers where rogue nations or terrorists may conceal weapons of mass destruction. But Levi maintains that situations where the United States would need to destroy such bunkers are rare. Furthermore, he maintains that using conventional weapons to disable such targets would be more effective in many cases, and would certainly cause less collateral damage. In addition, Levi warns that building new nuclear weapons would undercut America's responsibility to discourage nuclear proliferation.

As you read, consider the following questions:

1. In Levi's opinion, what do most arguments for bunker-busting nuclear weapons ignore?
2. What is the highest-yield weapon in the U.S. nuclear arsenal, according to the author?
3. How might military planners disable, rather than destroy, deeply buried bunkers, in Levi's view?

Michael A. Levi, "The Case Against New Nuclear Weapons," *Issues in Science and Technology*, vol. 19, Spring 2003, pp. 63–68. Copyright © 2003 by the University of Texas at Dallas, Richardson, TX. Reproduced by permission.

Does the United States need nuclear bombs to destroy enemy bunkers and chemical or biological weapons? For some people, the answer is clear. Strong proponents of nuclear weapons speak of the need to give the president every possible military option, and the Bush administration's 2002 Nuclear Posture Review reflects this affirmative response. On the other side, committed opponents maintain that no potential military capability could justify designing—let alone building or using—new nuclear bombs. For both camps, the details of the proposed weapons are irrelevant.

Yet neither of the simple arguments for or against new nuclear weapons is broadly accepted. The United States does not develop every possible weapon simply to provide the president with all options; policymakers have, for example, judged the military value of chemical weapons insufficient to outweigh the political benefits of forgoing them. On the other hand, the nation has never rejected nuclear use outright and has always reserved the possibility of using tactical nuclear weapons. Indeed, until the end of the Cold War, such weapons were central to U.S. military thinking.

Despite their disagreements, the people engaged in debate over new nuclear weapons have tacitly agreed on one thing: that these weapons would deliver substantial military benefits. Thus, they have cast the dilemma over new nuclear weapons as one of military necessity versus diplomatic restraint. But this is a false tension: New nuclear weapons would, in fact, produce few important military advances. Yet their development would severely undercut U.S. authority in its fight against proliferation.

Advocates of new tactical nuclear weapons have tended to focus shortsightedly on simple destructive power. In particular, most arguments for bunker-busting nuclear weapons ignore the difficulty of locating threatening bunkers in the first place. During the Gulf War of 1991, military planners painstakingly assessed the potential consequences of bombing Iraqi chemical weapons facilities, debating nuclear and nonnuclear weapons, as well as the option of leaving the bunkers alone. Ultimately, the military used conventional weapons to bomb every known facility. Subsequently, however, international weapons inspectors, aided by Iraqi defectors, discovered that those targets had been the mere tip of a vast Iraqi system for producing and storing weapons of mass destruction. Had the military used nuclear weapons to bomb all known chemical facilities during the Gulf War, the United States would have made barely a dent in Iraq's deadly capability while incurring massive political backlash as people died from the accompanying nuclear fallout.

The challenge of finding hidden targets is the norm, not an exception. In Afghanistan [in 2001], U.S. efforts to eliminate the [ruling] Taliban and Al Qaeda [terrorists] were hindered by the difficulty of tracking down their underground hideouts. Intelligence technology, which relied heavily on detecting mechanical equipment, power lines, and communications systems to identify hidden facilities, floundered in the face of a backward enemy who employed none of the technologies being searched for. [Terrorist] Osama bin Laden is still alive not because the United States lacked powerful weaponry, but because U.S. intelligence could not find him in the caves of Tora Bora.

Still, an inability to locate all enemy weapons stockpiles and underground leadership targets is not an argument for leaving alone those that can be found. But proponents of nuclear weapons have overstated the capability of the nuclear option even in cases where targets can be located, while underestimating nonnuclear potential. In particular, proponents have contended that nuclear weapons are needed to compensate for difficulties in precisely locating underground targets; that they are needed to neutralize chemical and biological agents and thus prevent their deadly use; and that only with nuclear weapons will there be no "safe havens" (no depth below which enemies are safe). However, each of these arguments can be debunked, as illustrated in the following examples.

Inadequate Intelligence

Libya has been suspected of producing chemical weapons at its Tarhunah complex, located 60 kilometers southeast of the capital city of Tripoli and hidden in tunnels and bunkers under roughly 20 meters of earth. The problem is that U.S. analysts have not been able to produce an exact blueprint of the underground chambers. This lack of precision leads some observers to argue that although the facility is, in theory, shallow enough to be destroyed with conventional arms, uncertainty concerning its location may require the large destructive radius of a nuclear weapon to compensate.

America's Nuclear Hypocrisy

It is ironic and hypocritical that the Bush administration has condemned both North Korea and Iran for their apparent efforts to develop nuclear weapons. The Bush administration itself is undermining the international nuclear nonproliferation regime.

The heart of the regime is the Nuclear Non-Proliferation Treaty (NPT). One of its main provisions is the promise by the nuclear weapon states, including the United States, to move toward nuclear disarmament. In return for that promise, the non-nuclear weapon states have pledged not to acquire nuclear weapons. . . .

Nevertheless, the Bush administration's 2002 Nuclear Posture Review calls for rebuilding key parts of the U.S. nuclear weapons production complex to permit the modification, upgrading, or replacement of portions of the existing nuclear force. It further proposes the development of new, low-yield, and presumably more usable nuclear weapons, such as a new nuclear earth-penetrating weapon. The alleged purpose of this weapon is to give the United States the capability to destroy hardened and/or deeply buried targets, such as the cave complex used by Al Qaeda [terrorists] in Afghanistan. . . .

Clearly, if the Bush administration were serious about halting the proliferation of nuclear weapons, it would accept the same standards of behavior that it is attempting to impose on non-nuclear weapon states.

Ronald E. Powaski, "Bush's Nuclear Hypocrisy," *Bulletin of the Atomic Scientists*, January/February 2004.

A nuclear weapon detonated at or near the surface produces a large crater and sends a massive shock wave into the ground. Underground facilities within this crater are destroyed, as are facilities slightly outside the zone by strong stresses that rupture the earth. Based on the intelligence community's knowledge (even given its uncertainty) about the Tarhunah facility, it is apparent that a five-kiloton ground-penetrating nuclear weapon could destroy it. This attack would produce a moderate amount of nuclear fallout, the precise nature of which would depend on whether the weapon was detonated inside the facility or in the surrounding earth. To be conservative, military planners would have to assume the latter. Such a blast would kill every human being within approximately 15 square kilometers, according to calculations by Robert Nelson of Princeton University. Although this zone would not reach Tripoli, concerns about fallout would require medical monitoring for civilians as far as 20 kilometers downwind from the facility. U.S. troops in the zone would have to halt operations or risk being exposed to fallout. Troops could not enter the immediate facility area to inspect damage or collect intelligence, even with protective gear, which is ineffective against nuclear fallout.

Alternatively, there are a number of nonnuclear approaches that are already available or could be developed for destroying or neutralizing this type of complex. If the main bunker could be more precisely located, then a single earth-penetrating conventional bomb could reach it. A missile the length of the current GBU-28 penetrator, modified to strike the surface at twice the GBU-28's current impact speed, could smash through the cover of earth and reinforced concrete and destroy the facility with conventional explosives. This suggests that the military should focus on improving intelligence capabilities, particularly the ability to precisely map underground targets that have already been located, rather than on devising ever more powerful weapons.

Even if the facility cannot be precisely localized, several conventional penetrator missiles used simultaneously could mimic the effect of a small nuclear weapon. One scenario would be to mount multiple sorties to cover the entire suspected facility area. In a more sophisticated approach, the military is now developing a "small-diameter bomb" that packs several penetrating missiles into the payload of a single aircraft—essentially, an underground version of the ubiquitous cluster bomb. Extending the small-diameter-bomb concept to missiles the length of the GBU-28 would enable simultaneous delivery of as many as 24 penetrating missiles, at least several of which would be expected to penetrate the facility.

Still other options are available. If the facility were operating, then conventional electromagnetic pulse weapons—

recently added to the U.S. arsenal—might be applied to destroy or disable equipment inside. Because an electromagnetic pulse can easily travel down a bunker's power and ventilation ducts, equipment inside would be vulnerable to attack. Such weapons could be delivered by cruise missile.

In an indirect approach to rendering the facility useless, cruise missiles could be used to temporarily block its entrances. It also would be possible to establish a "no-personnel zone" or "no-vehicle zone" around the facility. A range of intelligence assets, such as spy satellites, would be trained on the area surrounding the complex, and any attempt to move material into or out of the facility would be stopped. Although the facility itself might continue to produce weapons, those weapons could not be removed and used on the battlefield. These approaches would be limited by the need to continually devote assets to a single facility or to mount repeated attacks; if there were many simultaneous targets of concern, the method might not prove feasible.

In each case of applying conventional weapons, collateral damage due to chemical dispersal would be minimal outside the facility. Inside, chemical agents would be dispersed, but U.S. troops inspecting the area could mitigate the dangers from these by wearing protective gear.

Agent Defeat

Proponents of nuclear weapons for attacking stockpiles of chemical and biological agents, called "agent defeat weapons," typically argue that the biological or chemical fallout produced by a conventional explosive attack can be more deadly than the fallout produced by a nuclear weapon. This argument misses two crucial points: In many cases, nonnuclear agent defeat payloads can avoid spreading chemical and biological fallout; and the fallout from a nuclear attack, though perhaps smaller than the potential biological or chemical fallout, is still prohibitive.

Consider a hypothetical example from Iraq, which is suspected of retaining stockpiles of weaponized anthrax and is known to use hardened bunkers extensively.[1] A typical bunker

1. Since this viewpoint was written in spring 2003, U.S. inspectors in Iraq have determined that it did not possess biological weapons.

might be 20 meters in height and cover an area measuring 400 square meters, have walls that are five meters thick and a roof of reinforced concrete, and be buried under five meters of earth. Built during the absence of United Nations weapons inspections, the bunker's existence has become known to U.S. intelligence through satellite imagery captured during its construction. It is believed to contain several tons of anthrax in storage barrels, though in the absence of a continuing ground presence, this cannot be confirmed.

A 20-ton penetrating nuclear weapon (if it were developed) detonated at the floor of the facility would incinerate its contents, preventing the dispersal of anthrax. But it would also spread nuclear fallout. Deaths from acute radiation poisoning would be expected as far as one kilometer downwind. People nearer than four kilometers downwind would, if not evacuated quickly, receive a radiation dose greater than that received by a nuclear worker during an entire year.

Nonnuclear payloads might, however, spread less collateral damage while avoiding political problems. A penetrating bomb carrying a fragmenting warhead and incendiary materials could be used. The warhead would break the anthrax out of any exposed containers, and the heat from the incendiary materials would neutralize the anthrax. Containers that were heavily shielded might not break open, but although the anthrax would not be destroyed, neither would it be released. The bunker would remain intact.

Alternatively, a penetrating bomb carrying submunitions and neutralizing chemicals could be used. The submunitions would spread throughout the bunker and release the anthrax from its containers, even if it were stored behind barriers, and the neutralizing chemicals would render the anthrax inert. The bunker would probably remain intact, although it could be breached if it had been poorly constructed.

U.S. planners may not want to directly attack the bunker. Instead, a watch could be placed on the facility using satellite imagery coupled with armed unmanned aerial vehicles. Anyone or anything attempting to enter or leave the bunker would be destroyed, making the anthrax inside unusable.

Among proponents of new nuclear weapons, the most consistent error is the assumption that they would be silver bullets, leaving no underground facilities invulnerable to their effects. But such is not the case. Even the two-megaton B-83 bomb, the highest-yield weapon in the U.S. arsenal, would leave unscathed any facilities buried under more than 200 meters of hard rock. In contrast, functional defeat approaches—sealing off entrances rather than directly destroying the bunker—have no depth limitations.

To better understand this, consider North Korea's Kumchangri underground complex, which was once suspected of housing illicit nuclear weapons activities. The depth of the facility, built into the side of a mountain, is not publicly known, but its main chamber may quite possibly be deeper than 200 meters, putting it out of the range of even megaton-sized, earth-penetrating nuclear weapons. Even if the facility were only 150 meters underground, a one-megaton penetrating nuclear weapon would be required to destroy it, and the resulting nuclear fallout would have enormous consequences. If the wind were blowing southwest, then the North Korean capital of Pyongyang, 80 miles away, would have to be evacuated within hours of detonation to prevent the death of more than 50 percent of its residents from radiation poisoning. If the wind were blowing north or northwest, then residents of several large cities in China would have to be evacuated immediately. And if the wind were blowing south, then residents of several large cities in South Korea, as well as U.S. troops stationed in the DMZ, would have to be evacuated within hours to avoid numerous radiation deaths.

Alternatively, regardless of the facility's depth, military planners could seek to disable rather than destroy the facility. Cruise missiles could be used to collapse entrances to the bunker. Entrances, however, might be reopened quickly, requiring repeated sorties to keep the facility closed. Thennobaric weapons, which debuted in Afghanistan, could be used to send high-pressure shock waves down the tunnels, possibly destroying equipment inside the facility.

An "information umbrella" approach also might be applied. The United States, possibly together with allies, would declare that no North Korean vehicles would be allowed to come near the facility. This curfew would be monitored using surveillance assets, and any vehicle attempting to enter or leave the facility would be destroyed. . . .

Broader Discussion Needed

Though many people now maintain that the military has little interest in tactical nuclear weapons, policymakers continue to contemplate developing and deploying them. This will, unfortunately, remain the natural state unless political decisionmakers force a change. Although designers of nuclear weapons have a built-in imperative to seek nuclear solutions to military problems, there is little to be gained by the uniformed military from pushing back. It falls to Congress to actively solicit the advice of military thinkers on the utility or lack thereof of new tactical nuclear weapons.

[As of spring 2003], only the Senate Committee on Foreign Relations has devoted substantial hearing time to tactical nuclear weapons. But these weapons have not only political but military liabilities. To explore these issues, the House and Senate Armed Services Committee should convene hearings. . . . The committee should solicit input from retired military officers and from individuals who have spent time understanding both the nuclear and nonnuclear options. Only by making direct comparisons will policymakers be able to find agreement on a way forward.

"Deterrence is the practice of preventing aggression by threatening unacceptable consequences."

The United States Should Use Its Nuclear Arsenal to Deter Nations from Developing Weapons of Mass Destruction

Loren B. Thompson

In the following viewpoint Loren B. Thompson defends the U.S. strategy of using the threat of nuclear attack to deter terrorists and rogue nations from threatening the United States. Nuclear deterrence was at the core of America's and the Soviet Union's defense strategies throughout the Cold War, as each nation used the threat of nuclear annihilation to discourage the other from attacking first. Thompson believes that the terrorist attacks of September 11 demonstrated the post–Cold War need for a renewed effort to deter terrorists or rogue states from using weapons of mass destruction. Loren B. Thompson is chief operating officer of the Lexington Institute, a conservative advocacy organization, and a professor of security studies at Georgetown University.

As you read, consider the following questions:

1. By how much does President George W. Bush want to reduce the size of the U.S. nuclear arsenal, according to Thompson?
2. What is the core of America's deterrent posture, as described by Thompson?

Loren B. Thompson, "How to Stop Worrying and Love the Bomb," www.opinionjournal.com, March 17, 2002. Copyright © 2002 by Dow Jones & Company, Inc. All right reserved. Reproduced by permission.

Someone tuned in to the breathless media coverage of the Bush administration's nuclear report [in March 2002] could be excused for assuming that [nuke lovers] had taken control of the Pentagon. According to the scribes at the *New York Times*, America is behaving as a "nuclear rogue." "If Pentagon proposals become American policy, . . . countries could conclude they have no motive to stay non-nuclear," an editorial complained.

From the sounds of it, President [George W.] Bush is pushing dangerous policies that would move the world closer to nuclear war. The countries named in the Nuclear Posture Review quickly got their backs up. China said it was shocked, "deeply shocked" at its inclusion on the target sheet and wants a "clear explanation." Axis of Evil[1] member Iran explained that the report itself was equivalent to terrorism.

The Continuing Importance of Deterrence

Let's stop and take a deep breath. Are we actually going to nuke countries ranging from Russia to Libya to North Korea? No. What the government says it will do with nuclear weapons, and what it actually intends to do, are seldom the same thing. The public posture on nuclear use is called "declaratory" strategy. The secret war plans are "operational" strategy.

That's a difference worth bearing in mind. According to recent reports, the Bush administration wants to reduce the size of the nation's nuclear arsenal by about two-thirds while expanding the range of options for selectively applying such weapons. Some journalists have read the changes as evidence that Mr. Bush's advisers are lowering the barriers to employing weapons of mass destruction. In reality, the opposite is true.

The new stance is an effort to maximize the incentives other countries have to avoid using such weapons—not just nuclear weapons, but also chemical or biological weapons suitable for committing mass murder. The envisioned changes are an overdue response to shifts in the global secu-

---

1. President George W. Bush has named Iran, Iraq, and North Korea as the Axis of Evil.

rity environment that make devastating attacks on the American homeland more likely.

But because the core of U.S. nuclear strategy is an elusive psychological concept called deterrence, the proposed changes are easily misunderstood. That's nothing new: Every effort to adjust nuclear strategy to changing circumstances has elicited the same fearful responses from the media, whether it was Dwight Eisenhower's policy of massive retaliation, John Kennedy's assured destruction, Richard Nixon's flexible selective targeting, or Ronald Reagan's defensive initiatives.

A decade after the Cold War ended, it may seem disappointing to have to revisit the logic of strategic deterrence—many people hoped that the specter of nuclear holocaust would gradually slip into history. But the [September 11, 2001, terrorist attacks] demonstrated such aspirations are premature, and forced the administration to bolster the nation's deterrent posture.

Deterrence is the practice of preventing aggression by threatening unacceptable consequences. It has been used to channel conflict throughout history. Many historians believe that the reason Hitler did not use poison gas in World War II was his fear of retaliation in kind (he had been temporarily blinded by a gas attack in World War I).

After the advent of atomic weapons, the theoretical underpinnings of deterrence were elaborately systematized by scholars like Albert Wohlstetter and Henry Kissinger. The basic dilemma posed by such weapons was that their destructiveness made effective defense very difficult. If even a handful of bombs managed to get by defenders, they would cause vast carnage. A surprise attack could be so devastating that the target might lose the ability to retaliate.

Nuclear deterrence was conceived to stabilize this precarious balance. In essence, it sought to guarantee that no nuclear aggressor could escape destruction, thereby minimizing the incentive to attack. The concept had major limitations, especially when dealing with irrational or accident-prone adversaries, but once the Soviets achieved nuclear parity it was widely seen as the only viable option for assuring national survival.

The main problem with deterrence is that it is a psychological construct. It won't work unless the enemy believes you have the capability and will to make good on the threat of retaliation. During the late Cold War period, a great deal of thought went into designing nuclear forces that not only could retaliate, but could do so credibly. That meant not threatening nuclear Armageddon in response to limited provocations, because such behavior was unbelievable and hence a poor deterrent.

New Methods of Deterrence

Today's threats are far more diverse and less predictable than those of the past. States hostile to the United States and to our friends and allies have demonstrated their willingness to take high risks to achieve their goals, and are aggressively pursuing WMD [weapons of mass destruction] and their means of delivery as critical tools in this effort. As a consequence, we require new methods of deterrence. A strong declaratory policy and effective military forces are essential elements of our contemporary deterrent posture, along with the full range of political tools to persuade potential adversaries not to seek or use WMD. The United States will continue to make clear that it reserves the right to respond with overwhelming force—including through resort to all of our options—to the use of WMD against the United States, our forces abroad, and friends and allies.

In addition to our conventional and nuclear response and defense capabilities, our overall deterrent posture against WMD threats is reinforced by effective intelligence, surveillance, interdiction, and domestic law enforcement capabilities. Such combined capabilities enhance deterrence both by devaluing an adversary's WMD and missiles, and by posing the prospect of an overwhelming response to any use of such weapons.

George W. Bush, *The National Strategy to Combat Weapons of Mass Destruction*, December 2002.

Like the Soviets, President Reagan believed that the most potent deterrent was a credible capacity to fight and win nuclear wars. All of his strategic initiatives—better offensive forces, effective nuclear defenses, government continuity—were designed to support that goal. Much of the academic and policy community came to share Mr. Reagan's view, not because it wanted to wage such a conflict, but because it wanted to prevent one.

This all seemed like ancient history before September 11. U.S. nuclear strategy during the Cold War years was focused almost exclusively on the Soviets, so once communism collapsed nuclear forces were seen to be much less important. Although the Bush administration began reviewing the nation's nuclear posture within weeks after taking office, the main thrust of its efforts was to slash the size of the strategic arsenal by finding other means of deterring adversaries.

Part of a Broader Strategy

September 11 didn't so much change this impulse as temper it, by reinforcing the administration's awareness that not all mechanisms of mass destruction were nuclear, and not all potential aggressors were Russians. Mr. Bush's advisers still want to cut the nuclear arsenal, but they want to use what weapons remain to strengthen deterrence in a new world of more diverse threats.

One way the congressionally mandated Nuclear Posture Review would do that is by signaling potential perpetrators of mass murder—such as Iraq and North Korea—that evil behavior may elicit the ultimate punishment. Another way is to develop new weapons that can credibly address emerging threats such as deeply buried command bunkers or biolabs.

The core of the nation's deterrent posture will continue to be sea-based and land-based ballistic missiles, backed up by highly capable conventional and special forces. The modest refinements Mr. Bush proposes would simply seek to dissuade new classes of aggressors from attacking America and its allies. If deterrence fails, the U.S. would then seek to defeat those enemies at the lowest feasible level of violence.

Mr. Bush and his advisers have few illusions about their ability to bargain with the kind of people who make up [the al Qaeda terrorist network]. But even the most deluded aggressor usually has some fear that can be manipulated to restrain his actions. The proposed retooling of U.S. nuclear strategy would more precisely target such fears and make the prospect of warfare using weapons of mass destruction as remote as possible.

"The language in the new U.S. strategic posture portrays an image of an American military with a newly itchy nuclear trigger finger."

The United States Should Not Threaten Other Nations with Its Nuclear Arsenal

Theresa Hitchens

Theresa Hitchens is vice president of the Center for Defense Information, a nonpartisan think tank in Washington, D.C. In the following viewpoint she maintains that the U.S. strategy for dealing with national security threats has become too reliant on nuclear weapons. Hitchens writes that under President George W. Bush, the United States has declared that it will develop new types of nuclear weapons but will preemptively attack other nations that develop weapons of mass destruction. Hitchens warns that America's interest in developing new nuclear weapons, and its implied willingness to use them, may spur other nations to develop nuclear weapons of their own, thus making America less safe.

As you read, consider the following questions:
1. What nonnuclear states could potentially be targets of a U.S. nuclear attack, according to the author?
2. In Hitchens's opinion, what questions should the United States be asking in regards to its new nuclear strategy?

Theresa Hitchens, "Everyone Will Want One: Instead of Being Deterred by the New U.S. Policy, Enemies May Respond by Acquiring Their Own Nuclear Weapons," *Bulletin of the Atomic Scientists*, vol. 59, January/February 2003, p. 22. Copyright © 2002 by the Educational Foundation for Nuclear Science, Chicago, IL 60637. Reproduced by permission of the *Bulletin of the Atomic Scientists*: The Magazine of Global Security News & Analysis.

Is the United States now willing to launch a preemptive—or even a preventive—nuclear war? There has been little real public discussion, but the Bush administration's most recent strategy documents could be interpreted as lowering the traditional U.S. barriers to the use of nuclear weapons. Considering how potentially dangerous the international reaction to such a radical policy shift could be, it behooves U.S. policymakers and Congress to take a critical look at the wisdom of treading down this path.

A Dangerously Aggressive Stance

The administration released its classified Nuclear Posture Review (NPR) to Congress on December 31, 2001, and issued a new, more general, National Security Strategy on September 17, 2002. How radical is this policy shift? Neither document can be said to call explicitly for preemptive or preventive nuclear strikes. And, at the same time, the United States has never made a pledge not to use nuclear weapons first. But when the NPR is read as an implementation strategy for the goals embodied in the National Security Strategy, the specter of a United States ever more ready to use nuclear weapons first against an adversary or even a suspected attacker—state or non-state, nuclear armed or not—emerges quite clearly.

As the strategy bluntly states, "Our enemies . . . are seeking weapons of mass destruction . . . [and] America will act against such emerging threats before they are fully formed." The document further asserts that classic deterrence is unlikely to work against terrorists or rogue states and warns that the United States "cannot let our enemies strike first."

The National Security Strategy seeks to justify this new strategic posture by citing the recognized right under international law for a nation to defend itself by taking preemptive action against an "imminent attack." However, the strategy's language clearly stretches the traditional definition of "imminent"—seemingly to include preventing a nation or non-state actor from obtaining even the capability to attack the United States, particularly with weapons of mass destruction.

For example, the strategy states: "The greater the threat, the greater is the risk of inaction—and the more compelling the case for taking anticipatory action to defend ourselves, even if uncertainty remains as to the time and place of the enemy's attack. . . . The United States cannot remain idle while dangers gather."

And how will the United States achieve its goals? The answer includes, according to the strategy, transformation of the U.S. military to "provide a wider range of military options." This language echoes that of the NPR, which states that U.S. strategic forces must provide the president with "a range of options to defeat any aggressor," and calls for a more "flexible" set of nuclear weapons that "vary in scale, scope, and purpose" to counter emerging threats such as terrorists, rogue states, and the use of weapons of mass destruction.

Wolverton. © 2003 by Monte Wolverton. Reproduced by permission of Cagle Cartoons, Inc.

Perhaps one of the most interesting aspects of the NPR is the concept of a "New Triad," mixing nuclear and non-nuclear offensive options with missile defense. In the past, nuclear strike capabilities have been considered largely separate from non-nuclear capabilities, doctrine, and strategy. On the one hand, this could be a positive development—as the growing capabilities of conventional weaponry could decrease the perceived need for nuclear weapons for a number of future missions. On the other hand, there is the danger that the NPR's language will blur the distinction between the use of conventional and nuclear weapons—perhaps lowering the nuclear first-strike threshold.

Increased Risk of Nuclear War

Most clearly, however, the potential for preemptive or preventive nuclear war may be seen in the NPR's discussion of using nuclear weapons to "defeat" hardened and deeply buried targets. The NPR details the need to consider new "nuclear weapons options," including "possible modifications to existing weapons to provide additional yield flexibility in the stockpile; improved earth-penetrating weapons (EPWs) to counter the increased use by potential adversaries of hard and deeply buried facilities; and warheads that reduce collateral damage."

Finally, the NPR names North Korea, Iraq, Iran, Syria, and Libya as countries that could be involved in potential "contingencies" requiring nuclear weapons. This list is important in that it highlights the fact that non-nuclear countries are now considered potential nuclear targets—a policy directly counter to U.S. promises to eschew nuclear use against non-nuclear states, promises that crucially underpin the Nuclear Non-Proliferation Treaty.

Whether by intent or not, the language in the new U.S. strategic posture portrays an image of an American military with a newly itchy nuclear trigger finger, or at least a bent for coercive nuclear diplomacy. At issue, then, is how other nations will respond. Is it reasonable to expect that, with the world's most preeminent military power asserting its renewed placement of value on nuclear weapons, others will continue on a path of nuclear restraint? Will U.S. enemies be deterred by the threat of a preemptive/preventive nuclear strike, or will they instead be spurred to take their own "use 'em or lose 'em" posture?

Unfortunately, these important questions have yet to be taken up in earnest in Washington. But one cannot help but believe they are being answered—likely with negative results for U.S. national and international security—elsewhere in the world.

Periodical Bibliography

The following articles have been selected to supplement the diverse views presented in this chapter.

Drake Bennett — "Critical Mess: How the Neocons Are Promoting Nuclear Proliferation," *American Prospect*, July/August 2003.

Sidney Drell et al. — "A Strategic Choice: New Bunker Busters Versus Nonproliferation," *Arms Control Today*, March 2003.

Daniel Goure — "Nuclear Deterrence, Then and Now," *Policy Review*, December 2003.

Jonathan Granoff — "Power over the Ultimate Evil," *Tikkun*, November/December 2003.

Binoy Kampmark — "America's Nuclear Deterrence in the Age of Terrorism," *Contemporary Review*, April 2003.

Raffi Khatchadourian — "Saying No to Nuclear Arms," *Nation*, June 24, 2002.

David Krieger and Devon Chaffee — "Facing the Failures of the Nuclear Nonproliferation Treaty Regime," *Humanist*, September/October 2003.

John Parachini — "Non-Proliferation Policy and the War on Terrorism," *Arms Control Today*, October 2001.

Keith B. Payne — "The Nuclear Jitters: Fear Not Research, and Wise Deterrence," *National Review*, June 30, 2003.

George Perkovich — "Bush's Nuclear Revolution—a Regime Change in Nonproliferation," *Foreign Affairs*, March/April 2003.

Ronald E. Powaski — "Bush's Nuclear Hypocrisy," *Bulletin of the Atomic Scientists*, January/February 2004.

Nancy Small — "Is Nuclear Deterrence Still Moral?" *America*, September 29, 2003.

Henry Sokolski — "Taking Proliferation Seriously," *Policy Review*, October/November 2003.

CHAPTER 4

How Can the United States Defend Itself Against Weapons of Mass Destruction?

Chapter Preface

Among the various bioweapon threats, smallpox has received the most attention from both the media and from homeland security officials. Smallpox is extremely contagious, and like the common cold can be transmitted from person to person through the air or through contaminated clothing or surfaces. Antibiotics are not very effective in treating smallpox, and the disease is lethal in about 30 percent of cases. The development of a vaccine for smallpox stands as one of modern science's greatest achievements. In 1979 the World Health Organization officially declared that smallpox had been eradicated, but strains of the virus are stored in high-security research facilities in the United States and Russia, and homeland security officials are concerned that other samples of the smallpox virus could still exist elsewhere in the world.

The United States has over 200 million doses of smallpox vaccination, enough for every American. However, the smallpox vaccine has significant risk of side effects: Historically, between 14 and 52 of every 1 million people who receive the vaccine have experienced life-threatening reactions, and 1 to 2 out of every 1 million have died. That is why the United States stopped vaccinating children against smallpox in the early 1980s, and why the U.S. government's efforts to vaccinate five hundred thousand health care workers have met with heavy resistance. Fortunately, vaccination even *after* exposure to the smallpox virus is usually effective in stopping the disease.

The danger associated with smallpox vaccinations is just one example of how difficult it is for a nation to prepare for bioterrorism. The viewpoints in the following chapter explore some of the ways in which the United States is working to prevent and prepare for both nuclear and biological attacks.

> *"We and our elected representatives must take whatever steps are necessary to protect our nation from all forms of attack, which include ballistic missiles."*

The United States Should Build a Missile Defense System

Brian T. Kennedy

Brian T. Kennedy is president of the Claremont Institute, a conservative think tank in Claremont, California. In the following viewpoint, which he wrote in January 2002, Kennedy says that the terrorist attacks of September 11, 2001, raised public awareness about how vulnerable the United States is to attackers. While the attacks of September 11 were tragic, argues Kennedy, a nuclear missile attack would have been much, much worse. Therefore, he believes that the United States should build the means to defend against nuclear missile attack as soon as possible.

As you read, consider the following questions:

1. What is the government's primary constitutional duty, in Kennedy's view?
2. What two countries does Kennedy accuse of supplying nuclear technologies to rogue nations?
3. Why are space-based missile defense systems especially promising, according to the author?

Brian T. Kennedy, "Protecting Our Nation: The Urgent Need for Ballistic Missile Defense," www.claremont.org, January 1, 2002. Copyright © 2002 by The Claremont Institute. Reproduced by permission.

It will seem to many Americans that the national security concerns of the United States changed radically on September 11 [2001, when terrorists flew airplanes into the World Trade Center and the Pentagon]. But everything I have to say was true before that horrible day, and every bit of analysis since then confirms it.

On September 11, our nation's enemies attacked us using hijacked airliners. Next time, the vehicles of death and destruction might well be ballistic missiles armed with nuclear, chemical, or biological warheads. And let us be clear: The United States is defenseless against this mortal danger. We would today have to suffer helplessly a ballistic missile attack, just as we suffered helplessly on September 11. But the dead would number in the millions and a constitutional crisis would likely ensue, because the survivors would wonder—with good reason—if their government were capable of carrying out its primary constitutional duty: to "provide for the common defense.". . .

The Threat Is Real

The attack of September 11 should not be seen as a fanatical act of individuals like Osama Bin Laden, but as a deliberate act of a consortium of nations who hope to remove the U.S. from its strategic positions in the Middle East, in Asia and the Pacific, and in Europe. It is the belief of such nations that the U.S. can be made to abandon its allies, such as Israel and Taiwan, if the cost of standing by them becomes too high. It is not altogether unreasonable for our enemies to act on such a belief. The failure of U.S. political leadership, over a period of two decades, to respond proportionately to terrorist attacks on Americans in Lebanon, to the first World Trade Center bombing, to the attack on the Khobar Towers in Saudi Arabia, to the bombings of U.S. embassies abroad, and most recently to the attack on the USS *Cole* in Yemen, likely emboldened them. They may also have been encouraged by observing four government's unwillingness to defend Americans against ballistic missiles.

For all of the intelligence failures leading up to September 11, we know with absolute certainty that various nations are spending billions of dollars to build or acquire strategic ballistic missiles. Their purpose is to inflict from afar massive casualties on the United States, or to use the threat of doing so to blackmail us, for the purpose of forcing us to withdraw from our alliances around the world and retreat to the North American continent. Yet even now, under a president who supports it, missile defense advances at a glacial pace.

Asay. © 1998 by Creators Syndicate, Inc. Reproduced by permission.

You don't often hear these arguments in academic circles, and rarely even in political circles. They require talking about unpleasant subjects such as war and conflict and possible death, and I think it is the way of democratic peoples to look away from such subjects until they are forced to face them, as we Americans were forced to begin facing them on September 11. We were reminded on that day that the nature of international relations requires us to be prepared for war. And while at one time war was conducted with sword and spears, later arrows, later cannon and bullets, and later bombs, today it is waged with advanced weaponry that includes strategic ballistic nuclear missiles.

Who are these enemy nations, in whose interest it is to press the U.S. into retreating from the world stage? Despite the kind words of Russian President Vladimir Putin, encouraging a "tough response" to the terrorist attack of September 11, we know that it is the Russian and Chinese governments that are supplying our enemies in Iraq, Iran, Libya, and North Korea with the ballistic missile technology to terrorize our nation. Is it possible that Russia and China don't understand the consequences of transferring this technology? Are Vladimir Putin and [Chinese president] Jiang Zemin unaware that countries like Iran and Iraq are known sponsors of terrorism? In light of the absurdity of these questions, it is reasonable to assume that Russia and China transfer this technology as a matter of high government policy, using these rogue states as proxies to destabilize the West because they have an interest in expanding their power, and because they know that only the U.S. can stand in their way.

Recall that in February of 1996, during a confrontation between mainland China and our democratic ally on Taiwan, Lt. Gen. Xiong Guang Kai, a senior Chinese official, made an implicit nuclear threat against the U.S., warning our government not to interfere because Americans "care more about Los Angeles than they do Taipei." With a minimum of 20 Chinese intercontinental ballistic missiles (ICBMs) currently aimed at the U.S., such threats must be taken seriously. . . .

How to Stop Ballistic Missiles

For all the bad news about the ballistic missile threat to the U.S., there is the good news that missile defense is well within our technological capabilities. As far back as 1962 a test missile fired from Vandenberg Air Force Base was intercepted (within 500 yards) by an anti-ballistic missile launched from the Kwajalein Atoll. The idea at the time was to use a small nuclear warhead in the upper atmosphere to destroy incoming enemy warheads. But it was deemed politically incorrect—as it is still today—to use a nuclear explosion to destroy a nuclear warhead, even if that warhead is racing toward an American city. (Again, only we seem to be squeamish in this regard: Russia's aforementioned 9,000 interceptors bear nuclear warheads.) So U.S. research since President [Ronald] Reagan reintroduced the idea of missile defense in 1983 has been aimed primarily at developing the means to destroy enemy missiles through direct impact or "hit-to-kill" methods. American missile defense research has included ground-based, sea-based and space-based interceptors, and air-based and space-based lasers. Each of these systems has undergone successful, if limited, testing. The space-based systems are especially effective since they seek to destroy enemy missiles in their first minutes of flight, known also as the boost phase. During this phase, missiles are easily detectable, have yet to deploy any so-called decoys or countermeasures, and are especially vulnerable to space-based interceptors and lasers.

The best near-term option for ballistic missile defense, recommended by former Reagan administration defense strategist Frank Gaffney, is to place a new generation of interceptor, currently in research, aboard U.S. Navy Aegis Cruisers. These ships could then provide at least some missile defense while more effective systems are built. Also under consideration is a ground-based system in the strategically important state of Alaska, at Fort Greeley and Kodiak Island. This would represent another key component in a comprehensive "layered" missile defense that will include land, sea, air and space.

Arguments Against Missile Defense

Opponents of missile defense present four basic arguments. The first is that ABM [anti-ballistic missile] systems are technologically unrealistic, since "hitting bullets with bullets" leaves no room for error. They point to recent tests of ground-based interceptors that have had mixed results. Two things are important to note about these tests: First, many of the problems stem from the fact that the tests are being conducted under ABM Treaty restrictions on the speed of interceptors, and on their interface with satellites and radar.[1] Second, some recent test failures involve science and technology that the U.S. perfected 30 years ago, such as rocket separation. But putting all this aside, as President Reagan's former science advisor William Graham points out, the difficulty of "hitting bullets with bullets" could be simply overcome by placing small nuclear charges on "hit-to-kill" vehicles as a

1. The United States formally withdrew from the ABM treaty in June 2001, in part because of its restrictions on missile defense testing.

"fail safe" for when they miss their targets. This would result in small nuclear explosions in space, but that is surely more acceptable than the alternative of enemy warheads detonating over American cities.

The second argument against missile defense is that no enemy would dare launch a missile attack at the U.S., for fear of swift retaliation. But as the CIA pointed out two years ago—and as Secretary of Defense [Donald] Rumsfeld reiterated recently in Russia—an enemy could launch a ballistic missile from a ship off our coasts, scuttle the ship, and leave us wondering, as on September 11, who was responsible.

The third argument is that missile defense can't work against ship-launched missiles. But over a decade ago, U.S. nuclear laboratories, with the help of scientists like Greg Canavan and Lowell Wood, conducted successful tests on space-based interceptors that could stop ballistic missiles in their boost phase from whatever location they were launched.

Finally, missile defense opponents argue that building a defense will ignite an expensive arms race. But the production cost of a space-based interceptor is roughly one to two million dollars. A constellation of 5,000 such interceptors might then cost ten billion dollars, a fraction of America's defense budget. By contrast, a single Russian SS-18 costs approximately $100 million, a North Korean Taepo Dong II missile close to $10 million, and an Iraqi Scud B missile about $2 million. In other words, if we get into an arms race, our enemies will go broke. The Soviet Union found it could not compete with us in such a race in the 1980s. Nor will the Russians or the Chinese or their proxies be able to compete today. . . .

An American Focus

In conclusion, had the September 11 attack been visited by ballistic missiles, resulting in the deaths of three to six million Americans, a massive scientific effort would have immediately been launched to ensure that such an attack would not happen again. Just as firemen have been working around the clock at "Ground Zero" in New York City, teams of scientists nationwide would have been working around the clock to build and deploy a ballistic missile defense. America, thankfully, has a window of opportunity however narrow—to do so now, before it is too late.

Faced with a similar crisis in the 1930s, [British prime minister] Winston Churchill traveled the length and breadth of England to convince his countrymen that Britain should build massively its defenses in response to the growing Nazi threat. He and his colleagues called this effort "The Focus." Today we must begin an American Focus. We and our elected representatives must take whatever steps are necessary to protect our nation from all forms of attack, which include ballistic missiles no less than hi-jackings or terrorist bombings. This is the least we owe those fellow citizens who lost their lives in New York and Washington. Even more, is what we owe the Free World and our Constitution.

Let us begin in earnest.

> "We may be less safe if the President's
> [missile defense] program is implemented
> than if it is not."

The United States Should Not Build a Missile Defense System

George Rathjens and Carl Kaysen

In the following viewpoint George Rathjens and Carl Kaysen argue that America's plan to build a missile defense system is unrealistic and may harm national security rather than enhance it. The authors maintain that the technical difficulties involved in shooting down ballistic missiles are such that no missile defense system will ever be totally reliable. Rathjens and Kaysen warn that with a missile defense system in place, U.S. leaders might be tempted to take more aggressive stances against emerging nuclear powers such as North Korea; unfortunately, they contend, a catastrophe could result since the missile defense system will be unlikely to stop all enemy missiles. George Rathjens is a former director of the Advanced Research Project Agency of the Department of Defense. Carl Kaysen has served as a deputy special assistant to President John F. Kennedy for national security affairs.

As you read, consider the following questions:

1. What is North Korea's likely rationale for seeking nuclear weapons, in the authors' opinion?
2. According to Rathjens and Kaysen, what two questions must be considered in regard to an imperfect missile defense system?

George Rathjens and Carl Kaysen, "Missile Defense: The Dangers and Lack of Realism," www.clw.org, February 2004. Copyright © 2004 by the Council for a Livable World. Reproduced by permission.

[In December 2002] President [George W.] Bush announced that he was ordering the deployment of an anti-ballistic-missile (ABM) system, with the first sites to be operational in 2004 in Alaska and California. In 1967 President [Lyndon B.] Johnson made a strikingly similar decision. Both smacked of election-year domestic politics. President Johnson had reason to fear that Republican opponents would make a political issue in the 1968 election of a failure by him to begin deployment of ABM defenses. President Bush's core constituency of hawkish right wingers will be reassured by his decision.

Reality Check

Yet, notwithstanding very active systems development efforts in both administrations, there was not then, and there is not now even the remotest prospect that a near-term defense of population against a determined attack by a major power—then, the Soviet Union; now, Russia or China—would be effective. So, deployment is being rationalized now by the Bush Administration, as it was by Johnson's, as useful against emerging nuclear powers: then, China; now, North Korea—and possibly Iran.

The most fundamental problem is that the proposed system relies on a "hit-to-kill" interceptor to destroy incoming warheads above the atmosphere. We doubt that the problem of discriminating between warheads and decoys in the mid-part of their trajectories can be effectively solved in the near future, if ever. If it can not be, each American metropolitan area would have to be defended from a separate installation. But North Korea, or any other nation with a few nuclear-armed ICBMs [intercontinental ballistic missiles], would need hold hostage only a few American cities, perhaps only one, to have an effective deterrent.

Secretary of Defense [Donald] Rumsfeld has defended the President's deployment decision, arguing that, having "a limited capability to deal with a relatively small number of incoming ballistic missiles . . . is better than nothing", and that Americans should feel "marginally safer" with such deployment than without it.

Given the overwhelming retaliatory capability of the United

States, we question the premise underlying the Secretary's statements that North Korea (or perhaps another aspirant nuclear weapons state) would deliver a nuclear first strike against it once it had a capability to do so. It is more reasonable to assume that North Korea's rationale for acquiring a nuclear ICBM capability has been similar to that of the United States—to be able to deter another nation with strong military capabilities (in North Korea's case, the United States; in that of the United States, the Soviet Union) from involvement in regions of conflict in ways inimical to its interests.

A Lucrative Project for Defense Contractors

Top Ten Defense Companies Receiving the Largest Dollar Amounts of Pentagon Missile Defense Contracts, 1998–2001

Company	Total $
Boeing Co.	$3,503,913,000
Lockheed Martin Corp	$1,739,200,000
TRW, Inc.	$711,824,000
Raytheon	$601,938,000
Computer Sciences Corp	$410,520,000
Mevatec Corp	$218,524,000
Teledyne Technologies	$190,471,000
Science Applications Intl Corp	$168,403,000
Colsa Corp	$167,180,000
Sparta, Inc.	$134,805,000
Total	**$7,846,778,000**

Michelle Ciarrocca and William D. Hartung, "Axis of Influence: Behind the Bush Administration's Missile Defense Revival," World Policy Institute, July 2002.

Moreover, there is the possibility that at a future date, when an ABM system might actually have some capability, it could, in a crisis, be oversold to a president who might then make catastrophic decisions based on an assumed level of performance that would not be realized. This is reason enough for us to conclude that, contrary to Secretary Rumsfeld's observations, we may be less safe if the President's program is implemented than if it is not. While we appreciate that such an error may seem a remote possibility to many, we call attention to the fact that President Bush, senior, believed that during the 1991 Gulf War, Patriot interceptor missiles had been 96% effective in destroying Iraqi Scud missiles. After later assessment, it was apparent that few, if any, successful interceptions occurred; Secretary of Defense Cohen said, "The Patriots didn't work".

An ABM system, even a very imperfect one, might have some value as a hedge against accidental attacks. Even so, two questions must arise. First, whether the resources required might be more wisely used on homeland security and to meet other objectives, both military and civil. Second, whether, with the deployment, the leaders and the public of the United States would feel more secure about its involvement in crises in northeast Asia, where American interests clash with those of North Korea, than if the United States were not to proceed with the deployment proposed.

An affirmative answer to this last question depends on whether any deployed defense might be essentially 100% effective. This, however, will certainly not be the case with President Bush's announced deployment, nor do we believe it likely with any system that might evolve from it.

Like it or not, nuclear deterrence is likely to be with us during the first part of this century, as it was during much of the last. But, the United States may more often be the deterred rather than the deterrer should it seek to involve itself militarily in regions where there may be others with nuclear capabilities and interests opposed to it. We think it important that Americans recognize that the United States may not hold all the high cards and that it will have to face the reality that the costs of getting its way on all points of difference with adversaries may be higher than its citizenry are willing to pay. Beyond deterrence, its choices in dealing with North Korea as an emerging nuclear power will be by negotiation or preemptively destroying North Korea's offending capabilities, with all the risks of massive civilian casualties and political costs that that would entail.

It is illusory to see an ABM defense system as an escape from this dilemma.

"Nuclear terrorism is a largely preventable disaster."

The United States Should Secure the Materials Used to Make Nuclear Weapons

Graham Allison and Andrei Kokoshin

In the following viewpoint Graham Allison and Andrei Kokoshin argue that the United States and Russia must undertake a new, coordinated effort to track down and safeguard nuclear weapons and the materials used to build them. Dozens of nuclear weapons may have been lost in accidents during the Cold War, warn the authors, and many thousands more are vulnerable to theft from sites in Russia and emerging nuclear powers. In addition, the fissile materials necessary to power nuclear explosions are stored at hundreds of sites in dozens of countries. Allison and Kokoshin argue that measures need to be taken by the United States and Russia to ensure that these weapons and weapons-usable materials do not fall into terrorist hands. Graham Allison is director of the Belfer Center for Science and International Affairs at Harvard University's John F. Kennedy School of Government. Andrei Kokoshin is director of the Institute for International Security Studies of the Russian Academy of Sciences.

As you read, consider the following questions:
1. In what eight states are nuclear weapons known to exist, according to the authors?
2. By the authors' estimate, about what percent of containers entering the United States undergo X-ray?

Graham Allison and Andrei Kokoshin, "The New Containment: An Alliance Against Nuclear Terrorism," *The National Interest*, Fall 2002. Copyright © 2002 by *The National Interest*, Washington, DC. Reproduced by permission.

During the Cold War, American and Russian policymakers and citizens thought long and hard about the possibility of nuclear attacks on their respective homelands. But with the fall of the Berlin Wall and the disappearance of the Soviet Union, the threat of nuclear weapons catastrophe faded away from most minds. This is both ironic and potentially tragic, since the threat of a nuclear attack on the United States or Russia is certainly greater today than it was in 1989.

In the aftermath of Osama bin Laden's September 11 [2001 terrorist attacks against America] which awakened the world to the reality of global terrorism, it is incumbent upon serious national security analysts to think again about the unthinkable. Could a nuclear terrorist attack happen today? Our considered answer is: yes, unquestionably, without any doubt. It is not only a possibility, but in fact the most urgent unaddressed national security threat to both the United States and Russia. . . .

The argument made here can be summarized in two propositions: first, nuclear terrorism poses a clear and present danger to the United States, Russia and other nations; second, nuclear terrorism is a largely preventable disaster. Preventing nuclear terrorism is a large, complex, but ultimately finite challenge that can be met by a bold, determined, but nonetheless finite response. The current mismatch between the seriousness of the threat on the one hand, and the actions governments are now taking to meet it on the other, is unacceptable. Below we assess the threat and outline a solution that begins with a U.S.-Russian led Alliance Against Nuclear Terrorism. . . .

Means

To the best of our knowledge, no terrorist group can now detonate a nuclear weapon. But as Secretary of Defense Donald Rumsfeld has stated, "the absence of evidence is not evidence of absence." Are the means beyond terrorists' reach, even that of relatively sophisticated groups like Al-Qaeda?

Over four decades of Cold War competition, the superpowers spent trillions of dollars assembling mass arsenals, stockpiles, nuclear complexes and enterprises that engaged hundreds of thousands of accomplished scientists and engineers. Technical know-how cannot be un-invented. Reducing arsenals that include some 40,000 nuclear weapons and the equivalents of more than 100,000 nuclear weapons in the form of highly enriched uranium (HEU) and plutonium to manageable levels is a gargantuan challenge.

Terrorists could seek to buy an assembled nuclear weapon from insiders or criminals. Nuclear weapons are known to exist in eight states: the United States, Russia, Great Britain, France, China, Israel, India and Pakistan. Security measures, such as "permissive action links" designed to prevent unauthorized use, are most reliable in the United States, Russia, France and the United Kingdom. These safeguards, as well as command-and-control systems, are much less reliable in the two newest nuclear states—India and Pakistan. But even where good systems are in place, maintaining high levels of security requires constant attention from high-level government officials.

Alternatively, terrorists could try to build a weapon. The only component that is especially difficult to obtain is the nuclear fissile material—HEU or plutonium. Although the largest stockpiles of weapons-grade material are predominantly found in the nuclear weapons programs of the United States and Russia, fissile material in sufficient quantities to make a crude nuclear weapon can also be found in many civilian settings around the globe. Some 345 research reactors in 58 states together contain twenty metric tons of HEU, many in quantities sufficient to build a bomb. Other civilian reactors produce enough weapons-grade nuclear material to pose a proliferation threat; several European states, Japan, Russia and India reprocess spent fuel to separate out plutonium for use as new fuel. The United States has actually facilitated the spread of fissile material in the past—over three decades of the Atoms for Peace program, the United States exported 749 kg of plutonium and 26.6 [in] metric tons of HEU to 39 countries.

Terrorist groups could obtain these materials by theft, illicit purchase or voluntary transfer from state control. There is ample evidence that attempts to steal or sell nuclear weapons or weapons-usable material are not hypothetical, but a recurring fact. [In fall 2001], the chief of the directorate of the Russian Defense Ministry responsible for nuclear weapons reported two recent incidents in which terrorist groups attempted to perform reconnaissance at Russian nuclear storage sites. The past decade has seen repeated incidents in which individuals and groups have successfully stolen weapons material from sites in Russia and sought to export them—but were caught trying to do so. In one highly publicized case, a group of insiders at a Russian nuclear weapons facility in Chelyabinsk plotted to steal 18.5 kg (40.7 lbs.) of HEU, which would have been enough to construct a bomb, but were thwarted by Russian Federal Security Service agents.

In the mid-1990s, material sufficient to allow terrorists to build more than twenty nuclear weapons—more than 1,000 pounds of highly enriched uranium—sat unprotected in Kazakhstan. Iranian and possibly Al-Qaeda operatives with nuclear ambitions were widely reported to be in Kazakhstan. Recognizing the danger, the American government itself purchased the material and removed it to Oak Ridge, Tennessee. In February 2002, the U.S. National Intelligence Council reported to Congress that "undetected smuggling [of weapons-usable nuclear materials from Russia] has occurred, although we do not know the extent of such thefts." Each assertion invariably provokes blanket denials from Russian officials. Russian Atomic Energy Minister Aleksandr Rumyantsev has claimed categorically: "Fissile materials have not disappeared." President [Vladimir] Putin has stated that he is "absolutely confident" that terrorists in Afghanistan do not have weapons of mass destruction of Soviet or Russian origin.

Lost Nukes and Rogue States

For perspective on claims of the inviolable security of nuclear weapons or material, it is worth considering the issue of "lost nukes." Is it possible that the United States or Soviet Union lost assembled nuclear weapons? At least on the American side the evidence is clear. In 1981, the U.S. Department of Defense published a list of 32 accidents involving nuclear weapons, many of which resulted in lost bombs. One involved a submarine that sank along with two nuclear torpedoes. In other cases, nuclear bombs were lost from aircraft. Though on the Soviet/Russian side there is no official information, we do know that four Soviet submarines carrying nuclear weapons have sunk since 1968, resulting in an estimated 43 lost nuclear warheads. These accidents suggest the complexity of controlling and accounting for vast nuclear arsenals and stockpiles.

Nuclear materials have also been stolen from stockpiles housed at research reactors. In 1999, Italian police seized a bar of enriched uranium from an organized crime group trying to sell it to an agent posing as a Middle Eastern businessman with presumed ties to terrorists. On investigation, the Italians found that the uranium originated from a U.S.-supplied research reactor in the former Zaire, where it presumably had been stolen or purchased sub rosa.

Finally, as President [George W.] Bush has stressed, terrorists could obtain nuclear weapons or material from states hostile to the United States. In his now-infamous phrase, Bush called hostile regimes developing WMD [weapons of mass destruction] and their terrorist allies an "axis of evil." He argued that states such as Iraq, Iran and North Korea, if allowed to realize their nuclear ambitions, "could provide these arms to terrorists, giving them the means to match their hatred." The fear that a hostile regime might transfer a nuclear weapon to terrorists has contributed to the Bush Administration's development of a new doctrine of preemption against such regimes, with Iraq as the likeliest test case. It also adds to American concerns about Russian transfer of nuclear technologies to Iran. While Washington and Moscow continue to disagree over whether any safeguarded civilian nuclear cooperation with Iran is justified, both agree on the dangers a nuclear-armed Iran would pose. Russia is more than willing to agree that there should be no transfers of technology that could help Iran make nuclear weapons.

Opportunity

Security analysts have long focused on ballistic missiles as the preferred means by which nuclear weapons would be delivered. But today this is actually the least likely vehicle by which a nuclear weapon will be delivered against Russia or the United States. Ballistic weapons are hard to produce, costly and difficult to hide. A nuclear weapon delivered by a missile also leaves an unambiguous return address, inviting devastating retaliation. As Robert Walpole, a National Intelligence Officer, told a Senate subcommittee in March [2002], "Non-missile delivery means are less costly, easier to acquire, and more reliable and accurate." Despite this assessment, the U.S. government continues to invest much more heavily in developing and deploying missile defenses than in addressing more likely trajectories by which weapons could arrive.

Terrorists would not find it very difficult to sneak a nuclear device or nuclear fissile material into the United States via shipping containers, trucks, ships or aircraft. Recall that the nuclear material required is smaller than a football. Even an assembled device, like a suitcase nuclear weapon, could be shipped in a container, in the hull of a ship or in a trunk carried by an aircraft. After . . . September 11, the number of containers that are x-rayed has increased, to about 500 of the 5,000 containers currently arriving daily at the port of New York/New Jersey—approximately 10 percent. But as the chief executive of CSX Lines, one of the foremost container-shipping companies, put it: "If you can smuggle heroin in containers, you may be able to smuggle in a nuclear bomb.". . .

A New Alliance

The good news about nuclear terrorism can be summarized in one line: no highly enriched uranium or plutonium, no nuclear explosion, no nuclear terrorism. Though the world's stockpiles of nuclear weapons and weapons-usable materials are vast, they are finite. The prerequisites for manufacturing fissile material are many and require the resources of a modern state. Technologies for locking up super-dangerous or valuable items—from gold in Fort Knox to treasures in the Kremlin Armory—are well developed and tested. While challenging, a specific program of actions to keep nuclear materials out of the hands of the most dangerous groups is not beyond reach, if leaders give this objective highest priority and hold subordinates accountable for achieving this result.

The starting points for such a program are already in place. In his major foreign policy campaign address at the Ronald Reagan Library, then–presidential candidate George

W. Bush called for "Congress to increase substantially our assistance to dismantle as many Russian weapons as possible, as quickly as possible." In his September 2000 address to the United Nations Millennium Summit, Russian President Putin proposed to "find ways to block the spread of nuclear weapons by excluding use of enriched uranium and plutonium in global atomic energy production." The Joint Declaration on the New Strategic Relationship between the United States and Russia, signed by the two presidents at the May 2002 summit, stated that the two partners would combat the "closely linked threats of international terrorism and the proliferation of weapons of mass destruction." Another important result yielded by the summit was the upgrading of the Armitage/Trubnikov-led U.S.-Russia Working Group on Afghanistan to the U.S.-Russia Working Group on Counterterrorism, whose agenda is to thwart nuclear, biological and chemical terrorism.

Operationally, however, priority is measured not by words, but by deeds. A decade of Nunn-Lugar Cooperative Threat Reduction Programs [under which thousands of Russian nuclear weapons have been destroyed] has accomplished much in safeguarding nuclear materials. Unfortunately, the job of upgrading security to minimum basic standards is mostly unfinished: according to Department of Energy reports, two-thirds of the nuclear material in Russia remains to be adequately secured. Bureaucratic inertia, bolstered by mistrust and misperception on both sides, leaves these joint programs bogged down on timetables that extend to 2008. Unless implementation improves significantly, they will probably fail to meet even this unacceptably distant target. What is required on both sides is personal, presidential priority measured in commensurate energy, specific orders, funding and accountability. This should be embodied in a new U.S.-Russian led Alliance Against Nuclear Terrorism.

Five Pillars of Wisdom

When it comes to the threat of nuclear terrorism, many Americans judge Russia to be part of the problem, not the solution. But if Russia is welcomed and supported as a fully responsible non-proliferation partner, the United States

Dismantling the Former Soviet Nuclear Arsenal

The United States has spent about $7 billion over the past decade through a variety of . . . threat reduction programs. European countries, Canada, and Japan also contributed to these efforts, although in smaller amounts. As a result, Ukraine, Kazakhstan, and Belarus have been denuclearized. Over 800 strategic launchers, 97 heavy bombers, 24 ballistic missile submarines, and 815 ballistic missiles and related silos were destroyed pursuant to U.S.-Russian arms reduction agreements. The EU [European Union] as an institution spent more than €700 million on nuclear reactor safety in the former Soviet Union and billions of euros to help stabilize the successor states socially, politically, and economically. The world's largest anthrax production facility, located in Kazakhstan, was dismantled. The first prototype CW [chemical weapons] destruction facility in Russia is ready to start operating. Projects funded by the International Science and Technology Centers have engaged more than 50,000 WMD [weapons of mass destruction] scientists, helping to prevent the spread of their expertise into dangerous hands.

But enormous challenges remain. "Rapid" security upgrades have been completed at facilities containing only 46 percent of the approximately 603 metric tons of weapons-usable nuclear materials in Russia targeted by the U.S. Department of Energy's MPC&A [Material Protection, Control and Accounting] program, and "comprehensive" upgrades are only now getting under way. Less than one-seventh of Russia's total highly enriched uranium stockpile has been rendered unusable for nuclear weapons and virtually none of its plutonium. The same is true for the United States. None of Russia's nerve agent CW has yet been destroyed, a task that will also stretch out over the coming decade. Its former military biological weapons program continues to remain closed to outsiders, and physical protection against theft or seizure of biological pathogens is inadequate at a number of locations. Finally, thousands of weapons scientists and workers are still unemployed or underemployed. If current Russian downsizing plans are implemented, many will be laid off in the next few years, but it is unclear where they will find new jobs.

Robert J. Einhorn and Michèle A. Flournoy, project directors, *Protecting Against the Spread of Nuclear, Biological, and Chemical Weapons: An Action Agenda for the Global Partnership*. Washington, DC: Center for Strategic and International Studies, 2003.

stands to accomplish far more toward minimizing the risk of nuclear terrorism than if it treats Russia as an unreconstructed pariah. As the first step in establishing this alliance, the two presidents should pledge to each other that his government will do everything technically possible to prevent criminals or terrorists from stealing nuclear weapons or weapons-usable material, and to do so on the fastest possible timetable. Each should make clear that he will personally hold accountable the entire chain of command within his own government to assure this result. Understanding that each country bears responsibility for the security of its own nuclear materials, the United States should nonetheless offer Russia any assistance required to make this happen. Each nation—and each leader—should provide the other sufficient transparency to monitor performance.

To ensure that this is done on an expedited schedule, both governments should name specific individuals, directly answerable to their respective presidents, to co-chair a group tasked with developing a joint Russian-American strategy within one month. In developing a joint strategy and program of action, the nuclear superpowers would establish a new world-class "international security standard" based on President Putin's Millennium proposal for new technologies that allow production of electricity with low-enriched, non-weapons-usable nuclear fuel.

A second pillar of this alliance would reach out to all other nuclear weapons states—beginning with Pakistan. Each should be invited to join the alliance and offered assistance, if necessary, in assuring that all weapons and weapons-usable material are secured to the new established international standard in a manner sufficiently transparent to reassure all others. Invitations should be diplomatic in tone but nonetheless clear that this is an offer that cannot be refused. China should become an early ally in this effort, one that could help Pakistan understand the advantages of willing compliance.

A third pillar of this alliance calls for global outreach along the lines proposed by Senator Richard Lugar in what has been called the Lugar Doctrine. All states that possess weapons-usable nuclear materials—even those without nuclear weapons capabilities—must enlist in an international effort to guarantee the security of such materials from theft by terrorists or criminal groups. In effect, each would be required to meet the new international security standard and to do so in a transparent fashion. Pakistan is particularly important given its location and relationship with Al-Qaeda [terrorists], but beyond nuclear weapons states, several dozen additional countries hosting research reactors—such as Serbia, Libya and Ghana—should be persuaded to surrender such material (almost all of it either American or Soviet in origin), or have the material secured to acceptable international standards.

A fourth pillar of this effort should include Russian-American led cooperation in preventing any further spread of nuclear weapons to additional states, focusing sharply on North Korea, Iraq and Iran. The historical record demonstrates that when the United States and Russia have cooperated intensely, nuclear wannabes have been largely stymied. It was only during periods of competition or distraction, for example in the mid-1990s, that new nuclear weapons states realized their ambitions. India and Pakistan provide two vivid case studies. Recent Russian-American-Chinese cooperation in nudging India and Pakistan back from the nuclear brink suggests a good course of action. The failure and subsequent freeze of North Korean nuclear programs offers complementary lessons about the consequences of competition and distraction. The new alliance should reinvent a robust non-proliferation regime of controls on the sale and export of weapons of mass destruction, nuclear material and missile technologies, recognizing the threat to each of the major states that would be posed by a nuclear-armed Iran, North Korea or Iraq.

Finally, adapting lessons learned in U.S.-Russian cooperation in the campaign against bin Laden and the Taliban [in Afghanistan, which was aiding him], this new alliance should be heavy on intelligence sharing and affirmative counter-proliferation, including disruption and pre-emption to prevent acquisition of materials and know-how by nuclear wannabes. Beyond joint intelligence sharing, joint training for pre-emptive actions against terrorists, criminal groups or rogue states attempting to acquire weapons of mass destruction would provide a fitting enforcement mechanism for alliance commitments.

As former Senator Sam Nunn has noted: "At the dawn of a new century, we find ourselves in a new arms race. Terrorists are racing to get weapons of mass destruction; we ought to be racing to stop them." Preventing nuclear terrorism will require no less imagination, energy and persistence than did avoiding nuclear war between the superpowers over four decades of Cold War. But absent deep, sustained cooperation between the United States, Russia and other nuclear states, such an effort is doomed to failure. In the context of the qualitatively new relationship Presidents Putin and Bush have established in the aftermath of September 11, success in such a bold effort is within the reach of determined Russian-American leadership. Succeed we must.

"Biosecurity measures can raise barriers thwarting would-be bioterrorists from easily obtaining dangerous pathogens."

The United States Should Aid Global Efforts to Reduce the Bioterrorism Threat

Michael Barletta

Michael Barletta is a senior research associate in the Proliferation Research and Assessment Program at the Center for Nonproliferation Studies in Monterey, California. In the following viewpoint he discusses the concept of biosecurity, which he defines as measures to prevent terrorists from gaining access to pathogens and toxins, as well as the equipment and trained personnel necessary to produce bioweapons. Barletta explains that, ironically, biodefense research programs—designed to develop vaccines and drugs to deal with bioweapons—often present major biosecurity risks, since these programs involve all the materials and technologies needed to make bioweapons. Barletta calls on the United States to increase security at U.S. biodefense facilities and also to become more involved in developing standardized biosecurity measures that can be implemented on a global scale.

As you read, consider the following questions:

1. What is the FBI profile of the perpetrator of the 2001 anthrax attacks, as described by Barletta?
2. What international biosecurity body was formed in response to Iraq's chemical and biological weapons programs, according to Barletta?

Michael Barletta, "Biosecurity Measures for Preventing Bioterrorism," http://cns.miis.edu, November 27, 2002. Copyright © 2002 by the Center for Nonproliferation Studies, Monterey Institute of International Studies. Reproduced by permission.

One year ago [in 2001], anthrax mail attacks in the United States illustrated the ominous potential of bioterrorism, as faceless assailant(s) abused modern science to disseminate lethal pathogens to disrupt everyday life, cripple basic government functions, and spread fear. Bioterrorism—the deliberate use of microorganisms or toxins by non-state actors to sicken or kill people or to destroy or poison the food supplies upon which we depend—poses an uncertain but potentially devastating threat to the health and well-being of people around the world. Unless countered effectively, this threat may increase with the rapid pace of developments in science and biotechnology. While policymakers and medical service providers must prepare to treat victims of future bioterrorist attacks, in this as in most aspects of human health, prevention is far better than response after the fact. This essay . . . provides an introduction to biosecurity measures, a key element among policy efforts to address the threat of bioterrorism.

Biosecurity in the Context of Bioterrorism

The term "biosecurity" is used in quite distinct ways by different policy and scientific communities. For example, professionals in agricultural science and industry, and specialists in ecological research and policymaking, have very different concepts in mind when using this word. In the context of biological weapons threats in general and bioterrorism in particular, biosecurity can be defined in narrow terms: *biosecurity is the effective implementation of measures that aim to prevent would-be terrorists, criminals, and spies from gaining access to dangerous pathogens and toxins.* Related measures limit access to equipment, technologies, and information that could be used for malicious purposes involving biological weapons. . . .

Biosecurity is sometimes also used to refer to the much broader range of measures to prevent and respond to possible biological attacks, (e.g., biodefense; public health; law enforcement, etc.), but a focused definition refers to a subset of policies to deny unauthorized access to germs and toxins for illicit purposes. Experts at Sandia National Laboratories conceptualize biosecurity as falling into six categories of measures: physical protection, personnel reliability, scientific and programmatic oversight, pathogen accountability, transportation security, and information security.

Among the diseases that could be used as biological weapons, anthrax, botulism, plague, smallpox, tularemia, and viral hemorrhagic fevers are among those judged by specialists at the U.S. Centers for Disease Control and Prevention (CDC) to be of greatest concern. While most national and international authorities concur in identifying about three dozen pathogens and toxins as "select agents"—i.e., those presenting the gravest security threats given their potential for contagion or weaponized dissemination and probability of causing serious illness or death—there are differences among the select agent lists employed around the world, and disagreement over the significance of listed agents. All lists, wherever employed, must be updated regularly to respond to new information and developments. For example, since 1973, thirty new disease agents have been identified, including some for which no cure exists, notably HIV, Ebola virus, hepatitis C virus, and Nipah virus.

There is growing recognition in the United States and around the world of the need for effective biosecurity measures to mitigate biological warfare (BW) threats, and especially to reduce the threat of bioterrorism. Government officials, industry representatives, and nongovernmental analysts emphasize the need for focused and effective steps to prevent terrorists from misusing science, medicine, and biotechnology. Most recognize the need for centralized action at the national level to promote biosecurity; many stress the importance of developing and implementing consistent international biosecurity standards and measures.

Without standardized measures applied worldwide, terrorists could exploit unprotected or least-protected facilities to gain access to toxins and pathogens, and then use the material for bioweapon attacks in far-distant locations. Consider the mass-murder attacks of 11 September 2001, which demonstrated the ruthless transnational reach of al-Qa'ida terrorists. Given the group's ambition to acquire mass-destruction weapons, and its track record of killing fellow Muslims in conducting terrorist strikes, its operatives may be willing to unleash deadly epidemics against the population of the United

States or other countries that it considers to be enemies. If al-Qa'ida operatives were to gain access to a lethal contagious pathogen from a location anywhere in the world, they might employ suicidal or unwitting individuals as carriers to launch disease attacks from one country to another—despite the likelihood that an epidemic would spread via intercontinental air travel to eventually decimate Islamic peoples among other noncombatants. Given this prospect, al-Qa'ida's reported interest in obtaining the smallpox pathogen should be a matter of grave international concern. . . .

Although many countries are working to develop or upgrade and implement biosecurity measures and related legislation, these efforts vary in breadth and effectiveness, and significant gaps remain in even the best-secured states. Furthermore, some biodefense initiatives—the principal responses that have been launched by leading states—may unintentionally increase prospects for bioterrorism.

Biodefense Risks

Biodefense research, such as efforts to develop vaccines and drugs, is a necessary element among national efforts to prepare for bioterrorism and BW. Unfortunately, however, without better provisions for biosecurity the ongoing expansion of civilian and military biodefense programs will increase some bioterrorism risks. Because more people in more facilities will be trained to work on projects involving lethal pathogens and toxins, there will be greater risk that insiders within these facilities may abuse their access to dangerous biomaterials and sensitive information for criminal or terrorist purposes.

For example, the terrorist(s) who last year mailed letters containing anthrax spores in the United States used a virulent *Bacillus anthracis* strain held since 1981 by a military biodefense facility at Fort Detrick, Maryland. It is possible that this deadly strain may have been acquired directly from the facility, or from one of several other labs supplied with this bacterium to conduct biodefense research. The FBI behavioral profile of the unknown perpetrator is of a lone individual with a scientific background, laboratory access, and experience working with hazardous materials like anthrax bacteria. The technical sophistication apparently required to prepare the anthrax spores used in the attacks suggests that the assailant(s) might have been supported by a foreign biowarfare program, or alternatively, that the culprit(s) may have stolen material from a U.S. or foreign biodefense program that uses the agent for research. Revelations about the lack of oversight on dangerous projects, and unreliable internal security at a leading research facility, have raised questions as to the security of BW-relevant agents within U.S. biodefense programs. But whatever the origin of the anthrax material, and whether or not the anthrax mail attacks were inflicted by a lone insider-turned-terrorist, the ensuing investigation and disclosures have highlighted the inadequacy of existing measures to control access to deadly organisms.

Thwarting Acquisition

In the past, terrorists and criminals have acquired biological weapons agents in several ways, including collecting pathogenic microorganisms and toxins directly from natural sources; purchasing disease strains from culture collections; and infiltrating medical and bioresearch facilities or paying criminal accomplices to do so on their behalf. Non-state actors could also acquire deadly bacteria, viruses, and toxins from state BW programs as well as biodefense facilities. Eventually, terrorists might develop the capability to synthesize some pathogens in the test tube by means of genetic engineering techniques.

Thus, controlling access to pathogen cultures and toxins cannot entirely prevent the malevolent use of biology and medicine. But biosecurity measures can raise barriers thwarting would-be bioterrorists from easily obtaining dangerous pathogens and toxins. For example, physical security measures blocked a recent attempt to steal pathogens from a biodefense laboratory in Kazakhstan. Complicating and delaying acquisition of lethal agents would increase prospects that terrorists with ambitions to use biological weapons will be stopped by domestic law enforcement, foreign intelligence, or military action before they can launch bioterrorist attacks. Moreover, denying terrorists access to known lethal strains of pathogens may limit or even entirely negate their

Requirement for Biological Weapons

Skilled people
—E.g., microbiologists, biochemists, engineers, aerosol and containment specialists, lab technicians, etc.
—Behavior can be controlled through background checks, security guards, identity, badges, locks, video cameras, fences around facilities, etc.

Dangerous pathogens or toxins
—E.g., such "select agents" as those causing anthrax, botulism, plague, smallpox, tularemia, Ebola, etc.
—Access can be limited through physical control and accounting procedures on possession, use, sale, and transfer of select agents.

Dual-use technologies
—Tools, machines, and information for isolating, testing, producing, storing, and disseminating BW agents.
—Most are widely employed in industry and science, hence difficult to regulate; some import/export controls limit international transfers.

Biosecurity measures work to prevent skilled *people* from acquiring dangerous *pathogens or toxins* and employing dual-use *technologies* to make biological weapons.

Bioterrorists need all three prerequisites to cause harm; biosecurity measures succeed if they block any *one* of these.

Biological Weapons

Michael Barletta, Center for Nonproliferation Studies, November 2002.

efforts to cause harm. For example, the Japanese cult Aum Shinrikyo was unable to sicken anyone in its repeated attempts to use anthrax bacteria for bioterrorism, in part because the group's scientists had acquired and mass-produced a non-lethal strain of the organism. Fortunately, the group also failed in its effort to acquire samples of the Ebola virus for use in its bioweapons program.

In fact, simply delaying terrorist attacks could be invaluable; implementing effective biosecurity measures now could gain time for biodefense programs to develop better means to detect and diagnose biological weapons attacks, and to prevent and treat illnesses caused by bioweapons. Improved detection and treatment capabilities could reduce the harm that bioterrorists can inflict. Better detection, moreover, would have forensic value and increase the likelihood that bioterrorists would be quickly identified, apprehended, and punished. By contrast, the bioterrorist(s) who unleashed anthrax in fall 2001 benefited from the incubation period of the disease, and the time required for doctors to diagnose it as anthrax, to thus far escape detection and arrest. In turn, recognition of stronger detection and treatment capabilities could lead terrorists to decide that pursuing biological weapons would be ineffectual and personally or organizationally hazardous, and hence not worth pursuing.

To stymie aspiring bioterrorists, biosecurity efforts only need to block any one of three general requirements for bioweapon production: skilled people, dangerous pathogens or toxins, and dual-use technologies [which can be used for legitimate biotechnology purposes or misused for bioterrorism]. Although primarily aimed at non-state actors, effective biosecurity measures could also thwart procurement activities by states seeking to produce biological weapons. In the 1980s, weak controls on the transfer of biological agents enabled Iraq to acquire cultures and toxins for its BW programs from France, Germany, Japan, and the United States. Inadequate internal security measures also may have allowed Iraqi agents to infiltrate British microbiology laboratories to gain access to potential BW agents and BW-relevant expertise.

Iraqi exploitation of Western commerce and scientific cooperation for its chemical and biological weapons programs led to formation and strengthening of the Australia Group (AG), an export control coordinating body now comprised by 33 member states plus the European Commission. The AG is a crucial element in international efforts to limit access by proliferant countries to pathogens and toxins, as well as to equipment and supplies required for their weaponization. In June 2002, the AG tightened its guidelines on transfers of sensitive items related to biological and chemical weapons. That same month, the Group of Eight (G8) [Germany, Canada, the United States, France, Italy, Japan, the United Kingdom, and Russia] reached agreement on nonproliferation principles that included physical protection, control, and accounting for biological agents and other materials that could be used by terrorists to conduct mass-destruction attacks. The G8's nonproliferation activities currently focus on securing facilities in the former Soviet Union. In Europe, member states of the European Union have undertaken efforts on biosecurity that include development of a prioritized list of select agents, an agent inventory, and guidelines for surveillance and reporting on agent production, transfer, and processing.

As noted above, there are regulatory and legislative initiatives currently underway to promote biosecurity within the national borders of a number of countries. In the United States, these efforts include two new laws regulating lethal toxins and pathogens, an interagency working group refining laboratory biosecurity procedures, and formation of the Department of Homeland Security with responsibilities for biosecurity. Of course, stringent regulations and powerful agencies are not in themselves sufficient; biosecurity measures must be implemented effectively in order to actually reduce the risk of illicit misuse of biological agents. Distressingly, more than five years after initiation of the Select Agent Program to regulate transfers of pathogens and toxins within the United States—and over one year after the country suffered bioterrorist attacks with anthrax bacteria that many officials believe originated in a U.S. laboratory—implementation of the program remains seriously deficient.

Moreover, although U.S. regulatory efforts are necessary steps to reduce bioterrorism risks, U.S. measures alone cannot prevent terrorists from acquiring deadly pathogens, in part due to the operation of over 1,500 culture collections worldwide that possess, exchange, and sell disease specimens for legitimate scientific, medical, and agricultural research purposes. Many of these collections are in countries that are not members of the AG, and that may have negligible or ineffectual measures for biosecurity. In the past, even criminals and terrorists who possessed technical expertise in isolating disease organisms from natural sources have relied on culture collections to acquire deadly organisms.

In recognition of the global dimensions of the threat, there are also policy proposals for action on biosecurity measures at the international level. One approach would be to establish an encompassing convention to criminalize bioterrorism and related activities worldwide, with biosecurity measures and other provisions to strengthen enforcement of the prohibition against BW. Another mechanism could be an international scientific commission and governing body to develop biosecurity standards and oversee their enforcement, and also to provide oversight of research that might be misused for biological weapons purposes. More narrowly, an international inventory of anthrax bacteria and other pathogens could be initiated by the UN Security Council, under Article V of the 1972 Biological and Toxin Weapons Convention (BWC). Another option would be negotiation of a Biosecurity Convention focused on reducing risks of bioterrorism, separate from but in partial support of the BWC. A technically grounded, multilateral negotiation process could offer a politically feasible means for generating international biosecurity standards and winning the support necessary to put them into practice worldwide. . . .

Whatever initiatives are undertaken by national and international authorities, biosecurity measures should be designed carefully so as to avoid undue constraints on legitimate scientific and medical research and productive commercial activities, and they must be vigorously implemented in order to effectively forestall bioterrorist threats to the United States and to international security.

"*A strong public health system can quickly
identify the presence of a biological attack,
contain the number of patients, help restore
calm to society, and ensure the health of
the population.*"

A Strong Public Health System Can Manage the Consequences of a Biological Attack

Rebecca Katz

Rebecca Katz is a doctoral candidate at the Woodrow Wilson School of International Affairs and the Office of Population Research at Princeton University. In the following viewpoint Katz argues that the United States should strengthen its public health system in preparation for acts of bioterrorism. Currently, she warns, the nation's hospitals, infectious disease laboratories, and vaccine distribution systems are woefully underprepared for the disease outbreaks that could follow a bioterror attack. She believes that more federal funds should immediately be put toward improving the public health system's ability to rapidly detect and respond to infectious disease outbreaks.

As you read, consider the following questions:
1. What is the public health system, as defined by the author?
2. What would be the first sign of a biological weapon attack, according to Katz?

Rebecca Katz, "Public Health Preparedness: The Best Defense Against Biological Weapons," *Washington Quarterly*, vol. 25, Summer 2002. Copyright © 2002 by The Center for Strategic and International Studies (CSIS) and the Massachusetts Institute of Technology. Reproduced by permission of The MIT Press, Cambridge, MA.

Two major exercises have tested the U.S. government's preparedness for, and capacity to respond to, a large-scale, covert biological weapons attack. TOPOFF, led by the Federal Emergency Management Agency (FEMA) and the Department of Justice in May 2000, and Dark Winter, directed by CSIS [Center for Strategic and International Studies] in May 2001, found that the United States was ill prepared to detect and respond effectively to a bioterrorist attack in a way that would prevent the attack from escalating into a major security crisis. These exercises demonstrated the devastating impact a bioterrorist attack can have when initiated against a poorly prepared government: hundreds of thousands dead or sick, widespread panic, a resultant breakdown of civil society, and the suppression of individual rights in order to control the spread of disease.

TOPOFF and Dark Winter revealed how a biological weapons attack is unlike an attack utilizing conventional weapons or even another type of weapon of mass destruction. Although the Department of Defense and typical first-responders (local fire and police departments) ably handle the defense against, management of, and deterrence of most weapons, these actors are not sufficient for detection and control of a biological attack. Maintaining homeland security against a biological attack requires a strong civil defense rooted in the capabilities of a new player in the realm of national security: the public health system.

The public health system is a federal, state, and local infrastructure responsible for monitoring health status, diagnosing and investigating health problems, linking people to health services, enforcing health laws and regulations, assuring a competent health workforce, communicating with the public, disseminating information, and conducting scientific research. This system plays a vital role in an effective defense against biological weapons. A strong public health system can quickly identify the presence of a biological attack, contain the number of patients, help restore calm to society, and ensure the health of the population. Understanding the role of public health will allow policymakers to structure a comprehensive weapons defense, allocate funds appropriately, and set up collaborative efforts. . . .

Public Health Preparedness Today

If a terrorist group or hostile nation releases a biological weapon on the U.S. public, the first sign of an attack is likely to be the seemingly innocent event of a small number of people going to their private doctors' offices or the emergency room at their local hospitals, complaining of flu-like symptoms. Patients may arrive at various hospitals throughout a geographic region, reducing the likelihood that one hospital may raise suspicions that a cluster of disease is within the community. Once such a cluster has been identified, determining if the disease results from a natural epidemic or if a biological attack has taken place will most likely be initially impossible.

To determine exactly what is wrong with the patients, blood samples will be sent to local laboratories and then possibly to state or federal laboratories, depending on the initial suspicions of the physicians treating the patients or the inability of a local lab to identify an agent. This process can continue for a day or a month, depending on the capacity of the local labs (the size, personnel, and equipment available), the awareness of disease possibilities, and the agent itself.

Once officials have detected and diagnosed the disease, they must determine the number of people affected, treat the infected populations, and make efforts to contain the spread of disease. This process may be as simple as getting antibiotics to a finite number of infected people if the biological agent is not communicable (cannot be spread from person to person) or as complicated as tracking down possible contacts of patients, initiating vaccination campaigns, and enacting quarantine procedures for infectious patients. In order for the public health system to operate effectively during a biological weapons attack on the United States, it must include a strong infectious-disease surveillance system, vaccine development and pharmaceutical stockpiles, scientific research, communications networks, laboratory capacity, hospital readiness, and professional training.

Infectious Disease Surveillance

The longer it takes to identify the presence of an outbreak, the more people will become sick or die, at a greater cost to society. According to one study, if officials identify an anthrax attack on a population of 100,000 and distribute proper doses of antibiotics to the exposed population within 24 hours, approximately 5,000 people will die and the cost to society both in health care expenditures and economic loss will be $128 million. On the other hand, if officials do not identify the attack for six days and only then give doses of antibiotic prophylaxes to the exposed population, approximately six and a half times as many people will die (33,000) at a cost almost 205 times higher ($26.3 billion).

This example demonstrates the importance of early detection of an event, be it an epidemic of a naturally occurring disease, such as the occasional outbreak of meningitis on a college campus, or a biological attack, such as the anthrax letters of last fall. To identify such an event quickly, a multifaceted surveillance system is needed. Well before an attack occurs, public health departments around the country from the local to the state level must establish and enforce reporting mechanisms of diagnoses from hospitals and private physicians, findings from laboratories, and sales of prescription drugs as well as over-the-counter medication from pharmacies. Complete, real-time reporting from all of these areas, in addition to accurate historical trends to use for comparison, would enable public health departments to identify out-of-the-ordinary occurrences, as well as piece together an initial picture of the location and timing of events in a given region. Information from this system should be monitored at the federal level in order to analyze both regional and national trends.

Accurate reporting in this surveillance system will depend on trained physicians, competent local laboratories, and functional communication systems, as well as vigilance on the part of participants in the surveillance system, to ensure that information is continuously updated, either automatically or through personnel dedicated to this task. A comprehensive surveillance system relies on passive (having disease information reported to a central location) and active (searching for information on disease occurrences) surveillance and requires personnel to monitor the situation 24 hours a day. A national infectious disease surveillance system is only as strong as its weakest link. Thus, in order for the system to be effective, every region of the country must be connected and actively participate.

Today, a hodgepodge of surveillance systems operates around the country, with the nearly 3,000 local health departments, 50 state health departments, and several large municipalities all using different variations. The Centers for Disease Control and Prevention (CDC) maintains more than 100 surveillance systems, most of which operate independently of each other. Recognizing the need to manage information from local and state surveillance better, the CDC created the National Electronic Disease Surveillance System (NEDSS), which is designed to integrate a variety of disease databases. Although NEDSS is a start, by no means has it accomplished the task of integrating all the surveillance systems operating nationwide. A comprehensive system must be available to all and capable of reporting to the local, state, and federal level. This system must also be impervious to attack, from both outside and within the public health community. The Office of Homeland Defense, with the guidance and expertise of the CDC and health informatics professionals, is an appropriate choice to coordinate an integrated nationwide surveillance system.

Vaccine Development

Vaccination against known bioterrorist agents, specifically anthrax and smallpox, are part of a preattack defense and a postattack containment. Although engaging in large-scale vaccination programs of the civilian population prior to an attack is neither practical nor safe, vaccine availability if a large-scale attack did occur is important, particularly for smallpox. Because the smallpox vaccine is dangerous to people with compromised immune systems (e.g., people with HIV/AIDS, on chemotherapy, or with autoimmune diseases), a large-scale vaccination program is only practical if a viable threat exists that outweighs the danger posed by the vaccine itself. If a smallpox outbreak did occur, however, engaging in a regional vaccination program to contain the spread of the disease would be essential.

The United States once kept a stockpile of smallpox vac-

Project Bioshield

In my State of the Union address, I asked Congress to approve a comprehensive plan for research and production of needed drugs and vaccines, a plan that we call Project BioShield. My budget requests almost $6 billion to quickly make available safer and more effective vaccines and treatments against agents like small pox, anthrax, botulinum toxin, e-bola and plague.

We already have the knowledge and ability to manufacture some of the vaccines and drugs we need. Yet, we have had little reason to do so up until now, because the natural occurrence of these diseases in our country is so rare. But the world changed on September the 11th, 2001, and we've got to respond to that change.

In light of the new threats, we must now develop and stockpile these vaccines and these treatments. Right now, America must go beyond our borders to find companies willing to make vaccines to combat biological weapons. Two main drug therapies used to treat anthrax are produced overseas. We must rebuild America's capacity to produce vaccines by committing the federal government to the purchase of medicines that combat bioterror.

Under Project Bioshield, the government will have the spending authority to purchase these vaccines in huge amounts, sufficient to meet any emergency that may come. Project BioShield will give our scientific leaders greater authority and flexibility in decisions that may affect our security. Our labs will be able to hire the experts, get more funding quickly, and build the best facilities to accelerate urgently needed discoveries.

We'll have a better and safer smallpox vaccine, antibodies to treat botox, sophisticated devices that can confirm a case of anthrax infection almost instantly. We will ensure that promising medicines are available for use in an emergency. Like other great scientific efforts, Project BioShield will have many applications beyond its immediate goals. As scientists work to defeat the weapons of bioterror, they will gain new insights into the workings of other diseases. This will also break new ground in the search for treatments and cures for other illnesses. This could bring great benefits for all of humanity, especially in developing countries where infectious diseases often go uncontrolled.

George W. Bush, remarks on the Bioshield Initiative, Bethesda, MD, February 3, 2003.

cine, but much of that vaccine has deteriorated, leaving only 15.4 million original doses. Packaging and distribution problems could further reduce the number of available doses, although a recent study suggests that the existing 15 million doses can be expanded through dilution to at least 75 million and possibly 150 million. The federal government recently approved contracts for the production of enough smallpox vaccine to serve the entire domestic population. . . . Whether any of these stockpiled vaccines will be made available to foreign nations in the event that smallpox is released overseas, however, is unclear.

More research is needed to improve the currently available vaccines, as well as to develop and manufacture vaccines for other diseases categorized by the CDC as bioterrorist threats. Tests also must continue to determine if the available vaccines protect against more potent variants of diseases, such as the drug-resistant anthrax bioengineered by the Soviet biowarfare program.

In order to avoid chaos during an event, development and dissemination prior to an attack of vaccine priority and distribution plans is essential. These plans should incorporate the best methods for controlling the spread of disease, saving the most lives, and ensuring the utility of responders. The CDC has developed vaccination plans for smallpox containment, but plans do not currently exist for vaccination for other known biological weapons, nor have the details of distribution techniques and prioritization among nonpatients been established in all regions. The public health community should work with organizations such as the National Guard as well as local law enforcement and even local business to arrange plans to distribute vaccinations to large numbers of people. Authorities could use the same plans to distribute drugs and other medical supplies.

Pharmaceutical Stockpile

The CDC has taken the lead in creating the National Pharmaceutical Stockpile Program, which maintains a national repository of drugs and medical material to be delivered to the site of a biological attack. Mandated by Congress in January 1999, this stockpile can provide quantities of drugs and medical supplies that might otherwise be difficult to obtain rapidly in the event of an emergency. Originally funded with $52 million a year, this program can presently deliver packets of drugs and medical equipment, along with a small team to assist with distribution, to any U.S. site within 12 hours.

The program has developed remarkably well with such limited funds, but further resources are needed to enhance the program's ability to respond to a greater variety of situations. With additional funds, more drugs can be stocked in a larger variety of locations around the country, reducing the time between request and delivery of the stockpile as well as increasing the number of people that could be treated. Local authorities could also receive more intensive training in distribution strategies, and leaders could dispatch larger teams of experts in the case of an emergency. . . .

Hospitals

Currently, U.S. hospitals are operating at close to full capacity, and barely enough hospital beds and nurses are available to respond to the annual flu epidemic. Most metropolitan areas have a limited number of ventilators and beds in rooms especially designed to isolate infectious patients. The entire Washington, D.C., area has fewer than 100 of these isolation beds, all of which would be quickly filled in the event of a biological weapons attack of smallpox or some type of hemorrhagic fever, such as the Ebola virus.

All major hospital centers in the country should develop plans to handle a bioterrorist event. In the event of a large-scale bioterrorist attack, hospitals must first decide where to situate patients physically and then assess whether enough personnel are available to work in an emergency, as well as whether the hospital is equipped to quarantine patients if necessary. Hospitals might need to hire additional nurses and purchase equipment for use in an emergency. Because these expenditures may be inconsistent with individual hospitals' profit maximization policies, compensating hospitals from the bioterrorism preparedness funds may be necessary. . . .

Training

In almost all emerging infectious disease outbreaks, the local medical and public health personnel are the first professionals to identify the existence of a problem, and only then are federally trained experts involved. Having a cadre of experts at the CDC ready to be called when needed, however, is not enough. Physicians, nurses, epidemiologists, emergency medical personnel, and lab workers nationwide must also be trained to recognize the existence of a problem, even if only to know when to call federal experts.

Not enough epidemiologists and public health officials are trained to investigate every suspected outbreak at the local, state, or federal level. Funding should be given to schools of public health and to fellowship programs to ensure that a cadre of highly trained professionals are available. Officials should also allocate portions of local and state budgets to the hiring of infectious disease epidemiologists. Federal programs should also expand so that more people will be trained in advanced outbreak investigation. Currently, the CDC places Epidemic Intelligence Service members (highly trained professionals) in state health departments around the country. On average, however, only one person is placed in each state, and at least 12 states have no representative. Fortunately, officials have slated this program to receive a significant increase in funding, which they will hopefully use to place at least one person in every state and large metropolitan region, with preferably a small team of professionals in each state to coordinate disease investigations and communication with federal authorities.

In addition to training more epidemiologists, existing medical personnel must learn about the role they might play in a biological attack. Most U.S. physicians and first-responders today have never seen a case of smallpox or many of the other diseases listed as critical threats; an infection would thus challenge them to present a diagnosis of the disease without laboratory confirmation. Because rapid diagnosis and treatment is an essential component of bioterrorism response, physicians should become familiar with likely bioterrorist attack agents. Although some physicians initially resisted attending training sessions, they are becoming more willing participants as they perceive the threat of a bioterrorist attack and recognize the role they might play. In addition to the voluntary training of attending physicians, an organized, mandatory program should educate medical students, selected residents, and paramedics on the signs, symptoms, and treatment of agents identified by the CDC as possible biological weapons. Officials should also reinforce for these professionals the protocols for reporting diseases and the required actions in the event of a bioterrorist attack.

How to Appropriate the Increased Funds

The public health system has suffered years of financial neglect, leaving it disabled in its ability to manage outbreaks of infectious diseases effectively without quickly becoming overwhelmed. In 1992, 12 states had no one on the payrolls responsible for monitoring food-borne and waterborne diseases (the two easiest pathways for terrorists to release a biological weapon). A 1999 Harvard University study determined that public health leaders felt they were only performing one-third of the functions essential to protecting the health of the U.S. public, primarily because of insufficient resources.

In 1999 the Congress appropriated $121 million to the CDC to improve the national disease surveillance system. For fiscal year 2000, $277.6 million was set aside for the Department of Health and Human Services (which includes NIH and CDC) to improve the disease surveillance system, engage in research, stockpile drugs, and create vaccines. Bioterrorism funding for 2002 was raised to $1.4 billion, and the president's budget for 2003 proposes a 319 percent increase, to $5.9 billion.

For the first time in its history, the U.S. public health system is positioned to receive enough resources that, if spent appropriately, could improve the public health infrastructure to the point where the system could fulfill its mission to protect the public's health. . . .

Beyond improvements in the U.S. public health system, public health infrastructure around the world could be improved. The release of a biological agent in one part of the world will not be limited in its spread to national borders unless a nation's public health infrastructure is capable of containing the disease. Thus, from a security and a public health point of view, our nation's best interest lies in enhancing the surveillance and response capacity of public health systems around the world—particularly in areas with a possibly increased threat of biological attack.

A strong additional argument for funding the public health system for bioterrorism preparedness is the beneficial side effects of antibioterrorism programs. In the 1950s, officials allocated the CDC funds to establish an Epidemic Intelligence Service (EIS), designed to create a cadre of professionals who could serve as "an early-warning system against biological warfare and man-made epidemics." EIS has existed for 50 years and has played a key role in combating epidemics all over the world, including eradicating smallpox, controlling Ebola outbreaks, discovering how AIDS is transmitted, and studying U.S. public health problems. The EIS program has also trained many medical and public health leaders in the United States, including the most recent director of the CDC, deans of prominent schools of public health, and practicing physicians around the world. . . .

The Unique Bioweapons Challenge

The threat of a biological weapons attack on the United States is more real than at any time in the nation's history. The goals and actions of terrorists and hostile states have changed in a way that makes biological weapons use conceivable, while technological advances have made biological agents weaponization more feasible than in decades and centuries past.

Rapid detection and consequence management of a biological attack will be the primary responsibility of the public health system. As it stands today, a biological weapons attack would quickly overwhelm the public health system. In order for this system to be effective in its detection and response roles, officials should focus more attention toward strengthening the public health infrastructure in general and the infectious disease surveillance system in particular.

"Along with the ability to deploy about 600 people, [the Nuclear Emergency Search Team] also has about 150 tons of equipment at its disposal."

Nuclear Detection Teams Can Prevent Nuclear Terrorism

Jeffrey T. Richelson

Jeffrey T. Richelson is a senior fellow with the National Security Archive in Washington, D.C., and the author of *The Wizards of Langley: Inside the CIA's Directorate of Science and Technology*. In the following viewpoint he discusses the role of the federal Nuclear Emergency Search Team (NEST) in preventing nuclear terrorism. NEST operatives have a wide range of scientific specialties, as well as an arsenal of nuclear detection equipment. If a nuclear threat is received, writes Richelson, NEST operatives can be covertly deployed to locate and destroy a bomb. However, Richelson warns that NEST's effectiveness is dependent on intelligence—the more time that NEST has to deal with a threat, and the more information it has, the greater its chances of locating and neutralizing a hidden nuclear device.

As you read, consider the following questions:

1. Who is referred to as the "father of NEST," according to Richelson?
2. In what year was NEST established, according to the author?
3. What is one of the ways that NEST might disable a nuclear bomb, as described by Richelson?

Jeffrey T. Richelson, "Defusing Nuclear Terror," *Bulletin of the Atomic Scientists*, vol. 25, March/April 2002, p. 38. Copyright © 2002 by the Educational Foundation for Nuclear Science, Chicago, IL 60637. Reproduced by permission of the *Bulletin of the Atomic Scientists:* The Magazine of Global Security News & Analysis.

On October 16, 1994, the Federal Bureau of Investigation (FBI) received word that one of its informants was being held hostage by a domestic terrorist group, the Patriots for National Unity, in a New Orleans safe house. The next morning, after overhearing plans to kill the hostage, a raid by the FBI's hostage rescue team freed the informant. During a debriefing, the rescued informant revealed that members of the terrorist group were looking to obtain nuclear material and assemble several nuclear devices. The bureau also determined that one of the group's members may have leased a boat. In response to a possible nuclear threat, the FBI alerted a number of other federal agencies, including the Nuclear Emergency Search Team (NEST)—a special unit under the control of the Energy Department's Nevada Operations Office.

Fortunately, this entire scenario is fictional, just like the many incidents of nuclear terror portrayed in films and novels over the last 40 years: from Spectre's threat in the 1961 James Bond thriller *Thunderball* to employ stolen nuclear bombs against U.S. or British cities; to the Libyan-backed threat of atomic devastation in Larry Collins's *The Fifth Horseman* (1980); to the destruction caused by a terrorist nuclear device in Tom Clancy's *The Sum of All Fears* (1991); to the attempt by an aggrieved Serbian to incinerate the United Nations in the 1997 film *The Peacemaker* starring George Clooney and Nicole Kidman.

In the scenario described above, NEST was participating, along with the FBI, Federal Emergency Management Agency (FEMA), and several other organizations, in a "full-field exercise" designated "Mirage Gold." The purpose of the exercise was to test how successfully the agencies would respond to a nuclear terrorist threat—and if they could work together effectively.

Origins

The possible need to track down lost, stolen, smuggled, or "improvised" nuclear devices has concerned national security agencies for at least as long as novelists have been spinning fictional scenarios. A 1963 national intelligence estimate, The Clandestine Introduction of Weapons of Mass Destruction into the U.S., addressed the question of whether the Soviet Union was likely to attempt to smuggle biological, chemical, or nuclear weapons into the United States. The intelligence community concluded that "the Soviets almost certainly would not contemplate the use of clandestinely delivered nuclear weapons except as a supplement to other weapons in the context of general war," and that "the Soviets probably recognize that it would be impracticable for them to mount a clandestine nuclear attack on a sufficient number of [U.S. delivery vehicles] to reduce substantially the weight of a U.S. strike."

There was also, in the 1960s, concern about the possible consequences of a crash of nuclear-armed aircraft. According to Duane C. Sewell, commonly referred to as the "father of NEST," this led to the creation of a team based at Lawrence Livermore National Laboratory that could send qualified people to pick up the remains of the aircraft, detect the presence of a nuclear device, determine the area at risk, remove the bomb, and minimize the physical and political damage. When a B-52 carrying four thermonuclear bombs crashed near Thule, Greenland, in 1968, the value of such a capability was demonstrated. "Project Crested Ice" involved transporting two technicians and an instrument for detecting plutonium, suitably winterized to operate at temperatures of minus 60 degrees Fahrenheit, to the accident scene. Within 24 hours of arrival, they were able to locate the area contaminated with plutonium.

Then, in the summer of 1972, the terrorist group Black September seized, and ultimately murdered, nine members of the Israeli Olympic team. Among those who became seriously concerned over the prospect of nuclear terrorism was James Schlesinger, then chairman of the Atomic Energy Commission (AEC). He held a series of meetings exploring whether terrorists could steal plutonium and make a bomb with it, whether they could steal a bomb, and whether the United States would be able to locate it. In 1974, while those issues were being considered and investigated, the FBI received a note demanding that $200,000 be left at a particular location in Boston or a nuclear device would be detonated somewhere in the city. This note was not part of an exercise, but the real thing.

William Chambers, a Los Alamos nuclear physicist who was studying the detection issue, was instructed by the AEC and FBI to assemble the best team he could and head for Boston to search the city. The operation reflected its ad hoc origins. The group rented a fleet of mail vans to carry concealed equipment that could detect the emissions of a plutonium or uranium weapon. But the team found that they did not have the necessary drills to install the detectors in the vans. NEST field director Jerry Doyle recalled, "If they were counting on us to save the good folk of Boston . . . well, it was bye-bye Boston." Fortunately, it was all a hoax—FBI agents waited, but no one showed up to claim the bag of phony bills they left at the designated location.

The threat to Boston resulted in a secret November 18, 1974 memo from General Earnest Graves, the AEC's assistant general manager for military applications, to Mahlon E. Gates, manager of the commission's Nevada Operations Office. Titled "Responsibility for Search and Detection Operations," it authorized Gates to assume responsibility for the planning and execution of AEC operations to search for and identify "lost or stolen nuclear weapons and special nuclear materials, nuclear bomb threats, and radiation dispersal threats." Before the end of 1975, the NEST team was established to prepare for and manage such activities.

Capabilities

If necessary, NEST can deploy approximately 600 individuals to the scene of a terrorist threat, although actual deployments have rarely involved more than 45 people. According to a Nevada Operations Office briefing, deployed personnel come from a pool of about 750 individuals, most of whom work for Energy or its private contractors in other primary capacities. In addition to NEST members based at the team's Las Vegas headquarters, personnel are pulled from three Energy Department labs (Lawrence Livermore, Los Alamos, and Sandia), and from three contractors (Reynolds Electrical & Engineering, Raytheon Services of Nevada, and EG&G).

NEST personnel also have a wide variety of specialties. NEST briefing slides list 17 different categories of personnel, including four types of physicists (nuclear, infrared, atmospheric, and health), engineers, chemists, and mathematicians, as well as specialists in communications, logistics, management, and public information. As a result, the organization chart for a full NEST field deployment contains a multitude of divisions and subdivisions—what one might expect at a large government agency.

NEST and Dirty Bombs

Not all the challenges for the NEST searchers come from outside the border.

Radiological dispersal devices—known as dirty bombs—can be constructed from waste from nuclear power plants wrapped in conventional explosives. These would not produce a nuclear explosion. But, depending on the size of the package, large quantities of radioactive particles would be spewed into the environment.

"Detonation of a dynamite-laden casket of spent fuel from a power plant would not kill quite as many people as died [in the September 11, 2001, terrorist attacks]," [according to Bruce Blair, president of the Center for Defense Information]. "But if it happened in Manhattan, you could expect 2,000 deaths and thousands more suffering from radiation poisoning."

Can NEST intercept and disable this litany of deadly devices before they are used by terrorists?

The ease of detection depends greatly on the nuclear material used. Some will emit alpha radiation, which can be shielded by a single sheet of paper. Most beta rays won't make it through wood or dry wall. It's the neutrons and gamma rays, which can shoot out hundreds of yards, that offer the best bet for detection while driving up a city street or walking through a convention center, hotel or office building or flying low over a community.

Andrew Schneider, *St. Louis Post-Dispatch*, October 21, 2001.

If a nuclear terrorist threat is received, the NEST team first assesses the threat's technical and psychological validity. To determine if the technical details are accurate and indicate some knowledge of building nuclear devices (or were simply lifted from a Tom Clancy novel), NEST maintains a comprehensive computer database of nuclear weapon design information—from reports in scientific journals to passages from spy novels. Meanwhile, psychologists and psychiatrists examine the letter writer's choice of words and sentence structure to try to assess the writer's state of mind and the region from which he or she originates.

If NEST were to move into the field, it would not travel lightly. Along with the ability to deploy about 600 people, it also has about 150 tons of equipment at its disposal. NEST's air force consists of four helicopters equipped with radiological search systems, and three airplanes (a King Air B-200, a Citation-II, and a Convair 580T) modified for remote sensing missions. It can deploy vans with equipment capable of detecting the emissions from nuclear material. And by applying appropriate artwork to the sides of vehicles, its graphics department can help undercover vans blend into the flood of commercial vans on the road. When asked if the artwork would be the same as a legitimate company's or be imaginary—possibly allowing a terrorist armed with the Yellow Pages to determine that the van was a phony—a NEST spokesperson remarked that the search team seeks to insure that it does not "raise the suspicions of the terrorists."

NEST also has an arsenal of handheld nuclear detectors that can be concealed in any one of many attache cases, briefcases, lunch packs, and suitcases. The detectors can silently let a NEST member know that a radiation source has been detected by transmitting a signal to the member's concealed earphone.

In addition to equipment for detecting nuclear material, NEST also has diagnostic, disablement, and damage-limitation devices. Its diagnostic capability includes portable X-ray machines to peer under a bomb's outer shell as well as a hand-held device that looks like a Dustbuster and can pick up emissions to better estimate a threat. To disable a bomb, NEST might detonate explosives around it, or it could use a 30-millimeter cannon to blast the bomb into small pieces. The team can construct a nylon tent, 35 feet high and 50 feet in diameter, into which 30,000 cubic feet of thick foam can be pumped, which can mitigate the spread of radiation from a radiation dispersal device. According to a NEST team member, however, the foam is primarily intended to limit the damage from a non-nuclear detonation used to disable a nuclear weapon.

Deployments

Since NEST's creation, about 100 threats involving alleged nuclear devices or radioactivity have come to its attention. At least a dozen, and possibly more than twice that number, have resulted in deployment of NEST personnel. NEST, in general, will not confirm or deny when or whether it has deployed to a particular city or region. However, it has been reported that between 1975 and 1981 NEST personnel were sent to investigate threats in Boston, Los Angeles, Spokane, Pittsburgh, New York, Sacramento, Tennessee, and Reno.

The threat to New York came in July 1975 when terrorists claimed, "We have successfully designed and built an atomic bomb. It is somewhere on Manhattan Island. We refer you to the accompanying drawing in one-eighth scale. We have enough plutonium and explosives for the bomb to function. The device will be used at 6:00 p.m. July 10 unless our demands are met." As reported in the *New York Times Magazine*, the key demand involved $30 million in small bills.

NEST was impressed by the drawing. According to one account, it was sophisticated, precise, and "made by someone with more than a passing acquaintance with nuclear physics." But that did not lead the United States to part with real money. A dummy ransom package was left at the drop site in Northampton, Massachusetts, and FBI agents waited for someone to claim it. Nobody showed up and there was no further communication from the extortionists.

That same year, Fred L. Hartley, chairman of the Los Angeles–based Union Oil Company of California, received a note claiming that there was a nuclear device on one of the company's properties. The extortionist wanted $1 million; otherwise, the bomb would be detonated. Such a threat, away from the natural radiation of an urban area—where radiation can be emitted by freshly paved streets or Vermont granite in an office building—made it easier to use NEST vans in the search for a nuclear device.

"The guys were out there in their trucks listening to their earpieces," former NEST official Jerry Doyle told Larry Collins, the author of the first major article on the search team. "Suddenly one got an intensive reading, looked up and there, about 50 yards away, was a big bulky, unidentified wooden crate resting by a refinery fence. There was a moment of real panic," Doyle recalled. Fortunately, it was just a box left by some repairmen, and the signal came from natural radioactivity in the soil. The FBI managed to capture a suspect, who was tried and convicted, but was released after six months in prison.

NEST's deployment to Washington, D.C. during the bicentennial summer of 1976 may be the type of precautionary deployment that becomes more common after the September 11 attacks. Vans circled the streets and drove around federal buildings near the Mall, checking radiation levels. The FBI worried that a terrorist group might be tempted by the bicentennial's significance to threaten to explode or release nuclear material, but the summer passed without a threat.

Not all of NEST's deployments have involved nuclear terrorism. For three months in 1978, about 120 NEST personnel helped the Canadian government locate the remains of the Soviet Cosmos 954 ocean surveillance satellite that crashed into northern Canada. The following year, NEST equipment was used to monitor radiation in the vicinity of the Three Mile Island nuclear accident. . . .

Outlook

The catalyst for NEST's creation in the mid-1970s was the attempt to enlist nuclear terror in the service of extortion. And some NEST exercises still employ a nuclear extortion scenario, according to a current team member. But the premise for Mirage Gold was different, and consistent with today's greatest fear—that terrorists may not be interested in money or changing government policy. They may simply want to detonate a nuclear weapon.

It is also a premise that puts a much greater premium on intelligence. Nuclear extortionists have to threaten a particular city or area and give the threatened party time to react, giving NEST time to deploy and attempt to locate any bomb that might be in place. But terrorists could strike anywhere, and would give no warning. A NEST spokesperson acknowledged that without advance intelligence, the team would have nowhere to go. Exceptions may include deployments at high-profile events, such as the Salt Lake City Olympics, which would be obvious potential targets for terrorists. But to prevent detonation of a terrorist nuclear device in other circumstances would require warning from the FBI, Central Intelligence Agency, National Security Agency, or an allied intelligence service.

Of course, even advance warning is no guarantee of success, given the difficulty of locating a hidden nuclear device and the limited time that may be available. A comment in the Nevada Operations Office's after action report on Mirage Gold is chilling, not as a criticism of NEST members, with their diverse talents and dedication, but as an acknowledgment of a harsh reality. The report notes that it would be "a drastic mistake to assume that NEST technology and procedures will always succeed, resulting in zero nuclear yield."

Periodical Bibliography

The following articles have been selected to supplement the diverse views presented in this chapter.

Bulletin of the Atomic Scientists	"Missile Defense," November/December 2001.
Geoffrey Cowley	"The Plan to Fight Smallpox," *Newsweek*, October 14, 2002.
Philip E. Coyle	"Is Missile Defense on Target?" *Arms Control Today*, October 2003.
Nicole Deller and John Burroughs	"Arms Control Abandoned: The Case of Biological Weapons," *World Policy Journal*, Summer 2003.
Katherine Eban	"Waiting for Bioterror: Is Our Public Health System Ready?" *Nation*, December 9, 2002.
Economist	"Warding Off Missiles," December 4, 2003.
Economist	"Who Will Build Our Biodefences?: Vaccines Against Bioterrorism," February 1, 2003.
Craig Eisendrath, Gerald E. Marsh, and Melvin A. Goodman	"Can We Count on Missile Defense?" *USA Today Magazine*, September 2001.
Steven Johnson	"Stopping Loose Nukes," *Wired*, November 2002.
Charles C. Mann	"Homeland Insecurity," *Atlantic Monthly*, September 2002.
New York Times	"The Greater Nuclear Danger," September 27, 2002.
New York Times	"Heading Off Nuclear Terrorism," May 25, 2002.
Michael Scardaville	"The Cost of Securing the Homeland," *World & I*, August 2003.
Amanda Spake	"The Smallpox Conundrum," *U.S. News & World Report*, December 23, 2002.
Amanda Spake et al.	"Are You Ready?" *U.S. News & World Report*, February 24, 2003.
Time	"The Secretary of Missile Defense," May 14, 2001.
USA Today	"Antiterrorism Efforts May Bolster Public Health System," August 2003.
Kevin Whitelaw, Mark Mazzetti, and Richard J. Newman	"Wishing Upon a Star," *U.S. News & World Report*, November 19, 2001.

For Further Discussion

Chapter 1

1. What types of nuclear threat is John J. Stanton most concerned with in his viewpoint? What type of nuclear threat does Joseph Cirincione believe is exaggerated?

2. John Parachini argues that a bioterror attack is unlikely; Amy Sands, on the other hand, contends that several of the arguments Parachini puts forth are flawed. Whose position do you find more convincing and why?

Chapter 2

1. Did you have an opinion on the U.S. invasion of Iraq before reading the viewpoints by Thomas R. Eddlem, Robert Kagan, and William Kristol? Did either of the viewpoints influence your opinion of the Iraq war, and if so, how?

2. Both the viewpoints on the U.S. invasion of Iraq quote David Kay, the CIA official who led the search for weapons of mass destruction in Iraq. In your opinion, which authors make better use of quotes from Kay to support their views? Explain your answer.

Chapter 3

1. After reading the viewpoint by Jonathan Schell and C. Paul Robinson, do you believe that the United States should destroy its nuclear weapons? Why or why not?

2. After reading the viewpoints by Loren B. Thompson and Theresa Hitchens, do you feel that deterrence is a sensible strategy for the United States? Explain your answer.

Chapter 4

1. One of the main arguments against building a missile defense system, echoed by George Rathjens and Carl Kaysen, is that it may be technologically impossible to build such a system. Do you find this argument convincing? Why or why not?

2. Michael Barletta advocates securing the materials and technologies necessary to make biological weapons, while Rebecca Katz advocates improving the public health system's ability to deal with a biological attack. Based on the viewpoints, which measure do you think should be a higher priority for the U.S. government? Explain your answer.

Organizations to Contact

The editors have compiled the following list of organizations concerned with the issues debated in this book. The descriptions are derived from materials provided by the organizations. All have publications or information available for interested readers. The list was compiled on the date of publication of the present volume; the information provided here may change. Be aware that many organizations take several weeks or longer to respond to inquiries, so allow as much time as possible.

American Enterprise Institute (AEI)
1150 Seventeenth St. NW, Washington, DC 20036
Web site: www.aei.org

AEI is a think tank based in Washington, D.C., whose members support a strong and well-funded military and a "hawkish" approach to dealing with rogue states. AEI publishes the magazine *American Enterprise*. Other publications include papers "North Korea's Survival Game: Understanding the Recent Past, Thinking About the Future" and "In Iraq with the Coalition of the Willing."

ANSER Institute for Homeland Security
e-mail: homelandsecurity@anser.org
Web site: www.homelandsecurity.org

The institute is a nonprofit, nonpartisan think tank that works to educate the public about homeland security issues. The institute's Web site contains a virtual library of fact sheets, reports, legislation, and government documents and statistics on homeland security issues. It also publishes the *Journal of Homeland Security* and a weekly newsletter.

Arms Control Association (ACA)
1726 M St. NW, Suite 201, Washington, DC 20036
(202) 463-8270 • fax: (202) 463-8273
e-mail: aca@armscontrol.org • Web site: www.armscontrol.org

The Arms Control Association is a nonprofit organization dedicated to promoting public understanding of and support for effective arms control policies. ACA seeks to increase public appreciation of the need to limit arms, reduce international tensions, and promote world peace. It publishes news articles on foreign policy; fact sheets on missile defense, nuclear testing, and other issues, and the monthly magazine *Arms Control Today*.

Brookings Institution
1775 Massachusetts Ave. NW, Washington, DC 20036
(202) 797-6000 • fax: (202) 797-6004
e-mail: brookinfo@brook.edu • Web site: www.brookings.org

The institution is a think tank that conducts research and education in foreign policy, economics, government, and the social sciences. Its publications include the quarterly *Brookings Review* and periodic *Policy Briefs*, including "The New National Security Strategy: Focus on Failed States," "The New National Security Strategy and Preemption," and "A 'Master' Plan to Deal with North Korea."

Cato Institute
1000 Massachusetts Ave. NW, Washington, DC 20001-5403
(202) 842-0200 • fax: (202) 842-3490
Web site: www.cato.org

The institute is a libertarian public policy research foundation dedicated to peace and limited government intervention in foreign affairs. It publishes numerous reports and periodicals, including *Policy Analysis* and *Cato Policy Review*, both of which discuss U.S. policy on terrorism, weapons of mass destruction, and foreign policy.

Center for Arms Control and Nonproliferation
322 Fourth St. NE, Washington, DC 20002
(202) 546-0795
Web site: www.armscontrolcenter.org

The center serves as a "watchdog" of the U.S. Congress and Executive Branch on a range of arms control issues. It supports the United Nations disarmament and weapons inspections programs and opposes missile defense and the use of force to resolve international conflicts. The center's Web site offers news updates and commentaries on a variety of WMD issues.

Center for Defense Information (CDI)
1779 Massachusetts Ave. NW, Suite 615, Washington, DC 20036
(202) 332-0600 • fax: (202) 462-4559
e-mail: info@cdi.org • Web site: www.cdi.org

CDI is comprised of civilians and former military officers and serves as an independent monitor of the military, analyzing spending, policies, weapon systems, and related military issues. The center opposes both excessive expenditures for weapons and policies that increase the danger of war. It publishes the *Defense Monitor* ten times per year.

Center for Nonproliferation Studies
Monterey Institute for International Studies
460 Pierce St., Monterey, CA 93940
(831) 647-4154 • fax: (831) 647-3519
e-mail: cns@miis.edu • Web site: http://cns.miis.edu

The center researches all aspects of nonproliferation and works to combat the spread of weapons of mass destruction. The center has multiple reports, papers, speeches, and congressional testimony available online, including the papers "After 9/11: Preventing Mass-Destruction Terrorism and Weapons Proliferation" and "New Challenges in Missile Proliferation, Missile Defense, and Space Security." Its main publication is the *Nonproliferation Review*, which is published three times per year.

Center for Strategic and International Studies (CSIS)
1800 K St. NW, Washington, DC 20006
(202) 887-0200 • fax: (202) 775-3199
Web site: www.csis.org

CSIS is a public policy research institution that specializes in the areas of U.S. domestic and foreign policy, national security, and economic policy. The center analyzes world crisis situations and recommends U.S. military and defense policies. Its publications include the journal *Washington Quarterly* and the reports *Change and Challenge on the Korean Peninsula: Developments, Trends, and Issues* and *Combating Chemical, Biological, Radiological, and Nuclear Terrorism: A Comprehensive Strategy.*

Council on Foreign Relations (CFR)
58 E. Sixty-eighth St., New York, NY 10021
(212) 434-9400 • fax: (212) 986-2984
Web site: www.cfr.org

The council specializes in foreign affairs and studies the international aspects of American political and economic policies and problems. Its journal *Foreign Affairs*, published five times a year, includes analyses of current conflicts around the world. Articles and op-ed pieces by CFR members are available on its Web site, along with the report *A New National Security Strategy in an Age of Terrorists, Tyrants, and Weapons of Mass Destruction.*

Federation of American Scientists (FAS)
1717 K St. NW, Suite 209, Washington, DC 20036
(202) 546-3300
Web site: www.fas.org

The federation is a nonprofit organization founded in 1945 out of concerns about the implications of nuclear weapons for mankind. FAS members support arms control through international treaties. The federation has available on its Web site primary documents, fact sheets, and news reports concerning weapons of mass destruction and missile defense.

Foreign Policy Association (FPA)
470 Park Ave. South, 2nd Fl., New York, NY 10016
(212) 481-8100 • fax: (212) 481-9275
e-mail: info@fpa.org • Web site: www.fpa.org

FPA is a nonprofit organization that believes a concerned and informed public is the foundation for an effective foreign policy. Publications such as the annual *Great Decisions* briefing book and the quarterly *Headline Series* review U.S. foreign policy issues and FPA's Global Q & A series offers interviews with leading U.S. and foreign officials on issues concerning the Middle East, intelligence gathering, weapons of mass destruction, and military and diplomatic initiatives.

Heritage Foundation
214 Massachusetts Ave. NE, Washington, DC 20002-4999
(800) 544-4843 • (202) 546-4400 • fax: (202) 544-6979
e-mail: pubs@heritage.org • Web site: www.heritage.org

The foundation is a public policy research institute that advocates limited government and the free-market system. The foundation publishes the quarterly *Policy Review* as well as monographs, books, and papers supporting U.S. noninterventionism and the building of a nuclear missile defense system. Heritage publications on U.S. defense policy include *President Bush Strikes the Proper Balance on Non-Proliferation Policy* and *Compassionate Counter-Proliferation*.

Nuclear Control Institute
1000 Connecticut Ave. NW, Suite 410, Washington, DC 20036
(202) 822-8444
Web site: www.nci.org

The institute is an independent research and advocacy center specializing in problems of nuclear proliferation. It monitors nuclear activities worldwide and pursues strategies to halt the spread and reverse the growth of nuclear arms. Its Web site provides an

overview as well as many detailed reports of the problem of un-
guarded nuclear material.

Peace Action
1100 Wayne Ave., Suite 1020, Silver Spring, MD 20910
(301) 565-4050 • fax: (301) 565-0850
e-mail: paprog@igc.org • Web site: www.peace-action.org
Peace Action is a grassroots peace and justice organization that
works for policy changes in Congress and the United Nations, as
well as state and city legislatures. It also promotes education and
activism on topics related to peace and disarmament issues. The
organization produces a quarterly newsletter and also publishes an
annual voting record for members of Congress.

Union of Concerned Scientists (UCS)
2 Brattle Sq., Cambridge, MA 02238
(617) 547-5552 • fax: (617) 864-9405
e-mail: ucs@ucsusa.org • Web site: www.ucsusa.org
UCS is concerned about the impact of advanced technology on society. It supports nuclear arms control and opposes building a missile defense system. Publications include the quarterly *Nucleus*
newsletter and reports and briefs concerning nuclear proliferation,
including "The Troubling Science of Bunker-Busting Nuclear
Weapons" and "President Bush's Nuclear Weapons Policy: Illogi-
cal, Ineffective, and Dangerous."

U.S. Department of Homeland Security (DHS)
Washington, DC 20528
Web site: www.dhs.gov
DHS's priority is to protect the nation against terrorist attacks. Its
component agencies analyze threats and intelligence, guard America's borders and airports, protect critical infrastructure, and coordinate the U.S. response to future emergencies. The DHS Web site
offers a wide variety of information on homeland security, including
press releases, speeches and testimony, and reports on topics such as
airport security, weapons of mass destruction, planning for and responding to emergencies, and the DHS threat advisory system.

U.S. Department of State
2201 C St. NW, Washington, DC 20520
Web site: www.state.gov
The State Department is a federal agency that advises the presi-
dent on the formulation and execution of foreign policy. The State
Department's Web site includes pages providing background in-

formation on every country in the world, as well as news updates and speeches from senior department officials.

Web Sites

Missilethreat.com
www.missilethreat.com
This Web site is a project of the Claremont Institute (www.claremont.org), a conservative think tank that supports the building of a missile defense system.

Nuclear Files
www.nuclearfiles.org
This Web site, a project of the Nuclear Age Peace Foundation (www.wagingpeace.org), provides background information, analysis and access to primary documents on nuclear weapons, missile defense, and arms control treaties.

The White House Web Site
www.whitehouse.gov
This Web site offers an archive of President George W. Bush's speeches on national security, the war on terrorism, and other WMD issues.

Bibliography of Books

Yonah Alexander and Milton Hoenig, eds.	*Super Terrorism: Biological, Chemical, and Nuclear.* Ardsley, NY: Transnational, 2001.
William Blum	*Rogue State: A Guide to the World's Only Super-power.* Monroe, ME: Common Courage Press, 2000.
Michael E. Brown, ed.	*Grave New World: Security Challenges in the 21st Century.* Washington, DC: Georgetown University Press, 2003.
Richard Butler	*Fatal Choice: Nuclear Weapons and the Illusion of Missile Defense.* Boulder, CO: Westview Press, 2001.
Stephen J. Cimbala, ed.	*Deterrence and Nuclear Proliferation in the Twenty-first Century.* Westport, CT: Praeger, 2001.
Joseph Cirincione, ed.	*Repairing the Regime: Preventing the Spread of Weapons of Mass Destruction.* New York: Routledge, 2000.
Joseph Cirincione et al.	*Deadly Arsenals: Tracking Weapons of Mass Destruction.* Washington, DC: Carnegie Endowment for International Peace, 2002.
Malcolm Dando	*The New Biological Weapons: Threat, Proliferation, Control.* London: Lynne Reinner, 2001.
Gavin de Becker	*Fear Less: Real Truth About Risk, Safety, and Security in a Time of Terrorism.* Boston: Little, Brown, 2002.
Richard A. Falkenrath	*America's Achilles Heel: Nuclear, Biological, and Chemical Terrorism and Covert Attack.* Cambridge, MA: MIT Press, 1998.
Kathlyn Gay	*Silent Death: The Threat of Chemical and Biological Terrorism.* Brookfield, CT: Twenty-first Century Books, 2001.
Nadine Gurr and Benjamin Cole	*The New Face of Terrorism: Threats from Weapons of Mass Destruction.* New York: I.B. Tauris, 2000.
Robert Hutchinson	*Weapons of Mass Destruction: The No-Nonsense Guide to Nuclear, Chemical and Biological Weapons Today.* London: Weidenfeld & Nicolson, 2003.
Peter R. Lavoy, Scott D. Sagan, and James J. Wirtz, eds.	*Planning the Unthinkable: How New Powers Will Use Nuclear, Biological, and Chemical Weapons.* Ithaca, NY: Cornell University Press, 2000.
Robert Litwak	*Rogue States and U.S. Foreign Policy: Containment After the Cold War.* Washington, DC: Woodrow Wilson Center Press, 2000.

National Research Council	*Making the Nation Safer: The Role of Science and Technology for Countering Terrorism.* Washington, DC: National Academies Press, 2002.
Michael E. O'Hanlon et al.	*Defending America: The Case for Limited National Missile Defense.* Washington, DC: Brookings Institution Press, 2001.
Sheldon Rampton and John C. Stauber	*Weapons of Mass Deception: The Uses of Propaganda in Bush's War on Iraq.* New York: Jeremy P. Tarcher, 2003.
Scott D. Sagan and Kenneth N. Waltz	*The Spread of Nuclear Weapons: A Debate Renewed.* New York: W.W. Norton, 2003.
Jonathan Schell	*The Unfinished Twentieth Century: The Crisis of Weapons of Mass Destruction.* New York: Verso, 2001.
Martin Schram	*Avoiding Armageddon.* New York: Basic Books, 2003.
Henry Sokolski	*Best of Intentions: America's Campaign Against Strategic Weapons Proliferation.* Westport, CT: Praeger, 2001.
Henry Sokolski and James M. Ludes, eds.	*Twenty-first Century Weapons Proliferation: Are We Ready?* Portland, OR: Frank Cass, 2001.
Victor A. Utgoff	*The Coming Crisis: Nuclear Proliferation, U.S. Interests, and World Order.* Cambridge, MA: MIT Press, 2000.

Index